JAPAN'S ROAD
to the PACIFIC WAR

The Fateful Choice

Studies of the East Asian Institute • Columbia University

JAPAN'S ROAD
to the PACIFIC WAR

The Fateful Choice

JAPAN'S ADVANCE
into SOUTHEAST ASIA, 1939–1941

Selected translations from
Taiheiyō sensō e no michi:
kaisen gaikō shi

Edited by JAMES WILLIAM MORLEY

Columbia University Press · New York · 1980

The Japan Foundation, through a special grant, has assisted the
Press in publishing this volume.

Library of Congress Cataloging in Publication Data

Main entry under title:

The Fateful choice.

   (Japan's road to the Pacific war)
   Bibliography: p.
   Includes index.
   CONTENTS: Hosoya, C. The Japanese-Soviet
neutrality pact.—Nagaoka, S. Economic demands on
the Dutch East Indies.—Hata, I. The Army's move
into northern Indochina. [etc.]
   1. Japan—Foreign relations—1912–1945.
   2. World War, 1939–1945—Diplomatic history.
   3. Japan—Foreign relations—Asia, Southeastern.
   4. Asia, Southeastern—Foreign relations—Japan.
   5. Japan—Military policy.   I. Morley, James
William, 1921–   II. Nihon Kokusai Seiji
Gakkai. Taiheiyō Sensō Gen' in Kenkyūbu. Taiheiyō
sensō e no michi.   III. Series.
   DS845.F37   327.52   79-23486
   ISBN 0-231-04804-1

Columbia University Press
New York   Guildford, Surrey

The East Asian Institute of Columbia University

The East Asian Institute is Columbia University's center for research, education, and publication on modern East Asia.

The Studies of the East Asian Institute were inaugurated in 1962 to bring to a wider public the results of significant new research on modern and contemporary East Asia.

Contents

Editor's Foreword   ix

I. Northern Defense   1

    Introduction by Peter A. Berton   3
    One: The Japanese-Soviet
         Neutrality Pact by Hosoya Chihiro   13

II. Southern Advance   115

    Introduction by Robert A. Scalapino   117
    Two: Economic Demands
        on the Dutch East Indies by Nagaoka Shinjirō   125

    Three: The Army's Move
        into Northern Indochina by Hata Ikuhiko   155

    Four: The Drive into Southern
        Indochina and Thailand by Nagaoka Shinjirō   209

    Five: The Navy's Role in the Southern Strategy
        by Tsunoda Jun   241

Appendixes   297
    1. Text of Semi-Official Communication from
       Foreign Minister Matsuoka to Foreign
       Commissar Molotov, April 13, 1941   299

    2. The Matsuoka-Henry Pact, August 30, 1940   301

    3. Outline of Policy toward the South, April
       17, 1941   303

Notes   305

Glossary   335

Bibliography   341

Contributors   353

Index   357

Maps
    Northern Indochina 1940   161
    Indochina and Thailand 1940–1941   213

Editor's Foreword

Some years ago the Japan Association on International Relations (Nihon Kokusai Seiji Gakkai), which embraces Japan's leading scholars of international affairs, undertook an ambitious collaborative research project on the origins of the Pacific War from the 1920s to 1941. Under the leadership first of Kamikawa Hikomatsu,* professor emeritus of international politics at Tokyo University, and then of Tsunoda Jun, professor of diplomatic history at Kokugakuin University and head of the Shidehara Peace Collection of the National Diet Library, an impressive number of objective diplomatic and military historians were assembled. They were given access to a wide range of primary materials, including not only those of the International Military Tribunal for the Far East but also a mass of others hitherto unavailable from the former imperial army and navy, the Justice Ministry, and the Foreign Ministry. The private papers of Prime Ministers Konoe Fumimaro and Okada Keisuke, Ugaki Kazushige (who served as both army and foreign minister), Colonel Ishiwara Kanji, and others were now available. In addition, a number of leading participants in the events made themselves available for interview. Each scholar in the project was given personal responsibility to present the facts on a given subject as he saw them.

The result was a collection of remarkably objective essays, designed not to fit an overall interpretation of events, an approach that was consciously rejected, but, as one researcher put it, "to provide clues and materials for future historians." Published in 1962–63 in seven volumes by the press of Japan's largest newspaper, the *Asahi shimbun*, under the title *Taiheiyō sensô e no michi: kaisen gaikô shi* (The Road to the Pacific War: A Diplomatic History of the Origins of the War), the series was immediately acclaimed as the most informative, factually based account of Japan's road to war.

Japan's Road to the Pacific War is a translation of selected parts of that work. The principle of selection has been to include those essays or portions of essays that focus primarily on the policy of Japan rather than

---

* In accord with Japanese usage, Japanese names are given throughout this volume with the surname first.

other countries and draw on materials of an unusual character. While each essay stands on its own authority, its value has been greatly enhanced by a brief introduction by its scholar-translator.

In each case as faithful a translation as possible has been rendered, but translation is not a mechanical process. With languages and cultures as different as the Japanese and the American, minor omissions, revisions, or insertions have occasionally been made, with the approval of the author, to make the translated version more readily intelligible. In addition, for the convenience of researchers, footnotes have been clarified and occasionally changed to correct errors in the original or to indicate subsequently published sources that were originally used in archival form. An effort also has been made to standardize the spellings and identifications of the names of persons and institutions and the titles of documents.

While the maps are derived from those accompanying the original Japanese text, place-names are spelled according to the current usage of the National Geographic Society. Except for widely recognized romanizations, such as Peking, Nanking, or Canton, Chinese and Mongolian place-names are romanized according to the modified Wade-Giles system, retaining only essential aspirants. Personal names are rendered in the romanized form preferred by their users insofar as we have been able to ascertain them; otherwise, standard orthographical principles have been followed: modified Wade-Giles for Chinese, modified Hepburn for Japanese, and modified Library of Congress for Russian.

Many have contributed to this painstaking translation and editorial work, but for this and all volumes in the series, the contributions of Shumpei Okamoto and Dale K. A. Finlayson have been indispensible. In addition, for help on individual essays, we are pleased to express our thanks to Bamba Nobuya, Monica Brown, Joseph Gordon, Takane Masa'aki, and Ueki Yasuhiro.

The Fateful Choice relates how, following the victory of Germany in western Europe in 1940, the Japanese expansionists decided to move southward against the colonial empires in southeast Asia rather than northward against the Soviet Union—a choice which brought Japan ultimately into direct confrontation with the United States.

This is the second volume to be published in the series *Japan's Road to the Pacific War*. A list of the five volumes in the series is as follows:

Japan Erupts: The London Naval Conference and the Manchurian Incident, 1928–1932

The China Quagmire: Japan's Expansion on the Asian Continent, 1933–1941

Deterrent Diplomacy: Japan, Germany, and the USSR, 1935–1940 (published by Columbia University Press in 1976)

The Fateful Choice: Japan's Advance into Southeast Asia, 1939–1941

The Final Confrontation: Japan's Negotiations with the United States, 1941

J.W.M.

PART ONE

Northern Defense

Introduction

PETER A. BERTON

Japan and the Soviet Union did not cross swords in the Second World War except for a brief period during its last few weeks. Yet they were major participants in this world-wide conflict and this alone would make the study of their relations important. In the years before the war Soviet-Japanese relations were closely intertwined with the relations of both powers with Germany, and to a lesser extent with the United States, Great Britain, and China—in fact, all the major protagonists in the Second World War. Thus, a careful study of Soviet-Japanese relations is extremely important for an understanding of the origins of World War II, especially the conflict in the Pacific, and Japan's decision to attack the United States. Such a study, moreover, is significant for more than historical reasons. One of these nations is today a superpower; the other, the third largest economic unit in the world.

The present study by Hosoya Chihiro deals with a crucial two-year period in Soviet-Japanese relations, from the summer of 1939 to the fall of 1941, focusing upon the conclusion of a neutrality treaty between the two countries in April 1941. It spans the period from just before the Hitler-Stalin pact and the subsequent outbreak of war in Europe to a few months before the Japanese attack on Pearl Harbor and the beginning of the Pacific War.

A thorough study of Soviet-Japanese diplomatic relations requires access to the relevant national archives of the two countries (including, of course, those of the two foreign offices, the Gaimushō and the Narkomindel), as well as the diaries and memoirs of the principal decision makers and diplomats. On the Japanese side, it also requires the records of the Japanese military establishment: the Army and Navy ministries and the high command—the Imperial Army General Staff and the Navy General Staff. The role of the military in the decision-making process is especially significant because diplomatic negotiations between the two countries involved the settlement of large-scale armed clashes along the Soviet-Manchurian and Mongolian-Manchurian frontiers, and because at least since 1937 Japanese policy in the Far East was heavily burdened by military considerations. To a lesser extent, we would need relevant economic data, since Soviet-Japanese relations involved such economic issues as oil and coal concessions and fishing rights. For the Soviet side, the historian would need the personal papers of Stalin, as well as those of his right-hand man Vyacheslav Molotov, foreign commissar during the entire period under study, along with the records of the Politbureau and the Commissariat for Foreign Affairs.

Furthermore, inasmuch as Soviet-Japanese relations during this period were closely tied to Moscow's and Tokyo's relations with Berlin and to a lesser extent with Washington, London, and Chungking, the appropriate German, American, British, and Chinese foreign affairs archives and relevant memoirs are also, to varying degrees, important for a thorough study of our subject.

From this overview of needed historical data let us consider what is available. The historical records that survived the devastation of war and deliberate destruction at the hands of frightened Japanese and German officials were captured by the occupying powers. A good deal of this documentation turned up at the Nuremberg and Tokyo war crimes trials and is available in English translation. Other German and Japanese archival materials either have been published in English translation or are available on microfilm in the original. (See, for example, the *Documents on German Foreign Policy* series and the Library of Congress' *Checklist of Archives in the Japanese Ministry of Foreign Affairs, Tokyo, Japan, 1868–1945.*) A good deal of memoir literature appeared in post-occupation Germany and Japan, some of it designed to balance the war crimes documentation. Some hitherto unknown private archives have also come to light in both countries. In the case of Japan, moreover, the government has made a determined effort to gather all relevant archives, documents, and diaries and to interview both major policymakers and important witnesses in an ambitious undertaking to reconstruct the drama of the war and the years that preceded it.

The United States, even during the war itself, began to publish selected diplomatic correspondence relating to Japan (which also casts light on German-Japanese and Soviet-Japanese relations). More recently the *Foreign Relations of the United States* series covers the 1939–41 period in greater detail. Numerous first-hand accounts by American statesmen and diplomats supplement the official documentation. British and Chinese sources on the subject have not approached the quality and volume of American documentation, but they are not central to our investigation.

The greatest difficulty resides in the paucity of Soviet sources. Access to Soviet archives is denied to non-Soviet scholars, and published official Soviet documentation is extremely limited. The historical series of Soviet foreign relations has not yet reached the 1939–41 period. Most published collections of documents on World War II have been selected largely to support the official Soviet version of the prelude to the war and the war itself, and in some cases expressly designed to counter western collections of documents (for example, those on the Nazi-Soviet pact and Allied relations during the war). Crucial memoir literature is nonexistent, with Stalin and Molotov dead. (Memoirs of Soviet diplomats, such as those of Ivan Maisky, the Soviet ambassador to the Court of St. James, have been very disappointing.) These deficiencies in Soviet documentation did not impose any special obstacle for Hosoya or his associates writing in the *Taiheiyō sensō e no michi* historical series. Their focus was on Japanese policymaking.

From this brief description of primary documentation, let us turn now to a survey of scholarly studies of our subject. Hosoya's study of the Soviet-Japanese Neutrality Pact of 1941 and its background is the third study and the first in Japanese. The two preceding ones are Joseph Gordon's unpublished Master's thesis for the Certificate of the East Asian Institute of Columbia University entitled "The Russo-Japanese Neutrality Pact of April 1941" (completed in May 1955, 109 pp. typewritten), and Hubertus Lupke's *Japans Russlandpolitik von 1939 bis 1941* published in the monograph series of the Institute of Asian Studies in Hamburg in 1962 (189 pp.).

Gordon's study is entirely devoted to the Neutrality Pact, covering the period from May 1940 through the conclusion of the treaty in April 1941. Lupke treats not only the pact but the whole range of Soviet-Japanese relations from the outbreak of the Nomonhan Incident in May 1939 to August 1941. In fact, only about one-half of the monograph is devoted to the Neutrality Pact, the rest dealing with the settlement of the Nomonhan Incident, the demarcation of the Manchurian-Mongolian border, Japanese oil and coal concessions in northern Sakhalin, the fisheries problem, and economic relations between the two countries. Both Gordon and Lupke reproduce in their appendices a number of diplomatic documents, texts of treaties, as well as Soviet and Japanese draft proposals. Hosoya's study, like Gordon's, is focused on the Neutrality Pact, but its time span parallels Lupke's, starting with the Nomonhan Incident and ending a couple of months after Hitler's attack on Russia. In addition to these three studies there are a number of books in different languages dealing with either Soviet or Japanese diplomacy or with the related topics of German-Soviet, German-Japanese, and Japanese-American relations, but which make only passing reference to our subject.

Insofar as Soviet scholarly monographic literature is concerned, one should mention the detailed study of prewar and postwar Soviet-Japanese diplomatic relations, *Istoriia sovetsko-iaponskikh diplomaticheskikh otnoshenii*, published in 1962 by a high-ranking Soviet member of the United Nations Secretariat, Leonid Nikolaevich Kutakov. Like many Soviet monographs on foreign relations, this study is based in large measure on the Foreign Policy Archives of the USSR. Unfortunately, it sheds no light on the decision-making process in the Soviet Union, the negotiation positions of the Soviet leadership, and the evolution of policy in the light of interaction with other countries. To this basic defect we should add the fact that all Soviet scholarly historical writings by definition are required to propagate the latest official version of events and reflect the latest party line on the subject.

We now turn to a comparison of primary sources available to Gordon, Lupke, and Hosoya. Gordon and Lupke have utilized the microfilm collection of the Japanese Foreign Ministry archives, English-language documentation of the Tokyo war crimes trials, published collections of German and American diplomatic correspondence, plus a few other primary Japanese sources. Hosoya has used all these and more. He had access to the archives of the Foreign Ministry (that is, he was not restricted to the microfilmed files), the Military History Office in the National Defense Agency, and the War Crimes Materials Office in the Justice Ministry, as well as to private archives, notably the papers of former Prime Minister Konoe Fumimaro. Last but not least, one should note and welcome the interviews with former diplomats and political and military leaders in the work of Hosoya and his colleagues and associates on the origins of the Pacific War.[1]

Hosoya's basic contribution in this study is that precisely because of these sources (unavailable to either Lupke or Gordon or up to this time

to any foreign or Japanese scholar for that matter) he was able to go
beyond the diplomatic relations between Japan and the Soviet Union
and focus on the genesis and evolution of Japanese policy toward Russia
not only in the Foreign Ministry but, more importantly, also among the
military leadership. He has stressed the decision-making approach in
the study of diplomatic history and has added significantly to our knowledge of the prewar Japanese foreign policy decision-making process. He
has done much to explode the myth of civilian versus military, or army
versus navy, or northern advance versus southern advance confronta-
tions. By examining the differences within the Foreign Ministry with its
competing factions, the influence of conservative anticommunist politicians, and the fascinating divisions between the service ministries and
the high command, as well as within sections and factions of the Army
General Staff itself, Hosoya was able to reconstruct a highly complex
picture of power struggles, divergent ideologies, and competing objectives. He also exposes different motivations for advocates of a similar
policy, as occurred, for example, when both pro-Axis and anti-Axis
Japanese diplomats called for a treaty with the USSR. What is one to
make of so-called moderate politicians clamoring for an anticommunist
crusade, expansion in the north, and war against the Soviet Union, and
the rabidly anticommunist, expansionist, pro-Axis elements arguing for
an alliance with communist Russia? Or the attempts of the moderate
civilians to enlist the support of the traditionally anti-Russian generals to
counter such pro-Soviet policies?

Assessment of personalities and motives are always uncertain and
subjective. It will perhaps not be out of place here, therefore, to suggest
certain alternative views to some of those expressed so well by Hosoya. I
should be inclined, for example, to take a somewhat stronger stand on
Matsuoka than Hosoya has done, particularly in estimating his intentions
at the time of the outbreak of the German-Soviet War.

The records of the Japanese decision-making bodies indicate that
Matsuoka was in favor of breaking the Soviet-Japanese Neutrality Pact
and joining Germany in the attack upon Russia. During the Tokyo war
crimes trials, however, Matsuoka tried to defend himself by claiming
that he had advocated an attack in the north knowing that the military
would oppose it, a tactic that would help delay the Japanese attack in
the south. In presenting this evidence, Hosoya refrains from evaluation.
I believe, however, that the historical evidence is overwhelmingly

against Matsuoka's belated attempts at the war crimes trials to exonerate himself. Not only do the records of his conversations over the years place him squarely among the most rabid of Japanese expansionists, but in the specific case of relations with the Soviet Union one could add, for example, his statement to the German ambassador in Tokyo, General Eugen Ott, shortly after the conclusion of the Neutrality Pact, that "if war should break out between Germany and the Soviet Union, no Japanese Prime Minister or Foreign Minister would be able to keep Japan neutral. In such a case Japan would be impelled by national consideration to join Germany in attacking Russia."[2] These and similar statements Matsuoka made before and after the conclusion of the Neutrality Pact lead to the inescapable conclusion that in seeking a neutrality treaty with the Soviet Union Matsuoka was thinking (as Hosoya correctly describes) of the larger picture, but that he had no intention of committing Japan to strict neutrality.

Hosoya describes but I would stress more the monumental vanity and overconfidence in his own ability that Matsuoka shared with Ribbentrop, as well as a predilection for wishful thinking and the pursuit of illusory plans. Soviet archives, for example, illumine the personal style of Matsuoka, who during diplomatic negotiations used to pat his stomach and say that he was in favor of "soul to soul talks with responsible people" (the stomach, according to the Japanese, is the residence of the soul) and claimed that he stood for "straight and sincere exchanges of opinion" and that "only during personal meetings can ministers share secrets in accordance with time, place, and the problem under discussion."[3] But the Soviets were not impressed by these antics and regarded Matsuoka as basically anti-Soviet. As early as 1929 Soviet Ambassador Aleksandr Troyanovsky characterized Matsuoka as a "fanatical ideologue of Japanese imperialism."[4]

Pursuit of illusory plans was nowhere better illustrated than in Matsuoka's belief that the Tripartite Pact would intimidate the Soviet Union into joining the "four-power entente," or at least into signing a nonaggression pact with Japan, and that the "four-power entente" would in turn serve to pressure the United States into abandoning its hard-line policy toward Japan. What Matsuoka did not realize was that the tripartite alliance was likely to be counterproductive in arousing Soviet suspicions and hardening American determination. The signing of the Tripartite Pact followed the recall of Ambassador Tōgō Shigenori from Moscow and the suspension of Soviet-Japanese negotiations. The fact that Tōgō was only one of the many victims of Matsuoka's purge, which swept the foreign ministry and Japanese diplomatic posts, was overlooked in Moscow. What the Kremlin did perceive was that Matsuoka's appointment marked a significant change in the direction of Japanese foreign policy. The recall of Tōgō, aggravated as it was by the impending visit of German Special Envoy Heinrich Stahmer to Tokyo and the subsequent signing of the Tripartite Pact, caused consternation in Moscow.[5] Matsuoka must thus be faulted for not bothering to calculate the impact of his recall of the Japanese ambassador from Moscow during negotiations. Moreover, in view of the Soviets' understandably negative reaction to the tripartite alliance and their subsequent lack of enthusiasm for a nonaggression pact with Japan, one wonders about Matsuoka's ill-founded confidence in his plans to draw the Soviet Union to the Axis powers.

In fact, both Japanese and German hopes of Soviet cooperation in the delimitation of spheres of influence of the four powers were based on the naive assumption that they could satisfy the Soviet Union by offering territories like Iran, Afghanistan, or India, over which they had no control, while at the same time insisting that the Soviet Union abandon much more vital interests such as Finland and the Balkans, or northern Sakhalin and the Maritime Province Japan hoped to acquire to "round out" its own East Asia Co-Prosperity Sphere. Indeed, Soviet negative reaction to Ribbentrop's offer to Molotov in November 1940 can be clearly seen from Molotov's cable to the Soviet ambassador in London, dated November 17, 1940, in which he writes: "It seems that the Germans and the Japanese would like very much to push us toward the Persian Gulf and India. We declined the discussion of this question, as we consider such advice from Germany out of place."[6] It seems only poetic justice that Matsuoka paid with his career for his pursuit of illusory plans as well as his misplaced trust in Germany. (He was thrown out of the Konoe cabinet when Germany again betrayed Japan by attacking Russia, after leading Japanese leaders to believe that it was going to keep peace in the east at least until after the defeat of Britain.)

Soviet archival sources throw an interesting light on the relationship between Foreign Minister Matsuoka and the Japanese army leadership, which, as Hosoya indicates, was not always smooth. According to these sources, Colonel Nagai Yatsuji was made a member of Matsuoka's entourage on his European trip in order to "watch that in his talks with the Germans the expansive minister would not commit the Japanese army without its knowledge." Chief of the General Staff Sugiyama Gen allegedly reminded Colonel Nagai about this assignment at the sending-off ceremony at Tokyo Central Station, and Nagai discussed it with the foreign minister as soon as they had left Shimonoseki. Matsuoka supposedly reassured Nagai that he was well informed about the matter and that he would not make any commitments.[7]

Hosoya is quite right in linking Soviet-Japanese negotiations to Tokyo's and Moscow's relations not only with Berlin but also with Washington. For example, he suggests correctly that in relations with Japan the Soviet Union wanted just the right degree of closeness to give the Japanese enough security to advance in the south and yet not so deep an involvement as to worsen relations with the United States. At the same time Hosoya fails to tie this in with Japanese motives. For instance, he quotes extensively from the Japanese Foreign Ministry draft of policy for the adjustment of diplomatic relations with the Soviet Union, dated October 3, 1940, but fails to note that the fifth point in the "strategy" section of this document reads: "We shall make every effort to prevent a Russo-American rapprochement."[8]

In assessing Stalin's motives for signing the Neutrality Pact with Japan, Hosoya cites an impressive series of Soviet policy measures in the spring of 1941 that add up to an attempt to placate Hitler. Yet why would Stalin want not only to conclude a neutrality pact with Japan but also to dramatize his agreement with Matsuoka by personally seeing him off at the railroad station? This act would be likely to provoke precisely the kind of reaction by the United States that Moscow (according to secret documents captured by the Japanese and quoted by Hosoya) was trying to avoid in July 1940. Not having access to Soviet internal documents for 1941, we are left with the dilemma of whether the July 1940 position was in fact Stalin's policy, which he changed later by downgrading the importance of ties with the United States, or whether the earlier policy was the position of the Commissariat for Foreign Affairs (probably the policy of Solomon Lozovsky, who was then in charge of Far Eastern affairs). If the first is true, the question then is when and why Stalin changed his views. However, the second is more likely to be true. The April 1941 farewell gesture was probably Stalin's own, and may well have been opposed by the professionals in the Commissariat. Soviet histories shed no light on this problem, nor was my April 1969 interview with the Soviet historian Leonid Kutakov of much help on this point. Kutakov did, however, bring up the question of Soviet overtures to the United States for a united front against Japan in 1933 and 1939, which he said the United States had rejected. He thus implied that the Soviet Union was more or less forced to make its own arrangements with Japan because of American intransigence.[9]

Speaking of Stalin's motives, Hosoya claims that the pact "saved the Soviet Union from the danger of war on two fronts." (He also cites Lupke in support of this interpretation.) Despite Stalin's refusal to take defensive measures in the face of German preparations and warnings that an attack on Russia was imminent, from the Allies and the Soviet spy Richard Sorge, nevertheless it seems naive to believe that Stalin considered a paper agreement with Japan a guarantee against attack. One should rather agree with Soviet historians who say that the neutrality treaty "lessened the threat of a war on two fronts" and that the pact "played a certain role in restraining Japanese militarists"[10] or "made the attack more difficult."[11]

A few other, minor points might be noted. Hosoya depicts Lieutenant-General Tatekawa Yoshitsugu as one of the leaders of an anti-Anglo-Saxon, pro-Soviet group in Japan and asserts that this fact was taken into account when he was appointed ambassador to Moscow. Certainly he was not thus regarded by the Kremlin, which, according to Kutakov, could only look with suspicion on Tatekawa's early "virulent anti-Soviet position." Kutakov further cites the fear expressed by Imperial Household Minister Matsudaira Tsuneo that the Soviet government would not find General Tatekawa acceptable because of the anti-Soviet position he had taken in the League of Nations, but comments that "the Soviet government understood that the rejection of General Tatekawa would be used by anti-Soviet elements in Japan to sabotage the possible stabilization of relations between the two countries."[12]

Another aspect of Soviet-Japanese relations that Hosoya does not touch upon is Soviet intelligence, in particular the Richard Sorge spy ring, which operated successfully in Tokyo until the autumn of 1941, that is, throughout the entire period under study. Inasmuch as Sorge's confederate, Ozaki Hotsumi, was a member of Prince Konoe's brain trust, one wonders about Ozaki's potential impact through Konoe on Japanese policy, particularly on the question of war or peace with Russia after the German attack.[13] It is also interesting to note that the first Soviet accounts of the Sorge case, published in 1965 after a quarter century of total silence, indicated that Sorge kept warning Stalin about the possibility of a German attack, even giving June 22 as the date of attack,[14] that the Kwantung Army's preparations for war with the Soviet Union were not affected by the Neutrality Pact, and that the July 2 Imperial Conference had decided against an immediate attack on the Soviet Union. One of Sorge's last dispatches, on September 14, was to assure Moscow that the Japanese government had finally decided not to attack Russia during 1941.[15]

Hosoya also does not mention the potential impact of a gigantic Soviet sabotage operation carried out on August 2, 1941, in eastern Manchuria. According to John Erickson of the University of Edinburgh, the fact that a number of Japanese fuel and ammunition dumps were blown up, devastating an area more than seven miles across, could have inhibited a possible Japanese thrust into Siberia.[16] At the very least this explosion must have delayed the Japanese timetable of preparations for war, although the final decision in this case was mainly dependent upon the rate of withdrawal of Soviet forces from the Far East.

Soviet official statements[17] and historical writings[18] credit the Japanese defeat at Nomonhan with having played an important role in restraining the Japanese military from attacking the Soviet Union. While Japanese military documents quoted by Hosoya make no reference to this, it is quite possible that some of the advocates of a southern advance may well have been influenced by the strong Soviet resistance to the two Japanese probing actions in 1938 and 1939.

These minor points of interpretation or information do not detract from the immense value of Professor Hosoya's thorough and systematic study of the background of the Japanese decision to conclude a neutrality pact with Moscow in 1941.

ONE

The Japanese-Soviet Neutrality Pact

HOSOYA CHIHIRO

Translated by
PETER A. BERTON

Uneasy Relations on the Manchurian Frontier

The outbreak of the Manchurian Incident in September 1931 and the subsequent Japanese occupation of Manchuria drastically altered the balance of power in Northeast Asia and seriously affected Japanese-Soviet relations. The two nations had resumed diplomatic relations on January 20, 1925, when they signed the Treaty of Peking. Despite continuing mutual hostility between the ruling circles in both countries, as a result of historical confrontation and ideological differences, friendly relations continued for the next several years, as demonstrated by the conclusion of a fisheries treaty and an agreement on oil and coal concessions in northern Sakhalin. All this changed, however, when the Kwantung Army instigated the Manchurian Incident, occupied the area along the South Manchuria Railway, and proceeded to bring northern Manchuria under its armed control. Up to this time northern Manchuria had served as a buffer zone between Japan and the Soviet Union. Now Japanese and Soviet troops directly confronted each other along the entire Manchurian-Soviet border. This naturally heightened the tensions between the two countries and increased the anxiety among Soviet leaders that Japan was again about to embark on a military adventure against Soviet Far Eastern territory.

Immediately after the establishment of the Soviet government in late 1917, the Japanese army had occupied the entire Soviet Far Eastern region east of Lake Baikal, where it attempted to set up anti-revolu-

This essay originally appeared as "Nisso chūritsu jōyaku," in *Taiheiyō sensō e no michi*, vol. 5, part 2, sec. 2, pp. 227–331.

tionary regimes. When Japan moved into Manchuria in 1931, less than ten years had elapsed since its forces had withdrawn from Soviet territory. Moreover, at the end of 1931 the notorious General Araki Sadao became army minister, and a hard-line faction advocating a tough policy toward the Soviet Union emerged among the Japanese military leadership. While it is unlikely that this faction seriously advocated a so-called "preventive war against the Soviet Union," its hostility to Russia was well-known. It is also a fact that around this time rumors of an imminent war between Japan and the USSR achieved world-wide circulation. Under these circumstances, it is not surprising that Soviet leadership displayed considerable anxiety.

In response to the Manchurian Incident and subsequent developments, the Soviet government's policy toward Japan took two forms. First, conscious of their military inferiority to Japan in the Far East, they tried by diplomatic means to settle such problems as border disputes and the disposition of the Chinese Eastern Railway that all too often caused friction between the two countries. Second, they tried to change the balance of power in their favor by rapidly reinforcing their military strength in the Far East.

On the diplomatic front Foreign Commissar Maxim Litvinov, on December 31, 1931, proposed the conclusion of a Japanese-Soviet non-aggression treaty to Yoshizawa Kenkichi, the Japanese ambassador to France, who had stopped in Moscow en route home to become the new foreign minister. During the following year the Soviet government several times renewed its offer of a nonagression treaty.[1] Also in 1932 the Soviets told the Japanese they wanted to sell their share of the Chinese Eastern Railway in Manchuria, thus making clear their tacit acceptance of the extension of the Japanese sphere of influence into northern Manchuria. They further agreed to the establishment of a Manchukuo consulate in Moscow, according de facto recognition to the puppet state.

Parallel with such conciliatory measures toward Japan, the Soviet Union concentrated its energies on strengthening its military position by rapidly expanding its Far Eastern forces, by constructing fortified points along the entire border, and by completing the double-tracking of the Trans-Siberian Railway. These precautionary military measures, however, had the untoward effect of further provoking the Japanese army's traditional suspicion of Russia.

At the time of the Manchurian Incident the Japanese army already considered as unfavorable the balance of military power between its Kwantung Army and the Soviets' Far Eastern forces. After the incident, according to Japanese army General Staff estimates, this balance rapidly moved even further to the disadvantage of Japan. In 1935–36 the ratio of Japanese troops in both Manchuria and Korea to Soviet Far Eastern forces was one to three, and as low as one to ten in aircraft. From the standpoint of national defense, this estimate painted an extremely grave picture. To meet this challenge, some in the military talked of a preventive war against the Soviet Union, while others advocated a restoration of the balance of power through the reinforcement of Japanese troops in Manchuria.

In 1935 the Japanese army, aiming to bring its military strength in Manchuria and Korea to within 80 percent of that of the Soviet forces in the Far East, drew up a national defense plan calling for an increase to eight divisions in its military strength in Manchuria and Korea. This meant adding three divisions to the five it had maintained there ever since the Manchurian Incident. Thus, the psychology of suspicion and fear spurred expansion of the forces of the two antagonists, which, in turn, further aggravated mutual suspicions.

A Japanese-Soviet nonaggression treaty would probably not only have brought to an end this vicious cycle but would perhaps have had a good psychological effect as well. What, then, was the Japanese government's reaction to the Soviet proposals?

Some government officials urged that Japan accept the Soviet proposal "to stabilize relations between the two countries" in order to avoid diplomatic isolation and "do the utmost to bring about a final settlement of the Manchurian Incident." But the general trend was against a nonaggression pact with the USSR. Such a treaty, most officials feared, would permit the Soviets to put pressure on the northern fisheries and the northern Sakhalin concessions. They argued that "the Soviet Union will surely take a high-handed position that will hamper greatly Japanese military movements and the various installations in northern Manchuria." Therefore, "as a first step, satisfactory solutions must be sought to the fisheries, concessions, and other problems, settling at the same time the problems involving Japanese and Soviet interests in northern Manchuria; only then should Japan move toward the conclusion of a nonaggression treaty." This view, which prevailed, was greatly assisted by the tough stand of one faction within the army against both a nonaggression treaty and the purchase of the Chinese Eastern Railway. Finally, on December 13, 1932, the Japanese government rejected the Soviet proposals: "The time is not yet ripe to begin formal negotiations. Efforts should first be made, therefore, to solve the various problems pending between the two countries. As for the negotiations mentioned above, we believe that it would be better to wait a little and let the situation mature with time."[2]

This basic policy of "first settling pending problems" and opposing the conclusion of a nonaggression treaty continued for a long time. To improve somewhat the tense situation between the two countries, however, Tokyo in its reply proposed instead, as a formula for political agreement, the creation of a "Japan-Manchukuo-Soviet Union commission for the prevention of border incidents." Later, in 1935, Tokyo proposed the establishment of a demilitarized zone along the Manchurian-Soviet border. But these and similar Japanese proposals were not favorably received by the Soviet government. The vicious cycle of military expansion continued, although a ray of hope brightened the relations between the two countries when, after some difficulties, negotiations for the sale of the Chinese Eastern Railway resulted in an agreement formally signed by Japan, Manchukuo, and the Soviet Union on March 23, 1935.

The conclusion of the Anti-Comintern Pact between Japan and Germany in November 1936 led to a renewed and rapid deterioration in Japanese-Soviet relations. Thanks to its success in code breaking, the Soviet government became aware of the contents of the secret supplementary protocol according to which Japanese-German cooperation was directed not only against the Communist International but against the Soviet Union as well. Moscow attached great significance to this provision and, in retaliation, refused to go through with the formal signing of a Japanese-Soviet fisheries agreement that had already been initialed. Later the Soviets also increased their pressure against Japanese concessions in northern Sakhalin.

The conditions for the exercise of the northern fisheries rights, renewed through provisional annual agreements, became each year more restrictive. Japanese oil concessionaires in northern Sakhalin were compelled to curtail drastically their operations, while the coal concessions continued to exist in name only. The treatment of Japanese subjects in the Soviet Union became stricter, and with the closing of the four consulates in Odessa, Novosibirsk, Khabarovsk, and Blagoveshchensk, the number of Japanese consulates was reduced by half. Border incidents also increased in frequency, beginning with the clash at Kanch'atzu on June 19, 1937, and followed by the Changkufeng Incident in July 1938 and the Nomonhan Incident in May 1939. The border clashes became increasingly serious, and at Nomonhan there was actual danger of an all-out war. Japanese-Soviet relations, which had consistently deteriorated since the advent of the Anti-Comintern Pact, were on the brink of a complete breakdown by the summer of 1939.

In May 1939 border violations led to an armed clash between Outer Mongolian cavalry and Japanese troops in the Nomonhan sector of the Manchurian-Mongolian border. The situation gradually deteriorated when both the Kwantung Army and the Soviet-Mongolian command sent reinforcements and enlarged the scale of hostilities. By August several tens of thousands of troops, augmented by tanks and artillery, faced each other across the Mongolian plain. This confrontation, going beyond an ordinary border incident, actually threatened a full-scale all-out war between Japan and the Soviet Union. On August 20 Soviet troops began an offensive along the entire front and, owing to their superiority in tanks and artillery, all but annihilated the 23d Division, the nucleus of the Kwantung Army's newly formed 6th Army.

The conclusion in Moscow of the Nazi-Soviet Nonaggression Pact was announced at a time when Japanese and Soviet troops were locked in desperate battle at Nomonhan, and when relations between the two countries were at their lowest ebb. It was natural, therefore, that Japanese political and military leaders felt Germany had betrayed them by violating the spirit of the Anti-Comintern Pact. They were also apprehensive that the Soviets, feeling secure in the west because of the Nazi pact, might either embark on military adventures in the Far East or increase pressure on Japan from the north to make the settlement of the Sino-Japanese war more difficult. In response to this new state of affairs, Japan had to strengthen its precautionary defense position vis-à-vis the Soviet Union by reinforcing the Kwantung Army, especially in the Nomonhan area, and, at the same time, by trying to stop the hostilities at Nomonhan even at the expense of some concessions.

The authorities in Tokyo had wanted to localize the hostilities even at the beginning. Remembering the Manchurian Incident, the emperor in particular was much concerned about the arbitrary actions of the

Kwantung Army. He told the army General Staff that he strongly favored localizing the incident and suggested that, with the settlement of the incident, consideration should also be given to demarcation of the border.[3] On July 17 the Five Ministers Conference (composed of the prime minister and the foreign, finance, army, and navy ministers) decided to continue the policy of containing the incident and to attempt diplomatic negotiations to "alleviate the tense atmosphere and bring peace to the frontier." On July 21 instructions were telegraphed to Ambassador Tōgō Shigenori in Moscow to seek an opportunity to begin diplomatic negotiations for an armistice and for a demarcation of the border.[4]

The Kwantung Army argued that it was not advisable to start diplomatic negotiations while the military situation was not in Japan's favor. Since a similar view was expressed by Ambassador Tōgō,[5] the negotiations were postponed. It was at this point that news reached Tokyo of the conclusion of the German-Soviet Nonaggression Pact on August 23. As a direct result of this Nazi-Soviet bombshell, the cabinet of Baron Hiranuma Kiichirō fell. The cabinet of General Abe Nobuyuki, which succeeded, decided to open immediate negotiations with the Soviet Union. The new cabinet wanted to put a quick end to the Nomonhan Incident, even if under slightly unfavorable conditions, and from there to move toward the solution of the other problems pending between the two countries.

Thus, on August 31 instructions went to Tōgō ordering him to express to the Soviet government Japan's willingness to negotiate three matters: 1) a speedy settlement of the Nomonhan Incident; 2) the establishment of two commissions, one to demarcate the entire Manchurian-Mongolian and Manchurian-Soviet frontier, the other for the peaceful settlement of border disputes; and 3) the conclusion of a commercial treaty.[6] With the outbreak of war in Europe in early September, the Abe cabinet decided on a basic policy of nonintervention in the European conflict and an all-out effort to settle the Sino-Japanese war. A more positive attitude was also taken toward improving relations with the Soviet Union. On September 4 the following cable was sent to Tōgō: "Break the ice and start negotiations to achieve an overall adjustment of diplomatic relations. Parallel with this, try to settle the Nomonhan Incident quickly." Subsequently, on the 6th and 8th, Tokyo cabled three armistice proposals:

Plan 1: Until demarcation of the border, demilitarize the zone of hostilities in the vicinity of Nomonhan.
Plan 2: Until demarcation of the border, all troops in the zone of hostilities should not cross the line they occupy at the time of the cease-fire.
Plan 3: Until demarcation of the border, both sides should not cross the boundary line claimed by Outer Mongolia* (maximum concession).[7]

On September 9 Ambassador Tōgō met with Foreign Commissar Vyacheslav Molotov and transmitted to the Soviet government Japan's intention to negotiate a cease-fire at Nomonhan and its willingness to settle other pending problems, with an aim to achieving an overall adjustment of Japanese-Soviet diplomatic relations.[8]

The Impact of the Nazi-Soviet Nonaggression Pact

While the Japanese thus tried to improve their relations with the Soviet Union, the Germans, wanting to consolidate the New Order forces, were for their own reasons also strongly in favor of an improvement in Japanese-Soviet relations. Having concluded a nonaggression treaty with the USSR and having become involved in an armed conflict with Britain and France, the German government for a while gave up the idea of a military alliance with Japan, although it greatly valued Japanese cooperation. As a member of the Axis camp, Japan could prevent the entry of the United States into the war, and its naval strength was useful as a restraining force against Britain. Beyond that, one should not overlook the value of Japan as a supply route for important strategic materials.

From this viewpoint, even after the conclusion of the Nonaggression Pact with the Soviet Union, Germany assiduously engaged in diplomatic maneuvers to retain Japan as a member of the Axis bloc. To the Japanese, however, Germany's agreement with the Soviets presented an obstacle. As a result of the pact with Russia, Japan's traditional and hypothetical enemy, which, moreover, espoused an ideology incompatible with Japan's national polity, a deep distrust of Germany had arisen in Japan.

To soften the blow to Japan occasioned by the Nonaggression Pact,

* The vicinity of Nomonhan, about 13 kilometers east of the Halha river.

the German government conceived a plan to help improve Japanese-Soviet relations. To promote political understanding between Japan and the USSR, they reasoned, would certainly wipe out Japanese distrust of Germany and would be an effective strategem to revive the idea of Axis collaboration. In addition, if Japanese-Soviet rapprochement progressed to the conclusion of a nonaggression treaty, it would place both Japan and Germany on the same footing vis-à-vis the Soviet Union. Such action would not only rouse Japanese enthusiasm for cooperating with Germany but would help to form an anti-British, Axis-Soviet bloc. This reasoning led to brisk German diplomatic activity to bring about Japanese-Soviet understanding and a nonaggression pact between the two countries.

The problem of adjusting Japanese-Soviet relations had already been taken up during the negotiations leading to the German-Soviet treaty. On August 15 Molotov, in a conversation with the German ambassador in the Soviet Union, Friedrich Werner Count von der Schulenburg, asked "whether the German Government was prepared to influence Japan for the purpose of improvement in Soviet-Japanese relations and settlement of border conflicts." To this Foreign Secretary Joachim von Ribbentrop gave an affirmative reply.[9] Soon thereafter, on the night of August 23 when Ribbentrop was in Moscow to sign the Nonaggression Pact, the following exchange with Stalin was recorded:

> The Reich Foreign Minister stated that the German-Japanese friendship was in no wise directed against the Soviet Union. We were, rather, in a position, owing to our good relations with Japan to make an effective contribution to an adjustment of the differences between the Soviet Union and Japan. Should Herr Stalin and the Soviet Government desire it, the Reich Foreign Minister was prepared to work in this direction. He would use his influence with the Japanese Government accordingly and keep in touch with the Soviet representative in Berlin on this matter.
>
> Herr Stalin replied that the Soviet Union indeed desired an improvement in its relations with Japan, but that there were limits to its patience with regard to Japanese provocations. If Japan desired war, it could have it. The Soviet Union was not afraid of it and was prepared for it. If Japan desired peace—so much the better! Herr Stalin considered the assistance of Germany in bringing about an improvement in Soviet-Japanese relations as useful, but he did not want the Japanese to get the impression that the initiative in this direction had been taken by the Soviet Union.[10]

These two conversations show that the Soviet government had clearly transmitted to the German side its affirmative attitude toward adjusting relations with Japan and its expectation of Germany's good offices.

The night before his conference with Stalin, Ribbentrop met with the Japanese ambassador to Germany, General Ōshima Hiroshi. He asked for Ōshima's understanding concerning the forthcoming conclusion of the Nonaggression Pact with the USSR. It was his belief, he went on, that the best policy with which to confront Britain was the conclusion of a nonaggression treaty among Japan, Germany, and the Soviet Union and, if asked, he was prepared "to mediate a settlement between Japan and Russia." [11] On September 5, when Ōshima visited Hitler's headquarters on the eastern front, Ribbentrop again expounded his idea of a Japanese-German-Soviet joint front against Britain. [12]

Parallel with these *démarches* in Berlin, Ribbentrop's diplomatic efforts to form an anti-British bloc included an approach to Ambassador Tōgō in Moscow and persistent maneuvers directed at the Japanese ruling circles and organs of public opinion through Ambassador Eugen Ott in Tokyo. On September 6 and 7 Ambassador Schulenburg in Moscow held lengthy conferences with Tōgō. He argued that the improvement in Japanese-Soviet relations, and especially the solution of the Nomonhan Incident, would be of benefit to both Japan and the USSR, that the Soviet side was not opposed to negotiations, and that, if the need arose, Germany would at any time offer its good offices. Schulenburg urged repeatedly that negotiations with the Soviet authorities be started as soon as possible. [13]

On the other side of the globe, in Tokyo, Ambassador Ott urged Ribbentrop's views in numerous conversations with leading personalities in the Foreign Ministry, the armed forces, political groups, business circles, and the press. On September 16 he reported that "he found increasing appreciation of the necessity for a settlement between Japan and Russia." He also advised that, to encourage this trend and to bring about a Japanese-Soviet nonaggression pact, Germany might usefully influence the Soviet government to give up its support of Chiang Kaishek; to sign a long-term agreement meeting Japanese wishes with regard to the oil fields in Sakhalin; and to send an influential individual as ambassador to Tokyo. [14]

According to available records, Ott continued these efforts at least until May of the following year. He was joined in these maneuvers by former Ambassador to Italy Shiratori Toshio and by Ōshima, who was summoned from Berlin. For example, on May 10, 1940, Ott reported that in order to overcome the distrust between Japan and the Soviet Union, he was "endeavoring to promote personal contact between the Russian Embassy and influential Japanese."[15] This report illustrates Ott's attempts to win support for Ribbentrop's design.

What position did the Japanese government take with regard to the adjustment of relations with the Soviet Union and the conclusion of a nonaggression treaty? As we have already seen, the newly organized Abe cabinet determined to resolve the Nomonhan Incident as one item in a policy aiming at the overall adjustment of diplomatic relations with the USSR, and to this end, Tōgō met with Foreign Commissar Molotov on September 9.

At their second meeting, on the 10th, Molotov, in response to the Japanese proposal, indicated his approval of a commercial treaty and agreed to the creation of a border demarcation commission as well as a commission for the peaceful settlement of border incidents. He was opposed, however, to Japan's first proposal for a Nomonhan armistice agreement. Molotov argued that for many years there had been an accepted border in the vicinity of Nomonhan and that the troops of both sides should be withdrawn behind that boundary line. This was contrary to Tōgō's proposal, which did not recognize the same boundary line. At their third meeting, on September 14, when it became apparent that the two negotiators could not agree on the boundary issue, Tōgō submitted the second Japanese plan, according to which the boundary question would be settled later, but hostilities were to cease at the lines presently occupied by the two armies. Molotov accepted this proposal at their fourth meeting, on the 15th. The two sides thus came to an agreement with regard to the Nomonhan armistice, and a joint statement was issued on September 16.[16]

The negotiations between Molotov and Tōgō halted the armed clash at Nomonhan. They also led to an agreement to establish two commissions and to a promise to move toward the conclusion of a commercial treaty. With the signing of the Nomonhan armistice agreement Japanese-Soviet relations, which had steadily deteriorated since the Anti-Comintern Pact, changed in tone and gradually began to return to normalcy. In a sense they entered a new phase.

The Policy Debate

While the Abe cabinet, which had taken office on August 30, 1939, was inclined to move no further toward the Soviet Union than normalize the situation, there were those in Japan who felt that the time called for a much closer relationship. The pro-Axis ambassador, Shiratori Toshio, advocated a policy of attempting to conclude a nonaggression treaty with the Soviet Union and of moving from there to the establishment of a Japanese-German-Italian-Soviet four-power entente—in other words, the creation of an anti-Anglo-Saxon bloc. He held firmly to the view that the historical mission of Japanese diplomacy was the establishment of a New Order in East Asia and that, in any struggle between totalitarian countries seeking to change the international status quo and democratic countries trying to preserve it, Japan should ally itself with Germany and Italy. Further, in this analysis of the international political situation, the Soviet Union, as an anti-status quo power, stood in opposition to the status quo powers—Britain, France, and the United States. Since the Soviet Union, in this sense, was in the same position as Japan, Germany, and Italy, cooperation among them was mutually advantageous. Shiratori's "renovationist" ideas found many sympathizers among young Japanese diplomats, and a "renovationist faction," with Shiratori as its leader, gradually emerged as a power bloc in the Foreign Ministry.

In November 1939, in a speech entitled "The European War and Japan's Position," Shiratori claimed that in a memorandum submitted to the government at the beginning of July he had argued the necessity of forming a "four-power entente."[17] A very interesting document, possibly the same memorandum, has been found among the papers of Prince Konoe Fumimaro, which, if not written by Shiratori himself, was presumably written by one of his confederates. This typed manuscript, dated July 19, 1939, and entitled "How to Settle the China Incident Speedily and Advantageously," contains the following passages:

It is well known that at present the Chiang regime is supported by two pillars. These are, of course, Great Britain and the Soviet Union.

If one of these two pillars were to be removed, the China Incident could probably be settled in an unexpectedly short time. If the Soviet Union is the pillar removed, it is a definite possibility that in less than half a year the present incident could be completely brought to an end. . . .

It must never be forgotten that these maneuvers vis-à-vis the Soviet Union must be taken jointly with Germany. But if in the meantime, while we dilly-dally, Germany should separately come to an understanding with the Soviet Union, it would bring about the gravest crisis for Japan.

The following conditions should be presented to the Soviet government:

1) It must be made clear that Germany has no intention of moving into the Ukraine.

2) It must be made clear that the three allied countries—Japan, Germany, and Italy—are prepared to recognize the establishment of Soviet administrative districts in the areas of Shensi, Tibet, Yunnan, Sinkiang, and Kansu.

3) If the Soviet Union expresses the intention of moving south into Burma, the contracting parties, as a final concession, should be prepared to recognize such a move in an added secret clause.

4) If war should break out between Britain and the Soviet Union as a result of this, Japan, Germany, and Italy would collaborate with the Soviet Union, and [Japan should] propose to convene immediately a secret Japanese-Soviet-German-Italian military staff conference to plan operations against Britain, France, and the United States.

The strength of the communist forces in China has grown to the point where they cannot be ignored. Instead of getting into difficulties by attempting to eradicate them, a much wiser policy would be to include them in Soviet administrative districts, which would be set up under an agreement with the Soviet Union . . . .

The strength of the Japanese-Soviet-German-Italian combination diplomatically, militarily, and economically would not be at all inferior to that of Britain, France, and the United States.[18]

Although this policy was advocated as a solution to the Sino-Japanese war, it is noteworthy that such a four-power entente was proposed in Japan before the conclusion of the Nazi-Soviet Nonaggression Pact, when the Japanese generally regarded the Soviet Union as still the principal object of the tripartite cooperation among Japan, Germany, and Italy.[19]

A movement calling for a nonaggression treaty with the Soviet Union as an important step toward the realization of a four-power entente was activated by one segment of the Japanese right wing immediately after the conclusion of the Nazi-Soviet Nonaggression Pact.[20] With the support of the German embassy in Tokyo and especially with the return to Japan of Ambassador Shiratori in mid-October, the movement gradually began to gather strength.

Already at the beginning of September Shiratori had made known to the Germans his view that Japan would welcome their help in concluding a nonaggression treaty with the Soviet Union.[21] Upon his return home he immediately began to advocate the conclusion of a Japanese-Soviet agreement as a step toward the formation of a four-power entente. He expounded his views to important persons in the government, he appealed to financial circles and tried to arouse public opinion through speeches and panel discussions, and he collaborated closely with Ambassador Ott.[22] On November 16 Prince Konoe said that "pro-German and pro-Soviet sentiments are spreading among young officials, and one can say that this includes almost all the younger members of the Foreign Ministry."[23] Even if his judgment was not wholly accurate, it is probably true that support for the idea of Japanese-Soviet collaboration had grown in the Foreign Ministry and other government agencies. Above all, the mere fact that Konoe himself had realized this was of profound political significance.

That the idea of Japanese-Soviet cooperation reached even into political circles may be seen in the debates on foreign affairs during the 75th Session of the Imperial Diet in January 1940, when two diametrically opposed viewpoints were consistently expressed. According to the first, the basis of Japanese foreign policy rested on doing the utmost to come to a diplomatic settlement with Britain and the United States, while at the same time keeping a careful watch on the Soviet Union. According to the second, represented, for example, by Kiyose Ichirō, Japan had to strengthen cooperation with Germany and Italy while adjusting its diplomatic relations with the Soviet Union through German mediation.[24]

One should not overlook the fact that this growing movement toward Japanese-Soviet cooperation was related to the domestic struggle for political power. On November 19 the Osaka *Jiji shimpō* reported the creation of a pro-Soviet, anti-British national movement headed by Admiral Suetsugu Nobumasa, which raised the slogan of a New Order in East Asia based on a pro-Soviet diplomatic policy. This was probably an attempt to capitalize on the rising tide of enthusiasm for Japanese-Soviet cooperation among various sectors of the Japanese public, and to mobilize and utilize anti-British sentiment in an effort to break the power of the pro-Anglo-American forces. The sponsors of this movement included Shiratori, General Koiso Kuniaki, and two members of the House of Representatives, Tanomogi Keikichi and Miki Bukichi.

The government and the pro-Anglo-American group had to be extremely cautious in dealing with this movement, which utilized its demand for a nonaggression treaty with the Soviet Union and for a four-power entente against the Anglo-Saxon nations for domestic political purposes. They opposed it also from a deep ideological hostility to closer relations between Japan and the Soviet Union.

On September 3 former Foreign Minister Arita Hachirō referred to the movement in conversation with Baron Harada Kumao: "There is a very dangerous movement now afoot to align Japan with the German-Soviet nonaggression treaty and to confront Britain with a military alliance [among] Japan, Germany, and the Soviet Union. The right wing clique of converted left wingers provides the prime motive power behind this movement." [25] On September 22, with Harada present, Admiral Nomura Kichisaburō, who was slated to become the new foreign minister, met with General Araki Sadao and other military officers and a group of diplomats including Satō Naotake, Matsudaira Tsuneo, and Mushakōji Kintomo. Nomura noted that some of those who had earlier promoted a German-Italian alliance were now spearheading a movement for a nonaggression treaty with the Soviet Union and thereafter for a military alliance with Germany and the Soviet Union. He then turned to Araki and said: "We would like you to come to the forefront and lead a movement to counter the argument that we must sign a nonaggression treaty with the Soviets or that Japan, Germany, and the Soviet Union should now get together to beat the Anglo-Saxons." His request may be interpreted as part of a scheme of the Anglo-American faction to use the strength of the "ideological" right wing to block the activities of the "renovationist" right wing. [26]

At the beginning of his tenure as prime minister, Abe had supported the idea of Japanese-German-Soviet cooperation, including the conclusion of a nonagression treaty with the Soviet Union. [27] But gradually his enthusiasm waned, no doubt in part because of the activities, described by Harada, of those within ruling circles who opposed such a treaty. The appointment of Nomura to the post of foreign minister at the end of September made it evident that Japan would not go beyond the understanding reached by Tōgō and Molotov on September 15 in seeking rapprochement with the USSR. On October 25 the new vice foreign minister, Tani Masayuki, told Harada that "while Japan wanted to settle practical problems with the Soviet Union through diplomatic negotiations, a nonaggression treaty was of course out of the question."[28]

The new cabinet's basic policy in foreign affairs was outlined in a memorandum dated October 4, drafted by Vice Minister Tani and entitled "Foreign Policy to be Pursued in Response to the European War." It contained the following passage concerning Japanese policy toward the Soviet Union:

> Soviet policy on occasion takes sharp turns. Its bolshevization policy, however, remains consistent. Without dropping the vigilance we have displayed in the past, we should at this time make a special *attempt to calm Japanese-Soviet relations.** To achieve this, the basic principle would be direct negotiations with the Soviet Union, although Germany might be utilized as an intermediary.
> a) To reduce tension in diplomatic relations, the following measures should be considered: a solution to the general border problem, the settlement of pending problems, and the conclusion of a commercial agreement.
> b) To solve the general border problem, Japan, Manchukuo, the Soviet Union, and Mongolia should respect the border. In case of border disputes, [Japan] should not resort to force but rather try to settle them through peaceful negotiations. To achieve this, two commissions should be established: one to settle border incidents and the other to demarcate the border itself.
> c) *Although at the present time we have no intention of concluding a nonaggression treaty,* such a treaty should be considered in case a proposal should come from the Soviet Union.[29]

Prime Minister Abe, despite his earlier interest in a nonaggression treaty with the Soviet Union, now cooperated with the Anglo-American faction. On November 4 he told Harada: "The idea of using Soviet power to expel Britain and the United States is very bad. Not only materially, but especially spiritually, it does not amount to much."[30]

That same month Ambassador Tōgō in Moscow suggested to the newly appointed foreign minister that consideration be given to the conclusion of a nonaggression treaty with the Soviet Union.[31] His recommendations, however, differed fundamentally from the plan proposed by Shiratori and his group, who saw a Japanese-Soviet agreement as a

---

* Henceforth, unless otherwise indicated, italics are the author's.

step toward the conclusion of a four-power entente. Tōgō consistently opposed a tripartite alliance as well as the German mediation offered by Ambassador Schulenburg.[32] Tōgō's plan, in fact, had no relation to a tripartite pact. In his judgment the conclusion of a nonaggression pact with the Soviet Union would have two effects. First, it would lower Chungking's will to resist Japan and help to end the Sino-Japanese war. Second, it would cause the American government to reconsider its policy of applying pressure against Japan and contribute to improved Japanese-American relations.[33]

Tōgō's advice, however, was not accepted by Nomura. On December 28 the government adopted the "Principles of Foreign Policy," based on Tani's memorandum of October 4. And if one compares the sections concerned with policy toward the Soviet Union in these two documents, it becomes clear that the Japanese attitude toward a nonaggression treaty with the USSR had become even more negative.

> c) A nonaggression treaty should not be officially considered at least until the outlook for the two preconditions becomes clear: (the cessation of Soviet aid to China and the abandonment of menacing military preparations against Japan and Manchukuo). Therefore, such a treaty should not be proposed. In case of a proposal from the other side, however, we *should strongly emphasize that the urgent task is the settlement of the two preconditions rather than the conclusion of an agreement.* Such moves by the USSR should be utilized to facilitate the solution of pending problems, encouraging at the same time the adoption of a nonaggression posture.
>
> However, in order to deal more advantageously with the United States, we should *simulate an atmosphere of a Japanese-Soviet rapprochement.*[34]

Although journalistic writings labeled Nomura's foreign policy as a "dual American-Soviet diplomacy," this document shows that it was essentially a policy emphasizing relations with the United States, and that the purported Japanese-Soviet rapprochement was only an attempt to soften America's hard-line policy toward Japan.

On December 7 the Osaka *Mainichi shimbun* reported that "the United States is concerned about rumors of a Japanese-Soviet rapprochement, is in a dilemma over its hard-line policy toward Japan, and is making inquiries about the possible conclusion of a Soviet-Japanese nonaggression treaty." This gave the impression that the Japanese strategy of "dual diplomacy" had been successful. In reality, the United States was aware that the seeming rapprochement with the Soviet Union was merely a diplomatic weapon in Japan's negotiations with the United States. This can be easily seen in the November 24 meeting between the Japanese ambassador in Washington, Horinouchi Kensuke, and Secretary of State Cordell Hull. If Japan could find no means of obtaining economic cooperation from the United States, Horinouchi warned, liberal elements and business interests in Japan might be forced to seek such cooperation from the Soviet Union. To this Hull icily replied that "whatever surprise might be created in the United States by the development of closer relations between Japan and another power, it would not be equivalent to the surprise which was created when Hitler entered into closer relations with that same foreign power."[35]

Three plans had been put before the Abe cabinet to improve Japan's relations with the Soviet Union. The first aimed at normalizing Japanese-Soviet relations through the settlement of pending problems, such as demarcation of the border, and the conclusion of a commercial treaty and a long-term fisheries agreement. The second visualized the stabilization of diplomatic relations by moving one step beyond the settlement of pending problems to the conclusion of a nonaggression treaty along the lines proposed by Ambassador Tōgō. The third plan envisaged a nonaggression treaty as a stepping stone to the formation of a four-power entente.

The Abe cabinet, needless to say, chose the first plan. And insofar as the solution of pending problems was concerned, this period witnessed several developments that attest to the fact that Japanese-Soviet relations at least took a turn for the better. For example, on November 19 Tōgō and Molotov agreed to the creation of a commission charged with demarcation of the border in the Nomonhan area. The first meeting of the commission took place in Chita, December 7–25; the second followed in Harbin, January 7–30, 1940. Also, on October 4 Tōgō submitted a Japanese proposal containing the principles to govern a commercial treaty, and on November 15 Foreign Minister Nomura, in a meeting with the newly appointed Soviet ambassador, Konstantin Smetanin, proposed that negotiations for a long-term fisheries agreement should start.

The very fact that these negotiations got under way testified to a new era of understanding between Japan and the Soviet Union, although many obstacles still had to be removed before negotiations could progress harmoniously. Nevertheless, as far as the fisheries problem was concerned, a tentative agreement was reached on December 31 (the agreement for the previous year had not been signed until April 4, 1939). In conjunction with this, agreement was reached regarding the final payment in compensation for the Chinese Eastern Railway. It might be said that these were symbols of a new era of reconciliation between the two countries.

The Initiative of the Army General Staff

The day the Yonai cabinet was formed on January 16, 1940, Arita Hachirō outlined the foreign policies of the new cabinet. In an interview with the press, commenting on Japanese policy toward the Soviet Union, the new foreign minister stated: "Japan will continue the previously adopted policy of seeking a prior settlement of pending problems." He further made it clear that he intended to do his utmost to improve diplomatic relations with the Soviet Union through such measures as the establishment of commissions to demarcate the border and to resolve border incidents. At the same time, Arita revealed his negative attitude toward a nonaggression treaty. "If border settlement were to proceed in a comprehensive fashion," 'he said,' "it would have essentially the same results as a nonaggression treaty. A nonaggression treaty is a matter for the distant future and is not very useful." [36]

This argument that a nonaggression treaty in itself would be "not very useful" as a guarantee of the nation's security had some historical basis. But from the point of view of power politics one could hardly contend that, given the realities of international politics in the Far East, a Japanese-Soviet nonaggression treaty would have had no value. As Ambassador Tōgō had observed, there is no doubt that a political rapprochement between Japan and the Soviet Union at that time would have dealt a severe psychological blow to the Chungking regime, would probably have complicated relations between the Nationalists and Communists in China, and would have affected American policy toward Japan. Ambassador Tōgō's proposal merited careful consideration; it did not deserve a flat refusal.

Arita's judgment that a nonaggression pact was "not very useful" was not based upon objective examination of a treaty's political effects.

Rather it resulted from Arita's personal ideological antipathy to rapprochement with the Soviet Union and his fears that Shiratori and his supporters might take advantage of a treaty. In short, his subjective feelings had gained the upper hand. From the very beginning Arita's diplomacy was characterized by concern for the establishment of a new order in East Asia and cooperation with Britain and the United States and by a strong opposition to international communism, that is, to the Soviet Union.

As foreign minister earlier in the decade, Arita had consistently advocated "taking appropriate measures to save East Asia from the menace of bolshevization."[37] It was he who had concluded the Anti-Comintern Pact with Germany—a treaty directed not only against international communism but against the Soviet Union as well—and after it was signed had repeatedly urged that it be strengthened. Before his appointment as foreign minister in the first Konoe cabinet, Arita had participated in an organization called Comrades for the Strengthening of the Anti-Comintern Pact, organized by Tōyama Mitsuru, Admiral Abo Kiyokazu, Tokutomi Sohō, and other well-known anti-Soviet ultranationalists.[38] Arita thus had no objection to strengthening cooperation with Germany and Italy so long as its objective was opposition to the Soviet Union.

As a result, with the strongly anti-Soviet Arita as foreign minister and the pro-Anglo-American backing of the Yonai cabinet, it was hardly to be expected that positive diplomatic measures would be taken toward a rapprochement with the Soviet Union. At this time Kita Reikichi, a Minseitō member of the House of Representatives, wrote: "No Japanese has a common world view with the Soviet Union. Having led the nation until now to reject communism, we cannot today suddenly join hands with a communist country. And the sacred war against China would also lose its meaning."[39] This statement accurately represented the ideological opposition within Japanese ruling circles that barred the way to a political rapprochement with the Soviet Union.

Pressure within Japan for a political rapprochement with the Soviet Union came from those concerned with the dynamics of international power politics rather than from those motivated primarily by ideology. Years earlier, before German-Soviet cooperation culminated in the Rapallo Treaty of 1922, the German government had similarly hesitated on account of ideological prejudices. It had been the German armed forces who, motivated by a desire to build up German military power, took the initiative toward German-Soviet cooperation. In the same manner, the Japanese Army General Staff, concerned with settlement of the Sino-Japanese war, came forward at this time as the driving force toward Japanese-Soviet cooperation.

More than two years after the outbreak of the China War the Japanese army appeared to be bogged down and a drain on national resources. The outbreak of war in Europe provided the army with a fresh impetus to end the war. There were two reasons for this. First, the withdrawal from the Far East of British and French influence, which until then had constituted an obstacle in the prosecution of the war, created a more favorable situation for Japan. Second, the army realized that it needed to regain freedom of action if it were to respond to unforeseen developments that might arise because of the war in Europe. Moreover, the contradictions in Japan's wartime economy had become more acute in the autumn and winter of 1939, and Japan could not allow itself to be pushed into a drawn-out war.

In view of these circumstances, some officials in the Army Ministry began to argue for a gradual reduction of the Japanese expeditionary forces in China and for a voluntary cessation of the war. For budgetary reasons the Military Section developed a plan to shorten the military front in China. Even within the Army General Staff there was strong sentiment for an advantageous peace settlement with the Chungking regime, to be brought about through a variety of measures including military operations, plots, and an economic blockade. Concrete examples of this policy were the Nanning operation in the latter part of November 1939, the direct peace overtures to the Chungking regime in the Paulownia (*Kiri*) operation of February–September 1940, and the bolstering of the Wang Ching-wei puppet regime. Japanese-Soviet rapprochement was also advocated as a part of the General Staff's policy of attempting to settle the China War.

At this time, the Chungking regime was receiving economic assistance from abroad through three principal routes: Burma, French Indochina, and the northwest. With the outbreak of war in Europe it appeared feasible to cut the first two routes by applying diplomatic and military pressure against Britain and France. The northwestern route, needless to say, was the supply route from the Soviet Union. If Britain and France could be pressed to the wall and the first two routes of assistance cut, the Chungking regime would be forced to rely on the remaining route from the northwest, although its transportation capacity was estimated to be far less than that of the routes through Burma and French Indochina. The northwestern route was also, so to speak, a psychological pipeline symbolizing Chinese-Soviet friendship.

Thus, some on the General Staff thought, through a political rapprochement with the Soviet Union, to break down Chungking's will to resist, both by cutting the northwestern supply route and completing the economic blockade and by driving a wedge into Soviet-Chinese psychological solidarity.

Major-General Tsuchihashi Yūichi, who was appointed chief of the Intelligence Division of the Army General Staff in December 1939, leaned toward an economic blockade as a means of settling the Sino-Japanese conflict. Having grappled with the problem of closing the French Indochina route when he was chief of staff of Japanese forces in south China, Tsuchihashi in his new post was drawn to the idea of rapprochement with the Soviet Union in order to sever Soviet assistance to the Chungking regime.

At this time the mainstream on the General Staff still strongly favored a hard line toward the Soviet Union and a diplomatic policy based on ideological considerations. Tsuchihashi opposed this view on the ground that "ideology must be fought with ideology." He argued that there were real advantages in "considering the conclusion of a treaty so as to reach agreement with regard to the Soviet-Manchurian border," and he advocated the conclusion of a nonaggression treaty even at the price of concessions in the demarcation of the Nomonhan border. Tsuchihashi later recalled that he "personally drafted" a "New Diplomatic Policy" embodying these measures and at the beginning of April presented it at a meeting of General Staff division chiefs, where it was unanimously approved. His account, however, is disputed by Major Kōtani Etsuo who, as the head of the Russia desk of the Intelligence Division, was charged by Tsuchihashi with drafting a treaty for a reconciliation between Japan and the Soviet Union. Kōtani claims that he himself conceived the idea of a neutrality treaty as the formula for a political rapprochement.[40]

Since a nonaggression treaty had been specifically rejected in the "Principles of Foreign Policy" adopted in December by the previous cabinet, and since Arita, the new foreign minister, had taken the same

position, the military naturally anticipated difficulty in securing government approval. The Foreign Ministry explained its opposition to the
Army General Staff by arguing that Japan had previously rejected a Soviet proposal for a nonaggression treaty, and for Japan to bring it up now
"would be absolutely impossible, considering both the nation's 'face' and
consistency in its foreign policy."[41]

By April 1940 the General Staff's contribution to diplomacy, insofar
as Japanese-Soviet relations were concerned, was summed up in Tsuchihashi's "New Diplomatic Policy" and in Kōtani's draft of a Japanese-
Soviet neutrality treaty, which set forth a concrete plan for the adjustment of relations with the Soviet Union. General Mutō Akira, chief of
the Military Affairs Bureau, announced the Army Ministry's approval of
the Tsuchihashi draft, while Oka Takazumi, chief of the Intelligence
Division of the Navy General Staff, said that "the navy without reserva-
tion supports this plan."[42]

While responsible officials in both the army and the navy were
showing their acceptance of Tsuchihashi's plan, leaders in the Foreign
Ministry, from Foreign Minister Arita down, were still disapproving of a
political rapprochement with the Soviet Union. Arita replied directly to
General Tsuchihashi asking, "Tsuchihashi, do you think one can place
trust in agreements concluded with the Soviet Union?"[43] Arita's reaction to the army's maneuvers in support of rapprochement with the Soviet Union can be clearly seen in his statement to Baron Harada on May
23:

> I intend to do something about our problems with the Soviet Union so
> long as it does not adversely affect our relations with Britain and the
> United States. But this really cannot be counted upon. I think there are
> many among the military who dance to the tune of the popular front.
> After all, two or three professors who were expelled from the universities
> for being notorious Marxists are among the brains behind the military.
> They are trying to remodel the economy, talking about controls over
> profits or a wartime economic structure. This must also be watched.[44]

In contrast to the foreign minister's views, the renovationist faction
within the Foreign Ministry responded to the new situation created by
German operations against Norway and Denmark with a strong argument for "a certain political understanding" and "further strengthening

of cooperation and friendly relations with Germany and Italy." They also sought an adjustment of diplomatic relations with the Soviet Union.

On April 22 Shigematsu Nobuo, an official belonging to the renovationist group, prepared a document entitled "Principles of Foreign Policy, II," which was studied by a liaison committee on the 24th. Concerning Japan's policy toward the Soviet Union, the draft stated:

> c) When appropriate, [Japan should] demand that the Soviet Union abandon its aid to Chiang Kai-shek and cease its threatening military preparations against Japan and Manchukuo; in return, [Japan will] consider the conclusion of a Japanese-Soviet nonaggression treaty.
>
> d) Insofar as policies toward Great Britain and the United States allow, [Japan should] attempt to strengthen cooperation between Germany and the Soviet Union and at the same time plan to bring the Soviet Union into the war against Britain. To this end, if the need should arise, [Japan should] not be deterred from reaching a certain political understanding with the Soviet Union. In this case, circumstances permitting, [Japan should] consider the acquisition of northern Sakhalin and the Maritime Province.

Shigematsu's draft was revised on May 1, but the main points of policy toward the Soviet Union remained the same, with the sole addition of the following clause: "Consider the recognition of a Soviet or Chinese communist sphere of influence in Sinkiang and other areas in northwest China."[45]

This document presumably was not given the government's official approval. It is significant, however, that parallel with the activities in the army, a concrete plan was prepared within the Foreign Ministry, the aim of which was the conclusion of a Japanese-Soviet nonaggression treaty and further steps in the direction of a four-power entente. This was long before such activities came to the surface under Foreign Minister Matsuoka.

When Japan at last began to take positive action to bring about a rapprochement with the Soviet Union, the Soviet side appeared to suggest that it too desired to adjust diplomatic relations with Japan. On March 29, 1940, in a speech before the Supreme Soviet, Foreign Commissar Molotov touched upon relations with Japan. He said that judging from the conclusion of a provisional fisheries convention and Japan's consent to pay the last installment on the Chinese Eastern Railway, relations between the two countries were gradually turning for the better. Mutual agreement had not been reached on demarcation of the frontier in the Nomonhan area, however, in spite of the formation of a joint commission. Therefore, he regretted that he could not express great satisfaction in regard to an overall improvement of diplomatic relations with Japan.[46] It was also reported in the Osaka *Asahi shimbun* of April 18, 1940, that "on April 14 Soviet diplomatic officials requested through Ambassador Tōgō that the Japanese government give serious consideration to the fundamental improvement of relations between the two countries." Although a diplomatic document substantiating this newspaper report has not been found, on April 20 Foreign Minister Arita told Baron Harada: "The border problem is generally settled and I think it will be possible to fix the frontier. Since the Soviet Union is truly trying to solve the various problems and get closer to Japan, I would like to reach a settlement as soon as possible."[47] One might assume from this statement that the Soviet government had made some move to improve its relations with Japan.

But what would have motivated Soviet diplomacy to attempt a rapprochement with Japan at this time? Although sources to verify it are not available, one might conjecture that the Soviets wanted thereby to put pressure on the United States. Ever since the Soviet-Finnish war Soviet relations with Britain and France had deteriorated, while the American government had instituted a "moral embargo" and applied various economic pressures. There was a general increase of ill feeling toward the Soviet Union in the United States, and relations between the two countries had cooled perceptibly.

To improve this situation, the Soviet Union did two things: it began negotiations with the United States, and it tried to simulate a growing political rapprochement with Japan, doubtless in the hope of restraining the United States and softening American policy toward the USSR. Needless to say, one of the basic tactics of Soviet Far Eastern policy had been utilization of the confrontation and contradictions between Japanese and American "imperialisms." For instance, Molotov suggested to Laurence A. Steinhardt, the American ambassador to the Soviet Union, the possibility of cooperation between the American and Soviet navies against "our common foe," Japan.[48] On the other side of the globe, in Washington, Soviet ambassador Constantine Oumansky was negotiating with Secretary of State Cordell Hull for removal of the "moral embargo." Impatient at the impasse in the negotiations, he threatened that if American policy continued to discriminate against the Soviet Union, the latter would treat Japan more generously, and "might have to retaliate, especially in the Far East."[49]

Having taken note of Soviet attempts to improve relations with Japan, Foreign Minister Arita, at the end of April, sent instructions to Ambassador Tōgō to request the Soviet government to stop its aid to Chungking and cooperate with the Wang Ching-wei regime. Tōgō responded that it was unthinkable that the Soviet Union should unconditionally accept such a proposal without raising further questions in the negotiations. He therefore wanted first to ascertain the real intentions of the government with regard to the "limits of diplomatic adjustment between Japan and the Soviet Union."[50] Tōgō also used this opportunity to press his earlier proposal for a nonaggression treaty. He sent a second secretary from the Moscow embassy, Saitō Kiura, to Tokyo with instructions to size up the situation in the Japanese capital and try to convince influential people of the need to conclude a nonaggression treaty with the Soviet Union.[51]

In April and May 1940 the problem of Japanese-Soviet conciliation was a frequent topic of discussion not only among high officials but also among middle echelon administrative officials of the Army, Navy, and Foreign Ministry. For instance, it was reported that insofar as the basic policy of Japanese-Soviet rapprochement was concerned, there was by this time no disagreement among members of the Four Bureau and Two Division Chiefs Conference—consisting of the chiefs of the East Asia and Europe-Asia bureaus of the Foreign Ministry, the Military Affairs and Naval Affairs bureaus of the Army and Navy ministries respectively, and the Intelligence divisions of the Army and Navy General Staffs.[52]

Nonetheless, in spite of the positive attitude of the Army General Staff, Tōgō's reports to the Foreign Ministry, and the activities of the renovationists, Foreign Minister Arita did not change his negative attitude toward adjusting relations with the Soviet Union. In a speech to the International Association of Japan in Tokyo on May 4 Arita cautioned against a policy of conciliation. Ott reported his words as follows: "Russia, he said, had always talked of peace but at the same time prepared for war. At present also, Japan must take care that Russia did not pursue a policy of compromise only until she felt herself strong enough for the final clash."[53] On May 12, in a conversation with Baron Harada, Arita again expressed his opposition:

> Recently discussion of a Japanese-Soviet nonaggression treaty has become widespread . . . I don't want to worsen our relations with Britain and the United States, which are bad enough already, and I want to consider [the Soviet problem] with this in mind. Therefore, if a Japanese-Soviet nonaggression treaty would result in further worsening our relations with Britain and the United States, I think it should not be concluded.[54]

It was under these circumstances that the Army General Staff presented Kōtani's draft of a neutrality treaty to a conference of responsible officials. Compared with a nonaggression treaty, the neutrality pact embodied a lesser degree of political rapprochement, and the Foreign Ministry representatives doubtless assumed that as a "compromise" plan it had a chance of winning the approval of their superiors. Using his draft as a basis, Major Kōtani together with Andō Yoshirō, head of the First (Soviet) Section of the Europe-Asia Bureau, soon worked out an official draft of a neutrality treaty.[55] A rough draft of a Japanese-Soviet neutrality treaty, dated May 11, in the Foreign Ministry archives is probably the one prepared in this fashion. The draft consists of four articles:

> Article 1. The government of Japan and the government of the Union of Soviet Socialist Republics confirm the Convention Embodying Basic Rules of the Relations between Japan and the USSR signed on January 20, 1925, as the basis of mutual relations.
> Article 2. If one of the signatories is attacked without provocation by one or more nonsignatory powers, the other signatory will maintain neutrality throughout the duration of the conflict.
> Article 3. Both signatories will mutually respect peace and order in areas of special and close interest.
> Article 4. This treaty comes into force on the day of signature and shall remain valid for five years. The signatories at an opportune time prior to the expiration of this treaty will come to an understanding regarding the nature of cooperation between the two countries thereafter.

The following day, May 12, this draft was presented to a "conference of ministries concerned" (possibly the Four Bureau and Two Division Chiefs Conference). Here Article 3 was deleted and the revised draft approved with minor modifications.[56]

What happened next is unknown, although Kōtani recollects that a treaty based on his original draft sailed unexpectedly smoothly through the various ministries and that at the end of May, after it was approved by the cabinet, the foreign minister issued telegraphic instructions to Ambassador Tōgō. Tsuchihashi also recalls that at this time the representatives of the Army, Navy, and Foreign ministries worked together to hasten Japanese-Soviet negotiations.[57]

The government's instructions to Tōgō coincided with a rapidly changing situation in Europe. First the Dunkirk tragedy occurred, then the surrender of France. German troops entered Paris on June 14 and the following day the Soviets, after issuing an ultimatum, occupied Lithuania. Similar measures were taken next with respect to Latvia and Estonia, and all three Baltic states reverted to Russian rule. On June 26 in an ultimatum to Rumania the Soviet Union demanded the cession of Bessarabia and northern Bukovina, and a day later Soviet troops occupied the area.

As a result, German-Soviet discord over the Balkans began to come to the surface, while Soviet relations with other Western countries, which had been in a state of crisis because of the war against Finland, gradually began to improve. On May 24 Sir Stafford Cripps, a leader of the British Labour Party and an advocate of a British-French-American-Soviet "anti-fascist front," was appointed ambassador to Moscow, a sign of a change in British policy toward the Soviet Union.

These changes affecting the Soviet Union in the international sphere convinced Tōgō that circumstances were not suitable for proposing a neutrality treaty. As Tōgō saw it, at a time when the Soviet position was growing stronger, a Japanese proposal for a "weak political combination" devoid of a mutual nonaggression agreement, accompanied by a demand that the Soviet Union cease its aid to Chiang Kai-shek, was a one-sided proposition with very little probability of success.

Tōgō therefore responded sharply, advising in cables of June 19 and 22 that the proposal for a neutrality treaty be postponed. He still thought it would be possible to conclude a nonaggression treaty, however, and advocated this course of action. Should such a treaty materialize, he reasoned, it would have a favorable impact on the settlement of the war with China as well as on the problems of fisheries, oil, and other interests.[58] But Tokyo held firm and ordered Tōgō to carry out its original instructions.

On July 2, in a meeting with Molotov, Tōgō presented a Japanese draft of a neutrality treaty. This draft, consisting of three articles, is identical with that approved by the "conference of ministries concerned" on May 12, except for the addition of the following sentence at the end of Article 1: "Both parties proclaim their desire for the maintenance of peaceful and friendly relations and their mutual respect for territorial integrity."[59] This probably reflected Tōgō's views.

The adjustment of diplomatic relations with the Soviet Union, until then motivated by a desire to stop Soviet aid to Chiang Kai-shek, now acquired added significance when a new consideration arose. This was the policy of southern advance.

Germany as Honest Broker

To take advantage of the "golden opportunity that comes once in a thousand years" and to extend Japan's influence into Southeast Asia, it was imperative that the situation in Northeast Asia remain quiet and that the security of Japan's rear be guaranteed. "Tranquillity in the north" was a prerequisite of Japan's policy of southern advance, which, if worse came to worst, assumed an armed clash with Britain and the United States. It was even suggested that military combination with Germany and Italy and political cooperation with the Soviet Union would prevent armed British and American intervention in the event of Japan's expansion southward.

Thus, with the development of a new situation in Europe in June 1940, the problem of adjusting diplomatic relations with the Soviet Union came to be seen by the Japanese military as having a new strategic significance that went beyond merely isolating the Chungking regime. On June 12 the Navy General Staff prepared a plan entitled "The Empire's Policy in View of the Decline of Britain and France," which significantly began with policy toward the Soviet Union.

1) Overall diplomatic settlement with the Soviet Union;
2) Further disintegration of the Chiang regime; strengthening of military (air and land) operations and the blockade;
3) Declaration and realization of the empire's sphere of influence; and
4) Resolute incorporation into the empire of the mandated territories in the South Seas.[60]

"Defend the north, advance in the south" was the navy's traditional policy for expanding Japanese influence. But before attempting a southern advance, the navy wanted complete security in the defense of the north.

The navy's plan of June 12 was a clear expression of this concern. But the navy was not alone in recognizing the need to take positive diplomatic action vis-à-vis the Soviet Union before launching an advance in the south; the army too was increasingly conscious that such action was necessary. On June 24 Military Affairs Bureau Chief Mutō, in conversation with the German military attaché in Tokyo, brought up the Soviet problem in connection with the Japanese advance into French Indochina and stated that the Japanese army was aware of the need for Japan to adjust its diplomatic relations with the Soviet Union.[61] The original draft of the army's program for a southern advance, dated July 3 and entitled "Outline of the Main Principles for Coping with the Changing World Situation," contained the following passage: "In foreign policy, emphasis will be placed first on policies toward Germany, Italy, and the Soviet Union, with the special objectives of strengthening Japan's political solidarity with Germany and Italy and of *improving rapidly its relations with Soviet Russia.*"[62]

Thus, the army and navy were now agreed on the need for diplomatic moves toward the Soviet Union in order to achieve the "northern tranquillity" that was prerequisite to launching the southern advance. Amidst growing enthusiasm for a southern advance, both the government and many influential individuals outside of it became wedded to the argument for "northern tranquillity," and ideological objections to Japanese-Soviet understanding, as well as fears of its effect on internal security, gradually diminished.

On June 19 the Japanese ambassador in Germany, Kurusu Saburō, declared to Counselor Josef Knoll of the Political Affairs Bureau of the German Foreign Office, that "Japan is coming to realize more and more that her future lies in the south and that the foe in the north must be turned into a friend."[63] His statement was a reflection of domestic trends.

Molotov received the Japanese draft from Ambassador Tōgō on July 2 and expressed his agreement with the basic objectives of the Japanese proposal:

Your proposal, which attempts generally to stabilize Japanese-Soviet relations through agreement not to help a third power that might attack one of us, is of mutual benefit to both our countries.

He then continued:

Taking into account the present situation of Britain, France, and Holland, Japan is faced in the south with military and economic problems. Japan and the Soviet Union, who both play an important role in international affairs, should consider their mutual interests and rights and should stabilize and further strengthen relations between them. I believe that the present, changing situation favors such a course . . . The moment this has been done, countries like the United States will probably deal with both Japan and the Soviet Union more seriously and cautiously.

Molotov thus indicated his support for an improvement in Japanese-Soviet relations and even hinted his approval of Japan's policy of southern advance. With regard to stopping Soviet assistance to Chiang Kai-shek, however, one of the principal objectives Japan sought to achieve through the neutrality treaty, Molotov stated only that aid had been suspended but avoided any commitment for the future.

Tōgō: We would like to be given the understanding that the Soviet Union of its own accord was stopping aid to the Chungking government.
Molotov: Your allegation that we are presently giving aid to China is without foundation. Had we done so, the situation today would be different. And now especially, when the Soviet Union is concentrating on its own defense, it has no weapons to spare for other countries.
Tōgō: I am happy to conclude that the China problem is not an actual one for the Soviet government. As far as we are concerned, we wish that the Soviet government would continue to take such an attitude in the future. In view of the second objective of the draft of a neutrality agreement, it would be extremely fortunate if efforts were made to transmit this intention to our side.
Molotov: As far as the war in China is concerned, I do not think that Japan should become the victim of an unprovoked attack as stipulated in the draft agreement. In any case, I cannot say that the Soviet Union has never aided China in the past. The Soviet Union has in the past had need of Chinese nonferrous metals, and in this connection the Soviet Union at one time provided aid in the form of military aircraft and personnel. As for the present, there is need to administer new territories and great domestic demand for military supplies. As I have already said, we cannot be concerned about other nations.

As for the problem of fisheries and oil concessions, Molotov showed his disapproval of Article 1 by saying that "the question of the Japanese concessionaires' faithfully observing regulations must be settled first." The conference ended with Molotov promising to reply to the Japanese proposal as soon as possible.[64]

The Tōgō-Molotov conference clearly showed that in principle the Soviets had no objections to the conclusion of a neutrality treaty. However, their reaction to Japan's demands in return for a treaty—suspension of material aid to Chiang Kai-shek and the guarantee of concessions in northern Sakhalin—was not what the Japanese wanted to hear. It may be inferred from Molotov's comments that the Soviet leaders hoped through a neutrality pact to encourage Japan's southern advance policy, in order to intensify the confrontation between Japanese and American "imperialisms." But while one of the fundamental objectives of the Soviets was to reach a definite political understanding with Japan, thereby giving Japanese ruling circles a sense of security in the north and providing an impetus to the policy of southern advance, they could not carry rapprochement too far, lest there be a reaction from the United States government and a worsening of Soviet-American relations.[65]

Despite Molotov's initial favorable reaction, the Soviet government delayed its reply to the Japanese proposal. July went and August came and still there was no official reply. The reason for this delay was probably related to changes on the domestic political scene in Japan.

At the beginning of July rumors of a political change in Japan seem to have reached Moscow.[66] The resignation of the Yonai cabinet on July 22 must have caused misgivings concerning the new government's Soviet policy. The pivotal posts in the new Konoe cabinet were occupied by the so-called "Manchurian Group," who were regarded as advocates of a tough policy toward the Soviet Union. This was particularly true of the new army minister, Tōjō Hideki, who during his previous tenure as army vice minister had been an open advocate of two-front military operations against China and the Soviet Union.[67] The European situation had been further complicated by a German peace offensive against Britain, which must also have held up the Soviet reply.

During this transition period Molotov, in a speech before the Supreme Soviet on August 1, made a significant statement regarding Japanese-Soviet relations, in which he openly reiterated the basic attitude expressed in his meeting with Ambassador Tōgō. This may have been a trial balloon sent up to ascertain the new cabinet's policy toward the Soviet Union.

> It may be admitted that, in general, there are certain indications of a desire on the part of Japan to improve relations with the Soviet Union. Granted mutual recognition of the interests of both parties and provided both of them understand the necessity of removing certain obstacles which are no longer important, such an improvement in Soviet-Japanese relations is possible.[68]

The second Konoe cabinet's foreign policy was spelled out in the "Main Principles for Coping with the Changing World Situation," adopted by the Liaison Conference on July 27. This policy included the intention "of improving rapidly [Japan's] relations with Soviet Russia."

The phrase "improving rapidly" was undoubtedly vague, but there is no doubt that the new cabinet was prepared to take positive steps to adjust diplomatic relations with the Soviet Union. A memorandum adopted unanimously at a conference of his prospective army, navy, and foreign ministers, called by Konoe at his Ogikubo residence on July 19, contains the following passage:

> Concerning relations with the Soviet Union, Japan will conclude an agreement guaranteeing the border to be signed by Japan, Manchukuo, Mongolia, and the Soviet Union, to remain in effect for a period of five to ten years, and will make efforts to settle speedily the questions pending between that country and Japan. During the effective period of the proposed nonaggression pact, Japan will strengthen its military preparedness against the Soviet Union so as to be invincible.[69]

The day following the formation of the new cabinet Ambassador Tōgō counseled the government to continue the neutrality treaty negotiations. He stated that "in order to strengthen Japan's position vis-à-vis a third country, the conclusion of these negotiations is the most urgent task of Japanese foreign policy."[70] He further appealed to the government "to act quickly to bring these negotiations to an agreement" because "circumstances do not allow even a day's delay." Responding to Molotov's feeler of August 1, the new foreign minister Matsuoka Yōsuke on August 5 cabled Tōgō:

> The new cabinet desires that peace be maintained in East Asia and that Japan and the Soviet Union, taking a broad view of things, respect each

other's right to live. The government desires to conclude speedily the neutrality agreement that has been under discussion for some time. It would therefore like to have the Soviet government's precise reply to this proposal.[71]

Despite its formal decision to "improve rapidly" Japan's relations with the Soviet Union, it is clear that for the time being the new cabinet's policy was to continue the negotiations for a neutrality treaty started by the previous cabinet.

On August 14 Molotov gave Tōgō the Soviet reply, whose purport might have been anticipated from the foreign commissar's speech before the Supreme Soviet. While accepting the Japanese proposal in principle, the Soviets countered with significant revisions:

1) The first part of Article 1 establishes the Japanese-Soviet treaty of 1925 [Treaty of Peking] as the basis of relations between the two countries. The Soviet government sets forth the following objections. Ever since the Manchurian Incident, Japan has committed serious violations of the Portsmouth Treaty. As a result, we cannot consider the [Portsmouth] treaty to be valid in its entirety. Accordingly, further consideration is required to determine to what extent it can continue as a valid agreement. The oil and coal concessions in northern Sakhalin, in particular, must be liquidated. The Soviet government is prepared, however, to supply Japan with oil from northern Sakhalin, for a five-year period, and to provide just compensation to Japanese concessionaires for their investments.
2) We interpret the Japanese proposal as going beyond a neutrality treaty and being in actuality an agreement pledging nonaggression and nonparticipation in any coalition hostile to the other country.
3) The neutrality treaty provides Japan with maximum advantages. In improving the Japanese position in the north, it enables Japan to take positive action in the south. In contrast, the Soviet Union would gain few advantages. We would also expect complicated problems to arise in relations with other countries. By concluding a neutrality treaty with Japan, the Soviet Union would run the risk of damaging its relations with China and other countries greatly concerned with the Pacific and the South Seas. In this connection, we would like to know what measures the Japanese government is prepared to take to minimize the damage it is feared the Soviet Union would sustain through participation in such a pact.[72]

These, then, were the preconditions the Soviet government attached to its acceptance of the Japanese proposal for a neutrality treaty. The first point, in particular, demanded significant concessions from the Japanese. At his meeting with Molotov, Tōgō repeatedly called the Russian's attention to the suspension of Soviet aid to Chungking. To this Molotov replied: "Depending on the attitude Japan takes toward solving the various problems related to the neutrality treaty, the issue of Japanese-Chinese relations—that is, the issue of Soviet aid to China—can also be solved in the negotiations."[73]

Tōgō in his memoirs evaluated the Soviet response as follows: "The situation at the time was such that if negotiations regarding the northern Sakhalin concessions had ended in an agreement, an article could have been added regarding the suspension of Soviet aid to Chiang Kai-shek, which our side so ardently desired. The treaty could then have been immediately concluded."[74]

How did the Japanese government react to the Soviet reply? To answer this question one must first ask what decisions had been taken with regard to the implementation of Japan's southern policy and what the prospects were for a conflict with Britain and the United States. In this connection Ambassador Tōgō saw two choices open to Japan. In a memorandum of August 18, he expressed the following views:

> If there is a good chance of settling the China Incident and no danger of a clash with the United States by our expansion southward, there is no special need to conclude an agreement with the Soviet Union. One might as well continue in a nonthreatening, nonaggressive way . . .
> If, having taken a positive attitude toward the South Seas, Japan is resolved to use force should circumstances make it unavoidable, then we should follow Germany's example. Last fall Germany adopted the policy of "throwing away a sprat to catch a whale." It abandoned its political position in the Baltic states to advance in western and northern Europe. To conclude a political agreement [with the Soviet Union] is a necessity from the point of view of Japan's long-term interests.[75]

Obviously Tōgō was of the opinion that Japan should conclude a neutrality treaty even if the price were liquidation of the oil and coal concessions in northern Sakhalin. But on August 29 Tōgō became one of the many victims of Matsuoka's personnel purge; he received his recall orders.

The Soviet government's unyielding reply and news of the impending visit to Japan of the German special envoy Heinrich Stahmer led Foreign Minister Matsuoka to abandon direct negotiations with the Soviet Union for a neutrality treaty. He would continue to grapple with the problem of the "adjustment of relations with the Soviet Union," but from the standpoint of his own "grand design."

Matsuoka's cherished "grand design" had roughly the following dimensions. First, he would attempt to conclude a tripartite alliance with Germany and Italy. Then, building on the strength of the alliance, he would work for a Japanese-German-Italian-Soviet four-power entente. In seeking to adjust relations with the Soviet Union, he expected to utilize Germany's good offices and its supposed influence over the Soviet Union. Once a four-power entente had materialized, the coercive power of this combination would enable him to start negotiations with the United States in an attempt to reach agreement on various outstanding problems with that country, at the same time forcing the United States to refrain from intervention in Asia and Europe and inducing it to cooperate in joint efforts toward a peaceful recovery of these areas. While Britain and the United States were thus deterred by the strength of a tripartite alliance and a four-power entente, Japan would launch its policy of southern advance. Ultimately, he envisioned the establishment of a new world order in which Europe, Asia, and Africa would be divided into the *Lebensraum* of the four countries.

The idea of a four-power entente constituting an anti-British bloc had already been embraced by Foreign Secretary Ribbentrop in the fall of 1939. In Japan it was advocated by Shiratori Toshio and had been spelled out in the "Principles of Foreign Policy, II" prepared by the renovationist faction in the Foreign Ministry in April 1940. By the summer of 1940 the chorus of voices in favor of a southern advance had grown louder. At the same time the arguments for a four-power entente had become more persuasive and gained increasing support within the government. A memorandum of July 30, prepared in compliance with instructions from Matsuoka and entitled "On Strengthening the Cooperation between Japan, Germany, and Italy," contained the following passage:

Being destined to be the leader of East Asia in the postwar New Order, wherein it is anticipated that the world will be divided into the four great spheres of East Asia, the Soviet Union, Europe, and the American continent, Japan will cooperate closely with Germany and Italy, who will constitute the leading forces in Europe, to:

a) Restrain the Soviet Union on the east and the west and, inducing the Soviet Union to align its policies with the common interests of Japan, Germany, and Italy, endeavor to direct the Soviet sphere of influence into areas where there will be little direct conflict with the interests of Japan, Germany, and Italy, for example toward the Persian Gulf . . .[76]

Having thus planned a "rapid improvement" in diplomatic relations with the Soviet Union and a move toward a four-power entente, Matsuoka turned his attention to obtaining Germany's services as a mediator, on which he placed a high value, in order to implement this policy. In the fall of the previous year Ribbentrop had clearly indicated to Ambassador Ōshima the German government's willingness to act as mediator between Japan and the Soviet Union, and there is no doubt that Ribbentrop's proposal had made a strong impression upon Matsuoka. Moreover, the subsequent activities of the German embassy in Tokyo after this period reinforced his belief that the German government had not withdrawn its offer of good offices and that it would be possible to make use of presumed German influence over the Soviet Union.

On August 1, in a meeting with Ambassador Ott, Matsuoka attempted to verify the accuracy of his analysis.

Matsuoka: What does Germany want and what can it do as regards Soviet-Japanese relations?
Ott: Should Japan express a desire, Germany is ready to act as mediator. Personally, I think that it is wise to continue the Japanese-Soviet negotiations. As far as I know Hitler has no intention of fighting the Soviet Union.[77]

The fact that Stahmer stopped in Moscow on his way to Japan was to Matsuoka further evidence of the closeness between Germany and the Soviet Union and strengthened his view that Germany still intended to form a four-power entente.[78] He probably attributed the unsatisfactory reply to the proposal for a neutrality treaty to a mistaken attempt on Japan's part to deal directly with the Soviet Union and concluded, when informed of Stahmer's impending visit to Japan, that it would be better diplomatic procedure to bring about the tripartite alliance first and then, using the weight of this alliance and German mediation, proceed to negotiations with the Soviet Union.

At their second meeting on September 10 Stahmer told Matsuoka:

It is best to conclude an agreement [between] Japan, Germany, and Italy first and then immediately approach the Soviet Union. Germany is prepared to act as an honest broker on behalf of Japanese-Soviet friendship, and I don't think there are insurmountable obstacles on the road toward a rapprochement between the two countries. It can all be settled without much difficulty. Contrary to British propaganda, German-Soviet relations are good. The Soviet Union has satisfactorily fulfilled its agreements with Germany.[79]

Stahmer's guarantee that Germany would act as an "honest broker" between Japan and the Soviet Union strengthened Matsuoka's confidence in his plan, as well as his position vis-à-vis various domestic power groups.

On September 20 Baron Harada expressed his own misgivings to Prime Minister Konoe:

Rather than dealing with Germany first, we should find out whether a nonaggression treaty with the Soviet Union is possible. Only after making sure that is a definite possibility should we approach Germany. If we approach Germany first, we may then find that the Soviet Union is not agreeable and that it may be induced by the United States to hinder us. Considering all the issues involved, I feel very uneasy that things may not go according to our plans.[80]

Such fears that the conclusion of a tripartite alliance might lead to a serious confrontation with the United States and the Soviet Union were widespread in pro-Anglo-American circles in Japan at the time.

The navy was also deeply concerned about the effect of a tripartite agreement on Japanese-Soviet relations. Vice Navy Minister Toyoda Teijirō, in a meeting with Matsuoka, stressed the navy's strong desire to avoid automatic involvement in a war, adding that "another important matter is to draw the Soviet Union into the alliance."[81] On September 19, at an Imperial Conference, the chief of the Navy General Staff Prince Fushimi Hiroyasu expressed the navy's concern when he asked the cabinet representatives, "To what degree will this alliance contribute to the adjustment of Japan-Soviet relations?" Matsuoka replied:

We should like Germany to act as a mediator in the adjustment of our relations with the Soviet Union. Germany is willing to do this, inasmuch as the adjustment of Japanese-Soviet relations would be to its advantage. Last year at the time of the conclusion of the German-Soviet Nonaggression Pact the German foreign secretary asked Stalin about the future of Japanese-Soviet relations. Stalin answered that if Japan desired peace, then Russia also desired peace; but if Japan wanted war, then Russia also wanted war. From this we can assume that the Soviet Union is interested in adjusting its relations with Japan. In fact, Germany considers that it will be able to promote the adjustment quite easily.[82]

Such was the position taken by all members of the government, from Prime Minister Konoe on down, whenever discussion of a tripartite alliance came around to Japanese-Soviet relations.[83]

When the Privy Council's Investigation Committee met on September 26 to consider the Tripartite Pact, Councillors Kubota Seitarō, Minami Hiroshi, and Hayashi Raisaburō expressed their concern over the same point. Once more the government representatives present maintained that with the aid of Germany's good offices Japanese-Soviet negotiations would progress smoothly.[84]

Since Matsuoka placed such importance on Stahmer's "honest broker" statement, it is natural that he wanted to have this promise in writing. The fourth article of a secret protocol Matsuoka proposed to attach to the Tripartite Pact contained the following passage: "Germany and Italy will undertake *to use their good offices* to improve relations between Japan and the Soviet Union and *will make every effort to induce the Soviet Union to act in accord with the basic concept of the present treaty.*"[85] It was through this article that the Japanese government first conveyed to Germany its desire for a four-power entente.

When the tripartite alliance was realized, the idea of a four-power entente had already won the support of the army and navy. We have seen that Vice Navy Minister Toyoda stressed to Matsuoka the need "to draw the Soviet Union into the alliance." At a Liaison Conference on September 14 Vice Chief of the Army General Staff Sawada Shigeru presented the Supreme Command's two conditions for the tripartite alliance: "the need of four-power cooperation between Japan, Germany, Italy and the Soviet Union, and rejection of an automatic involvement in war."[86] It is clear that the Japanese government had determined on a policy of following the Tripartite Pact with an attempt to utilize Germany's good offices to form a four-power entente. But at the very time Stahmer was pledging that Germany would act as honest broker between Japan and the USSR, Foreign Minister Ribbentrop was telling Italian Foreign Minister Galeazzo Ciano in Rome that the Alliance was valid against both the United States and the Soviet Union.[87] It is, therefore, not surprising that the Germans amended the fourth article of the supplementary protocol, eliminating the reference to four-power cooperation: "That with regard to relations between Japan and the Soviet Union, Germany will do all in its power to promote friendly understanding and will offer its good offices to this end."[88] Thus did Germany communicate its negative attitude toward the idea of a four-power entente.

Since June relations between Germany and the Soviet Union had changed drastically, and Matsuoka's view of the situation no longer had any basis in reality. Nonetheless the German amendment failed to lessen his enthusiasm for his plan. And once the ceremonies marking the signing of the Tripartite Pact were over, Matsuoka turned to the next diplomatic business on his agenda—the four-power entente.

Japan Proposes a Nonaggression Treaty

By October 2, 1940, a week after the Tripartite Pact was signed in Berlin, the Foreign Ministry had prepared a "Draft Outline for the Adjustment of Japanese-Soviet Diplomatic Relations." This was a blueprint for a four-power entente to be "the next diplomatic engagement following the conclusion of the tripartite alliance."[89]

The substance of this draft lay in the following points: "We are in favor of drawing the Soviet Union into the course of [a concurrent] southern advance and aligning it diplomatically against Britain and the United States. . . . We recognize that in order to accomplish this a no-war, no-aggression relationship must be definitely established between Japan and the Soviet Union." A significant feature of the draft was that it abandoned the neutrality treaty formula and called for the *conclusion* between Japan and the Soviet Union of a *nonaggression treaty* similar to the German-Soviet Nonaggression Pact. Furthermore, while advocating negotiations for the division of spheres of influence, Japan was prepared to make some concessions along the lines of the Soviet government's reply of August 14.[90]

The main points of the document provided:

II. Basic Principles

1. Under the new treaty Japan and the Soviet Union are to enter into friendly relations based on a new foundation (*departing from the provisions of the Portsmouth Treaty and the Treaty of Peking*).

2. Japan and the Soviet Union are to conclude *a nonaggression treaty,* the essential points of which are as follows:

a) Both contracting parties will mutually respect each other's territory and sovereignty and will not commit aggression against each other.

b) If one contracting party is attacked, the other will remain neutral.

c) Neither contracting party will participate in any coalition directed against the other party.

d) Commissions for the settlement of the Soviet-Manchurian and Manchurian-Mongolian border incidents and for the demarcation of the border are to be established.

e) Disputes between the contracting parties are to be settled by a friendly exchange of opinion.

f) The treaty will be effective for ten years.

3. Japanese-Soviet economic relations are to be reestablished on a new foundation and regulated as follows:

a) Oil and coal concessions in northern Sakhalin as well as the importation of commodities therefrom are to be safeguarded.

b) While taking account of Soviet wishes, *Japan should secure fishing rights on a new foundation* designed to stabilize Japanese fisheries in the northern Pacific. *However, if all the oil from northern Sakhalin is secured, the abandonment of the fishing rights may be considered.*

[c and d omitted]

4. The Soviet Union will recognize Manchukuo, and Japan will recognize the recent Soviet fait accompli in western [sic] Europe.

5. The Soviet Union is to abandon its pro-Chiang attitude and activities and restrain the anti-Japanese activities of the Chinese communists. Japan is to acquiesce in the maintenance of the three northwestern provinces (Shensi, Kansu, and Ninghsia) as a Chinese communist base.

6. Japan and the Soviet Union mutually undertake not to take any action that might endanger law and order in the other country, as well as within the territory of China and Manchukuo.

In the sense that the above articles broadly incorporated the gist of the Soviet position, the document up to this point may be regarded as a Japanese counterplan. The succeeding articles, however, dealing with the establishment of spheres of influence and the formation of a four-power entente, suggested a plan for "improving rapidly" diplomatic relations between Japan and the Soviet Union.

7. Japan and the Soviet Union will come to the following understanding:
   a) The Soviet Union recognizes *Japan*'s traditional interests in *Inner Mongolia* and *the three provinces of north China;* Japan recognizes the Soviet Union's traditional interests in *Outer Mongolia* and *Sinkiang.*

   b) The Soviet Union acquiesces in Japan's future advance *in the direction of French Indochina and the Dutch East Indies;* Japan acquiesces in the *Soviet Union*'s future advance *in the direction of Afghanistan and Persia* (including *India* if circumstances should demand it).

   c) Japan, Germany, and Italy are to obtain Soviet cooperation in the building of a new world order; the inclusion of the Soviet Union in the alliance on an equal basis and its expansion into a quadruple alliance are not to be opposed.

8. As for northern Sakhalin and the Maritime Province, it is anticipated that at some future opportune time they shall come into Japan's sphere of influence by peaceful means—through purchase or exchange of territory. This matter, or the establishment of demilitarized zones, however, should not be brought up at the present time.

The third part of the draft was titled "Strategy." The Japanese recognized there that in the process of implementing their design they had to have a thorough understanding with Germany and that "German pressure from the west [had to] be used effectively." Furthermore, in the negotiations "the primary goal is to reach agreement on a nonaggression treaty, and if necessary to secure it, appropriate adjustment of economic relations should be considered."[91]

Thus, with the formulation of the "Draft Outline for the Adjustment of Japanese-Soviet Diplomatic Relations," the design of a four-power entente, incorporating the building of a new world order based on a broad division into spheres of influence, was set down in a concrete official plan.

On October 3 the Foreign Ministry's draft was considered by the Army Ministry and by a conference of responsible officials of the Army, Navy, and Foreign ministries.[92] No objections were raised to the basic policy set forth in the draft and, after making minor revisions, the conference decided to implement the policy. Because of the army's insistence, priority was to be given to concluding a nonaggression agreement, to be followed by negotiations regarding various outstanding problems.[93] These discussions resulted on October 4 in a revised draft that bore the same title and differed little from the previous one.[94] The new draft was submitted to the Four Ministers Conference, where, presumably, it was approved.

But deeply rooted opposition to a nonaggression treaty with the Soviet Union still existed among a certain segment of the Japanese public even after the signing of the Tripartite Pact. General Araki Sadao, for one, asserted that "in view of domestic and ideological effects a pact with the Soviets" would be a mistake.[95] The opposition failed to influence the policy of the government, which, in order to promote the desired negotiations, appointed Lieutenant-General Tatekawa Yoshitsugu as the new Japanese ambassador to Moscow.

General Tatekawa was prominent in the National Alliance for the Reconstruction of East Asia, which advocated anti-British and pro-Soviet policies, a fact that was taken into account when he was appointed.[96] Another leader of the alliance, Colonel (res.) Hashimoto Kingorō, wrote in a journal devoted to Soviet affairs:

> From a broad perspective, Japan should join hands with the Soviet Union, and the four countries—Japan, Germany, Italy, and the Soviet Union—should cooperate in the construction of a new world order. Our enemies are first Britain and second the United States. If the Soviets abandon their policy of aiding Chiang, a Japanese-Soviet nonaggression treaty should be signed. Diplomacy is not ideology.[97]

Thus, although Matsuoka's policy of promoting Japanese-Soviet cooperation faced opposition from certain quarters, within the government it was backed by the army and the navy and was strongly promoted by Shiratori and his renovationist faction in the Foreign Ministry; it also received the support of groups outside the government.

Ambassador Tatekawa assumed his post in Moscow on October 23. On October 30 he met with Molotov and formally presented the Japanese proposal for a nonaggression treaty, which read:

> Article I. Both signatories proclaim their mutual respect for each other's territorial integrity and pledge not to engage in aggressive activities toward the other, either independently or in concert with another power or powers.

Article II. In the event of military activity by any other power or powers against either of the signatories, the other signatory shall in no way support this third power or powers.

Article III. Both signatories shall exchange information on problems common to both countries and shall maintain close consultative communication in the future.

Article IV. Neither signatory shall participate in any coalition aimed directly or indirectly at the other.

[Articles V and VI omitted.][98]

Despite minor stylistic differences, the draft treaty was obviously based on the second article of the "Basic Principles" set forth in the draft policy of October 4 and was substantially the same as the German-Soviet Nonaggression Pact signed in August 1939. In presenting the proposal to Molotov, Tatekawa argued that the treaty should be concluded first and that the question of the concessions and other pending matters should be postponed. Molotov replied that liquidation of the concessions demanded prior settlement, but with regard to a nonaggression treaty, he said neither "yes" nor "no."[99]

Germany's Abortive Four-Power Entente Proposal

Meanwhile, on October 13 Foreign Minister Ribbentrop had entrusted to Ambassador Schulenburg, who was about to return to Moscow, a long letter to Stalin which the count duly presented to Molotov on October 17. Ribbentrop began with a general review of developments in Europe during the previous year and, after defending the justness of various German policies, invited Molotov to visit Berlin to discuss outstanding problems between the two countries. The most important problem to be dealt with, he went on, was the relationship of the Soviet Union to the tripartite alliance, in particular "the delimitation of spheres of influence" among the four countries.

Friendly relations between Germany and Soviet Russia as well as friendly relations between Soviet Russia and Japan, together with the friendship between the Axis Powers and Japan, are logical elements of a natural political coalition which, if intelligently managed, will work out to the best advantage of all the powers concerned . . . I would welcome it, if the trend toward reaching an understanding with the Soviet Union, which is becoming more and more clearly manifest in Japan, too, could lead to its logical goal.

In summing up, I should like to state that, in the opinion of the Führer, also, it appears to be the historical mission of the Four Powers, the Soviet Union, Italy, Japan, and Germany, to adopt a long-range policy and to direct the future development of their peoples into the right channels by delimitation of their interests on a world-wide scale.

In closing, Ribbentrop suggested that, depending upon the results of the Berlin conference, he might again visit Moscow and that a four-power conference might also be considered.[100]

On October 22 Stalin accepted the invitation on Molotov's behalf and suggested November 10–12 as the most suitable period for the foreign commissar to visit Berlin. Stalin went on to state: "I agree with you that a further improvement in the relations between our countries is entirely possible on the permanent basis of a long-range delimitation of mutual interests."[101]

There is, of course, no way of knowing the extent of Japanese influence on Ribbentrop's invitation to Stalin. Given the fact that since June German-Soviet relations had become notably cooler and that Ribbentrop's enthusiasm for cooperation with the Soviet Union must consequently have abated, it is possible that Japan's earnest desire to adjust its relations with the Soviet Union and to form a four-power entente may have had some influence on Ribbentrop.

When it became known in Tokyo that the Soviet government had agreed to send Molotov to Berlin and that its reply to Tatekawa's proposal was not necessarily favorable, Japanese leaders must have appraised German influence over the Soviet Union as even higher and, as a result, placed more reliance on German diplomatic mediation. About November 10, just before Molotov's visit to Germany, Matsuoka telegraphed Kurusu to request formally German mediation in negotiations for a Japanese-Soviet nonaggression treaty. Kurusu was further instructed to ask Germany to persuade the Soviets to issue, either jointly with Germany or separately, an advice urging that the Chungking regime make peace with Japan.[102] In Tokyo on November 11 Vice Minister Ōhashi Chūichi made a similar representation to Ambassador Ott, asking Germany:

1) To bring influence to bear on Soviet Russia to accept the proposed nonaggression pact.

2) To bring influence to bear on Soviet Russia to stop supporting Chiang Kai-shek.
3) To bring influence to bear on Chiang Kai-shek to make peace with Japan.

Ōhashi suggested that "Japanese policy would be best served if the foregoing ideas were presented to Soviet Russia . . . as being German suggestions."[103]

Ribbentrop agreed to Kurusu's request for mediation and showed the ambassador his "private plan" for a four-power entente, on the basis of which he intended to conduct negotiations with Molotov.[104] The essence of Ribbentrop's "private plan" was a division of most of the world into spheres of influence, with the South Seas being given to Japan, Iran and the area in the direction of India to the Soviet Union, central Africa to Germany, and north and northeast Africa to Italy. Since Matsuoka's message to Ribbentrop must by this time have been delivered by Stahmer, who had left Tokyo on October 7, it may be assumed that Ribbentrop saw it before formulating his plan. Matsuoka had assured Ribbentrop that Japan would agree "to a Russian sphere of influence in Outer Mongolia and Sinkiang" and "would raise no objections against the creation of a Russian sphere of interest in British India."[105] Upon receipt of Ribbentrop's "private plan," a Four Ministers Conference was convened at which the plan was formally approved. This action was then communicated to the German government.[106]

The German-Soviet conference in Berlin consisted of four meetings, on November 12 and 13. At the first, between Ribbentrop and Molotov, the German foreign secretary did most of the talking. Ribbentrop began by summarizing the German government's views of the progress of the war, which, he declared, was already won. He concluded that

because of the extraordinary strength of their position," Germany and Italy were not "considering how they might win the war, but rather how rapidly they could end the war which was already won." He then turned to the subject of Russo-Japanese relations in the context of the Tripartite Pact. Hitler, he said, "now was of the opinion that it would be advantageous in any case if the attempt were made to establish the spheres of influence among Russia, Germany, Italy, and Japan along very broad lines" and had concluded that "a wise policy would normally direct the momentum of their *Lebensraum* expansion entirely southward.

He ended the meeting with a summary of his plan for a four-power entente.[107]

At the next two meetings (on the afternoon of the 12th and the morning of the 13th) Hitler was also present, and during the second a heated exchange took place between him and Molotov over the Finnish and Balkan questions. Molotov made it clear that the Soviet government's primary concern was to reach a firm agreement with Germany regarding spheres of influence in Europe.

The foreign commissar seemed also to wish to avoid discussing Japanese-Soviet relations and did not seem to favor German mediation. At the close of this meeting he at last touched upon the recent improvement in Japanese-Soviet relations:

> He anticipated that the improvement would continue at a still faster pace and thanked the Reich Government for its efforts in this direction.

> Concerning Sino-Japanese relations, it was certainly the task of Russia and Germany to attend to their settlement. But an honorable solution would have to be assured for China, all the more since Japan now stood a chance of getting 'Indonesia.'[108]

Molotov's last meeting in Berlin was with Ribbentrop, on the night of the 13th in an air-raid shelter, after an air-raid alert had terminated a banquet at the Soviet embassy. There Ribbentrop presented to Molotov a draft agreement for a four-power entente, the private plan he had earlier shown to Kurusu. It consisted of a main agreement and two secret protocols. The provisions of the main agreement were:

Article 1

In the Three Power Pact of September 27, 1940, Germany, Italy, and Japan agreed to oppose the extension of the war into a world conflict with all possible means and to collaborate toward an early restoration of world peace. They expressed their willingness to extend their collaboration to nations in other parts of the world which are inclined to direct their efforts along the same course as theirs. The Soviet Union declares that it concurs in these aims and is on its part determined to cooperate politically in this course with the Three Powers.

Article 2

Germany, Italy, Japan, and the Soviet Union undertake to respect each other's natural spheres of influence. In so far as these spheres of influence come into contact with each other, they will constantly consult each other in an amicable way with regard to the problems arising therefrom.

Article 3
Germany, Italy, Japan, and the Soviet Union undertake to join no combination of powers and to support no combination of powers which is directed against one of the Four Powers. The Four Powers will assist each other in economic matters in every way and will supplement and extend the agreements existing among themselves.

A secret protocol would establish "the focal points in the territorial aspirations of the Four Countries," as follows: apart from Europe, Germany in central Africa and Italy in north and northeast Africa; Japan in the direction of the South Seas; and the Soviet Union in the direction of the Indian Ocean. A second secret protocol would contain an agreement among Germany, Italy, and the Soviet Union regarding Turkey and the Dardanelles.[109]

Ribbentrop turned next to the adjustment of Japanese-Soviet diplomatic relations, as Matsuoka had requested. Japan was anxious to conclude a nonaggression treaty with the USSR, he said, and to this end Germany would gladly accept the role of a mediator. He went on in the following vein:

> . . . if the nonaggression pact materialized the Japanese would be prepared to settle all other issues in a generous manner. . . . *The Japanese Government was disposed to meet the Soviet wishes half way in regard to the oil and coal concessions on Sakhalin Island,* but it would first have to overcome resistance at home. This would be easier for the Japanese Government if a nonaggression pact were first concluded with the Soviet Union.

In response, Molotov stated that

> . . . concerning Japan, he had the hope and conviction that they would now make more progress on the road to understanding than had previously been the case. Relations with Japan had always been fraught with difficulties and reverses. Nevertheless, there now seemed to be prospects of an understanding. The Japanese Government had suggested the conclusion of a nonaggression treaty to the Soviet Government—in fact, even before the change of government in Japan—in which connection the Soviet Government had put a number of questions to the Japanese Government. At present, the answer to these questions had not yet been received. Only   when   it   arrived   could   negotiations   be   entered

into—negotiations which could not be separated from the remaining complex of questions. The solution of the problem would therefore require some time.[110]

Thus, in spite of Ribbentrop's efforts, Molotov made it clear that liquidation of the Japanese concessions was a precondition to the conclusion of a nonaggression treaty; he had not retreated one step from the position held by the Soviet government up to this time. The real extent of German "influence" over the Soviet Union was now quite clear.

The formal Soviet reply to Ribbentrop's proposal was given to Ambassador Schulenburg in Moscow on November 26. While in principle it expressed Soviet willingness to participate in a four-power entente, it added the following stiff conditions:

1) Provided that the German troops are immediately withdrawn from Finland, which, under the compact of 1939, belongs to the Soviet Union's sphere of influence. At the same time the Soviet Union undertakes to ensure peaceful relations with Finland and to protect German economic interests in Finland (export of lumber and nickel).

2) Provided that within the next few months the security of the Soviet Union in the Straits is assured by the conclusion of a mutual assistance pact between the Soviet Union and Bulgaria, which geographically is situated inside the security zone of the Black Sea boundaries of the Soviet Union, and by the establishment of a base of land and naval forces of the USSR within range of the Bosporus and the Dardanelles by means of a long-term lease.

3) Provided that the area south of Batum and Baku in the general direction of the Persian Gulf is recognized as the center of the aspirations of the Soviet Union.

4) Provided that Japan [renounces] her rights to concessions for coal and oil in Northern Sakhalin.[111]

These conditions were judged by Hitler to be unreasonable. Confronted with the Soviet reply, the German government abandoned the idea of a four-power entente and, of course, its proposal to send Ribbentrop to Moscow. It was at this point that Hitler reached his final determination for war against the Soviet Union.

The Berlin conference was an important turning point in German-Soviet relations and in the history of World War II. As early as June 1940, when the Soviets occupied the three Baltic states and demanded that Rumania cede Bessarabia and Northern Bukovina, German-Soviet relations had entered a new phase and began gradually to show signs of disagreement. The Soviet Union had acted in response to the destruction of British and French military forces in western Europe and the resulting change in the balance of power. But its action, in turn, produced a German counteraction. To prevent the further expansion of Soviet influence in the Balkans, and particularly with the aim of securing Rumania's oil resources—a matter of life-or-death for Germany—the German government first dispatched a military mission to Rumania and later, on October 5, stationed mechanized units there. On the other front, at the end of September German troops landed in Finland under the pretext of sending reinforcements to northern Norway. Even outside observers could not fail to notice the cooling in the relations between the two countries. But Hitler's uncompromising determination to act against the Soviet Union had by this time gone much further.

As *Mein Kampf* had made clear, a consistent objective of Hitler's foreign policy was the expansion of German *Lebensraum* into Russia. His conciliatory moves toward the Soviet Union were due solely to the strategic necessity of conducting military action in the west. This was a mere tactic, and Hitler never abandoned his fundamental aim of expanding Germany's *Lebensraum*.

In spite of the destruction of allied military power on the western front, Germany could not carry out landing operations against Britain. Meanwhile, on the eastern front, the Soviet Union expanded its sphere of influence and was reported concentrating its forces in Bessarabia. Under these circumstances Hitler leaned toward rapidly solving the eastern problem by force. On July 31 the Führer revealed his thinking to the army leadership:

> But if Russia is smashed, Britain's last hope will be shattered . . . In view of these considerations Russia must be liquidated. Spring, 1941. The sooner Russia is smashed, the better.[112]

On November 12, the day the Berlin conference began, Hitler issued the following secret directive to the military: "Political discussions have been initiated with the aim of clarifying Russia's attitude for the time being. Irrespective of the results of these discussions, all preparations for the East which have already been verbally ordered will be continued."[113] Thus Germany prepared for war against the Soviet Union, while the Berlin conference gave Hitler an opportunity to make his final decision.

Until this time Hitler may have continued to hope that the Soviet Union would make the concessions necessary to achieve agreement on delimiting spheres of influence and therefore hesitated to make the final decision for war. There were opponents of such a war within the German government: Ribbentrop claimed to have been one of them. According to his memoirs, the foreign secretary was concerned over the deterioration in relations with the Soviet Union and tried to argue with Hitler the need to maintain harmonious relations. He claimed he was particularly opposed to a preventive attack on the Soviet Union. In order to achieve a friendly clarification and strengthening of relations with the Soviet Union, Ribbentrop first wanted to bring about a meeting between Hitler and Stalin. When he saw that this was impossible, he switched, as the next best policy, to a visit by Molotov to Berlin.[114] Molotov's stubborn stand at the Berlin conference, however, greatly annoyed Hitler, and the Soviet reply to Ribbentrop's private plan was deemed excessively demanding. The outcome of the conference, contrary to the expectations of Ribbentrop and others who had opposed an attack on the Soviet Union, was to convince Hitler that an understanding with the Soviet Union was impossible.

In this manner Hitler's decision to attack the Soviet Union became final. On December 18 he issued the famous order for "Operation Barbarossa," directing the armed forces to complete all preparations for the operation by May 15, 1941. German-Soviet relations had entered the final stage leading toward catastrophe.

Upon his return from Berlin, Molotov handed Ambassador Tatekawa the Soviet reply to the Japanese government's proposal for a nonaggression treaty. Referring to the Berlin conference, Molotov said he had heard from Ribbentrop that the Japanese government was most anxious to adjust its relations with the Soviet Union and was ready to compromise on the northern Sakhalin concessions. Following these preliminary remarks, he presented the Soviet draft of a neutrality treaty containing four articles plus a supplementary protocol.

Molotov explained the counterproposal of a neutrality treaty on the grounds that "Soviet public opinion could not conceive of a nonaggression treaty unaccompanied by a return of lost territories. The Japanese, however, would probably not consider it proper to discuss the problem of southern Sakhalin and the Kurile islands. Therefore, under the present circumstances, it is appropriate to negotiate a treaty of neutrality." [115]

The first two articles of the proposed treaty provided:

Article I. Both contracting parties proclaim mutual respect for territorial integrity and desire to maintain peaceful and friendly relations.
Article II. In the event of military activity by any other power or powers against either of the contracting parties, the other contracting party shall maintain neutrality throughout the duration of the conflict. [116]

This Soviet draft resembled the neutrality treaty previously proposed by Ambassador Tōgō (except that it omitted from the first part of Article I reaffirmation of the 1925 Treaty of Peking). In rejecting the earlier proposal, on August 19, Molotov had replied that the Soviet Union interpreted it "as going beyond a neutrality treaty and being in actuality an agreement pledging nonaggression and nonparticipation in any coalition hostile to the other country." Now that the Japanese government, taking Molotov's reply into consideration, had proposed a nonaggression treaty, it was the Soviet government that counterproposed a neutrality treaty.

The supplementary protocol provided for the liquidation of Japanese oil and coal concessions in northern Sakhalin. The Soviet government, however, agreed to grant Japanese concessionaires a fair compensation for their investments and to guarantee to the Japanese government for five years the annual delivery of 100,000 tons of northern Sakhalin oil. [117]

On November 20 Matsuoka cabled Tatekawa that it would be difficult to consider liquidation of the concessions and proposed instead the purchase of northern Sakhalin. [118] This proposal was, needless to say, out of the question, and Molotov flatly rejected it, saying that on his visit to Germany he had been told by the German foreign minister of the "Japanese government's intention to abandon the concessions." [119]

Ambassador Tatekawa advocated acceptance of the Soviet counterproposal, [120] but disagreement arose within the Japanese government and the high command. Some within the Foreign Ministry recommended seeking a neutrality treaty by shelving the concession issue; [121] others were prepared to abandon the concessions on condition of annual deliveries of 200,000 tons of oil. [122] Foreign Minister Matsuoka, as his instructions to Tatekawa showed, was an advocate of a hard line. At the

Imperial Headquarters-Cabinet Liaison Conference on December 12 he said that "adjustment of Japanese-Soviet diplomatic relations on the basis of loss of the concessions was impossible." [123] Apparently Matsuoka was confident that, either through German mediation or, if that failed, through personal negotiations, agreement could be reached without necessitating liquidation of the northern Sakhalin concessions.

The navy had from the beginning objected to liquidation of the oil concessions. [124] Northern Sakhalin provided good quality crude petroleum for naval vessels, and the navy's interest in it as a source of fuel dated back to the Siberian intervention. The quantity Japan extracted had decreased gradually from the peak of 310,000 tons in 1933 to about 55,000 tons in 1939. This was not a large quantity, but the navy still valued the source and was reluctant to give it up.

General army opinion, too, held that since the conclusion of the Tripartite Pact there was "no need to rush to pay compensation in order to adjust diplomatic relations with the Soviet Union." [125] One segment of the army, however, was willing to abandon the concessions. Its view had earlier been put forward at the October 3 discussions on the "Outline for the Adjustment of Japanese-Soviet Diplomatic Relations." [126] Chief of the General Staff Operations Section General Doi Akio and officials of the War Guidance Office now favored acceptance of the Soviet proposal, which the latter characterized as "a plan for giving up in name but not in essence." [127]

With the government unable to achieve unanimity, the stalemate in the problem of adjusting Japanese-Soviet relations became apparent to all. [128]

Matsuoka's Quest for a Four-Power Entente

To hold heart-to-heart talks with the European dictators, to gain the world's attention by exhibiting himself as a star on the diplomatic stage—this was truly a Matsuoka performance.

Even before the Tripartite Pact was signed, a diplomatic trip to Europe had been proposed by Matsuoka and sanctioned by Prime Minister Konoe, but the plan had been postponed. [129] Informed of the forthcoming Ribbentrop-Molotov meeting, Matsuoka, confident of Germany's influence over the Soviet Union, was probably happy to let the

German foreign secretary set the stage, and he may have believed that his later appearance to add the finishing touches to a four-power entente would assure his place in the limelight. Other factors as well delayed his European trip. He had initiated the talks with Ch'ien Yung-ming in the hope of settling the China conflict, and the issue of recognizing the Wang Ching-wei regime had reached a critical point. As foreign minister, Matsuoka could not leave Tokyo before these matters were resolved.

These problems, however, became somewhat less pressing when Japan's policy toward China took a new direction with the adoption of the "Outline of Policy to Deal with the China Incident" at the Imperial Conference of November 13 and the signing of a treaty with the Wang Ching-wei regime on November 30. Moreover, Matsuoka had grown impatient at the impasse in Soviet-Japanese relations when Ribbentrop's good offices failed to bring about the desired negotiations, and he became convinced that he himself must go to Europe to take direct charge of the situation. On December 19 Matsuoka told Ambassador Ott that he proposed to visit Germany in the latter part of January and on the 24th the German government replied that it welcomed the foreign minister's visit to Berlin.[130]

Before leaving for Europe, Matsuoka had to obtain government and high command approval of the objectives he hoped to achieve in negotiations with the German and Soviet governments. On January 6, 1941, therefore, he prepared the following document, entitled the "Outline for Negotiations with Germany, Italy, and the USSR":

1) We expect the Soviet Union to accept Ribbentrop's "private plan" and accordingly to align its policies with the anti-British policies of Japan, Germany, and Italy, as well as to adjust its diplomatic relations with Japan.

2) The conditions for a Japanese-Soviet diplomatic settlement are, in the main, as follows:

a) Japan is to purchase northern Sakhalin through German mediation. If the Soviet Union does not agree to this, Japan will relinquish the northern Sakhalin concessions in return for an agreement to be supplied during the next five years with 2,500,000 tons of oil. If necessary, Japan will offer help to increase production of crude oil in northern Sakhalin. Depending on circumstances, Japan is to choose one of these two alternatives.

b) Japan recognizes the Soviet position in Sinkiang and Outer

Mongolia in return for Soviet recognition of Japan's position in north China and Inner Mongolia. The relationship of Sinkiang and Outer Mongolia to the Soviet Union will be settled between that country and China.

c) The Soviet Union will cease its aid to Chiang Kai-shek.

d) Commissions for demarcation of the frontier and for settlement of border incidents between Manchukuo, the Soviet Union, and Outer Mongolia are to be arranged promptly.

e) Agreement in the fisheries negotiations is to be reached on the basis of the Tatekawa proposal [the commission plan]. Japanese fishing rights may be abandoned if necessary for an adjustment of Japanese-Soviet diplomatic relations.

f) The Soviet Union is to provide railway freight cars for a substantial volume of Japanese-German trade and agree to a reduction in the freight tariff.

3) Japan occupies a position of political leadership in the East Asia Co-prosperity Sphere and is responsible for the maintenance of order. As a rule, the peoples of this area should either maintain their independence or achieve it. The peoples of the present possessions of Britain, France, Holland, Portugal, etc., who are unable to become independent should be granted as much autonomy as their ability allows, and Japan should assume the responsibility for leadership and government. Economically, in this area Japan reserves for itself a preferential position insofar as resources for national defense are concerned. In other, general commercial enterprises, the principle of the Open Door and equality of opportunity will prevail, provided Japan enjoys reciprocal rights in other economic spheres.

4) The world is to be divided into four large spheres: the Greater East Asia sphere, the European sphere (including Africa), the American sphere, and the Soviet sphere (including India and Iran). (Australia and New Zealand should be left to Britain, which is generally to be treated as Holland.) At the postwar peace conference, Japan will advocate implementation of this division.

5) Japan will coordinate its actions and its policies with the German authorities in order to make it impossible for the United States to enter the war.

6) Germany and Italy (especially Germany) will restrain the Soviet Union and will immediately attack the Soviet Union if the latter attacks Japan or Manchukuo.

7) If Japan enters the European war, it will sign with Germany, Italy, and other allies an agreement not to conclude a separate peace.

8) Naval preparations should be completed as soon as possible, and the army will drastically reduce the front in China. Germany is to do its utmost to help Japan perfect its military preparations, while Japan will attempt to supply Germany with raw materials and foodstuffs.

9) Upon reaching Europe, Foreign Minister Matsuoka is to negotiate with the German, Italian, and Soviet governments in order to implement the above-mentioned points and is authorized to conclude agreements if necessary.[131]

Following its adoption by the Foreign Ministry, Matsuoka's draft was sent to the army and the navy for review. The Army General Staff studied it from January 13 to 18. On January 15 the Intelligence and Operations divisions made the following suggestions:

Intelligence Division:
1) Conclude another agreement to bind Japan and Germany closer together.
2) Return the northern Sakhalin concessions without hesitation.
3) Conclude a commercial agreement with the Soviet Union.
4) Eliminate the article calling for reduction of the China front.
5) Study the document further, as it contains points that deviate from the "Outline of Main Principles for Coping with the Changing World Situation" adopted in July 1940.
6) Postpone the foreign minister's departure until the "Outline for Dealing with the Southern Areas" has been approved.
7) Negotiate first through Ambassador Ōshima.
8) Join with Germany and Italy in a treaty against the Soviet Union if our objectives cannot be achieved.

Operations Division:
Explore the possibility of utilizing the tripartite alliance to settle the China Incident.

In the end the General Staff approved Matsuoka's draft, with the exception of Article 8, to which strong objections were raised on the grounds that it constituted interference with the prerogative of the high command. On January 18, according to the *Confidential War Diary*, there was "Unanimous agreement in the General Staff concerning Foreign Minister Matsuoka's European trip."[132]

On February 3 the Liaison Conference met to consider Matsuoka's negotiation plans. While the army and navy had no objection to the foreign minister's European trip, they demanded that it be postponed until after the end of February, when it was expected that negotiations with French Indochina and Thailand would be largely concluded. A new schedule was therefore agreed upon by which Matsuoka would depart in early March and return to Japan in mid-April.

With this timetable approved, the conference took up the "Outline for Negotiations" article by article. While the army and navy representatives urged caution with regard to increasing the transportation capacity of the Trans-Siberian Railway and to concluding with Germany an agreement aimed at preventing American entry into the war, needless to say, the strongest objection was directed against the proposal to "reduce the front in China." Army Chief of Staff Sugiyama Gen, Navy Minister Oikawa Koshirō, Military Affairs Bureau Chief Mutō Akira, and Naval Affairs Bureau Chief Oka Takazumi one after another stood up to register their opposition. Finally Matsuoka gave in, and the article was drastically revised to provide merely that Japan would "hold friendly consultations with Germany to promote an overall peace settlement with China."[133] No other changes were made and, with this revision, the "Outline for Negotiations with Germany, Italy, and the USSR" was approved by the Liaison Conference.[134]

It is clear that when this document was being drafted and approved in January and early February, the Japanese government believed German-Soviet relations to be much as they had been in early October, when the "Draft of Basic Principles for the Adjustment of Japanese-Soviet Diplomatic Relations" had been prepared. Tokyo was still operating on the assumption that a basis for a four-power entente existed with Germany and the Soviet Union and that Germany continued to exert an influence over the Soviet Union. According to the new policy, therefore, Matsuoka's mission was to induce the Soviets to accept Ribbentrop's "private plan," to reach an agreement on delimitation of the four powers' spheres of influence, and to try to solve, through German mediation, the difficult problem of adjusting Japanese-Soviet diplomatic relations. There was no sign that the Japanese government was aware of the change that had taken place in German-Soviet relations, especially since the Berlin conference, resulting in the order for Operation Barbarossa on December 18.

Why was Matsuoka's perception of the situation so wide of the mark? Was it due to a lack of intelligence information or defects in the intelligence network?

Matsuoka's purge of the Foreign Ministry on taking office had effectively decreased, even if temporarily, the efficiency of Japanese diplomatic operations and had doubtless weakened the ability of Japanese diplomats abroad to assemble and transmit intelligence. The actual order for Operation Barbarossa, issued on December 18, was of course a top military secret, but had Tokyo received any information at all concerning developments during the Berlin conference or the Soviet reply to the German proposals, its view of German-Soviet relations would probably have been closer to reality. A report drawn up by the First (Soviet) Section of the Europe-Asia Bureau is indicative of the quality of Japanese intelligence at this time. Quoting from the London *Times* of November 29, 1940, to the effect that even though certain economic agreements were concluded between Germany and the Soviet Union at the Berlin conference, "no broad political agreements were reached and the Kremlin, as heretofore, maintains an ambiguous attitude," the Soviet Section added its own evaluation that "this is close to the true situation."[135] Reports from the Japanese embassy in Moscow reinforced the government's misperception of German-Soviet relations. On January 27, 1941, Ambassador Tatekawa wrote of the continuing need to adjust Japanese-Soviet diplomatic relations:

> To further strengthen the tripartite alliance and to improve relations between the Allied countries and the Soviet Union *will aid the realization of the German foreign minister's proposal* . . . Since the difficult problem in adjusting diplomatic relations with the Soviet Union is the abandonment of the concessions in northern Sakhalin, I think we should take advantage of Ambassador Ōshima's assumption of duties in Berlin to ask the German government to intercede in the conclusion of an unconditional treaty of neutrality.[136]

Among the Japanese diplomats who were observing the Balkan situation, there were those who early noted abnormalities in German-Soviet relations and relayed the information to Tokyo. Ambassador Tōgō, for example, upon his return from Moscow met with Prime Minister Konoe on November 5 and reported: "It will be impossible to force the Soviet Union to recognize German and Italian leadership in Europe. German-Soviet relations have recently deteriorated, and it may be said that they were worse than our relations with the Soviet Union. As I have pointed out in my reports from Moscow, the settlement of outstanding problems between Japan and the USSR is inconceivable." Tōgō also expounded these views to Matsuoka on November 27, urging him to be cautious.[137]

Other reports of German-Soviet disagreement must have reached the Foreign Ministry, but they had no effect on Matsuoka's perception of the situation as he prepared his "Outline for Negotiations" in early January. Between the time his plan received the formal approval of the Liaison Conference on February 3 and his departure from Tokyo on March 12, however, Matsuoka seems finally to have become cognizant of the changes in German-Soviet relations and to doubt the feasibility of concluding a four-power entente. A detailed report from the Japanese consul-general in Vienna, Yamaji Akira, informed him that German operations in the Balkans had created discord between Germany and the Soviet Union and made Matsuoka apprehensive about the prospect for Japanese-Soviet negotiations.[138] Again, early in February, Ambassador Kurusu reported that when he had paid his farewell visit to Hitler, the Führer had hinted at the deterioration in relations, saying that "on the surface German-Soviet relations are cordial, but we don't know when they will change."[139] Hitler's words aroused disquiet within imperial court circles and must have been brought to the attention of the foreign minister. According to Lord Privy Seal Kido Kōichi, the emperor reacted as follows: "Should Germany in the near future start a war against the Soviet Union, our alliance obligations make it necessary for us to be prepared in the north. With our hands tied in the south, we would be faced with a grave problem. Policies toward the south require very careful consideration."[140]

Although he carried with him to Europe the "Outline for Negotiations with Germany, Italy, and the USSR," Matsuoka, on the eve of his departure from Tokyo, must have accorded greater importance to an adjustment of relations with the Soviet Union than to the creation of a four-power entente.[141]

Standing at Tokyo Central Station on the night of March 12, surrounded by his retinue headed by Sakamoto Mizuo, chief of the Europe-Asia Bureau, Foreign Minister Matsuoka looked like a successful general who, in high spirits, was about to leave on an expedition. Listening to the cheers of well-wishers, Matsuoka may have dreamed of the moment he would cross swords with the German and Soviet foreign ministers. Or perhaps he recalled the day eight years before when he had returned home to receive the nation's applause as the star performer in the drama of Japan's withdrawal from the League of Nations. Paying homage at the sacred Shrine of Ise the next day—as was the custom for high officials embarking upon or returning from important trips—Matsuoka prostrated himself and prayed for the success of his mission.[142] He commemorated the event in a short poem:

Spring journey:
it was a splendid day
when I went to pray at the shrine.

Intent on reaching its destination as soon as possible, the party took a plane from Taegu in Korea to Ch'angch'un (then known as Hsinching) in Manchuria and on March 17, in a violent wind storm, crossed the Soviet-Manchurian border. Provided with a luxurious special train by the Trans-Siberian Railway, Matsuoka started out in an excellent mood. He drank vodka and displayed his confidence in his diplomatic ability by telling his retinue how he would make puppets of Hitler and Stalin. The tedious Siberian journey lasted a week. As the train rushed through barren snow-covered plains, Matsuoka composed short poems, full of subtle twists of thought, or meditated silently while sipping weak powdered tea.[143]

On the afternoon of March 23, a day ahead of schedule, the train pulled into Moscow during a snow flurry. Matsuoka was full of vigor and displayed no anxiety concerning the forthcoming negotiations. Immediately after his arrival he held a press conference for Soviet and foreign correspondents and that evening attended a banquet at the Japanese embassy.

The following day Matsuoka received a number of ambassadors and ministers stationed in Moscow, an hour-long talk with American Ambassador Steinhardt drawing the most attention. Matsuoka assured Steinhardt that Japan had no intention of attacking Singapore nor did it have any territorial ambitions in that region or other areas to the south. He added that he would like to see President Roosevelt act as mediator of the Sino-Japanese war. The foreign minister thereby was laying the groundwork for the Japanese-American negotiations he proposed to arrange when his negotiations with the Soviets were completed.[144]

At four o'clock that afternoon Matsuoka visited the Kremlin, where he met with Molotov; in the middle of the conference they were joined by Stalin. Matsuoka avoided discussing with Stalin substantive problems relating to the adjustment of relations but attempted only to establish a psychological basis for the full-scale negotiations that were to follow his visit to Berlin. Matsuoka seems to have felt that he should not begin negotiations with Stalin and Molotov before meeting with the German leaders to ascertain their views on the Soviet situation and being able to judge for himself the possibilities for a four-power entente. Doubtless he also believed his Berlin visit would have a positive psychological effect on his negotiations with the Russians. On this occasion, therefore, he limited himself to cultivating friendly relations with Stalin and his associates and indulging his special talent for dropping suggestions that might pave the way for future negotiations. The Japanese, he admitted, did not believe in "political and economic communism" but by tradition were "moral communists." The confusion in contemporary Japanese thinking, he averred, was due to the penetration of Anglo-Saxon liberalism. A struggle with the Anglo-Saxons was therefore unavoidable if Japan were to recapture its traditional ideals and build a new order. The Soviet Union, which likewise took an anti-Anglo-Saxon position, obviously belonged in the same camp. Thus did Matsuoka cheerfully argue with the old bolshevik strongman that Japanese-Soviet cooperation was inevitable in the light of world history.[145]

Matsuoka's party left Moscow the evening of March 24 and arrived in Berlin the evening of the 26th to the welcoming cheers of Hitler Youth in a sea of Rising Sun flags. During the next three days of formal negotiations, he attracted the world's close attention, meeting three times with Ribbentrop and once with Hitler.

As in the case of the German-Soviet negotiations in November, the German interpreter Paul Schmidt has left a record of Matsuoka's negotiations. His record reveals that the primary objectives of the conferees diverged widely. For Matsuoka the main concern was the Soviet problem, whereas the Germans by this time had absolutely no interest in a four-power entente or in mediating Japanese-Soviet negotiations. Because their principal aim was to obtain Japanese participation in the war against Britain, they tried to exact a pledge for an attack on Singapore. Already, on March 5, the Führer's headquarters had issued to his military and naval commanders Directive No. 24 stating that "the aim of the cooperation initiated by the Tripartite Pact must be to bring Japan into active operations in the Far East as soon as possible," and German policy toward Japan at this time was conducted entirely with this end in view.[146]

Both Hitler and Ribbentrop reiterated to Matsuoka that Britain's surrender was only a matter of time, and a Japanese attack on Singapore would be decisive in bringing about defeat at an early stage. The best time to carry it out, in their opinion, was within the next two months. Military action at that time would also prevent America's entry into the war, since the American government would probably be unable to take countermeasures if the attack were made then. The German leaders made concerted efforts to obtain assurances from Matsuoka on this point.

Matsuoka, however, had anticipated their demands; moreover, he was already committed by the Japanese army and navy to make no promises to the German government regarding the exercise of military force. Therefore, while he showed understanding of the German arguments and expressed personal agreement with the rationale of a Japanese attack on Singapore, he replied that as a representative of the Japanese government he was forced to withhold a definite answer.[147]

Schmidt's record leaves the impression that the Soviet problem, which was the original objective of Matsuoka's visit, was given only a secondary place in the discussions, and that he made only a perfunctory proposal of a four-power entente. Matsuoka brought up the Soviet problem at his second meeting with Ribbentrop, when he asked "whether the Führer had ever considered the possibility of a Russian-Japanese-German alliance."

> The Reich Foreign Minister denied this and said that a closer collaboration with Russia was an absolute impossibility, since the ideological bases of the Army, as well as of the rest of the nation, were completely incompatible. The Soviet Union was still internationally minded while Japan and Germany thought nationally. Russia was undermining the family; Germany championed it . . . Germany would not provoke Russia; but if the policy of Stalin was not in harmony with what the Führer considered to be right, he would crush Russia.
>
> Matusoka replied that Japan was now taking pains not to provoke Russia. Japan was waiting for the completion of the German victory in the Balkans. Without the good offices of Germany and without her strength there was no chance for Japan to mend Russo-Japanese relations completely.
>
> . . . He then asked the Reich Foreign Minister whether on his return trip he should remain in Moscow for a somewhat longer period in order to negotiate with the Russians on the nonaggression pact or the treaty of neutrality. He emphasized in this connection that direct acceptance of Russia into the Tripartite Pact would not be countenanced by the Japa-

nese people. It would on the contrary call forth a unanimous cry of indignation all over Japan.

The Reich Foreign Minister replied that such an adherence of Russia to the Pact was out of the question and, moreover, recommended that Matsuoka, *if possible, should not bring up the above-mentioned questions in Moscow,* since this probably would not altogether fit into the framework of the present situation.[148]

At their last meeting Ribbentrop advised Matsuoka that "in view of the general situation it might be best not to go into things too deeply with the Russians . . . But one thing was certain: If Russia should ever attack Japan, Germany would strike immediately . . . so that Japan could push southward toward Singapore without fear of any complications with Russia." [149]

Matsuoka's talks with Hitler and Ribbentrop convinced him that relations between Germany and the Soviet Union were deteriorating. The Germans had not shown the slightest interest in a four-power entente nor in mediating Japanese-Soviet negotiations and even seemed opposed to Matsuoka's efforts to adjust diplomatic relations with Russia.

Matsuoka had begun to have doubts about the feasibility of a four-power entente before he left Tokyo. After his arrival in Berlin, Germany's obviously hostile attitude toward Russia and the events in Yugoslavia only increased his doubts. At this point Matsuoka must have realized that his plan for a four-power entente was no more than a fantasy.

Following his formal conferences with the German leaders, the next item on Matsuoka's schedule was a visit to Rome, where he and his party stayed from the evening of March 31 until the morning of April 3. On April 1 he met with Prime Minister Mussolini and Foreign Minister Ciano. For Matsuoka the Italian visit was only a courtesy call, but it was a useful occasion to publicize the solidarity of the Axis powers.

Matsuoka then returned to Berlin and met with Hitler on the 4th; the next day he had a final conference with Ribbentrop. As he began his return journey, he directed his attention to main-stage negotiations in Moscow.

The Neutrality Pact Is Negotiated

Meanwhile, the situation in the Balkans had suddenly become critical. At the end of February German troops began to move into Bulgaria, which the Soviet Union claimed was in its sphere of influence, and on March 1 the Bulgarian government was obliged, under duress, to join the Axis. German political pressure was also being applied against Yugoslavia. The Yugoslav government for a time resisted joining the Axis, but finally yielded to the German demands on March 25. On the 27th popular opposition exploded, resulting that day in an anti-German coup d'état that greatly disturbed the German government. Hitler's anger was further aroused when the new regime concluded a nonaggression treaty with the Soviet Union on April 5, and the following day he ordered the German army to attack Yugoslavia, destroy the new regime, and bring the area under complete German control.

As the German army swept into Yugoslavia and Greece, Matsuoka and his party crossed the new German-Soviet frontier in Poland. When the news reached him, Matsuoka realized that while the German army operations meant increased tension in German-Soviet relations, they represented a favorable development for the adjustment of Japanese-Soviet diplomatic relations. The new situation in the Balkans would force the Soviet government to stabilize its diplomatic relations with Japan in the east so that it might concentrate its energies in the west.

Matsuoka arrived in Moscow just before noon on April 7 and by four o'clock was engaged in full-scale negotiations with Molotov. Although he had abandoned his earlier expectations of German diplomatic support, he was probably optimistic that the crisis in the Balkans would induce the Soviets to come to a compromise agreement.

Matsuoka began by urging unconditional agreement on a nonaggression treaty and the purchase of northern Sakhalin by Japan, but Molotov in his reply refused to budge from the basic Soviet position as stated to Ambassador Tatekawa on November 18. A neutrality treaty, he repeated, was the proper formula, since it was difficult to envisage a nonaggression treaty not accompanied by a return of lost territories. He stubbornly stuck to the position that liquidation of the Japanese concessions in northern Sakhalin was an indispensable precondition to the conclusion of the treaty, and he dismissed as foolish the proposal to sell northern Sakhalin to Japan. Instead of making "gigantic strides toward the improvement of diplomatic relations," this first meeting saw only the restatement of the positions of the two countries.[150]

The second meeting took place two days later and lasted three-and-a-half hours. Matsuoka now retreated a step toward acceptance of the neutrality treaty formula, but emphasized that the treaty would have to be without preconditions. He pressed Molotov to perform a kind of diplomatic blitzkrieg by concluding the negotiations while Matsuoka was still in Moscow. As expressionless and dogged as ever, Molotov refused to abandon his demand for the liquidation of the northern Sakhalin concessions. He maintained that Tatekawa had already agreed to this and criticized Japan for changing its position. Matsuoka emphasized the strength of public opposition in Japan, citing various statements of General Araki, to a rapprochement with the Soviet Union in an effort to explain to Molotov the difficulties that liquidating the concessions would produce.

This second meeting likewise ended without agreement. In contrast to his original optimistic expectations, Matsuoka must have been disappointed at the lack of flexibility in Molotov's position. The Japanese foreign minister, in accordance with Article 2b of the "Outline for Negotiations with Germany, Italy, and the USSR," also brought up the question of spheres of influence in China, proposing a secret protocol that would place north China and Inner Mongolia within Japan's sphere of influence and Outer Mongolia and Sinkiang within the Soviet sphere. Molotov quietly sidestepped the issue with the remark that he would like "to leave this for some later date."[151]

At midnight Matsuoka's party left Moscow and spent the next day sightseeing in Leningrad. In his report to the emperor upon his return home, Matsuoka explained that he had made the visit to Leningrad and extended his stay for two reasons: "to allow time to increase the chances of concluding a treaty, and in case no agreement could be reached, to make Britain, the United States, and other countries at least believe that significant talks had been held between Japan and the Soviet Union." These diversionary tactics in Leningrad allowed Matsuoka and his party to admire Ulanova's performance in "Romeo and Juliet." Directly after the performance they again boarded the night train and returned to Moscow in the morning.

On the 11th, at 4 p.m., Matsuoka and Molotov met for the third time, a meeting that lasted over two hours. For the first time Molotov made a proposal that revised slightly the position taken in the November Soviet reply. In that proposal, the first article had read: "Both contracting parties proclaim mutual respect for territorial integrity and desire to maintain peaceful and friendly relations." After the words "territorial integrity" Molotov now inserted "and inviolability, as well as the territorial integrity and inviolability of Manchukuo and the Mongolian People's Republic, allies and neighboring states of the contracting parties." But there was no change in his position on the supplementary protocol providing for the liquidation of the northern Sakhalin concessions.

Matsuoka had no objection to the addition of the phrase concerning the territorial integrity and inviolability of Manchukuo and Outer Mongolia, but he argued that "Manchukuo's independence and the spirit of self-respect of its people" should be incorporated in a separate declaration. He continued to press for elimination of the protocol, although as a compromise he proposed to substitute for it a personal letter in English with the following contents:

> In reference to the Neutrality Treaty signed today, I expect and hope that a commercial agreement and a fisheries convention will be concluded very soon, and that at the earliest opportunity we shall endeavor, in the spirit of conciliation and mutual accommodations, to solve the question of the concessions in northern Sakhalin under the contracts signed at Moscow on December 14, 1925, with a view to removing all questions which are not conducive to the maintenance of cordial relations between our two countries.
>
> In the same spirit, I should also like to point out that it is well for our two countries as well as Manchukuo and Outer Mongolia to find in a short time a way to institute joint or mixed commissions of the countries concerned with the object of settling the boundary questions and of handling disputes and incidents along the borders.[152]

This was the Japanese government's last concession, Matsuoka warned, and if it was not acceptable, he would have no alternative but to depart in two days as scheduled, leaving the neutrality treaty unsigned. But first he wished to say farewell to Stalin.

That evening Matsuoka received a message from Stalin that arrangements had been made for them to meet at 5 p.m. the next day. Once again Matsuoka pressed for the sale of northern Sakhalin to Japan and advocated directing Soviet influence toward India and Iran; Stalin countered with a proposal that Japan cede southern Sakhalin to the Soviet Union. Within a little over ten minutes after this brief exchange, the two had reached an agreement. Matsuoka's draft was accepted insofar as the form of the treaty was concerned, but the supplementary protocol was to be withdrawn and significant changes made in the text of Matsuoka's personal letter. Stalin himself took a pen and amended the portion of the letter concerned with the northern Sakhalin concessions to read "shall endeavor . . . to solve *in a few months* the question of the *liquidation* of the concessions in northern Sakhalin." Matsuoka consented to this formulation and both sides reached agreement on this compromise solution.[153]

The signing of the Japanese-Soviet Neutrality Pact took place at the Kremlin the following day, the 13th, at 3 p.m. Both parties signed the main text of the treaty and made public the declaration pledging respect for the territorial integrity and inviolability of Manchukuo and Outer Mongolia. At the same time, Matsuoka presented the agreed-upon letter to Molotov, who produced a letter of acceptance.

It is worth reproducing here in full the text of the treaty, the Declaration, and Matsuoka's letter.

The Treaty

The Empire of Japan and the Union of Soviet Socialist Republics, guided by a desire to strengthen peaceful and friendly relations between the two countries, have decided to conclude a treaty of neutrality as follows:

Article I. Both contracting parties proclaim their mutual respect for territorial integrity and inviolability and their desire for the maintenance of peaceful and friendly relations.

Article II. In the event of military activity by any other power or powers against either of the contracting parties, the other contracting party shall maintain neutrality throughout the duration of the conflict.

Article III. This treaty will become effective on the day of ratification by the two contracting parties and will remain in effect for five years. This treaty shall be automatically extended for another five years if neither contracting party gives notice of abrogation by the end of the fourth year.

Article IV. This treaty will be ratified as soon as possible. Instruments of ratification shall be exchanged in Tokyo as soon as possible.

The Declaration

In conformity with the spirit of the Treaty of Neutrality concluded on April 13, 1941, between the Empire of Japan and the Union of Soviet Socialist Republics, the government of the Empire of Japan and the government of the Union of Soviet Socialist Republics, in order to insure peaceful and friendly relations between the two countries, solemnly declare that the Empire of Japan pledges to respect the territorial integrity and inviolability of the Mongolian People's Republic, and the Union of Soviet Socialist Republics pledges to respect the territorial integrity and inviolability of Manchukuo.

Matsuoka's Letter to Molotov

Excellency:

With reference to the Treaty of Neutrality signed today, I have the honor to state that I expect and hope that a commercial agreement and a fisheries convention will soon be concluded and that at the earliest opportunity we, Your Excellency and myself, shall endeavor, in the spirit of conciliation and mutual accommodation, to solve in a few months the question of the liquidation of the concessions in northern Sakhalin under the contracts signed at Moscow on December 14, 1925, with a view to removing the various questions not conducive to the maintenance of cordial relations between our two countries.

In the same spirit I should like to point out that it will be well for our two countries, as well as Manchukuo and Outer Mongolia, if we find at the earliest possible date a means of instituting joint or mixed commissions of the countries concerned, with the object of settling the boundary questions and of handling disputes and incidents along the borders.[154]

The ceremony was followed by a banquet, after which Matsuoka was scheduled to leave Moscow. Stalin personally appeared at the railway station to see him off. This was unprecedented insofar as Soviet government protocol was concerned, and the event was not lost on the diplomatic corps and newspaper correspondents. Stalin showered Matsuoka with expressions of deep affection, and in the end the two exchanged a farewell embrace.

There is no way of knowing what prompted Stalin to make this unprecedented gesture, but his action certainly showed that he was satisfied with the results of the negotiations. A neutrality treaty with Japan saved the Soviet Union from the danger of war on two fronts. It might also provide an opportunity to reestablish friendly relations with Germany and encourage Japan's policy of southern advance.[155]

Matsuoka took the Trans-Siberian Railway to Hailaerh in Manchuria, from where he flew to Tokyo via Dairen and Fukuoka, arriving the afternoon of the 22nd. He went immediately to the imperial palace to report to the emperor on his European trip and at 9 p.m. attended a Liaison Conference. Two days later he presented the treaty for ratification by the Privy Council, which approved it the same day.

Why was Matsuoka so anxious to reach an accommodation with the Soviet Union? His original plan to use Germany as a go-between in negotiations had collapsed in Berlin when, instead of offering to act as mediator, the German government had advised him to avoid a political rapprochement with the Soviet Union. Matsuoka must have realized, from the language of the German leaders as well as from the situation in the Balkans, that German-Soviet relations had deteriorated beyond redemption. Why then did he cling to the adjustment of relations with the Soviet Union and unhesitatingly make large concessions?

While it is true that he managed to remove the thorny issue of the northern Sakhalin concession from a supplementary protocol to the treaty, the fact that he recognized in an exchange of letters that the fundamental point of the "liquidation of the concessions" certainly signified acceptance by Japan of the Soviet position. On top of that, the final formula—a neutrality treaty—was the one Matsuoka had originally rejected. Thus the compromise of April 13 that made possible the adjustment of Japanese-Soviet diplomatic relations was based largely on concessions by Japan. As F. C. Jones has concluded, it was "a triumph for Soviet diplomacy and a defeat for that of Matsuoka."[156]

One might speculate that Matsuoka believed the treaty would strengthen Japan's position from the viewpoint of international power politics. On the day of the signing Matsuoka told Ambassador Schulenburg that "the conclusion of the Neutrality Pact was of very great importance for Japan. It would make a powerful impression on Chiang Kai-shek and would appreciably ease Japanese negotiations with him. Also it would result in an appreciable strengthening of the position of Japan as over against America and England." This was probably a frank expression of his feelings.[157]

Looking first at the China problem, the Neutrality Pact at the very least dealt a severe psychological blow to the Chungking government. On August 21, 1937, China and the Soviet Union had concluded a nonaggression treaty pledging that

> in the event that either of the High Contracting Parties should be subjected to aggression on the part of one or more third Powers, the other High Contracting Party obligates itself not to render assistance of any kind, either directly or indirectly to such third Power or Powers at any time during the entire conflict, and also to refrain from taking any action or entering into any agreement which may be used by the aggressor or aggressors to the disadvantage of the Party subjected to aggression.[158]

It was to be expected that the Neutrality Pact, and especially the joint declaration concerning the territorial integrity and inviolability of Manchukuo and the Mongolian People's Republic, would intensify China's distrust of the Soviet Union and widen the rift between the two countries. China was certain to view the declaration as an infringement upon its sovereignty and territorial integrity. It was also to be expected that the Japanese-Soviet rapprochement would aggravate the confrontation between the left and right factions within the Nationalist government and accentuate the conflict between the Nationalists and the Communists.[159]

Another important element in Matsuoka's decision was the need to achieve "tranquillity in the north" as a prerequisite to the policy of southern advance. Here his aim of strengthening Japan's position vis-à-vis the United States is of particular importance.

Matsuoka was convinced that there could be progress in the negotiations with the United States only if Japan's coercive power were increased and its resolution to confront the United States strengthened. He expected the tripartite alliance to have such an effect, and his persistent attachment to the idea of adjusting Japanese-Soviet relations was probably similarly motivated. Thus, it was necessary to create at least the appearance of Japanese-Soviet conciliation, even though some compensation had to be paid to the Soviets and the final agreement in the form of a neutrality treaty was a "weak political combination." It accorded with his program of proceeding from the tripartite alliance to the adjustment of diplomatic relations first with the Soviet Union and then with the United States. Matsuoka's three meetings with Ambassador Steinhardt in Moscow were a sign that he was putting into operation his design of using the two pacts as stepping stones to negotiations with the United States.

Finally, there was undoubtedly the motive of personal ambition. The nationwide fanfare accompanying his send-off would have created in Matsuoka a strong psychological resistance to returning home empty-handed. Moreover, his aspiration to head the next government made it important that the negotiations eventuate in success.

Some Soviet scholars maintain that during his conferences with the German leaders in Berlin Matsuoka was informed of Germany's intention to attack the Soviet Union, and that his real motive in concluding the Neutrality Pact was "to lull the Soviet people's vigilance."[160] In short, they accuse Matsuoka of practicing deceptive diplomacy. Another Soviet interpretation characterizes Matsuoka's negotiations in Moscow as a plot:

Matsuoka already knew of German preparations to attack the Soviet Union. The Japanese government expected that at the outbreak of a German-Soviet war the Soviet Union, trusting in its agreement with Japan, would move a substantial part of its forces from the Far East to the western front, whereupon the Japanese army would be able to seize Soviet territory in the Far East without difficulty.[161]

Did Matsuoka conclude the Neutrality Pact on the assumption that a German attack on Russia was imminent? Hitler ordered that the plan of Operation Barbarossa be concealed from Matsuoka, and there is no indication in the records of his talks in Berlin that Matsuoka was told of the plan to attack the Soviet Union. It is true that the Balkan situation and his conversations with Ribbentrop probably made him aware of the tensions in German-Soviet relations. He did not expect the confrontation to develop into a war, however, as can be seen from his statement to Ambassador Steinhardt in Moscow: "He thought it was for the purpose of frightening the Soviets into continuing supplies that the Germans had given out rumours of a possible attack."[162] That Matsuoka was indeed unaware of Germany's plans is made clear by his reaction to a cable from Ambassador Ōshima that reached Tokyo in June, indicating that a German attack upon the Soviet Union was certain. Despite Ōshima's report, Matsuoka stated to the emperor on June 6 that "the outlook for German-Soviet relations was 60 percent for the conclusion of an agreement and 40 percent for war."[163] In Sugamo prison after the war Matsuoka recalled that "until the war finally broke out, I had real doubts that such a war would occur. This was probably due to my wish not to see it happen."[164]

When war finally did break out, Matsuoka, at the June 25 Liaison Conference, advocated that Japan cooperate with Germany and immediately attack the Soviet Union. On this occasion he said regretfully: "I really concluded the Neutrality Pact thinking that Germany and the Soviet Union would not fight. Had I known Germany and the Soviet Union would fight, I would have taken friendly action toward Germany and would not have concluded the neutrality treaty."[165] Irrespective of what Matsuoka may actually have thought, this at least is what he said about the conclusion of the neutrality treaty with the Soviet Union.

The reaction in Japan to the signing of the Japanese-Soviet Neutrality Pact was mixed. When Prime Minister Konoe received news of the agreement, he looked pleased and remarked to Vice Minister Ōhashi: "Now I feel relieved at last . . . Matsuoka is really an able man" (he used the English word "able").[166] To the extent that stabilization of Japanese-Soviet relations increased Japan's freedom of action in China and the areas to the south, the pact was welcomed. It was natural that there were counterarguments from the right wing and other ideological opponents. It is significant, however, that some in the Privy Council and even in the Foreign Ministry sounded a warning that Japan would fall into a Soviet diplomatic trap if it thought the treaty provided security in the north and thus permitted an advance in the south.[167]

Among them was former Foreign Minister Shidehara who, hearing of Matsuoka's send-off by Stalin in Moscow, wrote on April 16: "When shepherds quarrel, the wolf has a winning game. One cannot but be astounded by the clever trick of incitement that allows the Kremlin to fish in troubled waters." He criticized Matsuoka's "eccentric diplomacy" and in another letter on May 5 outlined what in his view were the Soviet government's objectives in concluding a neutrality treaty with Japan. These were two-fold:

> a) With respect to American military action against Japan: As a result of the guarantee that the Soviet Union will not support the United States, Japan's position vis-à-vis the United States is strengthened, and following the trend of events, there is finally the possibility of provoking a war between Japan and the United States.
>
> b) With respect to German military action against the Soviet Union: As a result of the guarantee that Japan will not support Germany, the Soviet position vis-à-vis Germany is strengthened; moreover, the Soviet Union will benefit from the effect of that guarantee upon the treaty of alliance among Japan, Germany, and Italy.

In either case, Shidehara argued, the treaty was of advantage to and served the interests of Soviet diplomacy alone, therefore Japan should exercise strict vigilance in its future conduct of foreign affairs.[168]

A year earlier the Army General Staff had supported the formula of a neutrality treaty in adjusting diplomatic relations between Japan and the Soviet Union. When the treaty was actually signed, however, there was uncertainty as to its meaning and significance. The *Confidential War Diary* of the War Guidance Office contains the following entry for the day following the conclusion of the treaty:

April 14: The Neutrality Pact contributes neither to a military solution in the south nor to the avoidance of war with the United States. It simply provides us with the time we need before independently starting a war against the Soviet Union. Our leaders must be fully cognizant of this. We don't know what Stalin's true intentions are. Within the Intelligence Division there is strong debate regarding the significance of the treaty.

April 18: a) As a result of the neutrality treaty, the situation in the Far East is advantageous to Japan; b) . . . the neutrality treaty is advantageous for Japan's southern advance; c) it must also be said that Japanese diplomacy has become more positive and vigorous.[169]

At a meeting of the Privy Council Army Minister Tōjō made it clear that he had no intention of relaxing Japan's strategic posture vis-à-vis the Soviet Union. "In spite of this treaty," he stated, "we must increasingly perfect our military preparations against the Soviet Union. We must continue to apply pressure against the Soviet Union. It is in the nature of things that countries prepare against violations of treaty obligations."[170] But while the army continued to advocate military preparations in the north, the conclusion of the treaty nonetheless did create a sense of "tranquillity in the north" that provided psychological encouragement for the policy of southern advance.

Even though it appeared that the Neutrality Pact had fulfilled Matsuoka's hopes for promoting the southern advance policy, it is questionable whether it had the effect he intended either upon reaching a settlement in the Sino-Japanese war or upon achieving progress in the negotiations with the United States.

There is no doubt that the treaty came as a severe psychological shock to the Nationalist government in Chungking. On April 14 Foreign Minister Wang Ch'ung-hui issued a statement that the joint Japanese-Soviet declaration was invalid insofar as China was concerned, and since it conflicted with the nonaggression treaty between China and the Soviet Union, his government was preparing to lodge a protest with the Soviet government. The following day the Chungking newspapers all published editorials criticizing the Soviet Union. At the same time, Japanese reports indicated that Sun Fo and other advocates of close ties with the Soviets had suffered a blow, whereas Chang Ch'ün, Ho Ying-ch'in, and others in the pro-Japanese faction perceived an opportunity to seek peace with Japan.[171]

In view of this reaction, on April 16 Molotov firmly assured the Chinese ambassador in Moscow, Shao Li-tzu, that no change would take place in Chinese-Soviet relations.[172] And on April 25, to boost Chinese morale and resistance to Japan, the United States government announced a $50 million loan to Chungking. Although the conclusion of the treaty did create agitation in Chungking and a loosening of Sino-Soviet ties, the extent was less than Japan had expected. The impact would doubtless have been much greater in the summer of the previous year, when the Nationalists were in the midst of acute economic difficulties and before the conclusion of the Tripartite Pact had strengthened American and British determination to aid Chungking.

American authorities were clearly disturbed by the news of the Japanese-Soviet rapprochement. American Ambassador in Japan Joseph C. Grew and the *New York Times* assessed the treaty as a Japanese diplomatic success.[173] Secretary of State Hull spoke of it at a press conference on the 14th: "The significance of the pact between the Soviet Union and Japan relating to neutrality, as reported in the press today, could be overestimated. The agreement would seem to be descriptive of a situation which has in effect existed between the two countries for some time past. It therefore comes as no surprise."[174]

As in the case of the Tripartite Pact, however, there was no sign that the American government felt coerced by the Russo-Japanese pact into adopting a conciliatory policy toward Japan. On the contrary, fearing that the treaty had strengthened Japan's southern advance policy, the United States accelerated its own war preparations against Japan and adopted an even tougher stance in its negotiations with Tokyo. Matsuoka's plan of moving from the Tripartite Pact through Japanese-Soviet understanding to Japanese-American negotiations had failed. The subsequent negotiations with the United States made even clearer the extent of his miscalculation.

The Shock of German-Soviet Hostilities

Hitler believed that if Germany were to be able to concentrate all its power in the war against Britain and deal a fatal psychological blow to the British people's will to resist, it was first necessary to destroy the Soviet army. Having given the order for Operation Barbarossa, he became unshakeable in his determination to carry out an attack on the Soviet Union.

In accordance with German operations plans, by the beginning of 1941 preparations for war against the Soviet Union were proceeding along both the military and economic fronts. By the third week of February a total of 680,000 German troops were concentrated in Rumania, and on the last day of the month German troops moved into Bulgaria to take up positions at strategic points.

The schedule, however, had to be revised when the anti-German coup occurred in Yugoslavia on March 26–27. Enraged by the events in Yugoslavia, Hitler decided that it should be dissolved as a state and on April 6 he ordered the German armed forces to attack Yugoslavia and Greece. This new campaign in the Balkans meant that Operation Barbarossa would have to be postponed.

On April 13 German troops entered Belgrade, and on the 17th the Yugoslav army surrendered; on April 27 German tank corps occupied Athens. Although the Balkan operation had taken only three weeks and ended in a spectacular German victory, more time was now needed for the forces thrown into the campaign to be restationed against the enemy in the east. On April 30 Hitler issued an order changing the date of Operation Barbarossa from May 15 to June 22.[175]

Having decided on the new date for the attack on the Soviet Union, the German government threw all its energies into completing war preparations. Abandoning mopping-up operations in Yugoslavia, the Germans quickly moved most of their troops in the Balkans to the eastern front. By the end of May they began to take up strategic springboard positions; they also prepared a plan for the occupation of Russia. War preparations progressed steadily toward the target date of June 22.

Surprisingly, Stalin took no countermeasures against Hitler's preparations for an attack on the Soviet Union, despite the fact that during March and April rumors about the imminence of war between Germany and the Soviet Union grew increasingly persistent. On March 20 the United States government informed the Soviet ambassador in Washington, Constantine Oumansky, of a secret intelligence report on Operation Barbarossa it had received early in January; the report had been obtained by an American diplomat in Berlin from an anti-Nazi friend with contacts among high officials in the German government. Prime Minister Churchill, in a personal letter to Stalin in April, also tried to alert him to the significance of German troop movements in southern Poland.[176] Stalin, however, seems to have regarded the British and American warnings as a plot to sow discord between Germany and the Soviet Union.

Even after the start of the offensive against Yugoslavia, Stalin believed it would be possible to achieve a political understanding with Germany. The Soviets, it appeared, were certain that the rifts in relations between the two countries over the Balkan problem could be repaired by a conciliatory attitude on their part. On April 10, therefore, the Soviet government abandoned its previous policy of resisting German domination of the Balkans—a policy expressed in the conclusion of a nonaggression treaty with the anti-German government in Yugoslavia—and clearly adopted a "conciliatory policy" toward Germany.[177]

When Stalin showed up at the railway station to see Matsuoka off on April 13, he specifically sought out Ambassador Schulenburg and the acting military attaché. Brimming with charm, he told them, "We must remain friends."[178] His behavior symbolized Soviet policy toward Germany at the time. The Soviet government, furthermore, was generous in supplying Germany with strategic materials. An agreement on oil deliveries was signed on April 12, and on May 15 it was reported that the government had provided several special freight trains to deliver four thousand tons of raw rubber to Germany from the Far East.[179] On April 15 the problem of the disputed boundary between the two countries in the north was settled by a one-sided Soviet concession.

On May 6 Stalin replaced Molotov as chairman of the Council of People's Commissars, or prime minister, but the conciliatory policy toward Germany continued unabated. On May 9 the Soviet government withdrew its recognition of the Belgian and Norwegian governments-in-exile; it also expelled the Yugoslav ambassador and withdrew its recognition of the Yugoslav regime with which it had concluded a nonaggression treaty only a month before. On June 3 recognition was withdrawn from the Greek government-in-exile. Meanwhile, on May 12 the Soviet government announced its recognition of the pro-Nazi regime of Rashid Ali in Iraq. It is clear that the Soviet Union intended by these measures to impress favorably the German government and bring about a lessening of tension between the two countries. Had Stalin correctly appraised Hitler's intentions toward the Soviet Union, he would not have made the mistake of pursuing such a conciliatory policy.

Matsuoka's continuing attachment, following his visit to Berlin, to the idea of adjusting Japanese-Soviet relations may have contributed to the Soviet leader's miscalculation. Although Matsuoka conducted his negotiations with the Soviets entirely in terms of Japanese objectives, this may well have served to camouflage Hitler's intentions. Stalin may have assumed that Matsuoka had the complete understanding of the German government in his attempts to achieve a rapprochement with the Soviet Union and that a political agreement with Japan would promote the restoration of harmonious relations between Germany and the USSR. If Hitler were bent on war, Stalin must have reasoned, Matsuoka would have been informed of it during his conferences in Berlin and would not have wanted to conclude a neutrality treaty with Russia. This hypothesis is supported by the fact that Matsuoka's visit to Moscow coincided with a change in Soviet policy toward Germany.

The Soviet Union's conciliatory policy, however, had no effect on Hitler's plans to attack Russia. The strategic deployment of German troops on the eastern front continued, and on June 14 Hitler and the commanders of his armed forces met for a last conference on Operation Barbarossa to arrange the final details for execution of the attack.[180]

On the same day, in another effort to avoid war with Germany, Molotov handed Ambassador Schulenburg a communiqué that was to be made public by the TASS news agency the following day. To squelch rumors being circulated in the foreign press of an "impending war" between the USSR and Germany, the communiqué branded them "a clumsy propaganda maneuver of the forces arrayed against the Soviet Union and Germany." "In the opinion of Soviet circles the rumors of the intention of Germany to break the Pact and to launch an attack against the Soviet Union are completely without foundation, while the recent movements of German troops . . . must be explained by other motives which have no connection with Soviet-German relations."[181] But it shortly became clear that British and American intelligence had been correct and that the Soviet conciliatory policy had been based on wishful thinking.

The dramatic change in German-Soviet relations was obviously a matter of grave concern to Japan, which had a military alliance with Germany and a neutrality treaty with the Soviet Union. If hostilities were to break out between the two countries, Japan would have to choose between its conflicting obligations under the two treaties[182] and make a fundamental reexamination of its foreign policy in light of the new situation.

Rumors that war was imminent had been reaching the Japanese capital for some time, but the first report the government credited seriously was a cable of April 16 from Ambassador Ōshima in Berlin summarizing a conversation with Ribbentrop on the 10th. "Depending on Soviet behavior," the foreign minister had said, "it is possible that Germany may start a war against Russia even during the present year . . . At present Germany has sufficient military power for an attack upon Russia. If war should break out, there is a good prospect that military operations would be successfully completed in a few months. *Therefore, depending upon how the situation develops, I think it is to our advantage to strike before Russia completes its preparations.*" Ribbentrop's words spelled out Germany's intention to attack Russia even more clearly than had the hints given to Matsuoka in February. To confirm the statement, Ōshima had arranged to see Stahmer on the 14th and asked him whether Germany had changed its policy from giving priority to operations against Britain to concentrating first on attacking Russia. Stahmer, hinting at the imminence of the attack on the Soviet Union, replied: "As you know, since last autumn Hitler has drafted so many into the army that it was considered unnecessary [to shift policy priorities]. The army now has over 240 divisions. *An attack against Russia cannot be launched during the winter.* It may be to our advantage, depending on the Russian attitude, to attack Russia *simultaneously with an attack against Britain.*"[183] Ōshima's own conclusion was that there was a possibility that between May and October Germany would start operations against the Soviet Union parallel with an attack on Britain. As for Japan's policy in the case of a German-Soviet war, he advised:

> The Germans are so confident of their ability to wage a war against the Soviet Union that they do not necessarily expect us to join them . . . In that event, Japan should not hurriedly launch an attack in the north but should rather wait for a suitable moment. First of all, Japan should push straight forward along the great road to establishing the East Asia Co-Prosperity Sphere. We should concentrate [first] on the capture of Singapore, the British and American power base in the Far East, which is the fundamental obstacle to our plans.[184]

Having just concluded the Neutrality Pact with the Soviet Union, the Japanese government must have been at a loss as to how to appraise the situation correctly. That Ōshima's cable created a stir in government circles can be seen from the fact that Prime Minister Konoe immediately

sent Vice Foreign Minister Ōhashi to convey the information to the lord
keeper of the privy seal, Kido Kōichi, who in turn went to the imperial
villa at Hayama to report to the emperor.[185]

On April 22 Colonel Nagai Yatsuji, who had accompanied Matsuoka
to Europe, brought the military authorities another message from
Ōshima to the effect that the "German attitude toward the Soviet Union
is getting worse. It seems that they have made up their mind to attack
Russia."[186] The army authorities were unwilling to accept Ōshima's intelligence reports at face value, for they still had doubts about Germany's determination to wage war against the Soviet Union.[187] The
Confidential War Diary contains the following entry for April 21:
"Strange telegram; the situation is indeed complex and strange."

On May 13 the Japanese military attaché in Berlin, Banzai Ichirō,
conveyed to Tokyo confidential information from German army sources
that war between Germany and the Soviet Union was inevitable and advised the immediate recall of the military inspection group headed by
General Yamashita Tomoyuki.[188] The military now began to give greater
credence to the possibility of a German-Soviet war,[189] although a conference of division chiefs on May 15 declared that war "is not expected to
break out suddenly."[190]

Despite such warnings received throughout April and May, the government and the military failed accurately to appraise Hitler's intentions. Nonetheless the General Staff did take the reports and rumors
into consideration and prepared a draft policy on "Japan's Attitude in
Case of War between Germany and the Soviet Union."[191] Matsuoka too
was sufficiently concerned about the situation to send the following inquiry to Ribbentrop on May 28: "Taking into account present international developments affecting our country and our domestic situation, I
wish at this point that the German government would do all in its power
to avoid an armed clash with the Soviet Union. I say this frankly as a
friend. Could I have your frank views on this point by return cable?"[192]

On June 3 and 4 Ambassador Ōshima was invited to Hitler's mountain villa at Berchtesgaden, where both Hitler and Ribbentrop made
some rather important statements about their attitude toward the Soviet
Union:

> Hitler: German-Soviet relations are increasingly deteriorating and a
> German-Soviet war probably cannot be avoided. The Soviet attitude to-

ward Germany is outwardly friendly, but in reality it is in complete op-position. For example, the Soviets concluded a nonaggression treaty right after the coup d'état that followed Yugoslavia's entry into the tripartite alliance, and Soviet staff officers directly aided Yugoslav operations. These are clearly hostile acts directed against Germany, and such a Soviet attitude cannot be tolerated. I believe one should never make concessions to the Soviet Union. I am a person who will always draw the sword first if I am convinced of my opponent's hostility.

Ribbentrop: German-Soviet relations have particularly deteriorated of late and the possibility of war has greatly increased . . . Germany already dominates the European continent. If we should now defeat Russia, we will secure a position that Britain and America would not be able to touch. That is to say, to crush the Soviet Union is an absolute precondition for an attack on Britain . . . If Japan is encountering difficulties in preparing for a southward advance, Germany would welcome Japanese cooperation in the war against the Soviet Union.

These statements can be construed as an advance notice to the Japanese government of the German intention to attack the Soviet Union. Reporting on this meeting in a long dispatch dated June 5, Ōshima expressed his opinion:

1) Neither Hitler nor Ribbentrop said that the decision to attack the Soviet Union was final. Thus the door was left slightly ajar. But judging from the fact that I was urgently summoned the day after a conference with Mussolini and that Hitler, as the head of state, spoke as explicitly as I have reported in this cable, it is reasonable to conclude that the outbreak of war between Germany and the Soviet Union is already inevitable.

2) As for the timing of hostilities, neither was very explicit . . . To judge from Hitler's way of doing things in the past, however, once he has made up his mind, he proceeds quickly to implement his decision. Therefore, I think that the Rubicon will be crossed in a short time.[193]

Ōshima's report created a suddenly tense situation within the government and the military. But still Matsuoka refused to believe that war would break out between Germany and the Soviet Union. On June 6 he had predicted to the emperor that agreement between them was more likely than war.[194]

A Liaison Conference was convened on June 7 to discuss Ōshima's cable. Here, too, Matsuoka expressed disagreement with Ōshima's conclusions:

I don't disagree with Ōshima when he says that Hitler is intent upon destroying communism. But will he therefore make war now, or will he perhaps wait twenty or thirty years? I think we should also watch carefully for British-German conciliation. Even assuming that war should break out between Germany and the Soviet Union, I think that Germany, needing moral justification, will make demands before launching an attack.[195]

As for the army's assessment of the situation, Ōshima's cable of June 5 and Military Attaché Banzai's cable had strengthened the view among "both upper and lower echelons" that war was imminent.[196] The Soviet Union could be expected to throw its entire military strength into the struggle against Germany, and bitter argument therefore arose within the Army Ministry and the General Staff over the military measures Japan should take in such an event. The debate centered around three proposed courses of action.

The first advocated that Japan take advantage of the disappearance of the threat in the north "to advance decisively with military force in the south." Japan should occupy the southern part of French Indochina and at an opportune moment use this area as a springboard for an advance into Malaya and the Dutch East Indies. This strategy was strongly advocated by the Army Ministry's Military Affairs Section (particularly by Section Chief Satō Kenryō), while other supporters included General Staff Operations Section Chief Doi Akio and its Europe-American Section Chief Amano Masakazu.

The second strategy was termed "the principle of the green persimmon," from the notion that the best way to secure the fruits of the persimmon tree was not to wait for them to ripen but to shake them down while still green. Analogously, depending upon the movement of Soviet Far Eastern forces, this strategy called for the Japanese military to act in concert with Germany and join in the attack upon the Soviet Union. Japanese forces would occupy the Soviet Far Eastern territories and achieve the Japanese army's traditional strategic objective of security in the north. This program was urged by General Staff Operations Division Chief Tanaka Shin'ichi, who called for a positive policy of "intentionally creating a favorable opportunity for using military force."

The third option was termed "the principle of the ripe persimmon," it being a strategy not to take positive action but to wait for the fruit to ripen, that is, for events to mature before irreversible action was taken.

Advocates of this policy called for Japan to prepare for action in the future without directly intervening in the war against either the Soviet Union or Britain. Such a strengthening of Japan's war potential in both the north and south was likened to pitching a preparatory camp. Concretely, Japan should strengthen its military power in Manchuria and advance into southern French Indochina. Such a strategy was favored by the Military Section of the Army Ministry and the War Guidance Office of the General Staff.

Between the 5th and the 14th of June the Army Ministry and the General Staff daily held separate and joint discussions of the policy Japan should pursue in case of a German-Soviet war. Finally, on the 14th an army draft policy emerged. Entitled "National Defense Policy for Dealing with the Changing Situation," it embraced the "ripe persimmon" strategy, calling for the building up of a preparatory strategic position in both the north and the south and called for intervention in the war against the Soviet Union should the situation develop so as to present a good opportunity.[197]

Meanwhile the navy was conducting its own policy deliberations and on June 7 adopted the "Measures for Dealing with the New Situation in German-Soviet Relations." Based on its traditional principle of "Defend the north, advance to the south," this navy document opposed not only intervening in a German-Soviet war but also the strengthening of Japanese forces facing the Soviet Union; outstanding problems should be settled by pushing the Soviet Union to the wall, but exclusively by diplomatic means.

1) Should a new situation arise in German-Soviet relations, Japan should not intervene. For a while it should adopt a wait-and-see attitude and be prepared for changes in the situation.

2) The army's and navy's military postures vis-à-vis the Soviet Union should be maintained at present levels (except for the reinforcement of some units).

.   .   .   .

6) At an appropriate moment the Soviet Union should be induced diplomatically to take the following measures:

a) Permit the purchase of northern Sakhalin by Japan.

b) Suspend its aid of Chiang Kai-shek and make a public announcement thereof.

c) Guarantee not to cooperate militarily or politically with Britain and the United States in the Far East.

d) Enable Japan to acquire necessary commodities.[198]

Obviously there were issues still to be resolved with the army. On June 20 the following entry was made in the *Confidential War Diary:*

> The navy's summary of national defense policy has been received. Although there is not a great difference of opinion, the army advocates taking advantage of a good opportunity to act, while the navy advocates postponing a decision on whether to act or not until future developments can be taken into account. There are obvious differences between the army's and the navy's approach. The navy plan calls for completing military preparations in the south and leaving military preparations in the north at the present level.

The differences had not yet been reconciled when news flashed to Tokyo of the outbreak of war between Germany and the Soviet Union.

Japan Positions Its Forces for War

At dawn on June 22 the massed armies of Germany on the eastern frontier invaded Soviet territory. This was the opening of Operation Barbarossa.

News that war had broken out between Germany and Russia threw Japan's political and military leaders into a flurry of agitation. Foreign Minister Matsuoka received the news at four o'clock while attending a kabuki performance with the head of the Nanking government Wang Ching-wei. He left at once and went to the palace to inform the emperor. Matsuoka had earlier decided that in case of conflict between Japan's obligations under the Tripartite Pact and the Japanese-Soviet Neutrality Pact, the former should prevail. Therefore when he reached the palace he told the emperor: "Since war has broken out between Germany and the Soviet Union, Japan should cooperate with Germany and attack the Soviet Union. To carry out the attack, it is better that we refrain temporarily from action in the south. We shall have to fight sooner or later. Ultimately, Japan will have to fight simultaneously the Soviet Union, the United States, and Britain." The emperor was alarmed.[199] Events must have proved a psychological blow to Matsuoka as well, for he had concluded the neutrality treaty with Moscow on the assumption that Germany and Russia were not going to fight and hoped until the very last moment that war would be avoided.

The sudden change in German-Soviet relations in 1939 had caused the fall of the cabinet of Baron Hiranuma and, following this precedent, Konoe had considered the resignation en bloc of his cabinet in such an event.[200] He also weighed the possibility of seceding from the tripartite alliance,[201] noting in his diary:

> Previously, at the time of the Hiranuma cabinet, while Germany was discussing with us a tripartite alliance directed against the Soviet Union, it suddenly concluded a nonaggression treaty with this adversary. This was Germany's first betrayal of Japan. Now, having promised to treat the Soviet Union as a friend and having concluded the tripartite alliance with this promise as a precondition, Germany ignored our advice and started a war against the Soviet Union. This then should be considered their second betrayal. Japan therefore has the right and the justification to reconsider the tripartite alliance. I once asked the army and navy ministers whether the alliance should not be reconsidered in view of the events that have transpired since its conclusion. But our army has the greatest confidence in the German military and would hardly listen to such a view.

It is doubtful whether Konoe ever formally took up abrogation of the Tripartite Pact. Nonetheless Japan's political leaders were clearly much perturbed by the outbreak of hostilities. Army authorities, on the other hand, seem to have been less disturbed by the news and continued their discussions of the policy Japan should adopt in the new circumstance. When the news was received on the 22nd, principal members of the Army Ministry and the General Staff—including Operations Division Chief Tanaka, Intelligence Division Chief Okamota Kiyotomi, War Guidance Office Chief Arisue Yadoru, and Military Affairs Bureau Chief Mutō Akira—met at General Staff headquarters to discuss the situation. They unanimously agreed that no change was warranted in the national policy draft they had been discussing.[202]

The rapidly developing international situation, however, did demand a reconciliation of the army and navy views and the formulation, as soon as possible, of a national policy agreed to by both the government and the high command. Accordingly, the chiefs of the Military and Naval Affairs bureaus and of the Operations bureaus of both services met for four hours on the 23rd to deliberate on a new national policy. In the end the navy, which had opposed not only a war against the Soviet Union but even accelerating preparations for such a war, agreed to a compromise formula. On condition that preparations for a military solution in the north would not be at the expense of the southern advance, the navy acquiesced in the adoption of the army's "principle of the ripe persimmon" with regard to a build-up in the north. On June 24 an army-navy draft entitled "Outline of National Policies in View of the Changing Situation" was completed. With respect to policy toward the Soviet Union it stated:

> 3) Although the basis of our policy is the spirit of the three-power Axis, with regard to the German-Soviet war, *Japan should not intervene for the time being, but should continue its military preparations against the Soviet Union in secrecy* and deal with this situation independently. Should the German-Soviet war *develop extremely favorably for Japan*, the northern problem should be solved *through the exercise of military power*, securing thereby tranquillity in the northern regions.
>
> 4) In implementing the policy described in the preceding article, and especially in the case of a decision to apply military force, the maintenance of a basic posture needed for a war against Britain and the United States will not be jeopardized.[203]

Needless to say, the strict condition that Japan should intervene in the German-Soviet war only if the war developed "extremely favorably" for Japan and the fourth point of the draft represented an effort by the navy to prevent hostilities between Japan and the Soviet Union.

Once the army's and navy's views had been reconciled, it was the turn of the government and the high command jointly to consider the new national policy. At daily (except Sunday) Liaison Conferences between June 25 and July 1, heated discussion ensued. On June 25 the conference first of all adopted the "Measures for Advancing the Southern Policy," an army-navy document that approved the move into southern French Indochina.[204] The conferees then took up the army-navy "Outline of National Policies in View of the Changing Situation." During the conferences that followed, it was principally Matsuoka who, representing the government, asked questions and raised objections.

The foreign minister was especially troubled by the failure of the draft to state explicitly Japan's determination to join Germany in the war against the Soviet Union. He argued that Japan should prosecute the war in the north even if it meant temporarily suspending the southern advance, appealing both on the basis of Japan's moral duty as a member of the tripartite alliance and on the need to secure Japan a voice in any postwar settlement. On June 27 he declared:

If one expects the German-Soviet war to be a short one, Japan cannot sit and wait, moving neither to the north nor to the south. We should first go north. From a diplomatic viewpoint, it is out of the question to wait to settle our problems with the Soviet Union until Germany has taken care of the USSR. If the Soviet Union is dealt with promptly, America will probably not enter the war. . . . If we attack the Soviet Union, I am confident I can keep America in check by diplomatic means for three to four months. If we sit on the fence, in accordance with the high command's draft, we will probably be encircled by Britain, America, and the Soviet Union . . . He who would search for pearls must dive deep. Let us act resolutely.

Army Minister Tōjō: What about the impact on the China Incident?

Matsuoka: Until the end of the last year we thought of moving first south and then north. We thought that by moving south, China would be taken care of; but it didn't work out. If we advance in the north and get, say, to Irkutsk, or even only half the distance, it would have an effect upon Chiang Kai-shek, and I think an overall peace might ensue.

Tōjō: Do you think it is advisable to move north, even if it means giving up the struggle in China?

Matsuoka: I think it is advisable to move north, giving up to a certain extent the struggle in China . . . I advocate moral diplomacy. We cannot renounce the tripartite alliance. It was better, from the beginning, to give up the Neutrality Pact . . . We must act while Germany's situation in the war is as yet uncertain . . . I think we should first of all decide to move north and convey this decision to the Germans.

Army Chief of Staff Sugiyama: Moral diplomacy is fine, but at present we have committed a large force in China. To follow the straight road of righteousness is desirable, but actually it cannot be done. As far as the high command is concerned, we must first complete our preparations. We cannot now decide whether we should or should not do it. The Kwantung Army alone needs forty to fifty days of preparation. To put our present forces onto a war footing and then take the offensive would take even more time. By that time the situation in the German-Soviet war will have become clear. And if it is favorable, then let us act.

Matsuoka: I dislike the "extremely" [in the Army-Navy draft advocating war with the Soviet Union only if the situation developed "extremely favorably" for Japan]. I would like us to decide upon an attack on the Soviet Union.[205]

After the war Matsuoka defended his argument for war against the USSR by saying: "This was not my real motive. I argued in this way to trick the army and navy. I already knew well that the army and navy were entirely against a war with the Soviet Union. The navy was extremely fearful of the Soviet Union . . . My scheme at the time was to force the army and navy to abandon their decision to advance in the south and, thus, not to advance in either direction."[206] Whatever his real motive may have been, however, Matsuoka's strong advocacy of intervention in the German-Soviet war complicated the deliberations of the Liaison Conference.

That evening a meeting of army and navy bureau and division chiefs was held to discuss Matsuoka's views. The army, wanting to move part way toward the foreign minister's position, urged that the draft be amended to read: "Begin preparations *with a determination* to use military force." But the navy would not agree. On the 28th, therefore, the chiefs of the Military and Naval Affairs bureaus met with Foreign Minister Matsuoka and Vice Minister Ōhashi, and a compromise agreement was finally achieved. Matsuoka had to accept the principle that, for the time being, Japan would not intervene in the German-Soviet war but would sit on the fence and continue to complete its military preparations. There were two principal revisions of the original army-navy draft. One was to add to the injunction in Article 3 that Japan should "continue its military preparations against the Soviet Union in secrecy and deal with this situation independently" the phrase "and during this period conduct diplomatic negotiations with extreme caution." The second was the deletion of the word "extremely" in "should the German-Soviet war develop extremely favorably for Japan."[207]

On the afternoon of June 28 the Liaison Conference formally adopted the revised "Outline of National Policies in View of the Changing Situation." The next subject of discussion was the content of the communication to be sent to the German government. Once again Matsuoka argued that Japan should make clear its intention to enter the war, and once again he was forced to retreat in the face of opposition from the army and the navy.[208]

On the 30th the Liaison Conference was convened to make final preparations for an Imperial Conference scheduled for the following day, as well as to discuss the relatively technical matters of the text of the communication to the German government and the draft of a government statement. But Matsuoka, pleading new developments, made yet another attempt to change the national policy already agreed upon. He urged that the advance into southern French Indochina be suspended or delayed—in effect nullifying the army-navy policy paper on "Measures for Advancing the Southern Policy."

Matsuoka: Until today Germany's attitude has been to ask only for our cooperation in the German-Soviet war, but today Ambassador Ott showed me instructions from his government to request our participation in the war . . . Japan must decide on entering the war. How about dropping the idea of setting the south on fire? How about suspending the advance into southern French Indochina in order to advance in the north? How about postponing it for six months? If the high command persists in its determination to carry it out, I will acquiesce, since I previously agreed to it . . . I have forecast events several years in advance and I have never missed the mark. I predict that touching the south will be a very serious move . . . A great man can change his mind. Previously I have advocated a southern advance, but now I switch to the north.[209]

It was the German government's formal request that Japan enter the war, transmitted that day to the Japanese government by Ambassador Ott, that gave Matsuoka the opportunity to argue for reconsideration of the decision to move into southern French Indochina. Ribbentrop instructed Ott to make the following points to Japan:

1) War between Germany and Soviet Russia will not only bring with it the solution of more or less limited individual problems, but will bring as a consequence a solution of the Russian question in its entirety through a final battle.

2) The destruction of Russian power by our military action, which is to be expected within a comparatively short time, will also make Germany's victory over England an irrevocable fact. If Germany is in possession of the Russian oil wells and grain fields, a sufficient supply for the whole of Europe will thereby be ensured so that the English blockade will on the whole be of absolutely no avail. The direct land connection with East Asia will likewise be established on this occasion.

3) In this way all the preconditions are given that will render possible the new organization of the European sphere as intended by the Axis Powers.

4) The present situation also presents a unique chance for Japan. As Germany does this with respect to Europe, *so can Japan now through a military action against Soviet Russia create the prerequisites for the new order in East Asia planned by her.* After the removal of the Soviet power in the Far East also, the solution of the Chinese question will be achieved in the way desired by Japan without encountering any more difficulties.

5) From the standpoint of Japanese interests, *the idea of a drive toward the South* in the direction of Singapore, to be sure, is and remains also of great importance. *As Japan is not yet prepared for this and as a possibility for such a drive has not yet been presented in the present*

phase of the war, it is in the urgent interest of Japan not to leave unused this chance now offered to her for solving the Russian question in the Far East too. By doing this she would also free her rear for a drive toward the south.

6) In view of the speedy course of events to be expected, Japan should come to a decision in favor of a military action against Soviet Russia without hesitation. *A Japanese action against a Soviet Russia already beaten to the ground would be quite prejudicial to the moral and political position of Japan.*

7) It can be expected that the swift defeat of Soviet Russia, especially if Japan participates in it from the East, will be the best means for convincing *the United States* of the absolute senselessness of entering the war on the side of England, who *will then be completely isolated* and confronted by the mightiest combination in the world.[210]

In short, what the German government proposed was that Japan postpone the southern advance and, in concert with Germany, start military operations against the Soviet Union. Heretofore Ribbentrop had tried to influence the decision makers in Tokyo by arguing to Ambassador Ōshima the advantages Japan would reap if it entered the war and by continuing Ott's diplomatic maneuvers.[211] Now his request was put in an official communication to the Japanese government.

The deliberations that followed Matsuoka's proposal that the southern advance be postponed were agitated. Navy Minister Oikawa Koshirō suggested deferring the advance for perhaps six months; he was supported by Vice Chief of the Navy General Staff Admiral Kondō Nobutake. The army, however, and Vice Chief of Staff General Tsukada Osamu in particular, advocated resolute action. After four hours of debate and yet another conference between army and navy representatives, it was finally decided to reaffirm the original policy draft.[212]

Because of the delay caused by the German government's communication, the scheduled Imperial Conference was postponed for a day. On July 1 the Liaison Conference met to work out the texts of a reply to the German government and a Japanese government statement.[213] And on the 2nd an Imperial Conference was convened to act upon the "Outline of National Policies in View of the Changing Situation."

Prime Minister Konoe and Foreign Minister Matsuoka, as representatives of the government, and General Sugiyama and Admiral Nagano Osami, chiefs of the Army and Navy General Staffs respectively, representing the high command, explained the essential points of the proposed draft. During the question-and-answer period that followed, Privy Council President Hara Yoshimichi pleaded against provoking the United States. Japan, he said, should avoid direct military action during the advance into Indochina. He then went on to advocate strongly an attack upon the Soviet Union at the earliest opportunity:

> To force French Indochina to comply by holding the threat of military force in the background is all right, but to use direct military force peremptorily and be denounced as an aggressor is not good . . . Furthermore, we are probably all agreed that the outbreak of war between Germany and the Soviet Union presents Japan with a golden opportunity such as comes only once in a thousand years. Since the Soviet Union is sowing communism throughout the world, we will have to attack it sooner or later . . . The Japanese people are eager to fight the Soviets. On this occasion I would like us to attack the Soviet Union . . . Because of the Japanese-Soviet Neutrality Pact, if Japan were to attack the Soviet Union some might say that it was a breach of trust. But the Soviet Union habitually acts treacherously, and if Japan were to attack the Soviet Union, no one would denounce our action as perfidy. I have been constantly awaiting an opportunity to attack the Soviet Union. I want to avoid war with America. Even if we attacked the Soviet Union, I think America would not come in . . . I would like you to make preparations for somehow starting a war quickly. I shall not cease hoping that we formulate and implement such a policy.[214]

Hara's words surely deserved the applause of all those who desired Japan to follow an aggressive policy toward the Soviet Union. His statement set the seal on Japan's policy in the new situation created by the German-Soviet war. That same day the government made the simple announcement that "to cope with the present situation, an important decision with regard to national policy was made at today's Imperial Conference."[215]

The decision reached by the Imperial Conference on July 2 was not, in spite of strong German urging, for immediate intervention in the German-Soviet conflict. This did not, however, signify Japan's intention to carry out faithfully its obligations under the Japanese-Soviet Neutrality Treaty but was, from the beginning, only a bid for time. The "Outline of National Policies" had already determined that "should the German-Soviet war develop favorably for Japan, the northern problem should be solved through the exercise of military power, securing thereby tranquillity in the northern regions." The government was simply postponing the decision until the war situation became much clearer.

Even if developments were favorable for Japan, it could not plunge into a war without preparation. Therefore the "Outline," anticipating that Japan would ultimately enter the war, explicitly prescribed a preparatory strategic posture: "Japan should . . . continue its military preparations against the Soviet Union in secrecy." These preparations took the form of "Special Grand Maneuvers" by the Kwantung Army, or *Kantokuen* as they were known. Thus, Japanese policy toward the Soviet Union at this juncture called, first, for carrying out the *Kantokuen* program and, second, upon its completion (presumably in forty to fifty days), for a fresh reexamination of the situation and a decision on whether or not to enter the war.

What precisely would the Japanese army regard as a "favorable" situation? At the June 25 Liaison Conference Chief of Staff Sugiyama cited civil disturbances in the Russian Far East, the transfer of Soviet Far Eastern forces to the western front, or the collapse of the Soviet regime.[216] Of these, the most important was the second, the movement of Soviet forces westward. The General Staff considered that "generally speaking, the reduction by one half of the total Soviet war potential in the Far East would constitute the condition for invoking the use of military force against the Soviet Union."

When the General Staff drew up its 1941 plan for operations against the Soviet Union, it estimated the nucleus of the Soviet armed forces in the Far East as consisting of about 30 infantry divisions, 2,800 aircraft, and 103 submarines. Facing it, the Kwantung Army had 12 divisions and about 800 planes—an inferiority in military strength of just under 40 percent. The Japanese proposed to attack if the Soviet Far Eastern air force were reduced by two-thirds and Soviet ground forces by a half, that is, 15 divisions, estimates being that, since one Soviet division had about three-quarters the strength of a mobilized Japanese division, 15 Soviet divisions equalled about 11 Japanese divisions. If Japan were to field an attacking force twice this number, a total of 22 divisions would have to be prepared for operations against the Soviet Union. This, in turn, demanded a large mobilization.

The General Staff's plan envisaged two phases. The first called for the mobilization of 16 divisions—12 divisions of the Kwantung Army, 2 divisions of the Korea Army, and 2 fresh divisions from Japan proper—which would then be moved in a strategic deployment centering on northern Manchuria. The second phase involved sending 2 divisions from north China and the mobilization of 4 additional divisions from Japan proper. Along with these calculations, the following schedule for operations against the Soviet Union was drawn up: decision to mobilize, June 28; mobilization order, July 5; beginning of assembly, July 20; decision to enter the war, August 10; completion of the first phase of preparations, August 24; beginning of operations, August 29; completion of the second phase of operations, September 5; end of operations, middle of October.[217]

The *Kantokuen* plan was drawn up under the leadership of Operations Division Chief Tanaka Shin'ichi, a vigorous advocate of operations against the Soviet Union, who had argued for "intentionally creating a favorable opportunity" for an attack on the Soviet Union while it was engaged in hostilities with Germany. His position was strongly supported by the Kwantung Army in the field, and by young staff officers in particular.[218] This policy was opposed by members of the Army Ministry's Military Affairs Bureau, who called for a Japanese attack in the south. These officers did not like the dispersal of forces to the north and were apprehensive lest the Kwantung Army's maneuvers automatically escalate into operations against the Soviet Union. In preparing for the use of military force against the Soviet Union, they espoused the "principle of the ripe persimmon."[219]

This difference of opinion had first emerged in the process of formulating the Army's "National Defense Policy" of June 14. It now reappeared in the form of a confrontation over the scale of mobilization and transportation in the Kwantung maneuvers. The General Staff, from a local military operations point of view, argued for the mobilization of 22 divisions, while the Military Affairs Bureau, viewing the situation from a more general perspective, demanded that the maneuvers be reduced to 16 divisions, which was tantamount to only the first phase of the General Staff's plan.

The Imperial Conference decision of July 2 left the conflict unresolved. Eventually, on the evening of July 5, Army Minister Tōjō, who had from the beginning advocated an aggressive policy toward the Soviet Union, accepted in principle the General Staff's position and approved the Kwantung Army maneuvers plan. His decision brought to an end the confrontation between the Army Ministry and the General Staff and paved the way for issuance of the mobilization order of July 7.[220]

The details of the *Kantokuen* plan are not quite clear, although it seems to have called for the mobilization of 16 divisions for field operations and the completion in the rear of logistic preparations (weapons, ammunition, and provisions) for 22 divisions. To carry out this plan it was estimated that the mobilization order should call for 850,000 men and a shipping capacity of 800,000 tons. This was indeed mobilization on an unprecedented scale.

With the setting into motion of the Kwantung Army maneuvers, ships fully loaded with soldiers, weapons, and supplies began sailing one after another toward Korean and Manchurian ports. The Kwantung Army continued its preparations for military operations. Even in Japan proper a general defense headquarters was established on July 12 and consideration given to instituting a system of air defense.

Ambassador Grew described in his diary the domestic situation in Japan at the time:

> We learned that . . . in one electric-line company alone fifty motormen were taken within a week. We ourselves lost our second cook. Osaka reported that the annual tennis tournament and other athletic contests scheduled for this week have all been canceled . . . This movement became so intense that no foreigners were allowed to pass through the Inland Sea or to travel on trains which would necessitate their crossing the ferry between Shimonoseki and Fusan.[221]

Japan was clearly on the brink of war with the Soviet Union.

The Decision to Remain Neutral

The General Staff had stated that a decision to use force against the Soviet Union depended on a 50 percent reduction of Soviet forces in the Far East. Soviet troop movements, therefore, had to be carefully watched. Meanwhile, the Japanese embassies in Berlin and Moscow kept reporting overwhelming German victories and estimates that the war would soon end.

Ōshima, for example, on July 2 quoted Ribbentrop to the effect that "the majority of the best Soviet divisions, constituting the nucleus of the

Red Army, either have already been destroyed or are at present being encircled and will be completely destroyed in the near future . . . Everyone says the Soviet army cannot now carry out a strategic withdrawal. The war will be settled in an extremely short time."[222] Two days later Ambassador Tatekawa reported the decision to move the Soviet government from Moscow to a temporary capital—a sign of defeat.

The symptoms of the demoralization of the Soviet government and people are undeniable. Stalin's address to the people yesterday was warm but spiritless. One can see the loss of confidence in the nation's ability to defend itself in his request for a scorched-earth policy. The spirit of the people is poor and they do not display any patriotic fervor. Most of the draftees look depressed. They are dressed worse than Chinese coolies. They walk silently, with bowed heads, seeming not to have the energy even to speak to each other, let alone to sing patriotic songs. They look like sheep being led to the slaughterhouse . . . The atmosphere is laden with defeat. One cannot but feel that the fall of Moscow is now only a question of time . . . The German armies will probably continue their rapid attack and reach the Ural line by the end of September. This will likely mark the end of the first stage of operations, and the Germans will then probably occupy themselves with the reconstruction of European Russia. If the Stalin government can hold on at the Urals, it will still wield considerable power; but once it moves to Omsk, it will possess only undeveloped and limited human and material resources. It will then be reduced just to hanging on.[223]

But despite such reports from Europe of the complete annhilation of the Soviet army, Japanese military observers in the field reported that the movement of Soviet Far Eastern forces westward was much slower and much smaller than expected. At the July 2 Imperial Conference Chief of Staff Sugiyama reported that only some four Soviet divisions had been transferred to the west. On the 12th the head of the Russia (Fifth) Section of the General Staff, Isomura Takesuke, came to a similar conclusion, reporting that the forces dispatched westward included five infantry divisions (17 percent of available strength), five tank brigades (one-third), and some air units, the majority being from the Lake Baikal area. There were no signs of troop movements east of the Ussuri and north of the Amur river, the main front with Japan. On the contrary, the Kwantung Army reported that these defenses were being strengthened.[224]

The timing of operations against the Soviet Union was very important. Since extensive military operations were almost impossible in the winter snows of Siberia, the major war objectives had to be achieved before the onset of winter. Japan, therefore, faced a time limit in starting operations against the Soviet Union and, by the same token, in reaching the decision to begin operations.

By the middle of July the General Staff had become restless. It was argued that the preconditions to the use of military force should be relaxed so that attack would not depend on such a large reduction of the Soviet strength in the Far East. On July 15 the advocates of the "principle of the green persimmon" spoke up once again at a meeting of departmental heads, when the view was expressed that the decision to use military force should be based on an overall political evaluation, including the effect of the removal of Stalin's capital to the Urals.[225]

By July 16 the German Army Group Center under Field Marshal Fedor von Bock, which had attacked Byelorussia from Poland, had advanced 450 miles into Soviet territory and reached Smolensk, 200 miles from Moscow. Although the war was progressing favorably for the German army, it soon became noticeable that the German advance was gradually slowing. The Japanese General Staff, meanwhile, was concentrating on gathering intelligence reports, which, it hoped, would permit the use of military force against the Soviet Union. By the end of the month, however, the outlook had become increasingly pessimistic, and general opinion was that operations would have to be postponed until spring. Two entries in the *Confidential War Diary* illustrate the change in mood:

> July 22. It is exactly one month since the start of the German-Soviet war, but in spite of the smooth progress of German operations, the Stalin regime is proving unexpectedly resilient. There has also been no [westward] movement of Soviet Far Eastern forces. When will a good opportunity arise for war against the Soviet Union? The probability that the war will end with the conclusion of the present German operation is diminishing.
>
> July 25. In the First [Operations] Division, the arguments for an attack in the north this year are being heard less and less frequently.

The General Staff even began to fear that a preventive strike might be launched by the Soviet Union, interpreting the strategic deployment of the Kwantung Army along the Soviet-Manchurian frontier following implementation of the *Kantokuen* plan as an indication that a Japanese offensive was imminent. On August 2 a report from the Kwantung Army that Soviet troops on the eastern frontier had instituted a blackout on wireless communications led the General Staff to fear that this might presage an attack upon Japan. In the wake of this report a cable arrived from Kwantung Army Commander General Umezu Yoshijirō: "In case of a large-scale Soviet air attack, I will contact the high command, but in the meantime, in order not to lose a good opportunity, I anticipate that I will have to carry out at my own discretion an air attack on Soviet territory. I ask for advance approval of such action."[226]

The Soviet communications blackout and Umezu's request, raising the possibility of a general military clash between Japanese and Soviet forces, added a new dimension to Japan's Soviet policy.

Chief of Staff Sugiyama immediately cabled the following instructions to Umezu: "In principle, stop counterattacks at the boundary line. The high command expects the Kwantung Army to act with caution." But Operations Division Chief Tanaka and other General Staff advocates of a tough policy toward the Soviet Union advanced their views with renewed vigor. On August 3, following consultations with Army Ministry officials, they drew up a new draft of Japanese policy toward the Soviet Union. "In response to a serious Soviet attack," it declared, "fire will be returned immediately and a resolution to start a war reached promptly at a top-level conference."[227] The navy, arguing that such a policy was dangerous, once more took exception to the army draft, in particular to the "resolution to start a war."

Interservice talks on August 4–5 resolved these differences, and on the 6th the following policy entitled "Measures to be Taken by Japan to Deal with the Present Situation in Japanese-Soviet Relations" was approved by the Liaison Conference:

> 1) While instituting precautionary measures for defense against the Soviet Union, we must strictly avoid provocative actions. If incidents arise, they should be localized so that they will not escalate into hostilities between Japan and the Soviet Union.
> 2) In response to a serious Soviet attack our forces will return fire immediately but refrain from offensive action.
> 3) Response to the above eventualities will be decided upon promptly at a top-level conference.[228]

In accordance with this decision, an imperial order was issued to General Umezu authorizing him to launch air attacks against Soviet territory in the event of a Soviet air attack.[229]

Thus, although the idea of initiating operations against the Soviet Union during 1941 had been abandoned, even by the General Staff, by early August, the Soviet communications blackout led once more to serious discussion of the possibility of an armed clash.

The German-Soviet war and the westward movement of Soviet Far Eastern forces were not the only matters that did not develop in accordance with Japanese expectations. As a result of the Japanese move into southern French Indochina on July 28, the United States froze all Japanese assets in the country and placed a complete embargo on oil shipments to Japan. Suddenly war with the United States became a distinct possibility. In view of the crisis brought about by the fires Japan had lit in the south, it was imperative that tranquillity be maintained in the north. On August 9 the General Staff made the final decision that no military solution of the Soviet problem would be attempted during 1941.[230] Thus, the gigantic mobilization of men and matériel that had accompanied the Kwantung Army maneuvers lost their original purpose, serving only the secondary end of pinning down a large Soviet force in the Far East.

Nonetheless the crushing blows sustained by the Soviet forces early in the war with Germany had changed the balance of power between Japan and the Soviet Union to the former's advantage. The war, of course, put an end to Matsuoka's plan for conducting negotiations with the United States on the basis of the tripartite alliance and the Neutrality Pact, but the heavy pressures exerted on the Soviet Union from the west placed Japan in a favorable position to enlarge its objective beyond the mere solution of pending problems with the USSR—the northern Sakhalin concessions, a long-range fisheries agreement, and the cessation of Soviet aid to Chungking. Now the government and military sought to fulfill a long-standing Japanese ambition to extend Japan's influence and defense sphere northward—an ambition that had been frustrated at the time of the Siberian intervention.

While in Moscow, Matsuoka had agreed to begin negotiations for the liquidation of Japanese concessions in northern Sakhalin at the earliest opportunity. On May 31 he had restated this understanding in a letter to Molotov, sent via Ambassador Tatekawa: "As I stated previously in Moscow, I am prepared to reaffirm our determination to settle definitely the problem of the liquidation of the northern Sakhalin concessions at the very latest within six months."[231] Now that Russia was at war with Germany, however, the Japanese government could ignore all such promises.

Hostilities had no sooner broken out than the Soviet ambassador in Japan, Konstantin Smetanin, visited Matsuoka on June 24 to seek reassurance that the Japanese government intended to observe the Neutrality Pact. Matsuoka, according to Smetanin's diary, "evaded a frank answer . . . [and] strongly emphasized that the Tripartite Alliance was the foundation of Japanese foreign policy, and that if the present war and the Neutrality Treaty contradicted both this foundation and the Tripartite Alliance, the Neutrality Treaty 'would probably lose its validity.' "[232] Needless to say, Japan's attitude was a matter of the greatest concern to the Soviet government, which mobilized a widespread intelligence network to obtain information regarding Japanese intentions.[233]

The government's reply to the Soviet inquiry was formulated at the Liaison Conference on July 1 and communicated to Ambassador Smetanin the following day.

> . . . The Japanese government sincerely desires that the present war end as soon as possible, or at least that it be limited to areas outside the Far East, where Japan has important interests. With regard to its policy toward the Soviet Union, the Japanese government would like to state on this occasion that, except for considerations bearing upon its desire not to cause any misunderstanding among its allies Japan recognizes no pressing need to revise its policy . . .[234]

Although the statement expressed Japanese intentions not to intervene in the German-Soviet war, it did not say that Japan would observe the Neutrality Pact.

By the end of July Japan's prospects of achieving the objectives of its Soviet policy by military means had receded. At the same time, the argument was gaining strength that Japan should utilize the threat implied by the Kwantung maneuvers to win concessions from the Soviet Union by diplomatic means. One important factor in this softening of Japanese policy toward the Soviet Union was the replacement of Matsuoka by Admiral Toyoda Teijirō as foreign minister in the cabinet reorganization of July 18.

A suggestion that it was perhaps time to begin diplomatic negotiations with the Soviet Union was first made at a Liaison Conference on

July 26, and the question was again raised at the next conference on the 29th. On both occasions, however, the issue was not examined thoroughly, because the army and navy argued that it was premature.[235] Meanwhile, officials in the Foreign and Army ministries continued to work on a draft of a policy for diplomatic negotiations with the Soviet Union.[236] On July 31 the First [Soviet] Section of the Foreign Ministry's Europe-Asia Bureau prepared drafts of an "Outline for the Settlement of the Northern Problem" and "Guidelines for Diplomatic Negotiations with the Soviet Union."

The first document forecast that "before the end of the summer the German army will bring under its control the area west of the Urals or [at least] the area west of the Volga River. In spite of moving its capital east of the Urals, Stalin's government will not be rocked by sudden disturbances and will be able to pull together the remnants of the defeated Red Army. It will exercise control over the Red Army in the Far East, concentrate on the rebuilding of a bolshevik regime in Siberia, and continue to confront the German army." Japan, it went on, "should immediately enter into diplomatic negotiations with the Soviet Union and demand the removal of all obstacles to normal diplomatic relations between Japan and the Soviet Union, as well as the establishment of the East Asia Co-Prosperity Sphere." The document also specified that "in return the Japanese side will affirm its obligations under the Japanese-Soviet Neutrality Pact." The second document divided the achievement of objectives to be sought in negotiations into two phases, preceding and following the completion of the deployment of troops in accordance with the Kwantung Army maneuvers. After some revision, probably as the result of discussions with responsible army and navy officials, the following document was presented to the Liaison Conference on August 1:

Guidelines for Diplomatic Negotiations
with the Soviet Union—Draft
I. For the time being, Japan should conduct negotiations with the Soviet Union with regard to the following matters (being careful, however, not to restrict Japan's future course of action):

    1) The Soviet Union should abolish the Far Eastern Maritime Danger Zone or make certain that Japan does not suffer any losses.

    2) Insofar as Soviet territory in the Far East is concerned, the Soviet Union should not cede, sell, lease, or provide military bases to a third country.

3) In concluding a military alliance with a third country, the Soviet Union should not extend [by treaty] the area covered to the Far
East; the Soviet Union should also refrain from concluding with a
third country a military alliance directed against Japan.

4) The Soviet Union should cease its aid to Chiang Kai-shek and
to the Chinese Communist Party. This is to be accompanied by the
cancellation of instructions [to the latter] to resist Japan.

5) Japan should secure full operation of concessionary enterprises
in northern Sakhalin.

6) Detained Manchurian and Soviet personnel and [seized] commodities are to be exchanged.

7) Efforts to demarcate the boundary in the Nomonhan area
should be continued; negotiations regarding an overall boundary line
are to be postponed.

Note a: In the preceding, items 2, 3, and 5 are to be emphasized.

Note b: In return for these demands, Japan will pledge to observe
its obligations under the Japanese-Soviet Neutrality Pact.

II. Depending upon the extent of our military preparations against the
Soviet Union, and taking into consideration developments in the
German-Soviet war, the general world situation, and their effect upon
our future plans, Japan should negotiate with the Soviet Union on some
or all of the following matters:

1) A fisheries treaty (striving, in contrast to previous negotiations, to obtain Japan's original claims).

2) Purchase or cession of northern Sakhalin.

3) Lease or cession of the Kamchatka region to Japan.

4) Demilitarization, lease, or cession to Japan of the Soviet territory east of the Amur river.

5) Demilitarization of other Soviet territories in the Far East.[237]

This document, together with the "Outline for the Settlement of the
Northern Problem," was presented to the Liaison Conference as "An
Explanation of the Guidelines for Diplomatic Negotiations with the Soviet Union" for discussion at its meetings on August 1 and 4. The main
problem arose over Note (b), which specified that in return for its demands Japan would promise to observe the Neutrality Pact. Most of the
conferees objected strongly, arguing that such a pledge would violate
the Tripartite Pact. Finally, on the 4th, the following conditional formulation was adopted:

If the Soviet Union strictly observes the Neutrality Pact and does not
present a threat to Japan in the Far East, there is no objection to Japan's
observance of the Neutrality Pact. But if the Soviet Union does not ob-

serve the Neutrality Pact, if it does not show a friendly attitude toward Japan, or if it should give the Maritime Province, Kamchatka, etc. to a third country, the Neutrality Pact should be abrogated.

At the August 1 session a difference of opinion also arose between the army and navy over the question of whether the German-Soviet conflict would be prolonged. As a result, all references to the prospects for the war and to the Soviet domestic situation were eliminated. Finally, a third section entitled "Negotiation Policy" was added:

1) The solution of the northern problem should contribute to the successful completion of the national policy of establishing the East Asia Co-Prosperity Sphere. Accordingly, our objective should be to eliminate the threat from the north and to secure the resources of the region. *To achieve this objective, efforts will be made first by diplomatic means. A solution by force of arms, in accordance with our previously adopted national policy, will be attempted only if the situation develops favorably for our side.*

2) Diplomatic negotiations with the Soviet Union should be entered into immediately, and Japan should demand the removal of all matters and reasons which obstruct normal diplomatic relations between Japan and the Soviet Union and the establishment of the East Asia Co-Prosperity Sphere. *In return, Japan will declare that it will carry out its obligations under the Japanese-Soviet Neutrality Pact.*

3) At the start of diplomatic negotiations with the Soviet Union, Japan's position and role should be explained frankly to Germany. Furthermore, since it is feared that in a German-Soviet armistice, German demands on the Soviet Union might include matters related to the Far East (for example, the Trans-Siberian Railway or the port of Vladivostok), Germany must be approached with this possibility in mind.

4) Although it is urgent that our military preparations against the Soviet Union be completed so that we are able to cope with any change in the situation, we should guard carefully against the accidental outbreak of war. In accordance with previously adopted national policy, we will not take military action against the Soviet Union unless the internal and external situations develop favorably for Japan.[238]

It is clear from the adoption of the "Guidelines for Diplomatic Negotiations with the Soviet Union" that by early August the Soviet policy of the Konoe cabinet had undergone a change since the "Outline of National Policies" had been approved on July 2. Diplomatic negotiations, not military force, now received primary attention, and the pressure for intervention in the German-Soviet conflict had weakened.

The new policy resulted from the accelerated deterioration of Japanese-American relations occasioned by the Japanese move into southern French Indochina. This deterioration and the resulting economic strains in Japan again shifted the balance of power between Japan and the Soviet Union. Japan therefore could no longer pursue a high-pressure diplomacy against the Soviet Union.

Between the outbreak of the German-Soviet war and the Japanese move into southern French Indochina some five weeks later, there was probably a reasonable basis for pursuing a diplomatic policy that attempted to win concessions from the Soviet government in return for Japan's pledge to observe its obligations under the Neutrality Pact. But that time was past. By the time it was adopted, the policy enunciated in the "Guidelines for Diplomatic Negotiations with the Soviet Union" was unrealistic.

On August 5 Foreign Minister Toyoda presented Ambassador Smetanin with the Japanese demands, based on the new policy, and on the 13th Smetanin forwarded the Soviet government's reply:

1) The Soviet government expresses its satisfaction with the foreign minister's statement that Japan will observe the Japanese-Soviet Neutrality Pact.

2) The problem of the concessions should be settled in accordance with the Matsuoka-Molotov letters and the May 31 letter presented to Molotov by Ambassador Tatekawa.

3) Inasmuch as the Neutrality Pact does not apply to relations with third countries, the Japanese government has no basis for bringing up the question of Soviet-Chinese relations. The Soviet government recognizes, however, the need to confirm its previous statement made by Molotov to Ambassador Tōgō on July 6, 1940, to the effect that since the Soviet Union was pressed with its own defense preparations, it did not consider this to be an important problem.

4) The Japanese government seems anxious lest the Soviet Union conclude a military alliance directed against Japan, or one which would extend to the Far East. The Soviet government, however, will observe the Neutrality Pact. Situations such as Japan anticipates will definitely not occur.

5) The British-Soviet agreement was directed only against Germany. As Molotov has stated, it bears no relation to Japan.

6) The Soviet government will never lease or cede its territory in the Far East, nor will it offer military bases to a third country. Such rumors are merely propaganda by other countries attempting to estrange Japan

from the Soviet Union. On the other hand, the Soviet government would like an explanation for recent large-scale Japanese military preparations in Manchuria.[239]

This reply made it clear that, despite the new situation created by the German attack, the Soviet Union was not in the least prepared to retreat from its original position on the concessions, cessation of aid to Chungking, or other matters raised by Japan.

Neither diplomatic negotiations nor armed action had achieved Japan's aim of solving the northern problem. Negotiations reached a deadlock, and most of the men and matériel transported to Manchuria for the Kwantung Army maneuvers were still there when the Pacific War broke out in December.

On April 5, 1945, in accordance with the provisions of the treaty, Molotov notified the Japanese ambassador that the Neutrality Pact would not be extended when it expired the following year. Four months later, on August 9, the Soviet Union launched its attack upon the Kwantung Army. But for four years a state of neutrality, although an imperfect one, had been maintained between Japan and the Soviet Union.

PART TWO

Southern Advance

Introduction

ROBERT A. SCALAPINO

The fascination of the essays that follow lies in the evidence they provide both as to the substantive issues that formed the background to Pearl Harbor and to the deep, continuous conflict within all branches and levels of the Japanese government concerning the policies to be pursued. These studies make clear once again what has long been accepted as fact, namely, that China proved to be both the "insoluble problem" between Japan and the western Allies, particularly the United States, and the problem that provided the underlying rationale for the Japanese "southern advance."

By this time Japan had invested too much in its China policy to abandon it—therefore much more was invested and all was lost. It insisted that the United States in effect relinquish its ties with and support of Chiang Kai-shek's government. But despite indications (not discussed here) that the United States would acquiesce in Manchukuo and despite America's strong desire to avoid a conflict with Japan, the Roosevelt administration was not prepared to abandon the China with which it had had such lengthy diplomatic and political connections and whose territorial integrity it had championed verbally before the world.

The undeclared war against China—or as the Japanese preferred to label it, the second China Incident—was far more costly than had originally been anticipated. Nevertheless, by 1940 Japan had military control of practically all of coastal China, and the main body of the Nationalists had been driven deep into the interior. To hit effectively at Chiang's forces, the Japanese military were now to make out a case for the use of bases in French Indochina. As these essays make clear, however, the military requirements may have been less critical than the political ones, although they were easily meshed. The concept of a Greater East Asia Co-Prosperity Sphere was now central to Japanese policy—economic, political, and military.

Such a policy required a New Asia, one in which Japanese influence was paramount, and one, therefore, from which the West was largely excluded, or perhaps more accurately, admitted only on Japanese terms. We witness in the pages that follow a dramatic illustration of the domino principle at work. Deep involvement in and control over China required, at least in Japanese eyes, control over French Indochina. This in turn led to intimate involvement with Thailand, as succeeding sections indicate. Meanwhile, the "southern advance" had as its logical capstone control of the Dutch East Indies with their vital resources—and that would unquestionably necessitate the seizure of Singapore and Malaya.

Not all Japanese leaders, to be sure, were prepared to accept these policies, especially when they were put so boldly. Indeed, the debate over both tactics and strategy raged throughout the 1939–41 period with which this portion of the work is centrally concerned. Even among the militants, the hope was expressed from time to time that Japan's basic objectives in East Asia could be attained without a war between Japan and the United States. Yet almost every step led in that direction. But this study also emphasizes once again the importance for Japanese policies of American actions *and* inactions, both in their substance and in their timing. Among the former, none was more crucial than the American use of the embargo as a means of pressure upon Japan, particularly the threat of a total embargo on oil. As Japanese military spokesmen were frank to admit in this period, in the face of a total Allied oil embargo, Japanese reserves were scarcely sufficient for a year of warfare. Similarly, as the increasingly desperate negotiations with Dutch authorities indicated, Japan's need for many other essential military and industrial resources from the Indies made access to the area (as well as to French Indochina, Thailand, and Malaya) "a matter of life or death" for the empire, given current policies.

In reexamining this period through the eyes of Japanese documentary materials, it is difficult to avoid the feeling that one is involved in a massive Greek tragedy, with various actors—both Japanese and western—moving with ever greater desperation to avoid the disaster of total war, but with options being foreclosed, one by one, through a process of linkage going back to earlier decisions and, most fundamentally, to Japan's "continental policy." Of course, there were some actors who appeared almost to relish the prospects of an Armageddon—but even among these there appear to have been moments of doubt and ambivalence. As Tsunoda Jun sets forth so well, by 1939–40 the chain of events that seemed inevitable to many Japanese leaders was: occupation of French Indochina, leading to a more rigid American embargo, leading to a Japanese attack upon the Dutch East Indies, leading to war with the Allies, including the United States.

Even now it is difficult to say whether and how this outcome (slightly altered in terms of subsequent events) could have been reversed, given the situation as it was in that period. One is tempted to assert flatly that the time to have prevented the steadily escalating political-military confrontation was earlier, not in this era. Perhaps such fatalism is not warranted, however, and in a moment we will suggest one or two other possible scenarios. Clearly, certain Japanese decisions pertaining to Southeast Asia were made on the basis of misperceptions of trends with respect to the European war. The data presented here indicate that throughout this era certain key figures in Japanese military and intelligence circles in the West were prepared to write off the British (hence, the French and Dutch) chances for survival. Nor did they believe that in the aftermath of a successful German invasion of Britain, the British fleet in exile, even if combined with American naval forces, would constitute a match for total Axis military strength.

Yet even at a time when these views were dominant or at least highly influential in Japanese military and civilian circles alike, we are witness to a gnawing anxiety, especially within the navy, regarding the central question: "In the event of war with the United States, can Japan win?" And here we move toward insights into the manner in which critical decisions were made. It was commonly accepted at the highest levels that a protracted war with the United States would be most disadvantageous for Japan. In short, Japan, already exhausted by nearly four years of struggle in China, had the resources for a one- to two-year war, but after that the prospects were gloomy. Instead of examining carefully the likelihood that the war would in fact be a short, decisive one, fought under optimum conditions for Japan, contingency plans increasingly took on a strangely irrational, desperate quality, in which the central issue, "Can we win?" was shunted aside. Rather, it was as if Japan had finally painted itself into a corner. Such major figures as prime ministers and navy ministers, while having the gravest doubts about the outcome, finally accepted the position, "There is no alternative."

In these essays we get few glimpses of the response of the indigenous peoples of Southeast Asia to the moves and countermoves of the major powers, reminding us that this was still the age of western domination of most of the world. Japan, indeed, was the first nonwestern modernizing power to challenge that domination, and in so doing it provided a powerful impetus for the Asian nationalist, anticolonial movement, as is well known. That story is not told in the following sections, but we do get a most interesting vignette of the responses of the leadership of the one independent country of Southeast Asia during this period, Thailand. Prime Minister Luong Pibul Songgram, in the fashion of his predecessors, maneuvered desperately to preserve his nation's independence, on the one hand, and to take advantage of the end of French power on the other. Pibul tried to calculate where power and commitment lay, because Thailand's survival, in his view, depended upon being with the victors at all costs. Thus, when he could not get firm commitments from Britain and the United States, and when he came to the conclusion that Britain's days were numbered, he made an accommodation to Japan. But because it was an opportunistic alliance, not one based upon deep ideological or political commitment, he—or rather, Thailand—was able to shift to the Allies when the Japanese sun seemed to be setting.

While coming to appreciate the substantive issues dominating Japanese policy during this period, we can also come to understand the most extraordinary challenge to procedures and authority that took place, one involving almost every echelon of the Japanese government. To be sure, this was not a new phenomenon in Japan. It had been vividly and "successfully" displayed at the time of the Manchurian Incident. And indeed, the complex, subtle relation between juniors and seniors in Japanese culture has always been a vital factor with which to reckon in seeking to probe the Japanese decision-making process. The critical importance of the small group; the capacity of juniors collectively to put pressure upon seniors; the intricate, collective nature of decision making, with the use of intermediaries and the concern for consensus; and the premium placed upon "morality," *ergo*, the capacity of an individual to sacrifice himself, defying authority, willing to take the punishment, for the honor of his fatherland and race—all of these were prominent elements in the institutional-behavioral patterns of this era.

Thus, we observe orders being deliberately disobeyed by subordinates; critical decisions being taken without the proper authority; the leaking of classified decisions to unauthorized personnel in an effort to influence subsequent actions; and in the midst of all these events—and others—the most bitter antagonisms and feuds emerging, not alone between the military and civilian elements, or the army and the navy, but within each branch of government, and at nearly every level.

It is clear that in this period some individuals who opposed governmental policy—essentially those who felt it was too weak, vacillating, and compromising—decided to take matters into their own hands whenever they could. Naturally, they did this out of profound moral conviction and in the certainty that they were right, their opponents wrong.

Did they succeed? In the broadest sense, yes. It is true that men like General Tominaga Kyōji were disciplined, and by no less a person than Army Minister Tōjō Hideki himself. Tōjō was furious at the breakdown of discipline within the military, and particularly within the army. Yet only a short time later Tominaga and most of the others were back in critical positions, vindicated and lauded as heroes.

Thus, one gets here a very different picture from that often presented of the Japanese nation and particularly the Japanese military in this period as a highly disciplined, monolithic force, responding as one to the emperor's command. The refusal of the navy to support the army's unauthorized landing south of Hanoi is but one of the more dramatic examples of the crisis within the Japanese structure during this period. And in another sense, also, those who posed their own will against that of higher authority could claim an ultimate victory. They had succeeded by 1940–41 in imposing a creeping intimidation on their opponents. Thus a Yoshida Zengo could be forced into a nervous breakdown; a Yamamoto Isoroku could expect to be assassinated; and more importantly, rational dialogue almost ceased just at the time when Japan was moving step by step toward one fateful decision after another. A helplessness swept over the top elite—a paralysis of nerve and will. In the end, perhaps, this more than the objective factors was the truly decisive element in the march toward catastrophe.

A number of lessons might be drawn at this stage, acknowledging quickly that we are seeing here only a very small part of a massive and complex scene. First, despite its formidable development in recent decades, Japan was not truly competitive with the United States in the type of power that was involved in a total war of the mid-twentieth century. Nor were its military-political ties with the Axis sufficient to permit a true aggregation of power from this source. Essentially, Japan counted upon only one thing from Germany: victory in Europe. Viewed from this perspective, Japanese policies were not well meshed with Japanese capacities—*unless* war with the United States could be avoided. The Japanese, it should be emphasized, did *not* lose the war against the China; nor were their policies in Southeast Asia unsuccessful in the period prior to Pearl Harbor. On the contrary, taking advantage of the declining fortunes of France, the Netherlands, and Britain, Japan bid fair to become the new dominant force in East Asia. Nor was it oblivious to the force of Asian nationalism, as we have already noted. Indeed, Japan played skillfully upon anti-western (anti-white) sentiment in its relations with the peoples (as apart from the governors) of Southeast Asia.

Yet it was essential to avoid war with the United States. As indicated, a number of Japanese leaders instinctively knew this. And even toward the end many of them approached that war with more fatalism and resignation than enthusiasm. It is always possible to argue that had Japan taken the risks of a limited war—either confining its sphere of military operations to China and the Indochina-Thailand area, or taking the further risk of attacking only British and Dutch territories, studiously avoiding an assault upon American possessions—it might have avoided the type of conflict that ended in total defeat. Like most "ifs," one can neither prove nor disprove this contention. And even if it were true in the short run, it is quite uncertain as a long-run proposition. But as we shall see, during the 1939–41 period there was considerable disagreement as to whether the United States could be separated from Britain and the Netherlands. It seems reasonably certain, in any case, that one of the above tactics would have produced a less united America than came out of Pearl Harbor.

It is equally clear, however, that the linkage that led from China to Indochina to Singapore and the East Indies, and hence to the ABCD powers (the Americans, British, Chinese, and Dutch), was an extraordinarily difficult one to break, both for Japan and for its rivals. The concept of a Greater East Asia Co-Prosperity Sphere was not tacked on to Japanese policy as an afterthought. By this period, as we suggested earlier, it had become central to Japanese Asian policy. Both implicitly and explicitly, its thrust was in the direction of excluding the West from East Asia. Japan wanted its Monroe Doctrine. The problem, of course, was both that it did not possess the power to exclude the West without a struggle and that the Pacific-East Asia region was not the western hemisphere in power configuration, in geopolitical significance, and in many other respects.

Finally, in discussing lessons we must revert to an earlier theme. In the essays soon to be presented, the critical importance of maintaining procedures and authority patterns if a state is to retain control of its decision-making process is underlined. Perhaps that is even more critical in a democratic society than in an authoritarian one, but this era indicates conclusively that it was supremely important even when all supposedly lived under the heaven-embracing roof of the imperial system.

TWO

Economic Demands
on the Dutch East Indies

NAGAOKA SHINJIRŌ

Translated by
ROBERT A. SCALAPINO

Efforts to Forestall Allied or German Intervention

On September 3, 1939, Britain and France declared war on Germany. The European war had begun. Japan's concern over the future of the Dutch East Indies was naturally aroused. As early as October 2 Foreign Minister Nomura Kichisaburō ordered Ishii Itarō, the Japanese minister to the Netherlands, to investigate what the Dutch response would be if Japan indicated a willingness to reconfirm the territorial integrity of the Dutch East Indies and, further, to determine whether the Netherlands intended to seek a similar guarantee from the United States.

On the 6th Ishii met with E. N. van Kleffens, the Dutch foreign minister, who told him that the Netherlands did not desire a nonaggression guarantee from any power and did not intend to ask American assistance for the defense of the Dutch East Indies. Ishii therefore recommended to his government that, "regarding current policy, Japan should not go beyond finding solutions to the difficulties facing Japanese citizens and business firms involved in the Dutch East Indies."[1] But as tension between Germany and the Netherlands increased from the end of October, the Japanese government saw the need for a more active policy in the region.

Since January 1939 the Foreign Ministry, through its Europe-Asia Bureau, had been exploring opinion within the ministry in an effort to formulate alternatives in its southern policy. Judging that Germany would invade the Netherlands, whereupon the war would be extended

This essay originally appeared as "Arita seimei to Nichi-Ran'in keizai kōshō," in *Taiheiyō senso e no michi,* vol. 6, part 1, sec. 4, pp. 71–99.

to the Dutch East Indies, the ministry drafted a policy about the end of October. Its thesis was that if Japan did not act immediately after Germany invaded the Netherlands, Britain would occupy the Dutch East Indies in order to guarantee their security and, moreover, that the United States might commit itself to the protection of the area. Regardless of the Dutch attitude, therefore, the ministry concluded that Japan must establish its right to participate in any future settlement involving the Dutch East Indies and at the same time must prevent the powers involved from placing Japan in a disadvantageous position with regard to such a settlement. To this end a statement was drafted, to be communicated to the concerned powers upon the expected German invasion of the Netherlands.

Against this background, Nomura, on November 16, expressed to Ishii his fears that Britain or the United States might take military or political action to protect the Dutch East Indies at the request of the Netherlands government. Should the Netherlands become involved in the war, Japan would naturally have to endeavor to prevent its extension to East Asia. In order that the Dutch government not be given the impression that Japan intended to pursue its objectives in a militant fashion, Nomura ordered Ishii to begin discussions on economic issues at once. Ishii was to express Japan's intent to open negotiations and present concrete proposals to settle the economic problems that existed between Japan and the Dutch East Indies. He should explain that Japan's aim was to make adequate preparations to preserve peace in East Asia should a widening of the European war threaten to bring about a change in the status of the Dutch East Indies. Nomura further instructed Ishii to state that, if the Dutch wished a pledge of nonaggression from Japan or if there were strong signs that they were seeking protection from the United States, Japan would be prepared to underwrite the security of the Dutch East Indies by appropriate means—this, so long as the war in Europe was not extended to the Dutch East Indies, their status was not changed by special understandings with the powers, and Japan's economic requests were met.

On November 23 Ishii again called on Kleffens, who informed him that the Dutch government had no objection to negotiations based upon the Japanese draft statement; however, his government could not accept the proposal relating to the admission of Japanese workers and enterprises into the Dutch East Indies, since this was a matter of domestic policy. Ishii did not raise the question of a nonaggression guarantee at this time. The crisis appeared to have abated somewhat, with a slackening of the German attack on the western front, and it did not seem an appropriate time for Japan to pursue its political objectives. The negotiations came to a temporary halt until December 16, when Nomura told Ishii to resume discussions on the economic issues between the two countries and to ascertain the extent to which Japanese requirements, as set forth in an Outline of a Japan-Netherlands Agreement, in connection with commercial relations, the admission of Japanese citizens and enterprises, investment, and the control of public opinion in the Dutch East Indies, could actually be attained.

Nomura was not optimistic about the outcome of these talks. He felt that the Netherlands' refusal to negotiate on the issue of the admission of Japanese workers and entrepreneurs to the Dutch East Indies might well increase political friction between the two nations, and, in view of the general coolness in the Dutch attitude toward the negotiations, he did not expect the discussions to progress smoothly even if Japan presented concrete proposals.

On January 16, 1940, the Abe cabinet was replaced by a government headed by Yonai Mitsumasa, with Arita Hachirō as foreign minister. Without waiting for a new set of proposals to be drafted, Arita, on the 17th, asked Ishii to sound out the general Dutch position on negotiations, in view of the friendly relations then existing between the two countries. That same day Ishii met with Kleffens and brought up the question of a possible Japanese guarantee of the security of the Dutch East Indies. The Dutch government, he reported to Tokyo, was not necessarily uninterested in such a guarantee. He had not, however, shown the contents of the Japanese "Outline" to the Dutch foreign minister, and on the 27th Arita requested that he do so. Arita hoped to reach an agreement on general principles before Japan made a formal proposal for a treaty.

In a private message to Ishii on the 30th Kleffens reminded him of the pledges of respect for the Netherlands' insular possessions in the Pacific given in identical notes from Britain, France, Japan, and the United States, based on the Four Power Treaty concluded at the Washington Conference on February 4, 1922, and emphasized that the pledge would not necessarily become void even if the treaty itself should become ineffective. Barring unforeseen developments, therefore, the Netherlands did not want an additional Japanese guarantee of the territorial integrity of the Dutch East Indies.

The proposed guarantee having been rejected, Ishii now turned to the question of negotiations on economic matters. On February 2 he showed the "Outline of a Japan–Netherlands Agreement" to Kleffens, who promised an answer at some future date. On March 8 Vice Foreign Minister Tani Masayuki presented to General J. C. Pabst, the Dutch minister in Tokyo, an "Outline for Negotiations Concerning Diplomatic Relations between Japan and the Dutch East Indies." Its contents differed little from those of the earlier "Outline" shown to Kleffens.[2]

In spite of Japan's efforts both in Tokyo and at The Hague, the Netherlands delayed giving an answer. The government was preoccupied with the European war and could not take time to negotiate with Japan on colonial economic problems. Meanwhile, the major powers began to pay more attention to the future of the East Indies.

On April 9 German troops advanced into Norway and Denmark, thereby bringing the crisis closer to the Netherlands and Belgium. On the 15th Arita commented in a press interview:

> With the South Seas regions, especially the Netherlands East Indies, Japan is economically bound by an intimate relationship of mutuality in ministering to one another's needs. Similarly, other countries of East Asia maintain close economic relations with these regions. That is to say, Japan, these countries and these regions together are contributing to the prosperity of East Asia through mutual aid and interdependence.
>
> Should hostilities in Europe be extended to the Netherlands and produce repercussions, as you say, in the Netherlands East Indies, it would not only interfere with the maintenance and furtherance of the above-mentioned economic interdependence and of co-existence and co-prosperity, but would also give rise to an undesirable situation from the standpoint of the peace and stability of East Asia. In view of these considerations, the Japanese Government cannot but be deeply concerned over any development accompanying an aggravation of the war in Europe that may affect the *status quo* of the Netherlands East Indies.[3]

Immediately after he made this statement, Arita called in Pabst to explain it to him. The Dutch response was firm. The Netherlands had maintained its neutrality and "will not ask protection from any power, will not do so in the future, and will reject such an offer or intervention—from any power," announced Kleffens to Ishii on April 16. His government appreciated Japan's proposal but had no intention of leaving the matter of the Dutch East Indies to the care of other powers.[4]

As far as the United States and Britain were concerned, Arita had not clarified Japanese policy toward the Dutch East Indies, and both nations seemed uncertain as to Japan's true intentions. On the 17th Lord Lothian, the British ambassador to the United States, asked Secretary of State Cordell Hull what the American response would be and was given a summary of a public statement Hull intended to release that evening. The ambassador expressed satisfaction with its contents,[5] which were:

I have noted with interest the statement by the Japanese Minister for Foreign Affairs expressing concern on the part of the Japanese Government for the maintenance of the *status quo* of the Netherlands Indies.

Any change in the status of the Netherlands Indies would directly affect the interests of many countries.

The Netherlands Indies are very important in the international relationships of the whole Pacific Ocean. . . .

Intervention in the domestic affairs of the Netherlands Indies or any alteration of their *status quo* by other than peaceful processes would be prejudicial to the cause of stability, peace, and security not only in the region of the Netherlands Indies but in the entire Pacific area.

This conclusion, based on a doctrine which has universal application and for which the United States unequivocally stands, is embodied in notes exchanged on November 30, 1908, between the United States and Japan in which each of the two Governments stated that its policy was directed to the maintenance of the existing *status quo* in the region of the Pacific Ocean. It is reaffirmed in the notes which the United States, the British Empire, France, and Japan—as parties to the treaty signed at Washington on December 13, 1921, relating to their insular possessions and their insular dominions in the region of the Pacific Ocean—sent to the Netherlands Government on February 4, 1922, in which each of those Governments declared that "it is firmly resolved to respect the rights of the Netherlands in relation to their insular possession in the region of the Pacific Ocean."

All peaceful nations have during recent years been earnestly urging that policies of force be abandoned and that peace be maintained on the basis of fundamental principles, among which are respect by every nation for the rights of other nations and nonintervention in their domestic affairs, the according of equality of fair and just treatment, and the faithful observance of treaty pledges, with modification thereof, when needful, by orderly processes.

It is the constant hope of the Government of the United States—as it is no doubt that of all peacefully inclined governments—that the attitudes and policies of all government will be based upon these principles and that these principles will be applied not only in every part of the Pacific area, but also in every part of the world.[6]

France, the third signatory of the Four-Power Treaty, on the 19th responded to Hull's statement with the suggestion that it be strengthened by simultaneous assurances issued by the United States, Britain, and France to the Netherlands government declaring "their loyalty to the principles enunciated in the notes of February, 1922." At the same time they should inform the Japanese government "that they interpret Mr. Arita's declaration as confirmation of the assurances contained in the note transmitted February 5, 1922, to the Minister for Foreign Affairs of the Netherlands by the Minister of Japan."[7]

But the British and American governments appeared satisfied that no additional measures were necessary at the moment. When asked in the House of Commons for assurances that the maintenance of peace in the Netherlands East Indies would not be left up to Japan alone if the Netherlands were drawn into the war in Europe, Parliamentary Under Secretary of State for Foreign Affairs R. A. Butler responded that "the Japanese Government has made no claim to be solely responsible for the maintenance of peace in the waters of the Netherlands East Indies." In his press statement Arita had expressed his government's deep concern over any developments in Europe that might affect the status quo in the East Indies and, Butler added, "I need hardly say that upon this question His Majesty's Government hold similar views." On the 20th the American under secretary of state, Sumner Welles, replied to the French note that for the present there seemed to be no need to take measures such as it had proposed.[8]

The German government did not see any need to react to Arita's statement. The Japanese government, declared a Foreign Office memorandum, did not necessarily believe the balance of power in Southeast Asia was threatened but was merely following its usual "political practice" of wording "demands in abstract form at opportune moments when these did not imply a definite threat."[9]

Public opinion in Japan at the time was strongly in favor of a southern advance, and Arita's statement was thus motivated by the domestic as well as the international situation. The German ambassador in Tokyo, Eugen Ott, reported to his government that the statement had been forced upon Arita by the Japanese navy.[10] Arita himself stated, "There are many movements taking place in Japan. There are even those who believe a second Manchurian Incident should be attempted, this time in the Dutch East Indies. Since Japan must follow a cautious policy both inside and outside the country at this time, I decided to make this announcement."[11]

The American government feared that Japan might occupy the Dutch East Indies, thereby strengthening itself militarily and making possible its conquest of China without depending on imports from the United States. In addition, such a move would threaten American supplies from the Dutch East Indies, particularly rubber and tin.[12] In a discussion with Horinouchi Kensuke, Japan's ambassador to the United States, on April 20, Hull denied the ambassador's claim that Arita's words had been misinterpreted by the American press. Hull went on to express disapproval of Japan's application of its "so-called Monroe Doctrine." He was adamant that the principles of the Monroe Doctrine could not be applied to Japan's policy in East Asia. The American Monroe Doctrine was concerned only with the "physical safety" of the United States, while that practiced by Japan seemed "applicable to all other purposes and all objectives, including economic, social, political, et cetera."[13]

On May 4, just before the German advance into Belgium and the Netherlands, President Roosevelt ordered that the United States Fleet, then on maneuvers off Hawaii, remain at Pearl Harbor. Even if the United States were not prepared to respond to a Japanese attack in the Indies, it was hoped that the presence of the fleet in Hawaii would prevent such an attack, which, Washington believed, Germany and Italy might entice Japan to launch by signaling it would have a free hand in that area.[14]

On May 10 Germany advanced into the Netherlands. In a press interview that day Roosevelt was cautious concerning the United States' attitude toward the problem of the Dutch East Indies. Asked how the United States would respond if Germany or Japan were to move into the Dutch West Indies or the Dutch East Indies, he declined to answer, saying that such a question was only hypothetical.[15] On the same day Hull queried Lothian on the British reaction to a statement making clear to Japan that Britain and the United States "stand unequivocally for the maintenance of the *status quo* of the Dutch East Indies" and inquiring whether Japan intended to hold to its recently announced position concerning the region.[16] Anticipating such a move, Ambassador Horinouchi had that day cabled his government to act swiftly, since Britain and France might approach the United States on the matter.[17]

In Tokyo, the day after his country was invaded, Ambassador Pabst informed Arita in an official letter of the outbreak of war between the Netherlands and Germany, repeating once again his government's refusal to countenance any interference from other powers in its territories. His note stipulated that "the Netherlands hopes Japan will not intervene in any manner in the Dutch Indies, Surinam, and Curaçao. Neither the partial nor the complete occupation of these areas should have any legal influence on other parts of the world."[18]

Arita thereupon asked Pabst to call on him. It was Japan's hope, he assured the ambassador, that the Dutch government would hold to its resolve concerning the Dutch Indies. Japan had reminded the representatives of Britain, Germany, and France of its interests in this area and had reported this action to the representatives of the neutral nations, the United States and Italy. To the three nations at war with Germany— Britain, France, and the Netherlands—Japan warned that "any disturbance in the maintenance and promotion of economic relations between Japan and the Dutch East Indies cannot be tolerated by Japan. Japan sincerely hopes that your government will bear this in mind."[19]

While Arita was endeavoring to maintain the status quo in the Dutch East Indies, British and French troops landed on the 11th on the islands of Curaçao and Aruba in the Dutch West Indies at the request of the Dutch government, which was worried that the Germans in Venezuela would seize the oil refineries on Aruba. In response to this move, Hull hurriedly issued a statement reiterating the commitment he had made on April 17 and his government's assumption that "each of the governments which has made commitments will continue to abide by those commitments." The statement concluded:

. . . On April 17, 1940, in a public statement, I said:
"Intervention in the domestic affairs of the Netherlands Indies or any alteration of their *status quo* by other than peaceful processes would be prejudicial to the cause of stability, peace, and security not only in the region of the Netherlands Indies but in the entire Pacific area."
In view of these facts commitments and expressions of intention to respect the *status quo* of the Netherlands East Indies cannot be too often reiterated.[20]

The American government feared that Japan might use the British and French landings in the West Indies as a pretext to begin some action in the Dutch East Indies. On the day of the landings, therefore, Roosevelt made two requests of the British government. First, he asked that it announce it had no intention of interfering in Far Eastern affairs and expressed the hope that the Dutch government would similarly state that it had no need of outside assistance in its East Asian colonies. Second, once security had been restored in Curaçao and Aruba through the arrest of any Germans and certain local leaders there, he asked that Britain and France withdraw their troops as quickly as possible, leaving matters in the hands of the local government.

The British immediately acceded to his requests. On the 13th British Ambassador Robert L. Craigie called on Arita and, in reply to Arita's previous note, stated that his government recognized Japan's special interest in the Dutch East Indies, believed the Dutch forces in the area were sufficient to maintain the status quo, and had no intention of intervening. Arita responded that Japan would, of course, not interfere in the Dutch East Indies either.[21]

Arita's assurances were reinforced by the reports of American Ambassador Joseph C. Grew. While it was true, he cabled on May 14, that elements in Japan were advocating the occupation of the Dutch East Indies to obtain raw materials that might be withheld by the United States—an action that they acknowledged might lead to a more rigid embargo but not a declaration of war against Japan—Grew, like Craigie, believed Prime Minister Yonai and Arita to be opposed to such an occupation and not likely to be influenced by the extremists. Moreover, Grew stated, there was no evidence that Japanese troops were advancing southward.[22] American fears of a Japanese advance in the south were thus allayed, although anxiety concerning Japan's southern policy still remained.

On the 15th Pabst responded formally to Arita's request of the 11th, stating that his government was assured that Britain, France, and the United States would not interfere in the Dutch East Indies. A day later French Ambassador Charles Arsène-Henry similarly indicated that "the French government agrees with the Japanese imperial government's principle that the status quo in the Dutch East Indies is to be maintained."[23] Arita had now heard from all the countries involved, and for each the basic principle was that the status quo should be maintained.

Their actions, however, did not accord completely with this officially expressed principle. In a meeting with Sumner Welles on the 16th Lothian and the Australian minister, Richard G. Casey, urged that the U.S. fleet be dispatched to Singapore; meanwhile, Britain and Australia would issue a strong warning against any action by Japan.[24] The United States did not comply with their request, not desiring to become involved in a Far Eastern conflict.

Japan was also worried about German policy. In order to confuse relations between the United States, Britain, and France on the one hand and Japan on the other, Germany might announce its intention to annex the Dutch East Indies; or it might force a government under German control in the Netherlands to issue a new statement on the questions. In either circumstance, Japan would have to hold to its recent assurances by issuing a statement opposing Germany's action. It was also likely that Britain and France would take some action in response to such a development.

On the 15th the Japanese government therefore ordered its ambassador to Germany, Kurusu Saburō, to request unofficially that Germany take no action regarding the Dutch East Indies.[25] Kurusu went at once to the Foreign Office. Ribbentrop was out, so he met with State Secretary Ernst von Weizsaecker. Weizsaecker commented that the state of the Dutch East Indies might be compared "to the center of a typhoon where . . . there was calm as the contending air streams neutralized each other." There was no need to explain to Kurusu, he added, "where the real opponents of Japanese interests were. He was well aware of the fate which war at present had brought to the Netherlands' possessions in the West Indies."[26]

On June 22 the German government finally made an official reply to the Japanese request. In a written statement presented to Arita by Eugen Ott in Tokyo, Germany explained that it had remained silent on the matter because it had not been asked by Japan to clarify its attitude and had not thought it necessary to express its views of its own accord. It now asserted that since the war with the Netherlands was a European matter and did not concern the Dutch colonies, Germany "had no interest in occupying herself with such overseas problems." Germany "had always pursued a policy of friendship toward Japan," the statement went on, "and believed that in the past this policy had promoted Japan's interests in the Far East."[27] In short, Germany would not oppose Japan's freedom of action in the Dutch East Indies. This attitude was calculated to arouse American anxieties, for Germany hoped thereby to lay the seeds of conflict between Japan and the United States in order to reduce the threat to itself in Europe.

The United States still hoped that it could avoid involvement in a Far Eastern conflict. Roosevelt and Hull therefore ordered Grew to discuss the situation with the Japanese authorities at the first opportunity. In a talk with Arita on June 10 Grew stressed that relations between Japan and the United States would not improve as long as Japan continued to interfere with American interests in China and attempted to pursue its aims by military means. His government believed, he said, that a policy of free trade would be to the advantage of both Japan and the United States.

Asking that his remarks be "off the record," Arita assured Grew that he agreed with him "in spirit and in principle." However, his government was facing difficulties in endeavoring to cope with strong pressures for the development of more intimate relations with Germany and Italy. He then pointed to the presence of the United States fleet in Hawaii. Grew responded that Hawaii was American territory and the fleet represented "no threat whatsoever to Japan." Nonetheless, Arita asserted, it implied suspicion of Japan's intentions in the Dutch East Indies and the South Seas where, he reemphasized, Japan had no territorial ambitions.[28]

Two days later Arita declared in an oral statement to Grew that Japan was not using military force in China as an instrument of national policy and if reasonable conditions could be obtained, his government was prepared of its own accord to end the war there. In order to bring about such a settlement and an improvement in Japanese-American relations, other problems would also have to be solved, and he pointed to several questions as worthy of particular study: Was Japan pursuing a restrictive economic policy and, if so, what were the causes? If the war in China were ended, would restrictive economic policies there be ended also? Did not Japan's policy toward the Dutch East Indies, the neutrality treaty with Thailand, and the settlement of the Tientsin problem give evidence of Japan's peaceful intentions? Was America prepared to relieve the uneasiness between their two countries by negotiating a provisional commercial agreement? In addition, would the United States stop aiding Chiang Kai-shek and cooperate with Japan in the reconstruction of China? Finally, he asked, would it be possible for the United States to recognize the new conditions in East Asia, with Japan and the United States each preserving its own sphere of influence in the Pacific Ocean and both acting in concert to contribute to the peace of the world?[29]

On the 19th, following receipt of instructions from Washington, Grew replied in an oral statement emphasizing his government's view that concrete issues could be discussed only after the "underlying policies and principles" of each government were defined and understood. Security and national interest must be fostered by peaceful means alone, on the Asian as well as the American continent, and by economic policies based upon the principle of economic freedom. Thus, in response to the concrete issues posed by Japan, the United States repeated general principles. When Arita requested a specific response to the matters he had raised, the U.S. government proposed only an exchange of notes indicating a common desire that the status quo in the Pacific territories and possessions of the European belligerents should be maintained, or modified by peaceful means alone.[30]

At first Arita stated that he did not see how the suggestion could be accepted unless the other issues in Japanese-American relations he had raised were first solved. And on the 28th he rejected the proposed exchange of notes on the grounds that it would be contrary to Japan's policy of noninvolvement in the European war. To prevent the spread of hostilities to the Pacific, however, he now believed it "timely and appropriate" to discuss problems of concern to the United States and Japan only. And he again asked for Washington's response to the points he had made in his oral statement of June 12.[31]

On June 29, in a noon meeting with Japanese and foreign newsmen and in a broadcast at 2:30 that afternoon, Arita issued a statement that elaborated upon the Japanese ideal of forming a sphere of co-prosperity and co-existence and establishing peace and order within it. The statement continued:

Countries of East Asia and regions of the South Seas are geographically, historically, racially, and economically very closely related to each other. They are destined to help each other and minister to one another's needs for their common well-being and prosperity, and to promote peace and progress in their regions. Uniting all of these regions under a single sphere on the basis of common existence and insuring thereby the stability of that sphere is, I think, a natural conclusion. . . . Japan, while carrying on vigorously her task of constructing a new order in East Asia, is paying serious attention to developments in the European War and to its repercussions in the various quarters of East Asia, including the South Seas region. I desire to declare that the destiny of these regions in any development therein, and any disposal thereof, is a matter for grave concern to Japan in view of her mission and responsibility as the stabilizing force in East Asia.[32]

Arita's words made clear Japan's intention to establish an East Asian bloc and its opposition to the American principle of free trade. These differences between the two nations led to a temporary suspension of the talks between Arita and Grew.

Economic Demands: The Kobayashi Mission

Until the outbreak of the worldwide depression, the Netherlands had pursued a free trade policy insofar as its East Indian colonies were concerned. With the depression, the major powers had returned to a protective system, and British preferential trade policies and the American reciprocal trade system following the 1932 Ottawa Conference had, in particular, shut off the flow of goods from the Dutch East Indies to the United States and Britain, the two most important customers for products of the region. At the same time the Dutch East Indies began to raise protective barriers against the flood of Japanese goods into its markets. In September 1933 the local government issued an emergency import control law, and in November the Dutch government imposed restrictions on immigration into its colonies.

Japan thereupon initiated talks with the Dutch government, with the aim of concluding a commercial agreement concerning the East Indies. In negotiations between June and December 1934 Japan hoped to lay a firm foundation for the future by enabling its manufacturers to sell more products in the Indies and its nationals to enter the colonies and establish businesses there. At the time, agricultural exports from the Indies were falling and industries in the Netherlands itself were declining, and no agreement was achieved. Subsequent efforts to iron out their differences finally resulted in a marine transport agreement in July 1936, the Ishizawa-Hult trade pact of April 1937, and the Kōtani-Van Mook note supplementing the pact in January 1938. Economic relations between Japan and the Netherlands were thereby adjusted.

As the war in China dragged on, Japan came to desire even closer economic ties with the Dutch East Indies in order to lessen its reliance upon American and British goods. This became even more important after the bombing of Nanking in 1938, when the United States applied its so-called moral embargo on the export of aircraft to Japan, followed by further, increasingly stringent economic pressures that culminated on July 26, 1939, when the U.S. announced its intent to abrogate the 1911 Treaty of Commerce and Navigation. In November Japan sought a new adjustment of its economic relations with the Dutch East Indies.

The threat of a German military occupation of the Netherlands in the spring of 1940 suddenly made the security of the Dutch East Indies the focus of attention of the powers. Japan, however, could not afford to delay, since the American abrogation of the commercial treaty had gone into effect on January 26. On May 10 the German army advanced into Holland, and on the 20th Arita, in addition to several political demands, asked the Dutch government for definite assurance that it would sell Japan annually the following thirteen vital commodities: [33]

Commodities	Tonnages Desired Annually
Tin (including ores)	3,000
Rubber	20,000
Petroleum	1,000,000
Bauxite	200,000
Nickel	150,000
Manganese	50,000
Wolfram (tungsten)	1,000
Scrap iron	100,000
Chrome steel	5,000
Industrial salt	100,000
Castor beans	4,000
Cinchona (quinine)	600
Molybdenum	1,000

Ishii Itarō, who presented Japan's demands to The Hague, later wrote, "I felt as if I had gone to dun a dying person for a debt." [34]

On June 6 The Hague responded. It accepted the demands in general, except with respect to the entry of Japanese nationals. Concerning the thirteen commodities the Dutch government stated, "We are not opposed to guaranteeing the requests of the Japanese government." The demand for a million tons of oil exceeded the average annual tonnage exported from the Dutch East Indies during the preceding three years, but the Dutch government assured Japan that the oil could be supplied provided that contracts were made with the oil companies in sufficient time.

On the 28th Arita reconfirmed this pledge through Ambassador Pabst. He wrote: "We understand that the Netherlands government and the governor-general of the Dutch East Indies promise us firmly that at least the said amount of the aforestated thirteen commodities will be exported to Japan every year under whatever circumstances. We also assume that in executing this promise your government will take such means as are necessary and that the price will not be higher than the market price." [35]

These developments in Japan's policy toward the Dutch East Indies led to growing U.S. government concern and renewed efforts to apply economic pressure to bring about a change in that policy. With the fall of France in the summer of 1940 and the resulting crisis in Britain's position, councils within the American government became divided over the question of further economic sanctions. Navy Secretary Frank Knox, Secretary of War Henry L. Stimson, and Treasury Secretary Henry Morgenthau, Jr., headed the proponents of a total embargo on exports of oil and scrap iron to Japan. They were opposed by Under Secretary of State Welles, who contended that such action would goad "an already berserk Japanese Army into an attack upon an almost crippled Britain and an almost defenseless Netherlands" and lead to American involvement in the war. Moreover, neither the navy nor the army was prepared to resist the Japanese attack on Malaya and the Dutch East Indies that would inevitably follow such an embargo. [36] Temporarily accepting the arguments of the opponents of a total embargo, President Roosevelt on June 26 reversed an earlier decision and limited the licensing requirement to aviation fuel and No. 1 heavy melting steel and scrap iron. [37]

On July 11 Ambassador Grew issued a warning to the Japanese government concerning its policy toward the Dutch East Indies. Trade with the region, he stated, was important to many countries, including the United States, which had an interest in the continuance there "of the principle and the observance of equality of trade opportunity, as well as of that of enterprise." And he requested that his government be kept informed "as to the manner in which these principles are being applied" in Japan's negotiation with the Dutch authorities. Turning next to the proposal for an exchange of notes, he stated that it had been made in an effort to prevent the extension to the Pacific of the hostilities in Europe and would seek to reinforce Japan's position of noninvolvement in that struggle. As for the points raised in Arita's statement of June 12, he made it clear that the United States had no intention of abandoning Chiang Kai-shek's government, that world peace might be promoted only by policies that aimed at achieving order, justice, and stability through peaceful means and allowed for independence and free trade relations among nations in any part of the world, and that settlement of their disagreement on fundamental questions must precede normalization of commercial relations between them.[38]

Soon after this the Yonai cabinet fell, and on July 22 Konoe Fumimaro became prime minister for the second time. The new government faced the problem of appointing a head for an economic mission to be dispatched to the Dutch East Indies. Sakawa Shūichi was first suggested, but soon General Koiso Kuniaki of the Army Reserves, minister of overseas affairs in the previous Konoe cabinet, emerged as the primary candidate.[39] Despite the urging of Konoe and Foreign Minister Matsuoka Yōsuke, however, Koiso did not accept the position immediately.[40] His appointment was opposed by Minister Pabst, who protested against charges attributed to Koiso in the press to the effect that the Netherlands had exploited its East Indian colony and has "placed [it] under administrative pressure from a moral viewpoint," adding that "freeing the Oriental races [was] necessary and destined to be realized."[41] On August 4 the Dutch ambassador in Washington, A. Loudon, handed to James C. Dunn, adviser on political relations in the State Department, a request that the United States advise Japan that any attempt to realize the views attributed to Koiso "would be viewed by the American Government as infringing the *status quo* in the Pacific which . . . would be objectionable to the United States Government."[42]

Koiso's delay in accepting the post was primarily due to his disagreement with Konoe and Matsuoka concerning the character of the mission. Koiso's view was that the mission should travel by warship to the East Indies and that the negotiations should be attended by a full display of military power. He therefore demanded that a force of Japanese marines accompany the mission and that instructions be given to their commander enabling him to act immediately and independently, without reference to the high command in Tokyo, if military action were necessary. The navy, however, was reluctant to pursue such a policy. When Koiso asked whether the navy would dispatch troops to protect Japanese residents in the Indies, Navy Minister Yoshida Zengo replied, "Naturally the navy would transport troops if necessary, but before dispatching a large number of troops, we should be very cautious." Koiso persisted, "Can you dispatch warships?" To which Yoshida answered, "Right now it is not possible." Unable to resolve the differences, the government eventually turned to Commerce and Industry Minister Kobayashi Ichizō to head the mission, a decision it reported to Pabst on the 27th. Claiming that Britain and the United States were scheming with the Netherlands to abort the mission, the Japanese government placed strict controls on press reports of the Kobayashi mission.[43]

The United States, meanwhile, was considering ways to limit Japanese access to East Indian oil. On July 25 Maxwell M. Hamilton, chief of the State Department's Division of Far Eastern Affairs, anticipating that Japan would seek to shift from the United States to the East Indies as its primary supplier of oil, asked George S. Walden of Standard-Vacuum Oil to attempt to limit insofar as possible Japanese access to East Indian supplies. The Dutch, however, were fearful that American economic pressures would bring about the aggressive action on the part of Japan that the United States hoped thereby to prevent. In a meeting with Joseph W. Ballantine, vice chief of the Far Eastern Division, on July 31, to ask that action be taken to expedite permission for the shipment of military supplies purchased in the United States by the Dutch East Indies, Ambassador Loudon referred to increasing Japanese diplomatic pressure against the East Indies and implied that his government was concerned about Japan's reaction to restrictions on certain American exports.[44]

Two weeks later the American consul-general in Batavia, Walter A. Foote, reported that the authorities in the Dutch East Indies had, some ten days before, issued orders for the complete destruction of all refineries, wells, and petroleum stocks totaling 5 million barrels (of which half would be American) in the event of invasion by Japan. On the 21st he confirmed this report and said that the oil companies were negotiating with the government to prevent total destruction of the oil fields.[45]

Meanwhile, on August 16 Walden called on Stanley K. Hornbeck, the State Department's political adviser, to inform him that the Dutch East Indies government had requested an oil company official to participate in the talks with the Japanese. Hornbeck warned that the Dutch might be seeking to draw the American government and oil companies into the dispute with Japan but said he had no objection to a representative's being sent. When a member of the British embassy, who was also present, expressed the view that the Japanese demands would have to be acceded to, Hornbeck responded that "there was no need and no advantage to be gained by assuming a defeatist attitude; that if the negotiators go into the negotiations in such a frame of mind they will be in a hopeless position, as the Japanese would of course take the fullest advantage of that situation." He advised them to "approach the negotiations as a business negotiation," judging the Japanese requests "on their merits from a business point of view." Unreasonable demands by the Japanese would create a political problem, and in the face of threats the companies' attitude should be "that the farthest they could go would be to give passive acquiescence." Sir Harold Wilkinson, the representative of Royal Dutch Shell in the United States, noted that the Asiatic Petroleum Company faced the more immediate problem of direct Japanese demands for petroleum supplies including aviation fuel, which had been embargoed by the United States, and "doctored" crude that could be readily transformed into aviation fuel. While there was no basis for not complying with Japan's demands for unprocessed crude oil, Hornbeck replied, to supply it with aviation fuel or "doctored" crude could serve only to nullify the American action and, moreover, was not in the long-term interests of either Britain or the Asiatic Petroleum Company. Japan, he declared, "did not require high quality aviation gasoline for its present uses but only for possible later or ultimate use against the British." In addition, since the Japanese were calling for a contract of one year or longer, for a British company to sign a long-term agreement to provide aviation fuel that American companies were prevented from supplying could serve only to eliminate any chance for American companies to participate in the market should there be a change in the Far Eastern situation—an outcome to which the United States "could hardly be expected to give [its] blessing."[46]

As if responding to Hornbeck's concern, Lord Lothian visited Hull on the 26th. The British government, he said, had urged British oil companies in the Dutch East Indies "not to allow themselves to be pushed into a long-term contract with Japan, but to bargain hard both as to time and quantity." In view of the "defeatist state of mind" of the

Dutch government and oil companies in the East Indies, he proposed that the American government suggest the same thing to them and assure them that they need not fear military attack or occupation should they bargain hard with the Japanese. Hull promised to consider the suggestion and said he would urge the Far Eastern Division to collaborate in discussions with the Dutch government and oil companies.[47]

Both governments were thus agreed on their policy toward the negotiations between Japan and the Dutch East Indies. The Dutch government would be encouraged to prolong the negotiations as much as possible and to limit the quantity of oil to be sold and the length of the contract with Japan.

On September 11 Hull instructed Consul-General Foote in Batavia to reaffirm to the local authorities the American government's interest in maintaining the status quo in the Pacific except as changed through "orderly process," and to express the hope that he would be kept informed of developments, particularly in the economic field, in which the United States "would be prepared to give consideration" should difficulties arise as a consequence of the Dutch East Indies' being cut off from normal markets and sources of supply. On September 24 the chargé d'affaires of the Netherlands, Baron C. G. W. H. van Boetzelaer van Oosterhout, called on Welles to press his government's desire that the U.S. government place no drastic restrictions on exports to Japan while negotiations with the Japanese mission were in progress. Welles assured van Boetzelaer that American officials had given "fullest consideration" to the effect on the East Indies of possible measures against Japan, but stated that it would be in the interest of neither government if the United States were to adopt "an attitude of complete supine acquiescence in the continuing and ever-enlarging policy of Japan of aggression in the Pacific region." For the moment, however, further sanctions against Japan were not being contemplated.[48]

In the face of the united attitudes of the United States, Britain, and the Netherlands, the Japanese government instructed Kobayashi to negotiate solely on economic issues, without expressing openly Japan's political intentions. What these intentions were may be discerned in the "Principles for Negotiations with the Dutch East Indies" agreed to by the cabinet on August 27 and sent to Kobayashi. According to the "Principles," Japan was to: 1) make the Dutch East Indies part of the East Asia Co-Prosperity Sphere, 2) support absolute self-determination for the Indonesian people, and 3) "conclude with the Dutch East Indies concrete pacts for the defense of that territory in order to secure peace in the East Asia Co-Prosperity Sphere, including the Indies." But fearing that revelation of these political aims might bring the United States and Britain to the defense of the Dutch colonies, the Japanese government ordered its representative not to bring them up just then.[49]

The negotiations between Japan and the Dutch East Indies began on September 13, when the Kobayashi delegation was warmly greeted by the governor-general of the colony. But the governor-general refused to participate directly in the negotiations, appointing Hubertus J. Van Mook, the local director of economic affairs to represent the Netherlands, and Kobayashi cabled his dissatisfaction to his government: "I feel it is no use to negotiate with such a governor-general and my long trip here was in vain." Foreign Minister Matsuoka was also convinced that the details of the negotiations were being leaked to Britain and the United States.[50]

The distrust between the Netherlands and Japan was further increased on September 27, when Japan concluded the Tripartite Pact with Italy and Germany, already at war with the Netherlands. The talks proceeded unsatisfactorily for Japan, until on November 30 Kobayashi was summoned back to Japan without raising the political aims that had been of primary importance in his instructions.[51] Before his recall, Kobayashi pressed Van Mook on the issue of oil, asking for a five-year guarantee from the Dutch East Indies government of 3.75 million tons annually. Van Mook rejected this request. Japan had hitherto imported 600,000 tons annually, and such a drastic increase would either mean premature exhaustion of the East Indian wells or require cutting off exports to other countries, which would be against the principle of equality in trade.

Meanwhile talks had begun between Mukai Tadaharu, president of Mitsui Bussan, and the representatives of the oil companies in the Dutch East Indies. In early October Royal Dutch Shell and Standard-Vacuum Oil offered to supply 726,500 tons, an offer Mukai at first did not accept. But in the end he abandoned his original demands and on November 12 signed an agreement to this effect with the oil companies. In addition, a shipment of 580,000 tons had been contracted in Tokyo in July, and an additional 49,000 tons had been purchased through local transactions in Tokyo. Another 650,000 tons were scheduled to be sold to Japan by branches of the Rising Sun Company and Standard-Vacuum Oil in Japan, although contracts had not yet been signed. Thus Japan succeeded in acquiring some 2 million tons of oil. This fell far short of Japanese hopes, however, particularly in terms of aviation fuel, of which no new supplies were made available, and benzine. Moreover, the term of the contract was limited to six months, beginning November 1, 1940.[52] Faithful to the understanding with Britain and the United States, the Dutch authorities had insisted on short-term contracts and had refused to sell high-grade petroleum to Japan.

Japanese oil imports had averaged 5,370,000 tons annually from 1937 to 1940,[53] and the agreement on East Indian oil represented less than half of Japan's needs. For the remainder it was dependent on the United States. And despite the licensing restrictions in effect since July of 1940, in the last three months of that year alone Japan obtained from the United States over 6 million barrels (nearly 1 million tons) of petroleum products:[54]

October	1.7 million barrels	
November	2.9 "	"
December	1.7 "	"

In April 1941 Charles W. Yost, assistant chief of the Division of Controls, pointed out that since the restrictions had been imposed the previous July 26, the department had licensed about 9.2 million barrels (1.3 million tons) of gasoline, with applications for another 2 million barrels pending. "The amount already licensed represents more than twice the normal annual pre-war import of Japan *from all sources*," he noted, and together with the orders not yet licensed and with supplies contracted in the Netherlands East Indies, Japan's total import would be "at least *three times* her normal pre-war import" and would "make her completely self-sufficient in gasoline for an indefinite period of time." Moreover, despite America's ban on exports of high-grade aviation gasoline, he warned, "most of the 9,200,000 barrels referred to above is of satisfactory aviation quality or can be made so by a very simple process." Likewise with lubricating oils, Japan had imported from the United States more than twice its prewar quantities and was reliably reported to be transshipping "substantial quantities" across Siberia to Germany. Although exports to Japan of most other petroleum products had not increased significantly since the start of the European war, and crude oil exports had actually declined in 1940, Yost warned that this might change suddenly; meanwhile, Japan was concentrating on importing higher grade petroleum from which aviation fuel could be obtained.[55]

For the present, Japan was not faced with a crisis in oil supplies, although future prospects for American imports were a cause of concern. Following his return to Japan, Kobayashi reportedly expressed to Minister Pabst his satisfaction with the outcome of the oil negotiations with the Dutch East Indies, and late in January 1941 Matsuoka himself remarked in the Diet that Japan had "obtained more oil than we had expected."[56]

Economic Demands Heightened: The Yoshizawa Mission

On October 25 Pabst asked the Japanese government to draw up a formal agenda for the discussions between the trade mission and the government of the Netherlands East Indies. Japan's reply was delayed while the government sought a replacement for Kobayashi as head of the mission. Finally, on November 28 former Foreign Minister Yoshizawa Kenkichi was appointed.[57] As he left Japan, Yoshizawa was told by Matsuoka that the negotiations could be considered satisfactory if half of Japan's demands were obtained.[58] On December 28 Yoshizawa arrived in Batavia and, after meeting with the governor-general on January 2, began negotiations with the Dutch authorities. But the talks did not proceed well for Japan.

The Japanese delegation presented a wide-ranging list of proposals as an agenda for the negotiations. The Netherlands delegation refused to respond, considering that to accede to them would reduce the East Indies to the status of a Japanese colony.[59] Then, on January 21 and again on the 29th, Matsuoka, speaking in the Diet, included the Netherlands East Indies within the bounds of Japan's Co-Prosperity Sphere and made clear the necessity for a fundamental realignment of Japanese relations with the Netherlands East Indies.[60] On the 31st Pabst presented an oral protest to Vice Foreign Minister Ōhashi Chūichi, stating that his government rejected any idea that the Dutch East Indies were part of a new East Asian order under the leadership of any power.[61] Ōhashi responded that Matsuoka's speech had been "only an assertion of Japan, therefore the Netherlands authorities need not accept it. The economic negotiations in Batavia are a separate matter." His reply was reported to the authorities of the Dutch East Indies as a rejection of Pabst's protest. As a result, on February 3 the chief of the East Indies Information Bureau told newsmen the negotiations could not be continued. After a protracted dispute Yoshizawa issued a statement that the report concerning Ōhashi was not true, and peace was restored. But a new problem soon arose when remarks made in a press interview by Ishii Yasushi, vice chief of the Cabinet Information Bureau, were interpreted as indicating Japanese refusal to recognize the Netherlands government-in-exile in London.[62]

It would appear that the intent of the Netherlands government in criticizing the statements of Matsuoka, Ōhashi, and Ishii was to delay the negotiations. On January 22 Van Mook secretly informed Consul-General Foote that he would "endeavor to prolong the negotiations as long as possible in order to give Great Britain more time to bring about a change in the situation in Europe." And in Washington the Netherlands minister was in close contact with the State Department concerning the Japanese demands.[63]

Finally, on February 15 the negotiations in the East Indies were resumed between J. E. van Hoogstraten, the head of the Bureau of Commerce, and Japanese Consul-General Ishizawa Yutaka as well as between Yoshizawa and Van Mook. Two days earlier Yoshizawa had informed Matsuoka that in view of the increasing American pressure against Japan, Japan could not anticipate a favorable outcome to the negotiations, which might soon be expected to collapse, and that military action might be necessary to secure the commodities Japan had demanded. Replying on the 21st, Matsuoka appealed to Yoshizawa to do his utmost to acquire the needed goods. Stocks of these important commodities in Japan were very limited, he said, and if they could not be obtained from the Dutch East Indies, plans for the stockpiling of critical materials could not be realized.[64]

Matsuoka's anxiety was due to the economic sanctions applied by the United States, which, toward the end of 1940, were becoming increasingly severe. One item after another of strategic military importance was added to the embargo list following the establishment of the export licensing system in July: scrap iron on September 26 (effective October 10); iron ore, pig iron, ferro-alloy, and certain kinds of finished and semi-finished steel products on December 10 (effective December 30); copper, bronze, zinc, nickel, brass, caustic potash, and many semimanufactured products made from them on January 10, 1941 (effective February 3); and well and refining machinery, radium, and uranium on February 4 (effective February 10).[65]

The restrictions were of grave concern to the Japanese navy, which sent a message to the Japanese representatives in Batavia stating: "We must make clear our intention to cease our dependence upon American oil and put our reliance primarily on the Dutch Indies. Our needs cannot be met unless we succeed in obtaining imports of 3,150,000 tons of oil as we requested originally."[66] Meanwhile oil exports from the United States to Japan had begun to decrease: 1.6 million barrels in January 1941, 1.3 million in February, and 1.4 million in March.[67]

The problem, however, was not clearly understood by the Japanese representatives in Batavia. Moreover, Matsuoka was in Europe at the time, so communications between Tokyo and Batavia were poor. The Foreign Ministry and the military in Japan thought the achievement of Japan's commercial aims should be the primary concern of the negotiators for the present, although they agreed that efforts should be continued to meet Japan's other demands: for example, the entry of Japanese nationals and the establishment of Japanese firms in the Dutch East Indies. The representatives on the spot, on the other hand, thought such a policy change in the middle of the negotiations would be unwise, for it would reveal Japan's difficulties to the Dutch negotiators, who would take advantage of them. Finally, about March 3, when it had become clear that the Dutch were determined to resist Japan's demands, Yoshizawa advised Tokyo that it would be better to conclude a treaty at once, even if it were only temporary, obtaining what concessions they could, rather than break off the negotiations. But Konoe, who was acting as foreign minister in Matsuoka's absence, decided more might be obtained by sticking to the original demands instead of hastily concluding the negotiations. On March 26, therefore, he instructed Yoshizawa: "The situation has changed since Matsuoka left for Europe. The Dutch foreign minister and colonial minister (friendly to Japan) are reportedly going to Batavia in the near future after sounding out America's intentions. Therefore, though it may be very difficult, wait and watch for new developments, meanwhile pushing our original plan with an emphasis upon acquiring the necessary commodities. (Consultations with the military have been concluded.)"[68]

On March 29 the Netherlands adamantly refused to increase exports of five commodities, having evidence that Japan intended to re-export them to Germany. It would agree to supply only the following quantities (figures in parentheses indicate quantities requested by Japan):

Commodities	Tonnage Agreed On
Tin	3,000 (10,000)
Rubber	19,800 (70,000)
Copra	12,000 (70,000)
Palm oil	960 (30,000)
Castor oil	6,000 (10,000)

On April 2 Yoshizawa requested permission to return to Tokyo to consult with the government, but Konoe, fearful that his return might have an adverse effect, ordered him to stay. He instructed Yoshizawa to delay the withdrawal of Japanese military personnel for as long as possible.[69]

Matsuoka returned from Europe on April 22. Four days later Yoshizawa advised him that, if Japan definitely planned military operations, the negotiations should be used to provide a pretext; but, if one did not know when such force was to be applied, he feared that it would be absolutely impossible for Japan to obtain its demands, not only for the entrance of Japanese business but also for the acquisition of vital commodities. If Japan did not intend to employ military means, on the other hand, it had best seek a compromise to insure that at least some essential goods would be obtained.[70]

Japan in the meantime had begun to look to French Indochina for certain of its supplies and to this end had begun negotiations in Tokyo in December 1940 with representatives of the Vichy authorities in Indochina. French promises to provide 700,000 tons of rice from Indochina in 1941 greatly improved Japan's prospects with regard to its food requirements, but the negotiations over tin and rubber dragged on. On April 30 the rubber issue was finally settled, when, according to Grew, the French allotted 25,000 tons jointly to Japan and Germany, with a separate allocation of 15,000 tons to Japan.[71]

Although Germany and Japan were not agreed on their shares of the joint allocation, a portion was reportedly to be re-exported to Germany from Japan. Fearing that supplies from its East Indian territories would likewise be re-exported to Germany, the Netherlands delegation adopted a stronger attitude in the negotiations and attempted to restrict exports to Japan as much as possible.

Through the spring of 1941 the shortage of commodities in Japan became more and more serious. On May 2 Matsuoka informed Yoshizawa that the need for defense materials was urgent and although, he said, "I doubt that this can be attained," he ordered Yoshizawa to demand from the Dutch delegation increased amounts of the following commodities:

Commodities	Increased Tonnage Demanded
Crude rubber	30,000
Tin	8,000
Copra	30,000
Palm oil	20,000
Bauxite	368,000
Nickel	180,000
Manganese ore	27,000 (approximately)

Later that same day Matsuoka again cabled the Japanese delegates to obtain definite promises of 25,000 tons of rubber and 5,000 tons of tin. And on the 6th he instructed them that even 20,000 tons of rubber and 3,000 tons of tin would be better than nothing. What was important, he said, was that they should get a firm promise quickly, adding, "you must secure a promise that the stipulated amounts will be exported to Japan without fail." He informed them that while Japan could expect about 15,000 tons of rubber from French Indochina, imports from Thailand were uncertain; as for tin, he was not sure how much could be obtained from Indochina, and Thailand would supply less than 40 tons of ore per month in the coming year.

While Matsuoka urged the members of the mission to redouble their efforts in the negotiations, he was aware that the talks with the Dutch East Indies were dependent on the overall international situation and, in the final analysis, fundamentally bound up with Japan's relations with Britain and the United States. For in his cable of the 6th he stated: "Breaking the impasse in our relations with the Dutch East Indies is ultimately related to a change in our relations with the United States and Great Britain. If Japan's demands for exports are not acceded to by the

Dutch East Indies, we will face difficulty in our commodity stockpiling program. The military also attaches great importance to this matter. Therefore, it is urgent that this problem at least be solved by any means possible." He added, "Within the month we should obtain a somewhat clearer projection of the international situation."[72]

On the 22nd Matsuoka complained to British Ambassador Craigie that the negotiations had reached an impasse over rubber and tin exports. Despite Japan's concession in agreeing to accept 20,000 tons of rubber and 3,000 tons of tin which he claimed the Dutch government had the previous June promised to sell to Japan no matter what the circumstances, the Dutch negotiators now told Japan that exports of tin and rubber from French Indochina and Thailand would be taken into account in determining allocations of those materials by the Dutch East Indies. Matsuoka further refused to accede to Dutch demands for a guarantee against re-exports to Germany, which in any case, he asserted, were very small in comparison with total quantities purchased by Japan. He went on:

> For Japan, a major power, to accept the demand of the Dutch East Indies, a minor power, that we promise not to re-export materials to Germany would be a humiliation. Hence, we shall never give such a guarantee. Such a demand reveals how arrogant the Dutch East Indies has become. We cannot be sure what will happen with respect to Japan's foreign and domestic policies if the negotiations break down and the Yoshizawa delegation withdraws from the Indies. Violent anti-Dutch, and consequently anti-British and anti-American, sentiment will develop to the point where this minister may not be able to control it any longer. We hope, therefore, through your good offices, that your government will put pressure upon the Netherlands government and the Dutch East Indies authorities to reconsider this matter. We hope that you will so cable your country immediately.[73]

In this manner Matsuoka sought to put pressure on Britain to achieve Japan's aims in the Dutch East Indies.

On the same day Vice Foreign Minister Ōhashi met with Minister Pabst and accused the Dutch government of accepting suggestions from the United States and Britain for the reductions in rubber and tin exports. He warned that the Yoshizawa delegation might have to be withdrawn. Confronted by Pabst with the fact that rubber and tin were being re-exported to Germany, Ōhashi did not deny it, but he argued that the bulk of those items was being used for the expansion of Japan's own military industries.[74]

It soon became apparent that Japanese intimations that the negotiations might be broken off were not empty threats. On May 22, the day Matsuoka sought Britain's good offices to bring about a successful conclusion in the talks, the foreign minister announced to the Liaison Conference: "We intend to end the negotiations with the Dutch East Indies and to summon the Yoshizawa delegation home. I would like you to leave the question of timing to the foreign minister."[75] To judge from this statement, Matsuoka did not expect Craigie to put pressure upon the Dutch government; his request was simply a device to enable him to recall the Yoshizawa delegation while explaining publicly that Japan had done its best in the negotiations and no other diplomatic recourse now remained.

Moreover, given the close liaison that existed between the Netherlands and Britain and the United States throughout the negotiations, and Matsuoka's charges that the Dutch negotiators were following British and American advice, the foreign minister clearly did not expect Britain to act as he had requested.[76] That his suspicions were correct is apparent from a cable sent to Craigie on June 4 by the British minister in Bangkok and subsequently communicated to Grew. The Thai government, it was reported, had allotted 30,000 tons of rubber to Japan and would allot 18,000 tons to Malaya. He therefore suggested that rubber supplies from Malaya to Japan be stopped and that shipments from the Dutch East Indies be "reduced to the absolute minimum." Although the Netherlands had decided on the Japanese quota, since Japan had not been informed, it could still be reduced. He urged, Grew wrote, "that London consult the Netherlands government and that the British Consul General at Batavia urgently inform Van Mook."[77]

The Dutch, too, by this time expected the talks to break down at any moment. On June 3 Foreign Minister van Kleffens called on Sumner Welles in Washington and predicted that the Japanese would use the failure to reach an agreement on rubber as a pretext to end the negotiations and undertake further threatening activities.[78] Three days later the Netherlands government communicated its final reply to Japan; the terms, as expected, were unsatisfactory. The following day Craigie notified Matsuoka that Britain's efforts to mediate had failed.[79] On the 11th the Liaison Conference decided that Yoshizawa and the delegation would be recalled but that *no* formal rupture of the relations should occur, making possible a future resumption of discussions.[80]

Accordingly, on the 14th Matsuoka ordered Yoshizawa to end his negotiations and withdraw the delegation, but inform the Dutch authorities that economic relations between Japan and the Dutch East Indies should continue as before. Yoshizawa was to "avoid taking formal steps to break off relations between them. However, our delegation should clearly indicate to the Indies authorities that the negotiations are ended and that all envoys will be withdrawn." Yoshizawa carried out his instructions on the 17th, informing the Dutch delegates that thereafter any problems concerning the negotiations would be handled by Consul-General Ishizawa.

In the course of the negotiations agreement had been achieved on certain matters important to Japan, including the right to drill oil wells in the future and to export some commodities.[81] Japan failed, however, to obtain those materials most vital to the Japanese military program at the time.

THREE

The Army's Move into Northern Indochina

HATA IKUHIKO

Translated By
ROBERT A. SCALAPINO

Japanese Demands on French Indochina

Japan's first move toward the south was taken with the advance into northern French Indochina, before the policy of southward advance had been officially adopted with the "Main Principles for Coping with the Changing World Situation" in July 1940. Taking advantage of the French surrender in June, Japan had succeeded in closing the military supply route to the Chinese Nationalists through French Indochina, and a group of inspectors headed by Major-General Nishihara Issaku was sent to Indochina to supervise the closure. Nishihara was also expected to negotiate with the French authorities concerning the passage through Indochina and the provisioning of Japanese military forces, supplies intended for China, and the use of air and naval bases in Indochina. In effect, this meant the stationing of Japanese military forces in French Indochina.

The ostensible reason for these demands was to cut off supplies to the Chinese Nationalists, to prepare for an attack on K'unming, and to withdraw the Japanese military force stationed in Kwangsi province. But while the demands were drawn up within the framework of operations to end the China War, the officers in the Operations Division of the Army General Staff and those commanding the local armies obviously regarded them as an opportunity to launch a southward advance and thereafter schemed to steer national policies in this direction. In the end

This essay originally appeared as "Futsuin shinchū to gun no nanshin seisaku (1940-nen–1941-nen)," in *Taiheiyō sensō e no michi*, vol. 6, part 2, sec. 2–3, pp. 186–241.

they succeeded in bringing about the military occupation of northern French Indochina.

General Nishihara and naval leaders, on the other hand, sought to limit Japanese actions in the region to operations that would contribute to a settlement of the China conflict. Opposed to their viewpoint were army leaders holding more aggressive views, while others evidenced no definite opinions on the issue. Inevitably, the result was a confusion of aims and policies.

The navy in particular suspected the army of planning to invade French Indochina and Hong Kong, on the grounds that they were not part of the southern region as specified in the "Main Principles." For this reason the navy had insisted that they be included in those sections of the policy dealing with the southern advance. At the same time, the navy was more and more certain that the United States would not remain neutral if British territory were attacked and therefore began to question the entire policy of a military advance to the south. It was against this background of disagreement between the army and the navy over the southern advance that the incident involving the desertion of a force landed on the coast near Haiphong occurred. The appearance and development of this divergence in policy between the services will be of concern here, beginning with the shutting off of supplies to Chiang Kai-shek via Indochina and Burma.

The supply route to the Nationalists actually consisted of four major routes: the northwest, French Indochina, Burma, and the coast, as shown in the table. At the beginning of the China War the route through French Indochina was the most important, but later the Burma route became equally vital. Supplies obtained from Britain, the United States, Russia, France, and other countries through these routes enabled the government of Chiang Kai-shek to continue its resistance to Japan, even though it had withdrawn deep into Szechwan province and lost most of the important ports and industrial centers of China. It was not illegal under international law for China thus to be supplied with arms, for in order to prevent the United States' neutrality laws from coming into effect and prohibiting the export of American weapons to Japan and China alike, Japan had not declared war on China. Only two countermeasures were available to Japan: to request the countries involved voluntarily to cease their supplies to China, or to destroy the supply routes by bombing or by occupying the relay points.

THE SUPPLY ROUTES TO NATIONALIST CHINA

Route	Course	Monthly Volume of Traffic (in tons)		% of Total
		Before the European War	June 1940	
Northwest	USSR——Sinkiang——Kansu	200	500	2
French Indochina	Haiphong —— K'unming (via Tienyueh line)	12,500	15,000	48
	Haiphong——Lang Son ⎛——Paise ⎝——Nanning			
Burma (opened fall 1938)	Rangoon —— Lashio——K'unming	2,000	10,000	31
Coast	Central and south China		5,000	16
	Kuangchou Bay, Hong Kong		1,000	3
	TOTAL		31,500	100

—— Road
--- Railway

SOURCE: "Sambo Hombu no suitei chosa shiryō" (Estimates of the Army General Staff), in JDA Archives.

The coastal route had been relatively effectively closed by the navy, especially by its occupation of the ports, and the quantities supplied via the northwest were small. Thus the major problems were the routes through French Indochina and Burma.

The Japanese Foreign Ministry asked France and Britain to stop supplying armaments to Chiang, but those countries instead increased the flow of supplies while attempting to deny that they had done so. In February 1939 the navy occupied Hainan island and established a base for medium-range bombers, whereupon it began to bomb the route through eastern French Indochina into Kwangsi. Because of bad weather and other difficulties, however, the bombing failed to achieve its purpose.

The army then launched a drive on Nanning toward the same end, but China opened a new route via Paise that made the Nanning operation likewise ineffective. The medium-range bombers were moved to Nanning and now attacked the Tienyueh rail line but were unable—because of weather conditions, poor base facilities, and the difficulties posed by the mountainous terrain—to reduce the flow of supplies. Moreover, incidents resulting from errors forced a temporary halt to the bombing.

The outbreak of war in Europe strengthened Japan's position in the negotiations with the authorities of France and French Indochina. Toward the end of 1939 the chief of the Army General Staff Intelligence Division, Major-General Tsuchihashi Yūichi, and in January 1940 Lieutenant-Colonel Nishiura Susumu of the Military Section were sent to Hanoi with orders to stop the supplies to Chiang and to set up an inspection unit. Governor-General Georges Catroux agreed to supply the Japanese forces in Nanning, but little was achieved with regard to the supply routes until June 17 when, following France's surrender in Europe, the governor-general announced the suspension of all arms traffic to China. A month later British Ambassador Robert L. Craigie notified Foreign Minister Arita Hachirō that the Burma and Hong Kong routes would be closed for three months. Following the precedent in French Indochina, the army dispatched to the consulate in Rangoon Colonel Watanabe Saburō and five other inspectors who, it claimed, were members of the consular staff. They had little effect, however, as the British firmly limited their movements.[1] Nevertheless, by the summer of 1940 the crucial arteries through which supplies flowed to maintain Nationalist resistance to Japan had been temporarily blocked. The army also expected, through an agreement with Russia, to cut off supplies reaching China via the northwest. If this effort met with success, Japan would achieve, as a by-product of its first step in a southward advance, the strangulation of China. But at the same time the southern advance was to drive Japan inexorably from the China War into the Pacific War.

When France surrendered to Germany on June 17, 1940, Japan was presented with a favorable opportunity for its advance to the south. Within the Army General Staff there was strong support for the view that an immediate settlement of all pending issues should be forced upon the French authorities, who had hitherto adopted a temporizing attitude. On June 18, at a joint meeting of leaders of the Army Ministry and General Staff chaired by Army Vice Chief of Staff Sawada Shigeru, a heated discussion took place. One group headed by Operations Division Chief Tominaga Kyōji insisted upon a military invasion of French Indochina, while the Army Ministry took a more cautious position, arguing that such a course would be "against the spirit of the samurai." The meeting ended with the sole decision being to strengthen the blockade of Shanghai and Hong Kong. At a meeting of the Four Ministers Conference that same day Army Minister Hata Shunroku expressed the opinion that Japan should demand only that the French government cease sending military supplies to China and that the question of military operations not be raised unless the French refused.[2] Those advocating a more aggressive policy held their ground, however, and the foundations were laid for the later decision to launch a military invasion.

Before any action at all had been taken, French Ambassador Charles Arsène-Henry informed the Foreign Ministry on June 18 that the border between China and French Indochina had been closed the previous day. According to Arsène-Henry, Governor-General Catroux had been personally responsible for the decision, which was taken upon the ambassador's advice. Navy sources also indicate that General Tsuchihashi had put pressure on French officials in Tokyo to advise that the border be closed.

The Foreign Ministry thereupon decided to place before the French authorities a stronger demand than had been planned for June 18. In an interview with Arsène-Henry Vice Minister Tani Masayuki asked that the transit of all war materials cease permanently and that the embargo be insured by methods agreeable to Japan, such as sending a Japanese military commission to police the border. The next day Arsène-Henry asked Tani what articles Japan wanted stopped, since a permanent embargo on all materials would be impossible. He also agreed to the stationing of Japanese units to guard the frontier. Tani now expanded the embargo to cover the smuggling of Chinese goods stockpiled in French Indochina and all shipments for Kuangchou Bay ports. On the 22nd Arsène-Henry was given an organizational chart of the inspection unit, which was to include thirty officers and ten Foreign Ministry officials.[3] Total blockade of goods to China was to continue, he was told, until after an on-the-spot inspection to determine which articles were to remain on the embargo list.

Major-General Nishihara Issaku, who on June 25 was appointed to command the inspection unit sent to Indochina, was an honors graduate of the twenty-fifth class of the Army Academy in 1913. After completing the course of the Army War College, he had been sent to Tokyo Imperial University as a special student in the Faculty of Law. Thereafter he had been stationed at the embassy in France and on two occasions at the League of Nations. Thus, he was regarded as a soldier possessing a rich knowledge of international affairs and a member of the moderate group within the army. Not unexpectedly, he did not get along well with his classmate, the aggressive Operations Division Chief Tominaga, nor with the officers of the South China Army, who were scornful of his "diplomatic manner" and the fluency of his French.[4] Moreover, at the time of his appointment Nishihara was a member of the board of directors of the Army War College, while his new second in command, Colonel Koike Ryōji, headed the Second Section of the Inspectorate General of Military Education. Neither, therefore, was acquainted with the delicate internal factionalism within the army, an ignorance that was to give rise to many problems in the months to come.

The first difficulties were related to the contents of the directives given to Nishihara's unit by the chief and vice chief of the Army General Staff on June 23. These stated that their major task was to inspect cargo transported through French Indochina and, in addition, to conduct negotiations to obtain permission for the passage through French Indochina of the 22nd Army from Nanning and, if possible, the right to

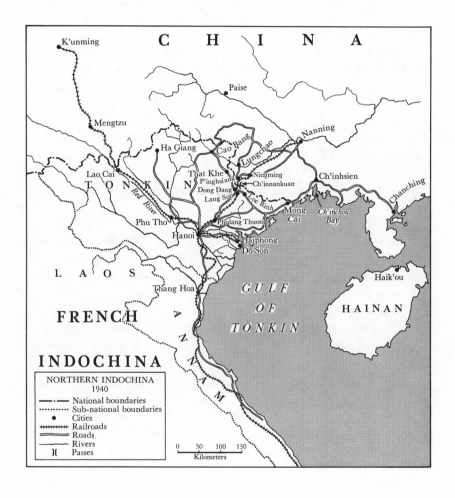

K'unming

C H I N A

Paise

Mengtzu

Ha Giang

Cao Bang

Nanning

Lungchao

Lao Cai

That Khe

Ningming

Ch'inhsien

Chanching

T O N K I N

P'inghsiang

Ch'innankuan

Red River

Dong Dang

Lang Son

Loc Binh

Phu Tho

Mong
Cai

Ch'inchou
Bay

Phulang Thuong

Hanoi

Haiphong

Haik'ou

Do Son

L A O S

Thang Hoa

GULF

HAINAN

FRENCH

OF

A N N A M

TONKIN

INDOCHINA

NORTHERN INDOCHINA
1940
—·— National boundaries
············· Sub-national boundaries
●   Cities
++++++ Railroads
═══ Roads
‒‒ Rivers
)(Passes

0   50   100   150
Kilometers

use air bases in Indochina. In explaining the directives, however, Operations Section Chief Okada Jūichi declared that the unit's primary mission was to secure permission by June 29 for the passage of troops; to this end, he said, Japan would not hesitate to use military force if necessary. When Koike pointed to the language of the directives, Okada responded, "Don't worry about semantics. Just interpret the orders in accordance with what I have said." But when on June 25 Nishihara made contact with the naval members of the commission, he was told that the item concerning the passage of troops had been eliminated from the navy's directives; moreover, with regard to the use of military force, the navy had demanded that, after any decision for military operations was taken, it be given two months for preparations. Nishihara was naturally surprised to find such a difference between the views of the two Operations divisions.[5] The fact was that the navy's views accorded closely with those of senior officers of the Army General Staff, the Intelligence Division, and the Army Ministry.

The directive on military passage had been deliberately dropped by the navy, which had been indignant upon learning that the army was preparing a separate secret directive when army and navy authorities were supposedly drafting joint instructions for the inspection unit. Thus, the instructions given to the head of the naval group, Captain Yanagisawa Kuranosuke, by Navy General Staff Vice Chief Kondō Nobutake instead related to the collection of operational data and information on China, especially the southwest and Chungking, to political activities aimed at drawing French Indochina into the Japanese camp, and to the conduct of subversive activities against the Kwangsi and Yunnan military cliques.

In this atmosphere of discord, the inspection unit left Haneda airport on June 26. Three days later they arrived in Hanoi, after being detained in Mingyeh by bad weather. On the 30th Nishihara began negotiations with Governor-General Georges Catroux.

Concerning the "major task," the embargo on military supplies, there were few problems, since French Indochina in principle had acceded to the Japanese demand, and inspectors were immediately dispatched to Haiphong and five other border posts. But over the additional aims of the mission—military passage and the use of military facilities—difficulties were expected.

At first the talks developed satisfactorily for Japan. On July 1 Catroux agreed to economic cooperation in return for Japanese acknowledgement of the territorial integrity of French Indochina, and the issue of border supervision was also resolved smoothly.[6] The French further agreed, on the 2nd, to the expulsion of the Chinese supervisors of military supply shipments to Chiang from French Indochina; on the 3rd, to the dispatch of investigators to leaseholds in Kuangchou Bay and to the transfer to Japan of stocks of materials originally destined for China; and on the 6th, to the extension of the submarine cable to Hanoi.

One reason the early negotiations went so well was the presence of Major P. Thiébaut, the French military attaché in Tokyo, who had accompanied the mission to Hanoi. The Japanese negotiators did not, however, anticipate Catroux's proposal at the July 4 session of a defensive alliance against Chiang in exchange for a Japanese pledge of the territorial integrity of Indochina.[7] This unexpected offer produced bewilderment in Tokyo. Members of the aggressive group within the army, who had urged the purchase of the Tonkin region,[8] now wanted to expand the proposal into an offensive-defensive alliance and, in addition, to require the French to promise cooperation not only against Chiang but against Britain as well.[9] Such cooperation was to include a military operation against K'unming and a wild scheme to provoke hostilities in the Shanghai International Settlement between Italy and France on the one hand and Britain on the other, thus bringing about the disarmament of the British forces. This idea, needless to say, was rejected. On July 7 the two vice chiefs of staff cabled Nishihara their approval of the proposal for a defensive alliance, adding: "In the name of joint defense, include in any agreement the utilization of military facilities and the right to station our troops in French Indochina."[10] As for a Japanese guarantee of Indochina's territorial integrity, they were prepared to state only that "we shall respect it." From this time on, Catroux grew suspicious and wary of Japan and in subsequent negotiations was less amenable to the Japanese demands.

On July 9 Catroux stated that he could not permit Japanese forces to be stationed in French Indochina or to utilize military facilities there because such concessions would amount to a Japanese occupation of French Indochina and would damage relations with the United States and Britain. Then, on the 11th he announced that further negotiations should be conducted with the French government, because he could not decide the issues on his own responsibility. With regard to the defensive alliance, he would have to receive instructions from France, since the proposal had been his personal idea. He also refused to extend the embargo to stockpiles of tungsten and antimony, which he said had been sold to the United States, and he requested that Japanese ships and planes not enter French Indochina without permission.[11]

At this point Colonel Satō Kenryō, the vice chief of staff of the South China Army (the so-called *Nami* or "Wave" Group), arrived from Canton to assist Nishihara in the negotiations. Satō had long been an ardent advocate of an attack on K'unming and had just returned from Tokyo, where he had presented a proposal for such an operation on behalf of the South China Army. To launch an attack into Yunnan province, it was necessary to obtain permission for the passage of troops via Haiphong and guarantees of supply and transport facilities. A defensive alliance, such as Catroux had proposed, would be to Japan's advantage, for it would enable a joint Japanese-French operation to be planned.[12]

On July 12 Satō and Nishihara met with Catroux, who was handed the following "Outline of a Japan-French Indochina Agreement" bearing the imprimatur of the South China Army:

Article 1: Japan and French Indochina agree to conduct joint operations against the government of Chiang Kai-shek.
Article 2: Basis of Joint Operations
  1) Japanese forces will attack China from French Indochina, while other Japanese forces will defend French Indochina jointly with troops of French Indochina.
  2) Troops of French Indochina will defend French Indochinese territory.
  3) In order to carry out such joint operations, French Indochina will provide Japan with rights of passage for Japanese troops and military supplies and with other necessary facilities.
  4) Japan will guarantee the independence of French Indochina and will cease military activities in French Indochina once the China Incident is settled.[13]

Despite Satō's strong urgings that he accept the proposal, Catroux insisted that he did not have the authority to determine such matters on his own. But he was also aware of the impossibility of an invasion such as Satō had proposed and knew that it was at total variance with Nishihara's intentions in the negotiations. Thus, while he evinced enthusiastic support for the plan and even offered to cooperate by setting up a supplementary supply system for the Japanese forces attacking China from Nanning,[14] he attempted to forestall an invasion from French Indochina by pointing out the difficulties involved. He provided aerial photographs to illustrate the difficult terrain that lay along the border between Yunnan and French Indochina, and on the 13th he made available an airplane so that Satō, Lieutenant-Colonel Arao Okikatsu of the Operations Section of the Army General Staff, and Commander Kami Shigenori of the Operations Section of the Navy General Staff could observe the situation along the border for themselves. When he saw the jungle-covered mountain ranges below, Satō too realized the impossibility of invading Yunnàn along the T'ienyueh rail line.[15]

The Operations Division of the Army General Staff and other staff officers of the South China Army had never been as enthusiastic about the proposed attack on K'unming as Satō. However, they saw the K'unming operation as a useful pretext for launching the southern advance. In the end, therefore, Catroux's cunning effort to keep Japanese troops out of Indochina failed. Moreover, after numerous visits to Hanoi, Satō was enchanted by the rich soil and excellent climate of Indochina and he became an ardent advocate of an advance into southern French Indochina.[16]

While the negotiations between Nishihara and Catroux were being conducted in Hanoi, in Tokyo the Army, Navy, and Foreign ministries were discussing the question of a politico-military and economic alliance with French Indochina. Just then the Yonai cabinet resigned, and on July 17 Prince Konoe Fumimaro formed his second cabinet, with the energetic Matsuoka Yōsuke as foreign minister. Matsuoka at once began negotiations with Ambassador Arsène-Henry on an agreement drafted by the Foreign Ministry on the 11th and agreed to by army and navy representatives on the 16th. Nishihara was ordered to conduct parallel talks on the subject in Hanoi. The terms of the proposed politico-military alliance were:

France will cooperate with Japan in establishing a New Order in East Asia and in reaching a settlement of the China Incident. In particular, at the present time France will permit the utilization of air bases in French Indochina (including the stationing of ground guard forces for this purpose) by Japanese military forces which will be dispatched for operations against China, and their passage through French Indochina. In addition, France will provide to the Japanese forces facilities necessary for the transport of arms and ammunition and other materials.

Japan will respect the territorial integrity of French Indochina.

In subsequent discussions debate centered upon the guarantee of French Indochina's territorial integrity, which Catroux had been so anxious to secure from Japan. On July 12 he had demanded that the foreign minister issue a statement or make a secret promise that the Japanese and French governments would cooperate 1) to maintain the status quo in French Indochina, 2) to prevent the extension of the European war to the Far East, and 3) to restore peace in East Asia.[17] But Matsuoka, no less than the aggressive faction within the army, was not prepared to give unnecessary promises, and on August 1 he himself opened talks with Arsène-Henry.

This left Nishihara in a difficult and uncertain position. He was further perplexed as to the true intentions of the army concerning the passage of military forces. Why had central headquarters been so adamant about the request? Was it a necessary prerequisite for the K'unming operation or the first step in a full-scale advance into French Indochina? The nature and specific details of military passage would differ depending upon its basic purpose, which would likewise affect the requirements for military facilities. And as the directives coming from various authorities in Japan had quite different implications, Nishihara found himself unable to proceed with the negotiations.

The report Nishihara cabled to Tokyo on July 25 revealed his indignation and exasperation. If Japan requested military passage without providing promises of territorial integrity, he stated, the negotiations were unlikely to produce satisfactory results. And if it nevertheless persisted in such extreme demands, it should make preparations for military operations while repatriating all Japanese civilians in French Indochina. If the French still refused to accede, Japan would have to use military force to obtain its demands.[18] Soon thereafter he was summoned to Tokyo by the General Staff, and on July 28 he left Hanoi, leaving Colonel Satō temporarily in charge of the negotiations.

Following the establishment of the Vichy government, Admiral Jean Decoux, the commander of French naval forces in the Far East, was appointed to replace Catroux as governor-general of French Indochina.

Catroux's acquiescence in the closing of the military supply route and his willingness to permit the stationing of the Japanese guard unit had produced dissatisfaction within his government, and by June 30 orders for his recall had been issued.[19] With Decoux's agreement, however, he continued his talks with the Japanese for three weeks, in an effort to prolong the negotiations.

On July 24 Catroux notified Nishihara of his resignation, and the first meeting between Nishihara and Decoux was held the same day. Nishihara's first impression of the new governor-general was of "an active military man, . . . a bureaucrat, and a very cautious man, obedient to the wishes of his government."[20] Decoux was to show more firmness than Nishihara's first impression had led him to believe.

At his first meeting with Nishihara, Decoux proposed that a committee be set up to continue the talks in place of the personal meetings that had hitherto been conducted. On July 27, when notified of Nishihara's temporary return to Japan, Decoux refused during his absence to continue discussions with Colonel Satō for a politico-military agreement. A day later he informed Satō in writing that he had no personal authority to conclude an agreement.

Irritated by Decoux's attitude, the excitable Satō reported to headquarters that he had decided to demand immediate acceptance of Japan's requests. In addition, he intended to repatriate the inspection unit and all Japanese residents in Indochina if no agreement with the French was reached, and he requested instructions concerning the timing of repatriation. Should Decoux continue his refusal to negotiate on the pretext that Satō was only an acting representative, he intended to repatriate the inspection unit immediately.[21]

Surprised and disturbed at the strong line Satō was taking, the military leaders in Tokyo informed him that fundamental policy would be decided when Nishihara had made his report, following further discussions between the army and navy. Repatriation would be decided upon and executed only by the central command. Satō cabled in reply that firm negotiations must be resumed as quickly as possible, because the talks were deadlocked and the conditions accepted by Catroux had gradually been set aside. He urged that August 5 be set as the deadline for resuming the negotiations, with a decision on repatriation being left to the man in charge of the negotiations. Headquarters responded that they would await the outcome of Matsuoka's talks with Arsène-Henry and reiterated that repatriation would be decided only by the central command.[22]

The firm attitude Satō adopted during Nishihara's absence was mainly the result of strong pressure by the South China Army, whose officers had criticized him for becoming "soft." The chief of staff, Major-General Nemoto Hiroshi, telephoned him daily to urge him to hold firm. Moreover, the time limit of August 5 had been suggested by staff officer Colonel Fujiwara Takeshi, who flew from army headquarters on July 31 to inform Satō that all preparations for military operations would be completed by that date.

The South China Army's Ambition

Let us turn at this point to examine the South China Army (the *Nami* Group), which was advocating such an aggressive policy in French Indochina. The commander at its headquarters in Canton was then Lieutenant-General Andō Rikichi, with Major-General Nemoto Hiroshi as chief of staff and Colonel Satō Kenryō as vice chief of staff. The Commander of the 22nd Army (the *Wa* or "Peace" Group) at Nanning, which was seized in November 1939, was Lieutenant-General Kunō Seiichi, with Major-General Wakamatsu Tadakazu as chief of staff. With them were the 5th Division (commanded by Lieutenant-General Nakamura Aketo), the 9th Brigade (Major-General Kusumoto Sanetaka), the 21st Brigade (Major-General Okamoto Shizuomi), and the Imperial Guard Division at Nanning (Lieutenant-General Iida Shōjirō).

The main force, the 5th Division, was famed for its toughness, having fought several important battles since the beginning of the war in China. Since the Nanning operation it had been conducting punitive expeditions against the Chinese forces aimed at securing the Ch'inning Road from Nanning to Ch'inchou Bay. Its strength in March 1940 was 25,271 men, increasing to 31,717 by the end of September, almost twice the complement of an ordinary division. The division's morale was excellent.

The purpose of the Nanning operation—to close the Kwangsi route for supplies to China—became less important following the development of the Paise route. Moreover, the condition of the Ch'inning Road was poor and guerrilla activities were prevalent. Thus the cost of supplying the division from the coast was high. To withdraw the Japanese forces without a specific reason, it was feared, would provide valuable propaganda for the Chinese. The Operations Division of the Army General Staff therefore suggested that the dispatch of the inspection unit to French Indochina be used as an opportunity to withdraw the 5th Division via French Indochina.[23] The real purpose of this plan, of course, was not merely to withdraw the 5th Division but to bring about the stationing of troops in northern French Indochina.

Such a maneuver had long been secretly contemplated within the Army General Staff. And on the pretext of "operational guidance," there had from the beginning been close liaison between the General Staff and the South China Army.

On June 10 Lieutenant-Colonel Takatsuki Tamotsu of the Operations Section, who had been dispatched to the South China Army from Tokyo, suggested that the 5th Division advance to Lungchou, and on the 13th General Nakamura was ordered to prepare the 5th Division for an advance to Lungchou and Ch'innankuan. On June 18, the day Arsène-Henry notified Japan of the voluntary closing of the Indochina border, the 21st Brigade left Nanning on the terrible road to Lungchou and Ch'innankuan.[24]

It is not clear precisely what "operational guidance" was given the South China Army by Takatsuki on this occasion. But a report based on hearsay information, sent to the central command by the 2nd China Fleet on June 19, read:

> The South China Army is first expected to occupy the border. Then it will demand, through diplomatic channels with accompanying demonstrations of military power, that all supplies to Chiang be stopped and that it be given the right to use the Yunnan railway for the K'unming operation. If these demands are not accepted, a military invasion of French Indochina will begin (mainly across the border but partly by sea), aiming at the occupation of French Indochina. The South China Army insists that such a military invasion will provide not only a quick solution of the China Incident but will also constitute the basis for a further southward advance. Its high morale tends to influence the central command toward its point of view.[25]

The South China Army had also drawn up a plan for an attack on Hong Kong and had begun constructing the air bases that would be required for such an attack.

The 21st Brigade occupied Lungchou on July 3 and Ch'innankuan on the 10th. On the 11th the 22nd Army ordered Nakamura to advance his division to Ningming to increase the pressure upon French Indochina, and to prepare for the occupation of Hanoi. The defense of Nanning was left to a brigade of the Imperial Guard Division when the 5th Division advanced to Ningming with the 9th Brigade on July 19.[26]

On July 20 at Ch'innankuan General Nakamura met with Nishihara, Acting General Mennerat, the French commander at Lang Son, and Major Thiébaut, who had come from Hanoi. It appeared to Nakamura that relations among the three were remarkably friendly. When he left Nanning, Nakamura had been told by 22nd Army Commander Kunō that the emperor desired that the Indochina border be strictly observed. Nakamura, however, was obsessed with the idea of a military occupation, and his troops had received rigorous daily training with this purpose in mind.

Although Nakamura was unaware of their contents, the plans cabled to Army Vice Chief Sawada by General Kunō on July 11 called for very severe measures toward the French. Nakamura's division, he said, would reach the border by July 20, at which point an ultimatum should be given to the Indochina authorities, whose "proposal for a defensive alliance is presumed to have been made in an effort to prolong the negotiations." The French, he concluded, "must permit the passage of Japanese forces as well as agree to the defensive alliance."[27] General Nemoto similarly pressed for an early conclusion of the negotiations. "Regardless of the outcome of the Yunnan operation or the details of preparations for it," he cabled on July 19, "we judge that it is urgent to secure the right to station troops in the name of that operation. The negotiations should be concluded sometime between July 22 and the end of the month, and the best time for a military invasion would be around the beginning of August, when military preparations will have been completed."[28] Thus, Nakamura advanced toward the border anticipating a war.

Not surprisingly, such an aggressive attitude on the part of the South China Army produced differences and friction with Nishihara, who pressed 21st Brigade Commander Okamoto for an explanation. Fearing that some disparity existed between the views of his commanding officer and central headquarters, General Nakamura at once asked Kunō to clarify the relationship of his troops to the Nishihara unit. "It is prohibited that the 5th Division contact the Nishihara unit or receive information from it," came the reply. "All information from that unit is to be referred to a level higher than the South China Army." The prohibition was so strict that Nakamura was required to take a written oath.[29] From then on all contact between the 5th Division and the Nishihara unit ceased. The antagonism that arose soon developed into a serious controversy.

Under these circumstances Colonel Satō arrived in Hanoi, followed on the 31st by Staff Officer Fujiwara with word that the 5th Division was prepared for an invasion at any time. The previous day General Nemoto had cabled Satō that central headquarters had "almost decided to use military forces." Satō was ordered to continue the negotiations on his own in Nishihara's absence, remaining in Hanoi until the invasion began. "We plan the military invasion of southern French Indochina at the next stage."[30] The telegram shows clearly the aggressive intentions of the South China Army and the arbitrariness and lack of self-control of the Army General Staff.

In his meeting with Decoux on August 2 Satō was stiff and uncompromising. He opened with a threat: "The Japanese side, in particular the South China Army, has been extremely offended by the recent impasse in the negotiations. Should this situation continue, conflict between Japan and France will be unavoidable. Only the formation of a political and military alliance will prevent a collision." Decoux's insistence that he had no authority to approve the passage of troops was nothing but an evasion of the issue, Satō continued. China was planning an invasion of French Indochina, and Japanese forces would then have to cross the border in self-defense, therefore the matter could not be prolonged.[31] However, Decoux was well aware of the internal split in Japan and failed to capitulate to Satō's threats, promising merely to study the situation further.

Meanwhile, by July 24 the main strength of the 5th Division had been mobilized at the border. On July 28 detailed planning for the invasion was begun at a conference of the chiefs of staff in Nanning, and three days later Nakamura was given the following order: "The 22nd Army will invade French Indochina. The 5th Division must complete necessary preparations by approximately August 10."[32] In Kwangtung three heavy bomber squadrons and one fighter squadron, totalling 130 planes, were placed on alert. But at the last minute the invasion was halted by order of the central command.

Preliminary Agreements Reached

With Nishihara in Tokyo and Satō's negotiations stymied by Decoux's calm and firm manner, the negotiating scene now moved to Tokyo, where Foreign Minister Matsuoka and Ambassador Arsène-Henry had begun talks on August 1. Matsuoka stated Japan's aims at their first meeting. His government, the foreign minister said, "desires that the government of French Indochina work with it in the establishment of a new order in East Asia and the settlement of the China Incident. In particular, it asks that the government of French Indochina permit the passage through its territory of Japanese troops sent for operations against China, the utilization of air bases in French Indochina, and the stationing of necessary guard units, and that it provide the facilities needed for the transport of Japanese troops and military supplies." Concerning Japanese trade and the entrance of Japanese nationals and products, he went on, they were to be granted "treatment equivalent to that given France, French nationals, and French products."[33] The first request was to be the basis for a politico-military alliance, the second for an economic alliance.

Matsuoka then gave further details of the Japanese requests. There was, he said, no intention of an invasion, since military passage and the related demands were needed for bringing about a solution of the China Incident and would be limited to what was required for the overthrow of the Chiang government. Arsène-Henry replied that, while Japan had not declared war against China, the request was equivalent to asking a neutral country to declare war on China. As for the economic alliance, would Japan in return give equal treatment to French nationals in Japan?

Matsuoka's words now assumed a belligerent tone: "Our present requests are based on absolute military necessity. Despite the fact that Japan has not declared war against China, if the French authorities do not accept our requests, we may be obliged to violate your neutrality . . . in the world today so many unexplainable things are happening that your agreeing to Japan's demands would not necessarily be interpreted as a declaration of war against China."[34]

On August 3 the French foreign minister informed Ambassador Sawada Renzō that France would accede if it could be done without humiliation. France might have been defeated, but it still took pride in its greatness as a nation. When he met with Matsuoka on the 6th, Arsène-Henry referred repeatedly to the Japanese "ultimatum" and urged that Matsuoka not force such a humiliation upon the French.

The French were particularly disturbed by Japan's failure to reaffirm the territorial integrity of French Indochina. Such a pledge was still at issue in debates within the Japanese government. We have already seen that Matsuoka refused to accept such a guarantee in the agreement drafted by the Army, Navy, and Foreign ministries in mid-July, and even when the navy asserted it had no objections to a guarantee, he did not change his position. Meeting with Arsène-Henry on the 15th, he was adamant that "France is at liberty to accept Japan's demands or not, but those demands are absolute." Even when told that France would accept all the demands if only an article guaranteeing French Indochina's territorial integrity were included, Matsuoka refused to compromise. He seemed resolved to force a breakdown of the talks. But in the end he gave way, and on the 30th an article purporting to "respect the territorial integrity of French Indochina" was included.

Details concerning the passage of troops and the utilization of military facilities were to have been stipulated in an official note from Vice Foreign Minister Ōhashi Chūichi given to Arsène-Henry on the 9th. But the note was vague and said nothing about routes of passage, numbers of troops, and so on, and Arsène-Henry complained that it gave the impression that an occupation of French Indochina was planned. After discussing the matter with the army and navy, the Foreign Ministry replied on the 10th that the troops would be transported through Tonkin; but it refused to give further details, insisting that such matters were "operational secrets."

In fact, Matsuoka himself did not know the details of the plans for troop passage, which were the exclusive prerogative of the supreme command, not even whether forces would be moved from north to south or from south to north. Despite this curious situation, the talks gradually came around to the main issues. The French position was set out on the 20th: provision of transport facilities would terminate as soon as the

China Incident was settled; troop passage was to be limited to specified areas near the border; other military issues were to be decided in on-the-spot negotiations, but the request for troops to guard the bases was rejected; in economic matters, Japan must be satisfied with third country treatment; Japan was to affirm the territorial integrity of Indochina.

The following day the Japanese position was detailed in a memorandum entitled "Details Concerning Military Demands," shown privately to Arsène-Henry by Europe-Asia Bureau Chief Nishi Haruhiko. This stated:

1) The number of air bases is to be at least three at all times.

2) Japanese military strength in Tonkin will not exceed 5,000 to 6,000, including the troops guarding the air bases, supply-transport forces for Japanese troops in China, and troops guarding the supply-transport forces.

3) The routes of passage for the China operation will be the Haiphong-Hanoi-Lao Cai and the Hanoi-Lang Son districts, and the number of troops involved in passage are not included in the restrictions set forth above.

4) The navy will be permitted to enter the port of Haiphong and to establish exclusive cable facilities.

In comparison with a plan prepared on the 16th by the navy, Nishi's demands dropped the guarantee of territorial integrity and added one air base and about 1,000 troops.

On the 25th Arsène-Henry called on Ōhashi to inform him that France had acceded to Japan's requests. Ōhashi pointed out that the use of air bases, the requirement concerning guard forces, and the routes of troop passage were not included in the official acceptance. Due to considerations of French dignity, these items could not be accepted formally, the ambassador replied, but they would be accepted in the field negotiations. He further requested that no public announcement of the agreement be made.

Ōhashi at once agreed not to publicize the agreement, and after conferring with the Army, Navy, and Foreign Ministry representatives he decided to accept the French scheme in principle. That evening Nishi presented Japan's "fourth plan" to Arsène-Henry. This was basically what the French had proposed earlier that day, with the addition of a concluding request "that the French government immediately issue the necessary orders to the authorities in the field."

After receiving further instructions from his government, Arsène-Henry replied on the 29th. In what was to be the final version of the agreement, the area in which facilities were to be provided to Japanese military forces was stipulated as being limited to "the Indochinese provinces along the Chinese border," as the Japanese version had provided; and in the directives to the commanders in the field, the facilities to be demanded were to be "limited to those items which are related to military operations in the Chinese provinces along the Indochina border." In addition, it was stated that the provision of facilities "does not have the character of a military occupation."

Japan accepted all these changes, and on August 30 the so-called Matsuoka-Henry Pact was concluded with the exchange of official statements between Matsuoka and Arsène-Henry. Although the negotiations had been conducted under the threat of action by the Japanese army in the field and a coercive attitude on the part of Matsuoka, Japan seems to have made a genuine effort to achieve a bloodless advance into French Indochina. In particular, at the final stage Japan acquiesced almost fully to the French demands. (See Appendix 2 for the full text of the Pact.)

Following the conclusion of the Matsuoka-Henry Pact in Tokyo on August 30, 1940, General Nishihara reopened negotiations with Governor-General Decoux in Hanoi. Three weeks had passed since Nishihara's return to Hanoi on August 9, and half a month since Colonel Satō had returned to Canton.

When Arsène-Henry reported on the 25th France's intention to accept an agreement, officials of the Army, Navy, and Foreign ministries at once began to discuss the on-the-spot negotiations. The first matter at issue was whether Nishihara should continue to head the negotiations or whether he should be replaced by the chief of staff of the South China Army, General Nemoto. In the end it was decided that Nishihara should remain in charge.[35]

The army and navy, however, were unable to agree on the instructions to be given to Nishihara. On August 27 Operations Division Chief Tominaga left for Hanoi, accompanied by Lieutenant-Colonels Arao Okikatsu and Miyama Yōzō and by Major Matsumae Misoo, and carrying to Nishihara a tentative draft plan from Imperial Headquarters.[36] Two days later the navy dispatched Lieutenant-Commander Shirahama Eiichi with a similar draft.

Imperial Headquarters had decided to send Tominaga to Hanoi to acquaint Nishihara with the developments that had taken place since his departure from Tokyo. In addition, Tominaga was to explain to him the details of the draft and assist him in the negotiations. As it turned out, Tominaga conducted negotiations entirely on his own, calling himself the representative of the army chief of staff.[37]

It is clear that Tominaga hoped to find a pretext to use military force in Indochina. This may be discerned from the fact that he stopped in Canton and brought Colonel Satō with him to Hanoi. Moreover, following a conference with Decoux on September 2, he showed to Satō alone a directive dated that same day from the army chief of staff bearing no headquarters number. The directive ordered, "The commander of the South China Army is to complete preparations as speedily as possible for an attack on northern French Indochina." It was signed by Prince Kan'in himself.[38]

Nishihara was uncertain how he was to proceed. He had gone back to Tokyo to ascertain the intentions of central headquarters but had found the internal situation so confusing that he returned to Hanoi concluding it would be best "not to make any definite decisions for the time being."[39] It is not surprising that he was easily swayed by aggressive young officers such as Tominaga.

The negotiations in Hanoi were resumed on the afternoon of August 30, when Nishihara and Tominaga showed Decoux the draft of an agreement based on the pact about to be concluded in Tokyo. Decoux, however, declined to negotiate on the ground that he had received no instructions from the Vichy regime. Nishihara demanded that, since the Tokyo pact would soon be approved, Decoux respond to the draft by the evening of September 2.

For two days Decoux held to his refusal to negotiate. Concluding that he had no intention of negotiating seriously, Tominaga on the evening of the 1st made up his mind that if a reply had not been received by the next evening, he, in the name of the chief of the Army General Staff, would "accuse the governor-general and the French authorities of insincerity, report to him our decision to undertake military operations, and warn him to evacuate all women and children from the Hanoi area within three days. At the same time we will request our consul-general to order all Japanese residents to withdraw from Hanoi." But when Arao asked the navy's representatives, Yanagisawa and Shirahama, to approve this decision, the two naval officers refused, saying that the use of force was a matter to be determined by imperial authority alone, not independently by officers in the field. Tominaga for the time being had to give up the idea of using force.

At 8:00 p.m. on September 2 a group of seven led by Tominaga went to the government offices in Hanoi to see Decoux. Tominaga, Satō, and Arao entered the conference room with Japanese swords in their hands, their eyes flashing. "We will meet you on the battlefield," Satō threatened Decoux, who was handed the following note: "The commander-in-chief of Japanese army and navy forces stationed in southern China has decided to station Japanese army and navy forces in French Indochina on and after September 5." This decision had been made by the officers on the spot alone. Decoux, however, was not intimidated, for he was aware of the internal circumstances on the Japanese side. He stated that instructions had arrived that evening from the Vichy government and he therefore wished to reopen negotiations the following day. After lengthy discussion, the Japanese finally agreed.

The next evening the French authorities presented the following draft pact to the Japanese:

1) The zone in which Japanese operations will be permitted is to be limited to the area north of the Red river. Japanese troops will be permitted to enter Hanoi.
2) Japanese troops in Tonkin must not exceed 25,000 in number.
3) Japan will pay all expenses involved in maintaining the troops stationed in Indochina.
4) Japanese troops may land only at Haiphong.
5) Japanese troops may use three air bases.
6) The installation of powerful permanent telegraph facilities will not be permitted, but the use of shipboard telegraph facilities is permissible.
7) Japanese troops are not to enter French Indochina until the final pact (covering detailed regulations, the date on which stationing is to begin, etc.) is concluded.
8) The following actions will be regarded as threatening actions, and if Japan undertakes them, France will take independent action and will stop the negotiations. (Such action will be taken if Japan violates the secret agreements.)
   a) Any attempt to cross the French Indochina border.

b) Assembly of troops near the French Indochina border.
c) Navigation by warships and commercial vessels in the coastal waters of French Indochina.
d) Flights over French Indochinese territory unless expressly authorized.

Except for the refusal to permit Japanese troops to enter Hanoi in item (1), this draft was accepted almost verbatim in the so-called Nishihara-Martin agreement concluded on September 4.

Tominaga, however, had decided that the French authorities were not "sincere" and resolved to carry out the earlier decision. On the 3rd he sent a wire to Tokyo charging, "The French are maneuvering to postpone the negotiations, and it does not appear that the problem will be settled easily. If no decisive action is taken on our part, they will make light of us. A decision is needed." Based upon his instructions and with the approval of Captain Yanagisawa and the South China Army, the wire continued, he had already informed Decoux on the 2nd that the stationing of troops would begin on the 5th. It concluded: "Otherwise our national prestige will be impaired. Pessimism concerning future developments is warranted."⁴⁰ That day the border inspectors were withdrawn to Hanoi and unofficial instructions were issued to prepare for the repatriation of Japanese residents.

Tominaga's wire came as a surprise to the authorities in Tokyo and antagonized the navy, which had been informed of his maneuverings by Yanagisawa and Shirahama. His claim to have received Yanagisawa's approval for his plan was denied by a message dispatched by Shirahama the day before, indicating their refusal to approve Tominaga's warning that armed force would be used. According to Shirahama, Tominaga had asked them not to report this to Tokyo. In the margin of this cable Operations Section Chief Nakazawa Tasuku wrote, "He is utterly absurd. I cannot but conclude that he is ambitious to obtain credit for himself."⁴¹ Such remarks testify to the navy's hostile feelings toward Tominaga.

Representatives of the navy and the army conferred immediately, then instructed Nishihara in the names of both vice chiefs of staff that the Foreign Ministry would issue a suitable warning to Arsène-Henry, instructions would be wired to Ambassador Sawada in France, and the German government would be requested through Ambassador Eugen

Ott in Tokyo to put pressure upon the Vichy government. In the meantime, no hasty action was to be taken and no troop stationing was to begin until an imperial order was issued.[42]

In the course of the army-navy discussions disagreement arose over the issue of troop stationing. The Operations Division of the Army General Staff asserted that an imperial order should be issued immediately, so that stationing could begin on September 5 and the troops on the spot would be able to operate freely. Army Vice Chief Sawada rejected this proposal, suggesting that Nishihara be instructed that "with regard to troop action, we are awaiting an imperial order based upon the Tokyo negotiations."[43] The navy, on the other hand, wanted the instructions to state: "Although it is permissible to use the stationing of troops as a diplomatic tactic, various conditions must be considered before it is carried out. If negotiations on the spot come to a standstill, final negotiations must be conducted by the central authorities." In the end, however, the formulation noted above was agreed upon.[44]

For the moment, Sawada avoided issuing the required imperial order. But he assumed that it was only a matter of time before armed force would be used, and from this time on his anxiety concerning events in French Indochina grew. On the evening of the 3rd he decided that if the French authorities attempted to delay the field negotiations, part of the 5th Division would be stationed in French Indochina; should the French resist, the full division would be ordered to carry out the operation. The stationing would begin around the 6th or the 7th. Sawada's plan was approved by Army Minister Tōjō Hideki and Foreign Minister Matsuoka. When he consulted the navy the next morning, however, the navy insisted it would need at least two weeks after the end of negotiations to make preparations. Meanwhile the delegates in Hanoi reported the French proposal of the 3rd, and the cabinet postponed a decision until the next day.[45]

The Army General Staff was worried that Japanese forces might cross the border without authorization from Tokyo, as the Korea Army had done at the time of the Manchurian Incident. It had therefore drafted a wire to the local forces explaining unofficially the government's intentions even before the cabinet had made its final decision.[46]

The negotiations in Hanoi were concluded at 11:00 p.m. on September 4, although a telegram anticipating the settlement was sent to

Tokyo at 5 o'clock that afternoon. The agreement was signed by Nishihara and General Maurice-Pierre Martin, the commander of the French forces in Indochina.

An order was now sent out to the 5th Division at the border to return to its base at Nanning. The order was not received, however, until 3:00 p.m. on the 5th, sixteen hours after the pact had been concluded. Why had it taken so long? The delay was to prove critical.

The Army Crosses the Border

The South China Army's 5th Division had been gathering north of the Indochinese border in anticipation of the order that a military stationing was to begin. Day after day it drilled in the hot weather, and as the negotiations in Toyko neared conclusion, newsmen gathered in the division's headquarters at Ningming. Soon General Nemoto too arrived. On August 27 General Nakamura wrote in his diary that "the day of battle is drawing near."[47]

Then, on the 31st, Tokyo informed the division that "an Indochina army will be organized by September 9, based upon a unit of the Imperial Guard Division." But the following day another cable ordered: "The entry of troops into French Indochina has been suspended. Stay at present positions and await further orders."[48]

Since the middle of August army authorities in Tokyo had been planning the establishment of an Indochina army, organized around the command staff of the 1st Brigade of the Imperial Guard Division, the 2nd Infantry Regiment of the same division, and other units. The new army would be sent to Indochina by sea, after which the 5th Division would withdraw through Indochina to Hainan. With the conclusion of the Matsuoka-Henry Pact, the stationing was expected to go forward smoothly; consequently the presence of the 5th Division was no longer necessary.

The 5th Division, however, had been waiting since June to occupy Indochina and was resentful that the Imperial Guard should now receive credit for the operation. According to Nakamura, some of the staff officers "turned pale with anger,"[49] and he had to warn his soldiers against rash actions.

Abruptly the situation changed once again. At 10:30 a.m. on September 4 the following order from the 22nd Army arrived:

1) Negotiations on the spot are at the point of breakdown.
2) The South China Army is about to complete preparations to invade northern French Indochina.
3) The 5th Division should prepare to destroy the opponent, to invade Hanoi swiftly, and to advance toward Lao Cai and Thanh Hoa in pursuit of the enemy.
   The date on which the advance is to begin will be given later.[50]

This order was based upon the unnumbered army order Tominaga had sent to the South China Army the day before. The 5th Division, however, had no way of knowing that it was not based on an order issued by the Army Division of Imperial Headquarters in Tokyo. It therefore prepared to take action any time after 0:00 hours on the 6th, and by the afternoon of the 5th a vanguard was advancing toward the deployment area near the border.

The genuine Order No. 452 of the Army Division (*tairiku-rei*) concerning the stationing arrived from Imperial Headquarters that day. It included the new Indochina Army commanded by Major-General Nishimura Takuma in the order of battle of the South China Army and instructed Commander Andō:

1) To perform its present duties, a part of the South China Army is to be stationed in northern French Indochina.
2) With the stationing of these troops, the troops occupying the Lungchou area may be withdrawn at an appropriate time.
3) Details will be provided by the chief of the Army General Staff.

That same day the Navy Division also issued an order (*daikai-rei*) to the commander-in-chief of the 2nd China Fleet: "to perform its present duties, a part of the fleet is to be sent to northern French Indochina." Simultaneously the Navy Division issued an instruction (*daikai-shi*) on the "Agreement between the Army and Navy High Commands Concerning the Stationing of Troops in French Indochina." Neither the orders nor the instruction was predicated on an entirely peaceful operation. The stationing was planned to be peaceful, but if force should prove necessary, it was permissible under the terms of the orders. Nor was it clear from the orders what was to happen if the negotiations broke down or were concluded just before the deadline. Furthermore, the army order was not accompanied by an instruction giving details of the operation. These failures were not corrected and were to cause great confusion when the actual stationing took place in late September.

The Nishihara-Martin Pact concluded on September 4 was merely an agreement concerning the "principal items relating to the Japan-French Indochina military accord." The date stationing was to begin, methods of transport, nature of bivouacking, means of supply—all these details remained to be negotiated, and the stationing was not to commence until they had been settled. This was clearly stipulated in the Nishihara-Martin Pact, which also provided that if Japan took threatening action during the negotiations, the pact would be nullified.

Throughout the day on the 5th Nishihara's delegation and a representative from the French side drew up a tentative draft of the detailed regulations on which official negotiations were to be held the following day. Although the army and navy command had agreed that the stationing would begin on a date to be decided by the commander of the South China Army and the commander-in-chief of the China Fleet, the Japanese side now demanded that the negotiations be concluded by the 6th and that the time be fixed for the stationing to begin. But at this point the 5th Division was reported to have crossed the border, and the negotiations were back where they had started.

On the afternoon of the 6th Colonel Satō was about to leave for Canton to begin the process of troop stationing, when he was informed that at approximately 12:40 p.m. a battalion at Ch'innankuan had crossed the border near Dong Dang and penetrated some 2 kilometers into Indochina. Satō and Arao flew immediately to the spot, where they found the Japanese forces had already withdrawn without bloodshed upon receiving a protest from the French army. Thereupon Satō went to Ch'innankuan and demanded an explanation from the battalion commander, Lieutenant-Colonel Morimoto Takuji.[51]

The 22nd Army had drawn an off-limits line on the Chinese side of the border to avoid any transgression of the border. Morimoto, who had been ordered on the 5th to return to his original post, decided to reconnoiter around the fort at Dong Dang, where a night attack had originally been scheduled, to acquire knowledge of the area for the future. He had therefore led his entire battalion across the line and advanced to the highlands near the border. In the process, however, they had become lost and halted. Just then a French army officer arrived and warned Morimoto that they had crossed the border, whereupon Morimoto ordered his troops to withdraw. He had, he claimed, no intention of crossing the border.

Both Satō and 5th Division Commander Nakamura were astonished at Morimoto's adventurism. Nakamura concluded that the lieutenant-colonel must have been "out of his mind . . . insane, wandering about in a daze,"[52] and he ordered him sent for psychiatric tests. Nakamura himself offered his resignation to the army authorities. Morimoto was courtmartialed by the South China Army at the order of Army Minister Tōjō,[53] and both Andō and Nakamura as well as Morimoto's brigade and regimental chiefs were removed from their commands once the issue of troop stationing had been finally settled.

The battalion's action provided the French side with a pretext for suspending the negotiations, and on the morning of the 7th Decoux told Nishihara and Tominaga that he would have to obtain new instructions from Vichy before the talks could continue. When the Japanese argued that an error made by a single military unit ignorant of the conclusion of the pact should not be a cause for ending the negotiations, Decoux simply quoted the terms of Article 8 of the pact. Tominaga had no recourse but to accept the fact that the negotiations were at an end. He and his party left immediately for Tokyo, while Colonel Satō returned to Canton.

Leaders in Tokyo now decided that no effort would be made to resume the negotiations until concurrence had been reached on the details of a final agreement. By September 13 army and navy representatives, with advice from Tominaga, who had returned on the 11th, had drawn up a plan entitled "On the Future Management of the French Indochina Problem," which was approved by the Four Ministers Conference on the afternoon of the 13th. The plan was:

1) Japan will express regret for the crossing of the border by its forces on September 6 and will state that action has been taken voluntarily against the persons responsible for the incident. At the same time we will strongly censure the authorities of French Indochina, whose procrastination in the negotiations was the cause of this incident. It will be announced to the French ambassador in Japan and the governor-general of

French Indochina that the stationing of Japanese military forces will begin at 0:00 hours on September 22 (Tokyo time), based upon the agreement reached in Tokyo on August 30 and upon the pledge given by Arsène-Henry to Ōhashi on August 25. It will further be stated that the stationing is to be carried out peacefully. We will demand that they cooperate in concluding an agreement on details of the stationing, in accordance with the aforementioned agreement and pledge and with the agreement concluded on the spot on September 4.

2) The empire's forces will be stationed in Indochina, beginning at 0:00 hours on September 22, by peaceful means. The stationing will be carried out regardless of whether the negotiations on the details have been concluded or are still in progress at that time. Japanese residents in French Indochina will be assembled at Haiphong and Saigon prior to the stationing in order to be withdrawn from the country at any time.

3) If the troops of French Indochina offer resistance, military force will be used.[54]

In short, it had been determined that the stationing would begin on the 22nd, regardless of the outcome of the negotiations.

Various problems still remained, some of which should have been noticed when the 5th Division crossed the border. For example, the new policy did not affirm that the stationing would be carried out in accordance with the terms of the agreement should negotiations be concluded before the 22nd, although perhaps this was thought self-evident. The fact that the deadline for concluding the negotiations was the same as the time set for beginning the stationing would create no problems if no agreement was reached. But how would word reach the troops if a settlement came just before the deadline? This matter was not considered. Matsuoka obviously approved the plan. Why did he not point out the deficiencies that should have been detected by someone with even the most elementary knowledge of diplomacy? It remained for the emperor to ask the obvious question. Having listened to the reports of the prime minister and the army and navy chiefs, the emperor turned to Prince Kan'in: "What will you do if the negotiations are concluded just before the deadline?" "Then a peaceful stationing will of course be carried out," Kan'in replied. Thereupon the emperor gave his reluctant approval.[55]

These ambiguities were carried over into Army Order 458 issued by Imperial Headquarters immediately after imperial approval had been obtained and into the joint agreement that formed the basis for the instructions drawn up by the Army and Navy divisions of Imperial Headquarters. This agreement was more detailed than the instructions issued but not executed at the beginning of the month. It stated that the objective was "to station troops in Tonkin province peacefully, to establish bases for the operations against China, and to shut off the supply route to China. But if the troops of French Indochina resist, Japan will exercise military force." The route the troops were to follow was also stipulated: "First, the main force will begin the stationing from Ch'innankuan by land; thereafter additional forces will land by sea. If military operations are necessary, troops other than those referred to above will land swiftly near Thanh Hoa." Tonkin province was specified as the major area of ground operations.

Based upon the imperial order of September 5, both the agreement and the instructions were phrased so as to be applicable to both a peaceful and a forceful troop stationing. While they seemed to expect the operation to be completed peacefully, in reality it was assumed that ultimately force would have to be used. Therefore, the peaceful stationing was to begin at 0:00 hours on September 22, with full preparations for combat having been made. Should the French Indochinese troops resist, military force would be used; if no resistance was offered, a peaceful posture would be adopted. This complicated procedure was required by the circumstances.

Simultaneously with Order 458, the following instruction was issued to the commander of the South China Army:

1) If the stationing is completed peacefully, the areas in which troops are stationed shall be limited to those around Hanoi and Haiphong.

2) Troops stationed in French Indochina shall be particularly careful to observe strictly the military code, so that they will favorably impress the French Indochina authorities and enable future operations in French Indochina.

3) Other details will be transmitted on the spot by Major-General Tominaga, chief of the Operations Division.

In specifying the region around Hanoi and Haiphong as the areas in which troops would be stationed, this instruction, like the army-navy high command agreement providing for a stationing from Ch'innankuan, completely ignored the Nishihara-Martin Pact. It reflected the intentions of the extremist faction within the Army General Staff, which hoped to take advantage of the border-crossing incident to bring the negotiations back to the terms of the Matsuoka-Henry Pact. In addition, Major-General Tominaga, one of the strongest advocates of such a course, was again sent to Indochina with responsibility to direct the delicate adjustment in relations between the diplomatic and military commands, guided by an imperial order containing the deficiencies we have noted above.[56]

On September 14 Tominaga left Tokyo for Hanoi by way of Canton. He was accompanied by Colonel Nakayama Motoo, chief of the General Staff Organization and Mobilization Section, Colonel Karakawa Yasuo, chief of the Europe-America Section, and Lieutenant-Colonel Arao, and by Lieutenant-Commander Shirahama of the Navy General Staff. On the 16th they transmitted the details of the stationing to the leaders of the South China Army. During this meeting Tominaga ordered Colonel Watanabe Kumeichi, chief of staff of the 5th Division, to rise and, with emphatic gestures, ordered him to accomplish the stationing without fail, irrespective of whether it was carried out following a successful conclusion of the negotiations, the negotiations had failed, or resistance was offered, in which case he should destroy the opposing forces and carry out the stationing.[57] He also distributed a document which, to judge from its style,[58] he himself had drawn up, without the approval of the army leadership in Tokyo. This ordered:

1) Method of troop stationing in French Indochina and related matters:
   a) If the authorities of French Indochina accept our demands completely and if there is sufficient time to transmit and change orders to all forces prior to the date of the stationing, only those forces dispatched to French Indochina by sea will be sent into the area.
   b) If the French Indochina authorities accept our demands before the time set for the stationing but there is not sufficient time to transmit and change orders, or if the French Indochina authorities do not accept our demands by the time set, troop stationing will begin in accordance with the operations plans approved by the emperor yesterday afternoon [September 15, although imperial approval was actually given on the 14th].
   c) The date upon which stationing will begin is any time after 0:00 hours on September 22 (Japan time), the exact date and time to be decided through consultations between the commander of the South China Army and the highest commanding officer of the China Fleet. The stationing will not be delayed any more than necessary, taking into account the general situation.
   d) In any case, it is to be carried out as peacefully as possible. But

should French Indochinese troops offer resistance, we will not hesitate to use military force to achieve our objectives.

e) After the objectives of the stationing have been achieved, troops
should be concentrated within important areas such as Hanoi and
Haiphong.

2) Objectives of the stationing:

a) To establish the bases necessary for our strategy of a China offensive.

b) To strengthen the operation to close the southwestern supply
route. (Terms such as "occupation" should not be used in discussing the objectives of this operation.)[59]

In answer to a question from Watanabe, Tominaga stated that the
peaceful stationing envisioned in section 1-a could hardly be expected.
Moreover, he underlined the situation set forth in 1-b, that if there was
not sufficient time to change orders already dispatched, a forceful stationing would be carried out even though the negotiations had concluded successfully.[60] With regard to the last point, Tominaga told Colonel Satō:

Major-General Nishihara will deliver to the office of the governor-general
the details concerning the stationing in the form of an ultimatum. The
time limit for reply will be twelve hours prior to the beginning of the stationing. If they have not replied by noon on September 21 or if they
propose amendments, we will regard this as a rejection of our proposal. If
by noon they answer that they accept our proposal completely, then a
peaceful stationing will be carried out. Otherwise a forceful stationing will
be carried out.[61]

Tominaga had advanced the deadline by twelve hours ahead of that set
by the Four Ministers Conference. His remarks were totally unauthorized and differed significantly from the view of central headquarters.

The South China Army, however, decided that a margin should be
allowed between the negotiating deadline and the time the troop stationing was to begin. It therefore directed that the stationing would
commence at 0:00 hours on the 23rd, twenty-four hours later than the
original plan.

That same day the leaders of the South China Army and the 2nd
China Fleet met to discuss the troop stationing. The army had planned
that the ground forces would begin operations at 0:00 hours on the 23rd,
and the sea forces before dawn on that date plus one day, that is, on the

24th. The navy, however, stated that there were powerful defenses at Do Son (southeast of Haiphong), where the troops were expected to land, thus the stationing there would have to be delayed briefly in order to allow for softening-up operations. The two sides were unable to reach agreement at this time.[62]

Commander Kami Shigenori of the Operations Section of the Navy General Staff, who was as aggressive as Tominaga, participated in the conference. In order to avoid discussions with the chief of staff of the 2nd China Fleet, Hara Chūichi, and staff officer Ōi Atsushi, who had taken a somewhat negative attitude to the stationing, he ordered Sugiura Kajū, the senior member of the fleet staff, and two others to attend the conference on the pretext that it was merely a preliminary meeting and therefore should involve lower staff personnel. Kami then thrust upon those present his plan for the stationing and immediately departed for Tokyo.[63] When the leaders of the 2nd China Fleet studied Kami's proposed plan, they discovered that it allowed insufficient time for the scheduled operations and, moreover, that it assumed a forceful stationing would be required. The leaders of the fleet were much offended by this plan, and it is here that the roots of the "desertion" mentioned earlier are to be found.

Negotiations Concluded

Negotiations between Nishihara and the French authorities had been suspended since the Morimoto battalion had crossed the border on September 6. On the 16th Tominaga's party arrived in Hanoi, and the negotiations were reopened the next day.

Tominaga showed Nishihara and Koike the instructions bearing the stamp of the army chief of staff and insisted in a high-handed manner that the negotiations should thenceforth be conducted in accordance with his plan, which was:

1) Japan will express regret at the border crossing incident.
2) The military demands to be presented to French Indochina will be those agreed to on August 30.
3) Negotiations in Hanoi will end on the morning of September 20. Therefore we will await in Haiphong the reply of the French authorities.

4) If a successful conclusion of the negotiations is not anticipated, the withdrawal of Japanese residents will begin on September 19.

He also explained that since Japanese forces had already been ordered to prepare for the stationing (the 5th Division had begun preparations on the 17th), if the negotiations were not concluded by the 18th, a forceful stationing would be carried out regardless of developments in the negotiations thereafter.

On the afternoon of the 17th the draft of a military pact was finally presented to the French negotiators. Under its terms the number of troops was increased from 5,000 to 6,000 to 25,000, five rather than three air bases would be utilized, and Hanoi and Haiphong were included in the stationing area. Tominaga obviously intended to ignore both Franco-Japanese pacts as well as the decision of the Four Ministers Conference.

The leaders of the army, the navy, and the Foreign Ministry in Tokyo were astonished when they received reports of these developments. Instructions were immediately sent out in Matsuoka's name ordering suspension of any withdrawal of Japanese residents, and Army Vice Chief Sawada gave orders that the Nishihara unit was not to be withdrawn on the 20th. Army Minister Tōjō was particularly angry and attempted to restrain the hotheads on the General Staff. He wrote a personal note saying: "Orders must be issued that even if the troop stationing is delayed, it is to be carried out peacefully. For this reason it does not matter if the stationing is delayed for two or three days." And he instructed the Nishihara unit to "remain on the spot and continue negotiations to the end." Should they meet death as a result, he concluded, "the central command would consider it unavoidable."[64]

The Operations Division of the Army General Staff, which was supporting Tominaga's policy, complained that Sawada's indecisiveness was allowing the General Staff to be pushed around by Army Minister Tōjō. The division's diary contains the following entry: "In recent days the army minister has encroached upon the prerogative of the supreme command too much. . . . He acts for the chief of the General Staff, and the vice chief is just like a second vice army minister."[65]

But despite the opposition within the General Staff and in Hanoi, Japan's policy on troop stationing was beginning to move toward making concessions, under the impetus of the Army Ministry and the navy.

Suspecting that certain elements within the army were trying to force a military operation in Indochina, the navy opposed the presentation of any demands that might result in a breakdown of the negotiations.[66] Then, on the 17th, in the Four Ministers Conference, Foreign Minister Matsuoka asked for a postponement of any deadline in the stationing until after the signing of the Tripartite Pact was officially announced, which he expected to be by September 21. He believed the pact would serve to deter any American intervention in Indochina. Tōjō and Navy Minister Oikawa Koshirō were willing to postpone the stationing for two days, but they met with opposition from both General Staffs, and in the end it was agreed that the stationing would begin at 0:00 hours on September 23. It was also decided that Matsuoka would officially inform Arsène-Henry of the date of stationing on the 19th rather than the 17th.

The South China Army had already planned to wait twenty-four hours after the deadline had passed before actually beginning the stationing, in order to avoid any confusion arising from the ambiguities that marked the earlier decision. But the possibility of confusion still remained, for both the negotiation deadline and the commencement of the stationing had been postponed for twenty-four hours.

The first instructions based upon this decision were delivered to Nishihara on the morning of the 19th. He was already confronted with a difficult decision: whether to follow the orders of the central command or those of Tominaga, a late-comer to Hanoi but exercising the authority of the army chief of staff. Now, one after another, he received instructions from the navy to avoid any breakdown of the negotiations, from the Foreign Ministry to hold up any withdrawal of Japanese residents, and from the Army General Staff to work for a peaceful solution and a stationing carried out by the Nishimura unit alone. And the next day a wire from both vice chiefs ordered that "as in the original plan, the negotiations should be carried out on the basis that no more than 5,000 to 6,000 soldiers will be stationed."

By this time considerable advance toward agreement in the negotiations had been made, but Decoux still rejected, on the grounds of orders from Vichy, the demand that the number of troops be increased.[67] By noon on the 20th Japanese residents had been withdrawn to ships in Haiphong harbor, and that afternoon Tominaga's group left for Haik'ou (Hoihow) harbor on Hainan, leaving only Nishihara and four other negotiators in Hanoi.

That evening General Martin made the following proposals to Nishihara:

1) A peaceful stationing through Haiphong would be permitted, beginning at 6:00 a.m. on September 23.
2) The passage of troops from Lang Son would be permitted, but details would be negotiated later. Stationing without advance consultation would not be permitted.
3) Troops should not be stationed in the city of Hanoi.
4) Five air bases, including that at Hanoi, might be used.
5) Any stipulation that Japanese troops would exercise military force if French Indochinese troops offered resistance was to be absolutely rejected.

These proposals showed that the French were anxious to reach agreement, but there was still a wide gap between them and Tominaga's demands. Nishihara now decided to seek instructions directly from the chief of the Army General Staff, and he immediately telegraphed Tokyo asking what response he should make to the French proposals. The next morning, with the deadline approaching, he and his companions left for Haiphong, where Tokyo's reply was received that afternoon:

1) The date and time stationing will begin is to be decided independently. Should the other party accept our demands, however, the above rule will not apply.
2) The number of troops should be limited to 5,000 to 6,000, as previously determined. The negotiations should not be broken off over this question alone.
3) There should be no stipulation that military operations will be conducted if the other side offers resistance to the stationing.

Thereupon Colonel Koike, Navy Captain Chūdō Kan'ei, and Minoda Fujio (Yosano Shigeru's successor as representative of the Foreign Ministry) left for Hanoi and reopened negotiations with Decoux's aide-de-camp, Captain Jouan.

Despite further concessions by Japan, who agreed to withdraw the demand that the 5th Division be among the troops stationed in Indochina and that troops be stationed in the city of Hanoi, the talks soon became deadlocked once more when Jouan requested that one air base be eliminated and that the stationing be postponed for one day. At midnight the Japanese delegates returned to Haiphong, and Nishihara decided that Japanese residents would have to be evacuated as planned. By the morning of the 22nd all Japanese had embarked for Hainan. Then, at 1:00 p.m. (Japan time, here and in the following account) Nishihara received a telephone call informing him that General Martin had signed the Japanese draft proposal, which was brought to Haiphong by Jouan at 2:30. Nishihara, however, was uncertain whether he should accept it, since the question of the passage of troops from Ch'innankuan was left for later negotiations. But the time for the stationing to begin was drawing near and Tokyo had just the day before expressed the strong hope that it would be completed peacefully, therefore he finally decided to agree. At 4:30 p.m., just 7½ hours before the deadline, Nishihara affixed his signature.

The Pact, based upon the Nishihara-Martin agreement of September 4, provided for: 1) The use of four air bases in Tonkin province—Gialiam airfield at Hanoi, Lao Cai, Phu Lang Thuong, and Phu Tho; 2) The stationing of up to 6,000 of certain contingents of Japanese troops for the purpose of guarding air bases and supplies, the area of stationing to be near the air bases and not in the city of Hanoi. Troops were to be landed at Haiphong, but no warships were permitted to approach the coast; 3) The passage of up to 25,000 Japanese troops through Tonkin province north of the Red river, with the date of passage, route from the border to Haiphong, and method of transportation to be decided in consultations between Japan and French Indochina.[68]

The negotiations had finally been concluded, but little time remained before the stationing was to begin. The forces involved must be told immediately that their operations were to be carried out peacefully. Already, on the 20th, the army and navy vice chiefs had underlined this point in instructions to Nishihara: "If negotiations are concluded by 0:00 hours on the 23rd, every precaution should be taken to inform the South China Army and the fleet, so there will be no cause for regret."[69] In particular, orders had to reach the 5th Division at the northern border as soon as possible, since that unit was no longer to be involved in the stationing and it was now necessary to make arrangements only for its passage through Tonkin to the coast. Major Ariga Jingorō of the inspection unit of the supervisory commission flew to Ch'innankuan immediately after the agreement was signed, and by 8:40 p.m. the news had been transmitted to an advance corps of volunteers there; Division Commander Nakamura received word around 11 o'clock.[70] The French Indochinese army also acted with dispatch to avoid any incident, and by

8:00 p.m. the French Indochinese border guard facing the Japanese forces at Dong Dang had been informed.

The army command in Tokyo was cabled at 1:30 p.m. that an agreement was imminent, and at 5 o'clock word of the successful conclusion of the negotiations was telegraphed from a destroyer anchored in Haiphong harbor. The former arrived in Tokyo at 2:35 and the latter at 6:05. Both were transmitted to the leaders of the Army General Staff, and a congratulatory wire signed by both chiefs of staff was immediately sent to Nishihara. The navy, however, received word first, for 1½ hours before Nishihara's second cable arrived, the Navy General Staff had been informed by Captain Chūdō. Also informed at the same time were the commanders of the South China Army, the 22nd Army, and the 2nd China Fleet. Thus, news that the pact had been signed should have been received by all the parties concerned six or seven hours before the time fixed for the beginning of troop stationing.

Why, then, was the order to halt the stationing not delivered to Nakamura until 40 minutes after stationing was to begin, that is, at 0:40 a.m. on the 23rd, when the attack on Dong Dang fort had already commenced?

The Army Moves Again

The fact that an agreement had been signed had reached Nakamura and 22nd Army Chief of Staff Wakamatsu by 11 o'clock. Thus, they should have known that only those forces dispatched to Indochina by sea were to be used in the stationing, which was now to be conducted peacefully. Upon receiving the news, however, Nakamura became agitated for, he explained, "I was strictly ordered that our corps was not to receive any instructions concerning troop dispositions from Major-General Nishihara. . . . I was even ordered to take a written oath on this matter." Continued Nakamura: "Particularly when my troops were deployed over a vast battlefield, the muzzles of our guns already aimed at the enemy, how was I to put into effect word arriving just one hour before we were to start shooting?" At 3:20 p.m. he had accompanied Major Yamada Yoshiji, a staff officer of the 22nd Army, and Major Yokoyama Hikosane, a member of Nishihara's commission, to a meeting at the border with officers of the French Indochinese army, who were given a final note concerning the stationing of Japanese forces in Indochina. And from the

22nd Army he had received orders that "X-day is September 23." The order for commencing a stationing by force had therefore been issued. Nakamura did not, however, think he should ignore Nishihara's report completely, so he asked Wakamatsu for advice. But Wakamatsu failed to give him any answer and shortly thereafter left for army headquarters in Ningming.

Was it then necessary to send an order down the chain of command—Imperial Headquarters to South China Army to 22nd Army to the 5th Division—in order to halt the military operations? It would have been difficult, following such a procedure, for an order to reach the terminus of the line by 0:00 hours on the 23rd, but given the capabilities of Japanese army communications at the time, it would not have been impossible. Moreover, the 22nd Army could have received the order from Imperial Headquarters simultaneously with the South China Army, and there was a telephone facility between 22nd Army headquarters and the 5th Division. But Imperial Headquarters did not utilize such convenient methods.

One reason for this was that the Operations Division of the Army General Staff wanted a military stationing and, apparently, deliberately sabotaged delivery of an order. A more important reason, however, was that Vice Chief Sawada judged that since Tominaga had been given the power to halt a forceful stationing, he did not now need to dispatch another army instruction from Imperial Headquarters.[71] Sawada did send a telegram in the name of the chief of the Army General Staff to South China Army Commander Andō, ordering, "Since the French Indochinese authorities have accepted our demands, the only troops to be stationed will be the Nishimura corps."[72] But this order was not issued as an army instruction of Imperial Headquarters and therefore was not binding on Andō's operational direction. A warning was also sent from the Navy General Staff to the commander-in-chief of the China Fleet lest any conflict occur as a result of a delay of orders.

As the time for the stationing to begin approached, combat command headquarters were established at Haik'ou on Hainan, where on the 20th Commander Andō and essential staff members of the South China Army command were joined by Tominaga and his party. Tominaga had instructed the South China Army that a military stationing would commence if the negotiations had not been concluded twelve hours before the deadline. But when noon on the 22nd arrived, Andō was reluctant to issue the order lest an agreement be reached even at that late hour. Finally, at 4 o'clock he ordered the commencement of military operations. This occurred after Nishihara had reported to Tokyo that an agreement was about to be concluded but before he telegraphed that it had actually been signed.[73]

When word of the agreement arrived, therefore, the South China Army was faced with the problem of nullifying the order immediately and substituting a peaceful stationing for military operations. In addition, at 7:00 p.m. Sawada's wire in the name of the army chief of staff came in, ordering that only the forces under Nishimura were to be stationed, not the 5th Division under Nakamura.

A similar cable was delivered to staff officer Ōi of the 2nd China Fleet, who went at once to the combat headquarters at Haik'ou to consult on the method of sea transport. There he found Chief of Staff Nemoto, Vice Chief Satō, staff officer Fujiwara, and Lieutenant-Colonel Arao discussing Sawada's cable. Unhappy with the idea of halting the military stationing, they were considering sending back the wire, since they were not bound by any instructions not issued as an order or an instruction of the Army Division of Imperial Headquarters.[74]

Tominaga, meanwhile, had been with Andō since noon, urging that the military stationing continue as planned. When word of the agreement arrived, followed by the wire from Sawada, Andō hesitated again. Exasperated, Tominaga flew to Canton and sent the following wires to Nishihara and Vice Chief Sawada:

> To Major-General Nishihara:
> 1) We were all surprised to hear that an agreement had been reached after preparations for the mobilization of troops had been completed. Under the circumstances, many errors can be anticipated.
> 2) Since we do not know the contents of the agreement, nothing can be done about it. Send the text and details of the agreement immediately to the commander of the South China Army.
> 3) Telegram 477 from Hanoi ignored the time limit and restricts the methods of stationing that have already been decided upon. It should not be enforced recklessly in accordance with your judgment alone. The commander of the South China Army is of the same opinion as I on this matter.

> To the Vice Chief of the General Staff:
> 1) Returned from Haik'ou to Canton at 7:00 p.m. and read Army General Staff telegram 79.

2) In order to halt an operations order issued by a commander under the direct authority of the emperor, send an imperial order or an army instruction of Imperial Headquarters based upon an imperial order. Although I previously sent the same wire to you from Haik'ou, since it may have been delayed I am sending it to you again. It is my belief that an instruction of the chief or the vice chief of the General Staff not properly authorized will cause confusion in the supreme command in the future.

3) I expect the contents of the agreement reached to be reported immediately.

The tone of Tominaga's telegram was so hostile that Sawada's subordinate refrained from showing it to his chief. But whatever the reason, Sawada's expectation that Tominaga would halt the military stationing was betrayed.

At South China Army headquarters the argument raged on. Discontented staff officers strained the interpretation of existing regulations to support their contention that a new order or an instruction based on such an order would have to be issued by the Army Division of Imperial Headquarters before plans for the military stationing could be changed. In addition, they planned to negate such an order, should it be sent, by arguing that it arrived too late to put into effect.

About this time Vice Admiral Takasu Shirō, commander-in-chief of the 2nd China Fleet, anchored his flagship, the *Chōkai*, at Haik'ou harbor and came ashore to discuss the situation with his old friend Andō. His arguments proved effective, and finally around 9:00 p.m. Andō resolved to issue a district army order to halt the military stationing.

The order arrived at 22nd Army headquarters at Ningming about 10:00 p.m., an hour after it was issued, yet it did not reach 5th Division Commander Nakamura until 0:40 a.m. despite the existence of telephone communications. Some 2½ hours had been wasted.

Nakamura had left his headquarters at P'inghsiang by car sometime after 11:00 p.m. on September 22 and at midnight was standing on the border south of Ch'innankuan, looking across to the fortress of Dong Dang. At 0:00 hours on the 23rd he gave the command to advance to Colonel Miki Kichinosuke, head of the advance corps, who was standing beside him.[75] The barriers were removed and the waiting Japanese forces rushed toward Dong Dang in the face of the fire of the French Indochina army.

Forty minutes later an express messenger from command headquarters in the rear arrived bearing an order from the 22nd Army: "The Nakamura division should cease its advance and return to its side of the border via an appropriate route." Nakamura has recorded that he, his subordinate staff officers, and even his orderly "were so shocked that no one uttered a word. All were gazing at me with pathetic faces." Nakamura immediately drafted a reply to General Kunō, pleading: "For the sake of the glorious history of His Majesty's army and this army corps, and given present circumstances, allow us to secure our present position so that we will not have to retreat, turning our backs to the foe. Then we will await the next order. This I beg you with the utmost sincerity." Just as he finished, about 1:15 a.m., Lieutenant-Colonel Gondō Seii, the chief staff officer in charge of 22nd Army operations, telephoned Nakamura to explain the army's intentions: "Because of the lateness of the order to halt the stationing, you have of course already crossed the border. Nonetheless, I request that your troops return to the border. If shooting has already started, you must naturally first handle the immediate situation and then return." Nakamura decided not to send his request. Surveying the situation along the front, he realized that the battle had started all along the line. It would be impossible to return his troops to their original positions until combat had been completed.[76] Then, fifteen minutes later, another order arrived from the South China Army directing Nakamura to advance his troops to the second target, Lang Son, beyond Dong Dang. To judge from these events, it seems likely that the 22nd Army had intentionally delayed transmitting the order until the fighting had started.

The report that the 5th Division had crossed the border arrived at Army General Staff headquarters around 2:00 a.m.[77] About an hour later Army Instruction 750 was issued from Imperial Headquarters:

> Until another order reaches you, the stationing of troops in French Indochina from Ch'innankuan must be halted. Troops which have already crossed the border should gather in their present positions. If shooting is already underway, confine the fighting to their immediate area. Troops which have crossed the border will be given directions respecting their actions in a subsequent order.

The instruction reveals the intentions of the Operations Division of the Army General Staff. Once hostilities had broken out, the officers in the division hoped to take advantage of the situation to complete a forceful stationing. Against the desires of Vice Chief Sawada, they accepted the 5th Division's action as a fait accompli, gave freedom of action to the troops on the spot, and thereby enlarged the war.

Once the fighting was under way, the deficiencies of the army instruction became clear. The 5th Division's front line was at Dong Dang at 9 o'clock the next morning, when further instructions arrived from the 22nd Army: "The army regards the region up to Lang Son as the immediate area of hostilities. . . . It is not necessary to get into difficulties by interpreting 'immediate area' narrowly. . . . It is not necessary to stop at Dong Dang if that proves difficult." The division was greatly encouraged by this.

The South China Army was not as enthusiastic about a military stationing as was the 22nd Army, and immediately after the latter had issued the above order, the South China Army sent further instructions to Nakamura: "Since French Indochina has accepted our demands, only the Nishimura force is permitted to be stationed there. The 22nd Army has been ordered to assemble within our border line [on the Chinese side]. Even if shooting has occurred, the troops must leave the battlefield."[78] Nakamura was puzzled over which instructions to obey. About 11:00 a.m. his troops seized Dong Dang. But the resistance had been intense, and Nakamura concluded that additional preparations were necessary before an attack upon Lang Son could begin. He therefore ordered the advance stopped temporarily.[79]

The 22nd Army, however, believed the Japanese forces should press their advantage and ordered Nakamura to attack Lang Son, arguing: "The French Indochinese troops not only have resisted stubbornly but also are engaged in various plots. Therefore, in order to terminate the fighting quickly, the core of resistance, Lang Son, must be attacked."[80]

The attack on Lang Son began the next morning, and by 7:00 p.m. on the 25th the defending forces under General Mennerat had surrendered. On the 26th, 22nd Army commander Lieutenant-General Kunō entered the fortress in triumph and combat ceased.

While the war on the ground spread from Dong Dang to Lang Son, the army and the navy were locked in bitter argument over the issue of landing the force under Nishimura. The September 22 agreement had stated that transport ships bearing the Nishimura corps might enter Haiphong harbor at 0:00 hours on the night of the 23rd to begin landing operations, although further negotiations were necessary concerning the details of disembarking and stationing. Accordingly, at noon on the 23rd the Nishimura corps left Ch'inchou Bay protected by the 1st Convoy Unit commanded by the 3rd Torpedo Squadron commander, Rear Admiral Fujita Ruitarō, and arrived off Do Son about midnight. Having heard of the 5th Division's attack, Nishimura decided to land and carry out a surprise attack before dawn.[81]

As the situation near the border worsened, Governor-General Decoux sent an emissary at 10:00 a.m. on the 23rd to appeal to Nishihara to halt the landing of the Nishimura corps. Nishihara sought instructions from Tokyo and agreed to postpone the landing.[82] The 2nd China Fleet ordered Fujita, after consulting the South China Army, to halt the landing until the border hostilities had ended and until then to remain ten nautical miles off Do Son.[83] A policy of peaceful stationing was also confirmed by the navy central command, which cabled the 2nd China Fleet that, inasmuch as efforts to obtain a regional settlement were being made, "the exercise of naval military operations should be performed only by special order, except as necessary for defense."

Despite these efforts by the naval command to restrain Nishimura, at midnight Admiral Fujita reported to the 2nd China Fleet that the corps "still seems to entertain the idea of a surprise landing and attack tomorrow morning." And he requested that they "consult with the South China Army to make certain that they are firmly ordered to wait."[84] Whereupon Fleet Commander-in-Chief Takasu cabled Commander Andō: "1) The stationing of the Nishimura corps will be decided later; 2) until then the corps is not to be permitted to land; 3) orders containing these instructions are to be sent immediately."[85] But Andō rejected the request, cabling Takasu that Nishimura's force was to be landed as planned as soon as possible in order to support the 5th Division and that the 2nd China Fleet was expected to cooperate fully.[86]

Increasingly suspicious of the intentions of the South China Army, the leaders of the 2nd China Fleet attempted to obtain from Imperial Headquarters the formal army order or instruction that would halt the landing of the Nishimura corps. Between midnight and dawn on the 24th a series of cables was dispatched to the Navy General Staff. Drafted by staff officer Ōi, who had just met and talked with Tominaga, Satō, and others at South China Army combat headquarters at Haik'ou, the cables accused the leaders of the South China Army of attempting "to destroy any effort at a peaceful settlement" and of interpreting "minute and unimportant sentences in orders from the central command in a manner advantageous to them. They equivocate," and, the warning continued, "it is quite probable that they are plotting to carry out military operations." Tominaga and the South China Army command, he charged, "do not seem to conceive of a peaceful stationing," and he urged that the army issue orders that could not be distorted.[87]

Naval headquarters supported the views of the 2nd China Fleet, which it instructed: "Although we have communicated with the Army Division of Imperial Headquarters, your fleet is to make every possible effort to prevent the combat from expanding, since it may be too late to obtain an army order or army instruction of the Imperial Headquarters." And a later telegram informed the fleet that "Lest we set a bad precedent for the future, it is not necessary for naval units to cooperate with the army."[88] Had not Nishimura decided at this point to postpone the landing, the desertion incident might have occurred then, on the morning of the 24th.

Just as the landing crafts were to be launched, Admiral Fujita received a wire from the 2nd China Fleet which he misinterpreted as stating that the South China Army was opposed to a landing on that day. Nishimura decided he had better check this report and postponed the landing for one day.[89] The 2nd China Fleet, however, feared that it would be confronted with the same situation the next day. It therefore sent another wire to central headquarters warning that, even though the Nishimura corps had been ordered not to land until the combat at Dong Dang had terminated and agreement had been reached between the army and navy, the landing might be carried out nonetheless.[90]

These forebodings soon proved justified. On the afternoon of the 24th Nishihara, Nishimura, and Fujita discussed the situation. Nishimura asserted that if the convoy entered the port of Haiphong, as instructed by the South China Army, the safety of the troops would be endangered. Therefore, his troops should be landed instead at Do Son, on the 25th, prepared for combat and ready to use this opportunity to occupy the city of Hanoi. Nishihara had no choice but to negotiate with the French authorities, who agreed tacitly that the stationing might be carried out on or after the 26th and that their forces in the landing area would retreat without resistance. Then, at 3:30 a.m. on the 25th Decoux's emissary once more visited Nishihara, who was aboard the destroyer *Nenohi* anchored in Haiphong harbor, to request that the stationing be postponed yet again, in view of the fact that the hostilities had spread to Lang Son the previous afternoon. Nishihara and Shirahama viewed the French request favorably and reported it to central headquarters. Navy Vice Chief Kondō met with Sawada and confirmed that both would attempt to insure that a peaceful stationing was carried out. But the South China Army had no intention of postponing the stationing.

Cognizant of the real intentions of the South China Army, Nishimura decided on his own initiative to land on the morning of the 26th. He secretly discussed his strategy with Admiral Fujita, who promised to command the vessels involved in the landings and to bombard the forts at Do Son from the sea and from the air. When Fujita informed the leaders of the 2nd China Fleet, however, they refused to approve the plan and instructed him to consult with Nishimura to halt it. "If he does not accept our request," Fujita was ordered, "inform him that we cannot cooperate with him and leave the port."[91]

On the evening of the 25th the Navy General Staff persuaded the Army General Staff to issue Imperial Headquarters Army Instruction 745:

> Based upon Imperial Headquarters Army Orders 452 and 459, you are instructed as follows: The troop stationing in northern French Indochina is to be carried out peacefully in accordance with the following procedures:
>
> 1) Combat at Ch'innankuan is to be terminated immediately north of the That Khe-Lang Son-Loc Binh line.
> 2) The stationing from Haiphong is to be carried out in the following way:
>   a) If negotiations for a peaceful stationing are completed by 12:00 hours on September 26 (Japan time), the landing will commence at Haiphong at the latest at 8:00 hours (Japan time) on September 27 and be completed swiftly.
>   b) If negotiations referred to in (a) are not successfully completed by 12:00 hours on September 26 (Japan time), prepare for combat near Do Son and land swiftly. The time and method of landing will be discussed and decided upon by the army and navy commanders on the spot.
>   c) After landing, troops are to gather near the landing spot and prepare for subsequent operations.
>   d) If combat occurs at the time of landing, it is to be limited to that area and ended quickly.

At 9:30 p.m. the 2nd China Fleet received a similar Navy Order 237 and immediately sent the following instruction to Fujita:

Withdrawal from the port as instructed in our previous wire is to be accomplished in the following manner.

Show Army Corps Commander Nishimura Imperial Headquarters Navy Order 237 and tell him to halt the stationing by force. If he does not agree, withdraw the fleet from the port. Above instruction based on Navy Order 237.[92]

Before the order arrived, however, at about 5:00 p.m. Nishihara had been informed by the French that the hostilities at Lang Son had ended, therefore the order to stop the stationing could be canceled and a peaceful stationing might begin on the morning of the 26th. But when Nishihara conveyed this message to Nishimura, the latter ignored him and refused to reply. Thereafter the Nishihara unit was completely disregarded by the other forces on the spot.

Nishihara appealed for support to Kanda Masatane, chief of the General Affairs Division of the Army General Staff: "If Imperial Headquarters does not control the forces on the spot so that they observe strictly the agreement I have concluded in accordance with the orders of Imperial Headquarters, it will make no difference how many agreements I obtain. Moreover, we will forfeit the confidence of people at home and abroad. Please take these matters into consideration and take such measures as seem desirable."[93] He also warned that he suspected the South China Army of issuing secret orders for Nishimura to attack Hanoi after landing at Haiphong and concluded that at the core of the plot were Tominaga and Arao.[94]

When Admiral Fujita received the instruction from Imperial Headquarters, he showed it to Nishimura saying that if landing operations were not halted, his vessels would have to withdraw from the port, an event that would leave a stain on the history of army-navy cooperation. Fujita argued until midnight, when Nishimura declared with finality that unless a specific order issued by the army supreme command arrived by 3:00 a.m., the landings must be carried out as scheduled. No countermanding order was received, and around 4:10 a.m. the landing of the Nishimura corps commenced. Once the landing crafts had been launched, the 1st Convoy Unit left the anchorage and withdrew to

Haik'ou, together with the *Nenohi* on which Nishihara had been quartered.

What then had happened to Army Instruction 745 issued by Imperial Headquarters? Under normal circumstances it should have reached Nishimura before midnight on the 25th. It appears that the instruction did arrive at the South China Army combat headquarters at about 10:00 p.m., where a perplexed staff officer Fujiwara handed it to Vice Chief of Staff Satō. Without consulting his chief of staff or commander, Satō decided to ignore it, rationalizing that "it would take at least an hour or two to recode it and for the Nishimura corps then to decode the message, . . . and by that time the troops would be leaving the anchorage or boarding the landing crafts." Moreover, to halt the landing a third time not only "would be harmful to the dignity of the army" but might "confuse the troops who are about to land so that some unexpected incident might occur."[95]

The leaders of the Nishimura corps, however, were apprehensive that an order to halt the landings would arrive at any moment. As the launching craft were being boarded, therefore, Nishimura and his chief of staff, Chō Isamu, went to the ludicrous length of hiding themselves in the ship's store and under a life boat, respectively, so that the order could not be given to them if it arrived.[96]

Thus the issue of stationing troops in northern French Indochina reached its denouement. The Nishimura corps landed and advanced unopposed to the city of Haiphong on the afternoon of September 26. Their objective was attained. But at a price, for the Navy General Staff, indignant and resentful at this action, on the afternoon of the 26th issued a navy order of Imperial Headquarters reaffirming the withdrawal of the 2nd China Fleet and refusing to cooperate further in military operations in French Indochina.[97]

The Discipline Problem

In the end, it was the army that lost face, in particular those leaders of the General Staff who had allowed themselves to be manipulated by Tominaga and the South China Army. At last criticism of Tominaga's arbitrary actions was voiced aloud. On September 25 Tominaga returned to Tokyo, where he was met at Odawara station by Operations Section Chief Okada, who informed him of the atmosphere within the army and advised him to restrain himself in both words and actions. At Sawada's office, with General Affairs Division Chief Kanda and others also present, the vice chief told Tominaga: "We request your resignation as chief of the Operations Division. I will take over your duties." Enraged, Tominaga tore the gold braid of a staff officer from his uniform and left the room.

The episode, however, was not yet concluded, for on September 26 there occurred the accidental bombing of Haiphong. The first report was sent in by Nishihara, who transmitted French protests that Haiphong had been bombed that morning by nine Japanese planes. It soon became clear that the incident had been a mistake, caused when one plane in a bomber squadron flying over the city had misinterpreted a banking maneuver by the command bomber and dropped a bomb, killing or injuring several Annamese. But to the navy, already angered by the army's repeated violations of the orders of the supreme command, the news only confirmed its suspicions. It immediately reported the incident to the emperor, adding that the Nishihara unit had been withdrawn. Summoning Sawada before him, the emperor blamed him for what had occurred.

Sawada had been considering the dismissal of Andō from his command of the South China Army, charging him with responsibility for the Morimoto battalion's crossing the border and for the stationing of the 5th Division after the agreement had been reached.[98] Now, pressured by Army Minister Tōjō and Intelligence Division Chief Tsuchihashi he decided to dismiss Andō at once and appoint Lieutenant-General Ushiroku Jun in his place. At the same time he issued an Imperial Headquarters army order prohibiting any bombing in French Indochina.[99]

But Andō's dismissal did not have the desired effect. Far from regretting their actions, Tominaga and his supporters and the South China Army staff officers developed an implacable enmity toward the navy and the Nishihara unit. The desertion incident led to a harsh exchange between the South China Army and the 2nd China Fleet that developed into a general confrontation between the central commands of the army and navy. Within the army, Nishihara, as an army man, came in for particularly vehement censure for having reported the accidental bombing of Haiphong "without investigation." Also at issue was a wire Nishihara had dispatched to the army and navy vice ministers and vice chiefs of staff from the 2nd China Fleet flagship *Chōkai* on the night of the 26th. This wire read: "The line of supreme command has fallen into disorder; we have lost public confidence within and outside the country. In order to control the situation in the future, I believe that I and other officers must return to Tokyo to report on these matters."[100] While it accurately conveyed the grievances the members of the inspection unit had accumulated over a period of three months, the telegram so angered certain members of the General Staff Operations Section that they demanded that Nishihara be dismissed from active service. The *Confidential War Diary* laments, "They do not behave as army officers should, they know nothing at all and make outrageous assertions. Ah! The world is going to the dogs!"

On September 27 Imperial Headquarters ordered Nishihara to return immediately to Hanoi to negotiate with the French Indochina authorities concerning the stationing and passage of the Nakamura and Nishimura forces. Nishihara, however, presented his resignation and asked that the inspection unit be abolished. "The French Indochina authorities think the present situation has been caused by those of us who are in French Indochina," he said, adding that they "are totally suspicious and resentful of us." But Major-General Suzuki Sōsaku, chief of the General Staff Supply Division, persuaded him to resume his task, and on the 29th Nishihara returned to Hanoi to reopen negotiations with Decoux and Martin. Soon thereafter his request to resign was accepted by the authorities in Tokyo and the former military attaché at the Japanese embassy in France, Major-General Sumita Raishirō, was appointed as his successor. On October 4 Sumita took Nishihara's place in Indochina. Grateful for Nishihara's actions, the army's leaders permitted him to return to his former post as a director of the Army War College, but because of the hatred of Tominaga and his supporters, Nishihara never again exerted much influence within the army.

On the eve of Sumita's departure, Army Minister Tōjō emphasized to him the need for cooperation between the military and diplomatic commands and between the army and the navy. For the present, he said, the occupation of northern French Indochina was not being contemplated and policy toward French Indochina was to be handled separately from policy toward the southern areas in general. Finally, the army minister warned, there should be no military interference with economic questions, with indigenous Indochinese issues, or with matters pertaining to Japanese civilians in Indochina.[101]

The negotiations between Sumita and the French authorities progressed smoothly and the headquarters of the Nishimura corps, numbering some 600 officers and men, was established in the city of Hanoi. Toward the end of October the 5th Division, which had grouped at Lang Son, went via Haiphong to Shanghai as a general reserve force under Imperial Headquarters.[102] By October 3 naval air forces had moved into the air base at Hanoi, from where they began to bomb K'unming on the 7th. The remnants of the 22nd Army were ordered to withdraw from the Nanning area, which no longer served any strategic purpose, and by the middle of November had returned to Canton or Taiwan via Ch'inchou Bay, although Tominaga and the South China Army had asserted that such a withdrawal was impossible. On October 19 the army was dissolved and Commander Kunō placed on the reserve list.

Thus, after three months of confusion, the problem of stationing troops in northern French Indochina was finally settled. But many serious problems still remained: the lack of coordination between political and military strategies, the failure of cooperation between the army and navy, extremism within the leadership of the Army General Staff, and lax military discipline. In particular, the army was suffering from the tendency of junior officers to dominate or ignore their seniors in the process of decision making. The disease, which appeared at this time among Tominaga's supporters, had infected the army since the time of the Manchurian Incident but by now was so widespread that the death of the Japanese empire was inevitable.

The situation convinced many top leaders within the army that major surgery was required. Following the conclusion of the Tripartite Pact, on October 3 Prince Kan'in resigned after eight years as chief of the Army General Staff. Sawada likewise resigned as vice chief, becoming commander of the 13th Army in Shanghai. Moreover, under the leadership of Army Minister Tōjō personnel changes were made comparable to those that occurred following the February 26 Incident.

Within the Army General Staff, Tominaga was transferred to the headquarters of the Eastern Zone Army and later to the military school at Kungchuling in Manchuria. Operations Section Chief Okada was appointed a regimental commander in Korea, while Lieutenant-Colonel

Takatsuki was appointed a staff officer in the North China Army and Lieutenant-Colonel Arao an instructor in the infantry school. It was obvious to everyone that their manipulations had caused the confusion surrounding the stationing in French Indochina and aroused Nishihara's fear that distrust of the army would be created both at home and abroad. Intelligence Division Chief Tsuchihashi, who had been in charge of communications between Nishihara and the Army Ministry and had tried to restrain the Operations Division, was made vice chief of staff of the China Army.

The leaders of the 5th Division down to the regimental level were held responsible for the border incident. Within the South China Army and the 22nd Army, however, only the commanders were transferred to reserve status; no blame was attached to their staff officers. "It is important at this time," Tōjō had said, "to restore discipline in the line of command. As army minister I shall administer reward and punishment justly; no one is to interfere in this matter."[103] But despite his firm stand on restoring discipline, Tōjō did not go so far as to blame Colonel Satō and other staff officers on the spot.

Furthermore, within a year even those officers who had been transferred from key positions in the Army General Staff to less important posts had been restored by Tōjō himself to influential posts in the Army Ministry and General Staff. Tominaga eventually became chief of the ministry's Personnel Bureau and subsequently vice minister. Satō was appointed chief of the Military Affairs Section and then chief of the Military Affairs Bureau. Indeed, both men became Tōjō's trusted associates. Not surprisingly, those who were aware of the true situation felt such an outcome "strange."[104] Nonetheless, these personnel changes did result in a decline in the tendency for junior officers to assert their views over those of their superiors and strengthened the position of the army minister and leaders of the General Staff.

It must not be forgotten that there were in the navy also middle-ranking officers who supported the aggressive aims of their counterparts in the army, although their maneuverings were less conspicuous. Among them were members of the so-called Axis faction, including Commander Kami Shigenori of the General Staff Operations Section and from the Naval Affairs Bureau of the Navy Ministry Commander Shiba Katsuo of its First (War Preparations) Section and Captain Ishikawa Shingo, who was appointed chief of the Second Section, dealing with foreign and defense policy and liaison with the army, when the bureau was reorganized in November. These men became the central figures in the powerful anti-British and anti-American faction that came to be an influential force within the navy.

The episode also brought a realization that there existed defects in the structure by which the army's wartime operations were directed. Hitherto the task had been performed by the General Staff Operations Section, which tended to give first priority to war operations to the neglect of political strategy.[105] The personnel changes of late 1940 provided the opportunity for creation of a new unit on the model of the Navy General Staff, where war guidance was under the direct control of the chief of the Operations Division. Therefore, the War Guidance Office was established at this time, headed by Colonel Arisue Yadoru and charged with directing overall war strategy, under the direct control of the vice chief of staff. It proved an effective organ and served frequently to restrain the Operations Division.

The more important task of establishing a unified command for army-navy operations or, as some army leaders had proposed, of unifying the General Staffs was never accomplished.[106] When the Pacific War broke out, Japan still faced the problem of disunity between its services.

The stationing incident was also important in that it marked Japan's first step on its southward advance. Such an advance and the occupation of Singapore could have been no more than a dream unless a bridgehead was built across French Indochina. Nor could Japan have contemplated waging war against the United States. Given the implications of this step, it is not surprising that such controversy arose at headquarters in Tokyo and on the spot and that it was attended by great confusion in Imperial Headquarters.

The operation seems in fact to have begun amid the excitement stimulated by profound changes attending the German blitzkrieg in Europe, without the necessary material and strategic planning that should have preceded it. The situation was exacerbated by the army's long-standing weakness in the delicate task of coordinating diplomatic and military policies, the inevitable result being that confusion spread.

FOUR

The Drive into Southern
Indochina and Thailand

NAGAOKA SHINJIRŌ

Translated by
ROBERT A. SCALAPINO

The Thai-Indochina Border Dispute

With the outbreak of the European war, French concern was aroused
for the security of France's territories in the Far East. In December
1939, therefore, the French minister to Thailand, Paul P. Lépissier, has-
tened to open negotiations with the Thai government for a nonaggression pact, and on June 12, 1940, such a pact was signed. On the same
day Thailand also concluded a nonaggression pact with Britain as well as
a treaty of friendship with Japan pledging mutual respect for one another's territorial integrity.

The armistice between Germany and France, however, led to renewed pressure by Thailand along its border with French Indochina and
intensification of the historic border conflict between the two countries.
In July Thai troops were positioned on the border along the Mekong
river. Japan had begun negotiations with France for the passage of Japanese troops through northern Indochina, and Thailand was greatly concerned about the outcome.

Fearing a Japanese annexation of French Indochina, Thailand began
to sound out foreign opinion concerning its reacquisition of territory in
Indochina previously ceded to France. On August 15 Deputy Foreign
Minister Nai Direck Jaiyanama handed to the new American minister,
Hugh Gladney Grant, an informal request from Prime Minister Luong
Pibul Songgram (who was also serving as foreign minister) for the Ameri-
can government's reaction to such an event. Direck indicated that Brit-

This essay originally appeared as "Nanka taisei no juritsu," in *Taiheiyō sensō e no michi*,
vol. 6, part I, sec. 5, pp. 99–140.

ain, Germany, and Italy were also being consulted and that Japan would soon be approached. Grant further reported that Thailand was planning to dispatch a military mission to Japan and another to Germany and Italy.[1] Thus, Thailand cleverly approached both the Axis and the anti-Axis powers simultaneously.

When Sir Josiah Crosby, the British minister, was approached on the matter, he advised the Thai government to avoid friction with Japan in order not to be drawn into the conflict with China. At his suggestion the mission to Tokyo was broadened to include a civilian member and both missions were to be designated "goodwill" missions, with the group visiting Europe including London on its itinerary.[2]

Two days later, when Grant presented his credentials to Pibul, the prime minister made it clear that while Thailand was satisfied with the existing situation in French Indochina, should another nation, such as Japan, attempt to seize control, he would demand the return to Thailand of the ceded provinces. The mission to Tokyo would discuss the matter with the Japanese as well as with the French authorities in Indochina. And on the 19th Grant reported that, according to reliable information, Pibul had asked the French minister to urge his government that the ceded region be omitted in any settlement with Japan. In reply to Pibul's inquiry and Grant's cables, Under Secretary of State Welles, on the 21st, instructed Grant to emphasize America's "belief that the adjustment of problems in international relations should be made by processes of peaceful negotiation and agreement," principles in which the Thai government had concurred, and to state that the Thai inquiry "should be considered and dealt with in the light of those principles."[3]

The French authorities in Indochina were growing increasingly concerned about the Thai attitude, and in early September the governor-general, Admiral Jean Decoux, declaring his intention to resist Japanese aggression, approached the British consul-general in Saigon to request that Britain exert its influence to prevent military action by Thailand in Indochina. In response to this request, Sir Josiah Crosby, on the 4th, privately asked Pibul to exercise restraint in Indochina. Crosby suggested to Grant that similar diplomatic overtures by the United States might be helpful. Meanwhile Direck had informed Grant that Thailand proposed to discuss its territorial claims only with the French authorities, not with the Japanese, and had so informed the French minister in Bangkok.[4]

On its way to Japan the Thai delegation stopped in Saigon and Hanoi, where the head of the mission, Deputy Minister of Defense and Assistant Commander-in-Chief of the Army Colonel Luang Prom Yodhi, appealed to Decoux for greater cooperation between their two countries in view of the Japanese threat to both nations. As a condition of such cooperation, he demanded the cession to Thailand of that portion of Laos on the right bank of the Mekong. Assuming that Prom was simply sounding out the French attitude, Decoux declined to give a substantive answer.[5]

On September 11 the State Department called in the Thai minister to Washington to express its concern about reports that Thailand was planning military action in Indochina. Such action, the department said, could only precipitate further aggression against Indochina "and thus inevitably result in a further spread of hostilities which this Government feels would ultimately be disastrous to Thailand and would certainly impair the friendly relations . . . so long enjoyed" between their two countries. The hope was expressed "that the Thai Government will, as in the past, adhere to the universal principles of fair dealing and good neighborliness" to which the U.S. government was committed. Grant was instructed to comment along the same lines in Bangkok.[6]

Thailand now undertook a vigorous propaganda campaign on the Indochina issue. Pamphlets demanding the return of territory incorporated within Laos and Cambodia were distributed in French Indochina. While the French ambassador in Bangkok lodged a protest against these activities, the French government was more apprehensive about Japan's reaction and on the 11th ordered Ambassador Arsène-Henry in Tokyo to raise the issue with the Japanese government and urge it to take a firm stand on the Thai demands. The French hope was that Japan would compel Thailand to withdraw its demands. Two days later Arsène-Henry was ordered to again ask the Japanese to intervene and to state that France held them responsible for the agitation by the Thais.[7] This charge of Japanese involvement was repeated on the 16th when the ambassador, in a meeting with Vice Foreign Minister Ōhashi, once more requested that Japan attempt to restrain Thailand. Ōhashi rejected the accusation, asserting that the border troubles had arisen because France was dragging its feet in the negotiations with Japan.[8]

While Britain was quick to ratify the nonaggression pact with Thailand, France was not. Although it had been discussed by the previous governor-general, General Georges Catroux, and Lepissier in Thailand, agreement had been reached and the pact hastily signed. Decoux, who had not received the details, criticized it bitterly.[9] Controversy over the pact also arose within France. On September 11, therefore, the Vichy government proposed that the pact be put into effect immediately without the usual formal exchange of instruments of ratification. The Thai government thereupon requested prior agreement on the following issues: 1) rectification of the Mekong frontier and settlement of other administrative questions, matters that had already been agreed upon in principle; 2) acceptance of the Mekong as the frontier as far as Cambodia, involving the retrocession to Thailand of territories on the right bank of the river; and 3) the return to Thailand of portions of Laos and Cambodia. The second point had been proposed because of Thai fears that the Japanese would march into Indochina and appear on the Thai frontier, while point three, although earnestly desired by Thailand, was not regarded by France as a precondition to bringing the pact into force.[10]

In mid-September the Vichy authorities agreed to permit Japanese troops to be stationed in northern Indochina, and it was anticipated that a military pact concerning Indochina would soon be concluded between France and Japan. It was only natural that Thailand's attitude with respect to French Indochina should harden. The British attitude had also begun to change, and Crosby told Grant that, should the Japanese establish a sphere of influence in Indochina on the Thai frontier, Britain might weaken in its "resolve to urge and insist that the Thai adhere strictly to the policy of the maintenance of the *status quo* in Indochina." While he pressed upon Crosby the need for a united policy to influence Thailand, Grant concluded that Britain was about to apply a "policy of appeasement" in the affair and expressed the fear that America's "policy of consistent dealing" would in this case "leave us out on a limb in splendid isolation while our friends compromise with the issue."[11]

On the 17th Grant was called to Pibul's residence and given a copy of an aide-memoire on the Indochina matter. Pibul expressed the hope that the United States would consider sympathetically the Thai proposals to the French government and stated the strong feelings of the Thai people concerning the territories, both in Thailand and in the French territories that Thailand desired returned. He assured Grant that Thai patrol forces had been sent solely to prevent trouble with the

INDOCHINA AND THAILAND
1940-1941

—·— National boundaries
·········· Sub-national boundaries
●   Cities
++++++ Railroads
——— Rivers
▒▒▒▒ Territory ceded to Thailand by
the Thailand-France Treaty
of Peace, May 9, 1941

0   100   200
Kilometers

YUNNAN

Mengtzu

CHINA

Lao Cai

Lang Son   KWANGSI

TONKIN

BURMA

Dien Bien Phu
Hanoi
Haiphong

Mong
Cai

Luang Prabang

GULF
OF
TONKIN

HAINAN

INDOCHINA

Vientiane

Mekong

LAOS

THAILAND

River

Hue
Tourane
(Da Nang)

Pakse
Bassac

Bangkok

Angkor

Battambang

CAMBODIA

Sattahip

Ko Chang Is.

Nhatrang   Cam Ranh
Bay

GULF OF
SIAM

Pnompenh

COCHIN CHINA

Saigon

SOUTH CHINA
SEA

French along the border and had been removed at least 25 kilometers from the frontier. Even if the French government should refuse the Thai request, he did not contemplate taking action by force. But when Grant asked for assurance that Thailand would not resort to force under any circumstances, Pibul answered that the Thais in the contested areas might take matters into their own hands. And if a third party should attempt to enter the scene, "it might become necessary for the Thai Government, for the protection of its national interests, to 'occupy' certain territory." Thus Pibul refused to limit his freedom of action in Indochina. The following day Hull instructed Grant that "no useful purpose" would be served by further approaches to the Thai authorities at that time, and if the subject was raised by Thailand, he was simply to reiterate the position Washington had taken previously.[12]

On the 19th the American chargé in France was informed that the French government had rejected the Thai demands, although the questions relative to the Mekong would be referred to a mixed commission to meet as soon as the nonaggression pact was ratified. In addition, France had declared its firm resolve "to defend against any pretensions and any attack . . . the political status and territorial integrity of Indo-China." In Thailand, on the 21st, Deputy Foreign Minister Direck informed Grant of the receipt of the French rejection the previous day.[13]

Sir Josiah Crosby was alarmed at the situation in Thailand. He feared that Britain and the United States would be confronted with a Japanese *fait accompli* in Indochina and that if they continued to insist on strict maintenance of the status quo, Thailand might go over to the totalitarian powers. Or, should a change occur in Indochina and Thailand fail to recover the territory it claimed, he believed the Thai Government would fall. He had therefore asked London for permission to indicate to Pibul that, "while the British Government is strongly opposed to a change in the *status quo* in Indochina, nevertheless if such a change should 'regrettably and unavoidably occur' the territorial claims of Thailand would not be considered unsympathetically by the British Government."[14]

Grant, too, was fearful of the rising militaristic spirit among Thai civilian officials, who, he believed, were merely puppets of the military leadership. During a meeting with Prime Minister Pibul, he observed that the door to the adjoining room remained open, so that army officers could listen to their conversation. At one point, Grant reported, Pibul had remarked that "they might kill me if I do not follow their desires."

Grant concluded that "the military clique is waging a war of nerves on him, that this mild mannered man is in the firm grip of his own ambitious army and navy officers and that Japan looms in the background of the whole business." While Grant felt that Pibul and his advisers wished to retain the goodwill of the United States and Britain—who, the prime minister had emphasized, seemed "sympathetic" to Thailand's claims— the American minister was convinced that the final decision would be made by the military, and "when the military group decrees that Thai troops shall march, they will march and Japan will provide the cue."[15]

Meanwhile, crisis loomed between Japan and France in Indochina. On September 19 Japan presented a new demand that France permit Japanese forces to be stationed in Indochina, threatening to invade three days later if the demand were not met. Despite the signing of an agreement at Hanoi on the 22nd, Japanese troops from Kwangsi entered Indochina and clashed with the French forces near Lang Son. Thailand seized this opportunity once more to press its territorial demands and on the 25th requested the Vichy authorities to reconsider its claim for the "adjustment of the frontier."[16] But this second request too was rejected by the French government, although it indicated willingness to negotiate on the question of several small islands in the Mekong.[17]

The incident at Lang Son was settled before it developed into prolonged hostilities. The French authorities agreed to the stationing of Japanese troops in the north and the Kwangsi forces were returned to Japan via Haiphong, strictly observing the terms of the agreement. Thus the confusion Thailand had expected in Indochina did not develop. Thailand had miscalculated.

What role had Japan played in Thailand's dispute with Indochina? On August 7 Japanese army authorities, desiring to expand the role of their attaché in Thailand—Colonel Tamura Hiroshi, a man well acquainted with Thai affairs—discussed with him how a military agreement with Thailand might be achieved. It was decided that Tamura should sound out possible Thai interest, although no concrete proposal was drafted at the time. In September, when Thailand made its first proposal to France for settlement of the border dispute with Indochina, Japanese army officials suggested mediation of the issue. Seeing this as an opportunity to establish close political and military ties with Thailand, Tamura began secret discussions with Prime Minister Pibul on a military pact.[18] It was these talks that led to France's charges of Japanese collusion with Thailand. Japanese army attention was focused on Indochina at this time, however, with the General Staff pressing for the right to station troops in the north, and the Thai military pact was therefore not of major concern. In addition, the Japanese government did not want the Thai claims raised during its negotiations with the French authorities, and it feared that support for Thailand's position would jeopardize future French cooperation with Japan. Thus, when the Thai "goodwill" mission, during its visit in September and October, raised the question of the lost territories, the Japanese government declined to give any concrete answer.[19]

In the weeks that followed the settlement, skirmishes were frequent along Thailand's border with Indochina and it was feared that more serious hostilities might erupt at any time. The American minister continued to press on the Thai authorities his government's conviction that it was in Thailand's interest to maintain the status quo in Indochina and refrain from the use of force to achieve its aims. Meanwhile, the U.S. government began to cut off the flow of military supplies to Thailand. On October 4 Maxwell Hamilton informed the Thai minister in Washington that because of its own defense needs the United States was revoking export licenses for certain commodities previously granted to Thailand; on the 9th ten dive bombers destined for Thailand were requisitioned in Manila; and on the 19th licenses were revoked for the export of six single-seat fighter planes as well as for spare parts.[20] This policy of embargo and insistence on the status quo was regarded by Thailand as evidence of an unfriendly and unsympathetic attitude on the part of the United States.

Britain, however, had a different outlook on the Thai demands, being concerned primarily about the consequences of a Japanese-Thai agreement. In early October Lord Halifax, the British foreign secretary, sent a message to Pibul stating that while the British government advocated the strict maintenance of the status quo in Indochina, should Japan extend its control over Indochina and Thailand feel compelled to reach an agreement with Japan in order to protect its interests, the British government "would expect Thailand to refrain from taking any action which would be prejudicial to the interests of Great Britain in this area, such as granting Japan permission to establish air bases in Thailand that could be used against British possessions."

On October 10 Pibul replied in a meeting with Crosby that as long as he was prime minister, Japan would not be permitted to establish air bases in Thailand. He then went on to predict that within a year Japan would have "complete control" of Indochina, therefore Thailand must protect its national interest by coming to terms with Japan for the recovery of its former territories. The only effective opposition to Japan's "new order," he stated, would be a power bloc composed of Britain, the United States, and Holland.[21]

Grant was adamant that Pibul's assurances could not be trusted, and he charged Britain with "planning another Munich" in admitting to Pibul that Thailand might have to come to an agreement with Japan. Any agreement between Thailand and Japan, he told Crosby, "implies a deal between them which means that Thailand will give something in return for what she gets from Japan and that probably means ultimately the domination of Thailand by Japan, the establishment of a puppet government by the Japanese, and in such case, I ask, of what value is the Prime Minister's promise not to take any action that would be prejudicial to British interests in this area?"[22]

Responding to Britain's views on the relations between Thailand and Indochina, the State Department, on October 23, emphasized its consistent efforts to dissuade Thailand from attempting to alter the status quo by other than peaceful means. And in a tacit plea that Britain reconsider its attitude, the department expressed gratification at Britain's reiteration of those principles to Thailand. On November 11, as if to indicate the absence of realism in America's simple adherence to principle, the British embassy conveyed to the State Department an extract from a cable from London of November 4 stating that unless Thailand were reinforced by Britain and the United States, it would not resist a Japanese invasion of its territory.[23]

In French Indochina, meanwhile, Governor-General Decoux was worried about future action by Japan as well as the likelihood of an attack by Thailand. In June Decoux dispatched to Washington a purchasing mission to discuss with officials in the State Department the possibility of obtaining military supplies in the United States, and similar approaches were made through the French embassy in Washington. The mission's efforts met with no success, and in early September it was recalled.[24] Hull was concerned lest war matériel supplied to Indochina should ultimately fall into the hands of the Japanese.[25] Moreover, he pointed out to the French ambassador, Gaston Henry-Haye, ninety planes purchased by France in the United States were sitting unused in Martinique and might easily be diverted to Indochina. Henry-Haye replied that this would probably not be permitted under the terms of the German-French armistice.[26] But on October 9 he reported that both the German and the Italian armistice committees were willing to allow troops and arms to be transported to Indochina; doubtless, he told Welles, because they desired "to prevent Japan from extending herself too far in Southern Asia and thus facilitating a Japanese attack upon the Netherlands East Indies which Germany desired to retain for herself."[27] Another reason may have been that Hitler wished to see the United States embroiled with Japan and therefore less able to aid Britain.

Despite his assurances to the British and American envoys, Prime Minister Pibul had begun to turn toward Japan, particularly after the signing of the Tripartite Pact, when the two western nations failed to respond positively to his requests. In late October army attaché Captain Torigoshi Shin'ichi returned secretly to Japan to report that on September 28 Deputy Prime Minister Wannitt had told him that Pibul had decided to rely upon Japan. Three days later he had asked Pibul whether this report was true and was told, "What Wannitt has told you is what I really intend." Pibul would ask Japan to mediate the border dispute with Indochina, Torigoshi reported, would allow Japanese troops to pass through Thailand if necessary, and would provide assistance in the form of goods and supplies. Torigoshi had been ordered by the army to obtain Pibul's written promise to this effect, but Pibul had demurred. "If a written promise is required, I will have to put the matter before the cabinet and then it might leak out." For this reason Torigoshi had hurriedly returned to Tokyo in secret. Matsuoka agreed that an oral promise was sufficient and is reported to have remarked that "secret matters leak out when they are put to the cabinet in Japan too."[28]

On November 5 the Four Ministers Conference decided to ask Wannitt to come to Japan to discuss the following points approved by the conference:

1) Japan will consider favorably Thailand's demand for restoration of its lost territories. In particular, Japan will, at the proper time, consider mediating the conflict between Thailand and France (including French

Indochina) concerning the restoration of the Luang Prabang and Pakse areas.
2) Thailand will be induced to cooperate with Japan in the establishment of the New Order in East Asia.
   a) Thailand will reform its internal structure gradually, so that an alliance with Japan can be effectuated smoothly.
   b) Conferences will be held to decide upon various areas of cooperation.
   c) Thailand is to recognize Manchukuo.
3) In order that Japan may secure needed commodities, a broad economic pact is to be concluded, including a barter trade agreement and an agreement on industrial development.
4) The Japan-Thailand Treaty of Friendship is to be ratified swiftly.[29]

Although Wannitt did not go to Japan, these points seem to have been communicated to Thailand. On November 15, however, the situation was complicated when Japan's chargé in Thailand, Asada Shunsuke, reported to Tokyo that Thailand had secretly agreed to an alliance with Britain and the United States. Under the terms of the alliance, Asada said, Thailand would participate in the joint defense of the South Pacific and, if the United States entered the war, would either join on the side of the United States and Britain or sever diplomatic relations with the Axis nations. Should war break out between Japan on one side and the United States and Britain on the other, Thailand would make available naval and air bases and secure provisions, in return for which the United States would grant the loans that Thailand was requesting.[30]

These allegations were strongly denied by Pibul, who stated emphatically that Thailand's attitude toward Japan would not change, even if the United States and Britain were to propose an alliance. The report was also denied in a press interview given on the 18th by Under Secretary of State Welles, who speculated that some Japanese plot must have been behind such rumors. And in Britain, Parliamentary Under Secretary Butler similarly declared to Ambassador Shigemitsu Mamoru that there was no truth in the report. On the 19th the British government issued an official denial, claiming the rumor had been spread deliberately to ascertain Britain's and America's response to it.[31] The incident suggests that Japan, the United States, Britain, and France were all increasing their activities in Thailand at this time.

On November 21 the Four Ministers Conference reached agreement on the following "Policy toward Thailand and French Indochina Concerning Mediation for Thailand's Recovery of Its Lost Territories":

Policy
The Empire will act swiftly to mediate the dispute between Thailand and French Indochina and will cooperate with Thailand to recover its lost territories, in order to establish a closer relationship with Thailand and, by manipulating France, to advance and expand the influence of the Empire in French Indochina. Thus, the Empire aims at establishing a lead position in Greater East Asia.

Outline for Its Realization
1) Concerning Thailand
Thailand is to accept our demands (the Four Ministers Conference decision of November 15) swiftly, and mediation for the recovery of Luang Prabang and Pakse will begin immediately. Japan will promise to restore to Thailand other lost territories (particularly British territories) in the future. In connection with this economic aid and munitions supplies are to be considered.

Note: If Thailand should not respond positively to our demands, it should be caused to do so by intimations that Japan might otherwise promote closer ties with French Indochina, that the imperial power will be expanded toward southern French Indochina, that munitions will be supplied to French Indochina and will be cut off from Thailand, and that relations between Japan and Thailand will worsen.

2) Concerning French Indochina
a) French Indochina is to be persuaded to accept the annexation of Luang Prabang and Pakse by Thailand, with a guarantee that Thai demands for the recovery of lost territories will be limited to a minimum and that Japan will support the territorial integrity of French Indochina thereafter. Simultaneous efforts will be made to cause Indochina to accept military cooperation with Japan in the southern portion of Indochina.

Note: (a) If French Indochina does not accept our demands, it should be hinted that the Empire will give more active support to Thailand and will oppose both the American and British maneuvers now being initiated vis-à-vis Thailand and the British policy vis-à-vis southern French Indochina. Furthermore, if necessary, it should be indicated that the agreement between Matsuoka and Arsène-Henry* might be abandoned, using as a pretext the delay in achieving an agreement on economic cooperation.

(b) If Thailand rejects our demands, wholehearted support should be

---

* On the Matsuoka-Henry Pact, see the preceding essay, "The Army's Move into Northern Indochina."

given to French Indochina and active military cooperation should be planned.

b) An outline of the negotiations with France will be communicated to Germany and, if necessary, we should seek German pressure upon France to influence the French government to the advantage of Japan.[32]

According to this policy, Japan would seek to obtain its political and military demands in playing Thailand and Indochina against each other. And in keeping with the final part of the decision, Vice Foreign Minister Ōhashi told Ambassador Ott on the day it was adopted that while America and Britain were maneuvering to win Thailand's support, Japan had offered to mediate the border dispute with Indochina, and he asked Germany for help in approaching France.[33]

Japanese Mediation

On November 28 the anticipated conflict broke out when troops clashed along the Laotian border. On December 2 Matsuoka told Ambassador Arsène-Henry that Japan was prepared to mediate a settlement, but on the 19th the French government indicated officially that it was not prepared to cede any of its territory.[34]

Thailand, meanwhile, had approached Germany. On the 9th State Secretary Weizsaecker told Thailand's minister, P. Pamon Montri, that Germany was opposed to any military solution of the dispute and would support a settlement reached between Thailand and France directly or through Japanese mediation. He expressed support for Thailand's demands for border adjustment and encouraged its claims for readjustment of the Burmese border. Later that month, in Rome, Foreign Minister Galeazzo Ciano took the same position in talks with Montri.[35]

Increasingly concerned about Japan's intentions in Thailand and French Indochina, Secretary of State Hull on December 12 instructed the American chargé in France, Robert D. Murphy, to suggest informally to the Vichy authorities that they discuss the situation with Germany with a view that the latter might exert a "restraining influence" upon the Japanese government. Jean Chauvel, chief of the Far Eastern Division of the French Foreign Office, was "mildly surprised" at this suggestion that France should deal with Germany but promised to consider it carefully and sympathetically. The Germans had not pressured France to accede to the Japanese demands, according to Chauvel, who was of the opinion that they preferred to see Indochina remain intact as part of the French colonial empire. When Murphy suggested to Foreign Minister Paul Baudouin that an approach be made to Germany, however, Baudouin felt it was the "last thing" France should do. The Japanese, he believed, had "manifested a certain pride in retaining an independence of action in the Orient" and "would resent any suggestions from Germany." Moreover, the Germans were unlikely to wish to interfere with Japanese plans in the Orient.[36]

Encouraged by Japan's offer of mediation and German support for its demands, the Thai government on December 14 issued a communiqué stating that it took "pleasure in entering upon negotiation with French Indochina in order to end peacefully the dispute prevailing between the two countries." The Thai nation, it said, "has no wish to disturb the peace of anyone but we will have to wipe out of existence all the injustice which French Indochina has done to us."[37]

While declining the Japanese offer of mediation, Chauvel was reportedly encouraged by the moderate tone of the Thai communiqué and prepared to discuss frontier demarcation along the Mekong. He was puzzled, however, by the attitude of the British minister in Thailand, who had refused to make any effort to restrain the Thais and, indeed, had suggested that it was "much more to British interests for the defense of Singapore to see aggressive Thailandese troops on the Mekong as a defense against Japanese forces pushing through Indochina with the Malay peninsula as their probable objective." In contrast, he felt that Grant had had a "calming effect" upon the Thais, and in conversation with Murphy he emphasized the need for economic cooperation and military support from the United States. Any possible encouragement to the French "to crystallize their natural desire to put a bold front in Indochina would," Murphy urged Washington, "be most timely."[38]

But British policy had begun to change. By the end of the year Britain had ceased to give tacit support to the Thai demands, seeking rather to cooperate with the United States in Indochina and to encourage French resistance to Japan and Thailand. When Governor-General Decoux dispatched his aide-de-camp, Captain Jouan, to Singapore for talks with the British governor-general and fleet commander between December 25 and 31, an informal economic agreement was reached for the resumption of trade and for limiting Japanese and German access to commodities from Indochina. Jouan also indicated that efforts by the United States, alone or jointly with Britain, to mediate the conflict with Thailand would be welcomed.[39]

Japan, meanwhile, had stepped up its supplies of planes, weapons, and munitions to Thailand. And in Japan consideration was once again being given to a military alliance with Thailand. Both the army and the navy drew up their own drafts of an alliance, while the Foreign Ministry prepared a draft based upon the navy's version. This Foreign Ministry draft was accepted by the services with some amendments[40] and on December 26 was adopted by the Liaison Conference as the "Policy of the Empire toward Thailand and French Indochina."*

Policy
Close, inseparable relations between Japan and Thailand should be established swiftly. At the appropriate time pressure should be put upon French Indochina to accept our demands. The adjustment of diplomatic relations between French Indochina and Thailand should be promoted.

Outline
a) Negotiations with Thailand for both a political-military pact and an agreement on economic cooperation should begin immediately.
b) Negotiations with French Indochina should begin immediately and Japan's economic, military, and political demands presented to it. Our economic demands, above all, must be accepted at once. Settlement of the Thailand-French Indochina border dispute must also be demanded.

If France does not accept our demands, we must be prepared to abandon the Matsuoka-Henry agreement and take the necessary steps accompanying the destruction of that pact.

Note: Concrete procedures concerning items (a) and (b) will be decided later.[41]

Thus Japan began to increase its pressure against French Indochina.

On January 7, 1941, the British chargé in Washington, Nevile M. Butler, called on Under Secretary of State Welles to hand over an aide-memoire setting forth the British government's views on the situation in Indochina and Thailand. Britain's policy, it stated, was governed by two principal concerns: first, that the dispute should be settled peacefully and without delay; second, that a settlement should not be brought

* For further explanation of this document, see the following chapter, "The Navy's Role in the Southern Strategy."

about through Japanese mediation, with or without German aid. In order that neither party be under any obligation to Japan and that a final settlement strengthen the French against Japan, Britain hoped the dispute could be solved either by direct negotiations or with British and American help. Both sides would have to make concessions, with the French ceding the territory originally claimed by the Thais plus a few islands in the Mekong, and the Thais agreeing to settle for something less than their maximum requirements and giving adequate guarantees that no further demands would be made. The British government was of the opinion that the French would be willing to make territorial changes in resolving the dispute and had indicated, through Jouan, that they would welcome mediation. Any delay in reaching a settlement would only be to the advantage of Japan, at the expense of the nations of the region and, ultimately, of Britain and the United States. Asking for an early response to the British views, the memoire concluded with the warning that while mediation must begin "with all possible speed," any open proposal would only provoke Japanese and German counter-action, therefore "the negotiations would ostensibly have to be undertaken directly between the two parties, British and American influence being exercised in the background."[42]

In keeping with these aims, Parliamentary Under Secretary Butler called in the Thai minister in London the following day to warn him that Thailand, by accepting aircraft and instructors from Japan, ran the risk of Japanese encroachment and involvement in "very wide and dangerous problems." "It was one thing for the Thai Government to interest themselves in frontier adjustments on the Mekong River," he said, "but quite another to play the Japanese game by becoming the base for Japanese operations in a possible extension of the war." Would the British government come to Thailand's assistance if it were attacked? the minister asked. While declining to discuss the question, Butler responded that "any Japanese encroachments were undesirable" and stressed the importance to Britain of preserving a free market in Thailand, in particular the trade in tin and rubber with the British colonies. But he made no commitment of British support against Japan. On the 11th the commander of the China Squadron was ordered to inquire confidentially of Decoux concerning the scope of negotiations he would be willing to un-dertake and how such negotiations could be brought about most rapidly.[43]

On January 10 the American government replied to the British aide-memoire. While the United States, it said, shared Britain's wish that the dispute between Thailand and French Indochina be settled peacefully and without delay, it doubted that a permanent settlement was possible under present circumstances. And while recognizing "the value of endeavor by diplomatic processes to influence the course of events in directions consistent with this Government's principles and objectives," it did "not perceive what useful contribution along the lines of mediation it could make at the present time," although it would be prepared to offer "friendly counsel" should that appear useful in the future.[44] In short, the United States agreed with Britain in principle, but it preferred to wait and see how the situation developed before taking any action.

Meanwhile, the two parties to the dispute were attempting to bring about direct negotiations. On January 8 Roger Garreau, the French chargé in Thailand, proposed to Deputy Foreign Minister Direck a mutual withdrawal of forces from the frontier. He rejected Direck's demand that the French accept in principle the right bank of the Mekong as the boundary but indicated that it might be placed on the agenda for negotiations. On the 13th Prime Minister Pibul laid down three conditions for a truce: 1) the Thai forces were to remain in the positions they then held; 2) France should agree in principle to the retrocession of territory on the right bank of the Mekong; and 3) the joint negotiating commission was to be convened as soon as possible.[45]

At the time it was reported that Thai troops had penetrated into Cambodia. Thailand therefore hoped to settle the border dispute quickly, while it was still in an advantageous position. For the French it was becoming increasingly urgent to obtain munitions for their forces in Indochina.

On January 10 Ambassador Henry-Haye met with Welles to request the unblocking of sufficient Indochinese funds to obtain munitions for French Indochina. Welles promised to give the request "full consideration" but reiterated that the United States would release no planes for Indochina until France agreed to ship those still in Martinique to Indochina. Henry-Haye then urged that the American government intervene with the Thai government in an effort to prevent the outbreak of open warfare. Welles replied that Hull intended to convey to the Thai minister the following day the American view that Thailand was allowing Japan to maneuver it into a position that would eventuate in "outright vassalage." He also informed the ambassador that Britain had agreed "in principle and under certain conditions" to permit shipment of the planes from Martinique to Indochina, and he advised that France seek the necessary authority from Germany. This, Chauvel informed American Ambassador William D. Leahy on the 13th, was being done "immediately and urgently."[46]

The same day Hull instructed Leahy to communicate to the French Foreign Office his disquiet at the latest reports of renewed fighting along the Indochinese border. It was obvious to Washington "that the fundamental factors in this situation are the activities and aims of aggressor nations which are alert to seize upon conditions of strife to further their own purposes," and both the French and Thai authorities must "recognize these fundamental factors and pursue courses which take them fully into consideration with the object of averting developments which sooner or later are likely to result in domination by aggressor nations of their territories in one form or another—economic, political, or military." Hull issued a similar warning in an interview with the Thai minister.[47]

Despite Britain's efforts to bring about a solution of the Indochinese crisis, French Foreign Minister Pierre-Etienne Flandin remained uncertain as to British intentions in the region. Both the British press in Singapore and the British minister in Bangkok, he stated in a memorandum to Leahy, seemed to support the Thai claims, while "British propaganda circulates rumors relative to an extension of Japanese ascendency in Indochina thus inciting Thailand to take its own measures of guarantee."[48] Unable to count on material aid from the United States and facing continued attacks in Indochina from Thai forces well supplied with Japanese munitions, Flandin now began to consider seriously a new Japanese offer of mediation.

On January 15 Matsuoka called Arsène-Henry to the Foreign Ministry to raise unofficially the question of mediation. The following day a similar proposal was made to René Robin, a former governor-general of Indochina who was then conducting commercial negotiations in Japan, by Matsumiya Jun, the leader of the Japanese delegation at the talks, who warned Robin against any effort to solicit such aid from the United States or Britain.[49]

At dawn on the 16th French Indochinese troops launched an attack against Thai forces on the Cambodian border but were thrown back with heavy losses. In a surprise attack on the Thai fleet at Ko Chang island in the Gulf of Siam, however, the French fleet won a major victory. Upon recieving word of the defeat, Prime Minister Pibul on the 17th appealed to the new Japanese minister to Thailand, Futami Yasusato, for additional Japanese support, saying that Thailand was seriously threatened by the Indochinese initiative. Meantime, Deputy Foreign Minister Direck had informed Futami that Crosby had proposed mediation by his government. Futami therefore advised Matsuoka to act speedily.[50]

On the 19th, charging that France was plotting to obtain American and British mediation, Matsuoka told Arsène-Henry that his government would be better advised to ask Japan to mediate the dispute. The foreign minister hinted that, should France again refuse Japan's offer of mediation, Japan would be forced to take a very strong attitude.[51]

That same afternoon, just before this meeting, the Liaison Conference approved an "Outline of Emergency Measures to Deal with the Thailand-French Indochina Border Dispute," which read:

1) *Policy*
Thailand must be forced to reject the British offer of mediation. Simultaneously the Empire should exert efforts to settle the dispute immediately by putting pressure on both parties.

2) *Toward Thailand*
a) Thailand must be forced to reject the British offer and made to understand Japan's offer of mediation concerning the recovery of its lost territories.
b) Japan should put pressure upon French Indochina to conclude an armistice immediately.
c) At the appropriate time, Japan must secure an agreement in principle from Thailand concerning a new Japan-Thailand pact, particularly a military pact.

3) *Toward French Indochina*
a) A proposal for an armistice should be made immediately to France and the French Indochina authorities.
b) Japan should indicate to French Indochina that any recourse to British mediation would violate the Matsuoka-Henry pact and threaten the stability of the Far East, the establishment of the New Order in Greater East Asia, and settlement of the China Incident, and that the Empire therefore cannot ignore such a move on the part of French Indochina.
c) After outlining this position to France, Japan should bring necessary pressure to bear upon French Indochina. The methods of pressure and military operations will be decided upon separately.[52]

The phrase "necessary pressure" referred to a proposal to stage a demonstration by Japanese war vessels in the South China Sea and to double for a limited time the Japanese force in French Indochina in the course of transferring troops stationed in the north. Matsuoka was opposed to this decision, fearing that it would bring about a reaction on the part of Britain and the United States and cause the policy to fail. In the end he agreed to a joint army-navy proposal to make Thailand reject the British offer of mediation and to stage military exercises to pressure the belligerents, particularly French Indochina, to cease hostilities. But he remained hesitant concerning a military pact with Thailand, emphasizing the difficulties involved, and finally succeeded in amending the "Outline" to provide for its proposal at a later date.[53]

The following day, therefore, Matsuoka made an official offer of Japan's good offices to Arsène-Henry, stipulating a cease-fire as a precondition to mediation. The French ambassador pointed out that France would find it difficult to accept Japan's offer if retrocession of territory along the Mekong were a precondition. Matsuoka answered that it was not. Arsène-Henry thereupon promised to recommend to his government and Governor-General Decoux acceptance of Japan's offer.[54]

In Bangkok on the 21st Minister Futami placed the proposal of mediation before Pibul, who accepted it immediately. On the 22nd further pressure was brought to bear on Arsène-Henry by Vice Minister Ōhashi, who threatened that the Japanese forces in Indochina, whose strength at the moment was being doubled in the course of rotation, might be provoked into action if the French delayed in accepting Japan's proposal.[55]

Britain was growing increasingly alarmed at what it saw as a Japanese threat to the autonomy of Indochina and Thailand. In an aide-memoire handed to Hull on January 22 the fear was expressed that, unless something were done to limit Japan's influence in the region, Indochina would soon be swallowed up and Thailand reduced to a puppet state. Should Britain and the United States allow such aggression to take its course, Japan would eventually be in a position to launch an attack upon Malaya and the Dutch East Indies—and only war could then put a halt to the Japanese advance. Britain proposed that, in order to retard Japan's policy of "infiltration and absorption," their governments must "at each successive stage of Japan's advance" display some reaction making clear that they "are not prepared to remain passive while Japan attempts to alter the *status quo* in the Far East." It further asked the United States to exercise its influence with the French government to begin negotiations in Bangkok or, if it were unwilling to do that, to reiterate yet again its "well-known view . . . regarding the settlement of disputes by negotiations" and appeal to the disputants to reach an agreement. Britain, it said, had been doing its best to impress upon the Thais its desire that negotiations take place, indicating that any threat, direct or indirect, to British possessions would result in "immmediate reaction from His Majesty's Government." The memoire contained records of the British approaches to Thailand through the minister in London and to Governor-General Decoux through the British naval commander in Singapore.

Hull responded that while the British views would be given "very full and careful consideration," he doubted that his government could do anything more than it was doing. "Japan probably is directing and controlling the course and attitude of Thailand toward the Indochina situation," he said, and "in these circumstances it may be very difficult to get the ear of the Thai government."[56]

Britain's efforts to limit Japanese influence in an Indochina settlement came too late, for France had already decided to accept Japan's offer of mediation. In a conversation with Leahy that same day, Flandin stated that France was "no longer in a position to refuse." Rejection, he said, would mean increased Japanese support to Thailand, threatening Indochina with rapid collapse and leading in the end to its submission to both Thailand and Japan. He asked the United States to exercise influence on Japan so that no territorial changes would be brought about in Indochina through Japanese mediation, and he made a final plea for delivery of urgently needed arms and munitions.[57] Unable to expect support from Britain and the United States, France saw in Japanese mediation the best hope of preserving its territories.

On the 17th the Japanese government had informed Ott of its intention once again to offer to mediate the dispute.[58] It explained its reasons in a note Ambassador Kurusu handed to Weizsaecker in Berlin on the 18th:

The Government of French Indochina has lately shown by various indications that it is seeking to establish relations with England and the United States. For instance, it is now about to buy airplanes in the United States;

in the question of maritime traffic between France and French Indochina, it has requested England's consent; in the boundary conflict
with Thailand, it is seeking Anglo-American mediation, etc. This attitude
is in conflict with the French Government's recognition of Japan's hege-
mony in the Greater Far Eastern sphere. The Government of French Indochina is striving to establish close relations with the nations which are
unfriendly or hostile to Germany; this endeavor has detrimental effects
on Japan and in particular on the relations between the German Reich
and the Vichy Government. The Japanese Government has therefore earnestly called the attention of the French Government to this attitude of
the Government of French Indochina.

Weizsaecker responded that while there was no evidence that French
Indochina had caused harm to the relations between Germany and the
Vichy government, it was in the interests of Germany that peace and
order be maintained in French Indochina.[59]

Japan was also concerned that the planes in Martinique not be permitted to reach Indochina, a question that had been put before the
German-French Armistice Commission in Wiesbaden.[60] On the 23rd
Kurusu asked the German government "to work on the Vichy regime.
Japan's southward advance to Singapore," he said, "is impossible without going through the Malay peninsula, and in order to utilize this land
bridge Japan must go through Indochina and Thailand. For this reason,
Great Britain must be prevented from exercising influence upon Thailand."[61] Germany did not approve transport of the planes from Martinique, and on the 28th Leahy was informed by the French colonial
minister that Germany had also declined to approve the sending of any
troops to French Indochina. In other words, Germany would not permit
France to strengthen its position in Indochina.[62] Germany had acceded
to Japan's request.

On the 24th Arsène-Henry officially accepted Japan's offer of mediation. This did not mean, he told Matsuoka, that France would passively
concede Luang Prabang and Pakse to Thailand, simply that it was prepared to halt military operations as soon as Thailand agreed to a cease-
fire, and that Thai and French troops must first of all be withdrawn to
their own territories. Three days later he acceded to the principles of
mediation set down by Japan. The talks, held on a Japanese light cruiser
anchored off the port of Saigon, began on the 29th and an armistice was
signed at 8:00 p.m. on the 31st.[63]

With the failure of its efforts to prevent Japanese involvement in a settlement, Britain now tried to exert some influence over the outcome of the negotiations. On January 30 Nevile Butler proposed to Stanley Hornbeck that their governments should signify to Japan their continuing interest in the matter. This was followed on February 3 by a note to Pibul warning against any compromise of British interests in the region and expressing Britain's opposition to any military alliance between Thailand and Japan, to the establishment of Japanese bases in Thailand, or to economic concessions by Thailand to Japan. On the 7th Pibul assured Crosby that Thailand would continue to respect its treaties with Britain.[64].

On January 30 the Liaison Conference met to consider Japan's future policy in the light of the new circumstances. Its earlier "Outline of Emergency Measures to Deal with the Thailand-French Indochina Border Dispute" of the 19th had provided that "necessary pressure" should be brought to bear upon French Indochina. The Japanese navy and army had thereupon begun to assemble troops and make strategic preparations for an advance southward, with northern French Indochina, Hainan island, and Taiwan as the bases for operations. For the Japanese military, mediation of the border dispute between Thailand and French Indochina would provide a stepping stone for Japan's advance southward to Malaya and the Dutch East Indies. Foreign Minister Matsuoka, however, still seemed to regard the negotiations themselves as the primary objective. For while he talked of the need for resolution to attack Singapore and wage war against Britain, his real intention may have been to check the military.

With the offer of mediation accepted and talks about to begin in Tokyo, the Liaison Conference now approved a new "Outline of Policy toward French Indochina and Thailand." This decision committed Japan to a policy of establishing close military, economic, and political ties with Thailand and Indochina for its "self-preservation and self-defense." Japan, it said, should take whatever measures were necessary to realize these objectives, even military action against French Indochina. Mediation of the border dispute should provide the opportunity to strengthen Japan's position of leadership over Thailand and French Indochina and to bring about the conclusion of military pacts with both states.

In the course of discussions on this "Outline" Matsuoka expressed strong opposition to a passage providing for the launching of military operations by the end of March. In the end the passage was eliminated and a supplementary decision simply stated that the objectives of the policy "should be achieved" by about the end of March or the beginning of April and that diplomatic efforts should be exerted to that end. Should French Indochina refuse to conclude a military pact, a separate decision would then be reached concerning military operations.[65] To the Japanese military, mediation of the dispute between Thailand and French Indochina was a chance to establish Japan's dominance in the region, a dominance which military leaders saw as a necessary preparatory step in the southern advance. The navy in particular had certain concrete objectives, such as the use of Camranh Bay as a naval base and the establishment of an air base near Saigon. But its leaders hesitated to reveal the extent of their ambitions and therefore acceded to Matsuoka's position with euphemistic references to the need to insure the maintenance of trade and transportation, for guarantees to prevent further disputes between Thailand and French Indochina, and so forth.

On February 6 Vice Minister Ōhashi confided to Ambassador Ott that in the course of the mediation conference Japan intended to sign secret pacts with France and Thailand pledging the latter two not to conclude military or political pacts with third powers. France's obligation, of course, would relate only to Indochina, since it had already signed the armistice pact with Germany. He added that Japan's action was based upon the principle of the tripartite alliance and aimed at eliminating British and American influence in East Asia. The German government, therefore, should welcome Japan's action, which would also be reported to the Italian government. On the 17th Weizsaecker cabled Ott to indicate that Germany welcomed Japan's proposal of mediation.[66]

The conference opened in Tokyo on February 7. Thailand put forward a claim to almost all the territory it had lost since 1867, a demand that France of course could not accept. The conferees were thus confronted with an immediate deadlock in the negotiations, and the armistice that had originally been due to end on February 11 was extended until the 25th. On the 17th Japan proposed a compromise,[67] but this effort to end the stalemate failed and on the 24th Japan put forward another plan, requesting that both sides respond by the 28th and setting noon on March 7 as the final deadline for the armistice.[68] "Now there can be no room for further amendments or reservations," Matsuoka told the negotiators firmly. On the 26th Thailand gave full approval to the Japanese plan, but France refused at first to accept it. The conference remained deadlocked as March 7 drew near.[69]

On February 23 the Liaison Conference discussed the question of what Japan should do if its mediation proposal were not accepted. The issue was raised by Army Chief of Staff Sugiyama Gen, who asked, "Should our military plans be put into effect as previously decided?" Navy Minister Oikawa Koshirō advised caution: "Since the situations in Britain and the United States as well as in Thailand and French Indochina have changed since the policy toward Thailand and French Indochina was adopted, further study is necessary before we undertake military action." Navy Vice Chief Kondō Nobutake agreed: "Military action should be undertaken only as a last resort. At this point I hope Japan will avoid a confrontation with Britain and the United States."

The two service vice chiefs conferred the following day, and on the 25th Tsukada Osamu reported to the Army General Staff that he had asked Kondō the real reason the navy had taken a "soft attitude" at the Liaison Conference. Kondō had emphasized that he had referred to military action against the "great south"—that is, against Malaya and the Dutch East Indies—but the navy "had not changed its mind concerning military action related to current policies toward Thailand and French Indochina." Nonetheless, the Army General Staff was under the impression that while it had decided to mobilize, the navy was still reluctant to decide on military action.[70]

Finally, on the 28th agreement was reached on "Actions to be Taken if France Rejects Our Final Mediation Proposal," which was adopted by the Liaison Conference on March 1.

1) The Empire will demand that France accept our plan by noon on March 5.

2) Military demonstrations against French Indochina will be increased and the repatriation of Japanese residents and guards in the Saigon area will begin, to be completed during the period of the armistice. The military demonstrations will be accompanied by displays of air power.

3) If France does not accept our final mediation plan by the deadline of March 5, the Empire will commence military action against French Indochina. This military action will be carried out on the basis of the "Outline of Policy toward French Indochina and Thailand," Point 3, No. 5, Sec. 3, which received imperial approval on February 1, 1941.

4) Military action will begin from March 8, but the precise date will

be decided after tactics toward French Indochina have been determined. Should France accept our mediation proposal after March 8, we will stop military action.

5) If France has not accepted our final mediation plan by March 5, from March 8 on we will approve freedom of action for Thailand to seize such territory as is awarded in our meditation plan. Military assistance, including weapons, munitions, and technical advice, will be supplied to Thailand.

6) Concerning mediation hereafter, there will be no change in the final mediation plan during the armistice period.

Note: (a) With regard to Sec. 4, plans after the dispatch of troops will be decided in accordance with the situation at the time. (b) The final mediation plan is that presented on February 24.

This then was Japan's final decision. It remained only to await the French answer. France held out as long as it could, but on March 6 it accepted the mediation plan "in principle" and a communiqué was issued prolonging the armistice and putting its procedures into effect. Japan's continued efforts to obtain the agreement of both Thailand and France finally suucceeded on March 10, and on May 9 a peace treaty was signed.[71]

The Stationing of Troops in Southern Indochina

In a meeting of the Liaison Conference on March 11 Matsuoka disclosed that Thailand had proposed a military alliance with Japan. This issue, he said, should be dealt with separately, otherwise a military alliance with Thailand would oblige Japan to give France compensatory guarantees. He proposed instead that the existing friendship treaty between Japan and Thailand be expanded, adding, "At any rate, I have told the representative from Thailand that a military pact would have to be considered separately from the present treaty."[72] It is interesting to note that it was Thailand, not Japan, which proposed a military alliance, and it was Matsuoka who refused the proposal. Thailand succeeded in winning back its sizeable lost territories in Laos and Cambodia without paying compensation to Japan in the form of a military alliance. Japan, however, secured from France and Thailand a pledge not to conclude a treaty with any third power hostile to Japan.

On June 11 the high command of the army and navy reached agreement on "Measures for Advancing the Southern Policy," a document that was presented to the Liaison Conference that day. At the meeting Matsuoka refused to agree to Sugiyama's demands that he begin negotiations with France for the stationing of troops in southern French Indochina. Such action, he feared, would arouse both Britain and the United States and force Britain to move into Thailand. At another meeting the following day Navy Chief of Staff Nagano Osami said that if French Indochina refused to accede to Japan's demands, or if the United States, Britain, or the Netherlands interfered, military measures would have to be adopted. But Matsuoka continued to oppose the stationing of troops in French Indochina. Negotiations to establish air and naval bases had to come first, he asserted, and then the question of stationing troops could be discussed.[73] On the 16th he reiterated this position, arguing that any effort to station troops in French Indochina would create international distrust of Japan. But in the end he yielded to the military, and on June 25 the Liaison Conference adopted the "Measures for Advancing the Southern Policy."

1) The imperial government, keeping in mind existing circumstances, will advance the policy already approved with respect to French Indochina and Thailand. In particular, a military relationship with French Indochina, aiming at the security and defense of East Asia, must be established as soon as the representatives to Indochina return.

Through the establishment of a military relationship with French Indochina, we should aim at the attainment of the following:

a) The creation or use of air bases and ports at specified places in French Indochina or the stationing of necessary troops in southern French Indochina.

b) The provision of necessary conveniences for the stationing of imperial troops.

2) Diplomatic negotiations will commence in order that the preceding items may be attained.

3) Military means will be used if the French government or the Indochinese authorities do not accept our demands.

4) In order to carry out the preceding items, plans for military operations must be prepared.

At Matsuoka's insistence the phrase "even at the cost of war with the United States and Britain" was eliminated.[74]

Three days before this decision was taken, the German army had invaded the USSR, producing a major change in the international situation. On July 2, therefore, the Imperial Conference met to consider a new policy document. The second article of this "Outline of National Policies in View of the Changing Situation" stated:

> The Empire will continue the diplomatic negotiations with respect to the southern area necessary for its self-preservation and self-defense and will promote various other policies. If necessary to the attainment of these policies, the Empire will prepare for war with the United States and Britain. We will first carry out various policies with respect to French Indochina and Thailand, on the basis of the "Outline of Policy toward French Indochina and Thailand" and "On the Promotion of a Policy toward the South," and thereby strengthen arrangements for the advance toward the south. To obtain these objectives the Empire will not hesitate to engage in war with the United States and Britain.[75]

This new decision set down Japan's determination to wage war against the United States and Britain if necessary. And while it confirmed the policy of southern advance, it also left open the possibility of operations in the north should a favorable situation develop.

Early in July Governor-General Decoux learned, through a conversation between Captain Jouan and Major-General Sumita Raishirō, chief of the Japanese military mission to French Indochina, that Japan would demand the right to establish bases in southern French Indochina. He reported this immediately to his government, which alerted Ambassador Arsène-Henry in Tokyo.[76] Matsuoka had intended on July 5 to instruct Japan's ambassador to France, Katō Sotomatsu, to negotiate directly with the Vichy authorities, because he feared Arsène-Henry would leak news of any negotiations on the subject to his American and British colleagues. It soon became apparent, however, that Craigie had already been informed of Japan's intentions, and Matsuoka postponed the cable to Katō. But the foreign minister grew anxious lest the British invasion of Syria in early June be reported in Indochina and sent the instruction to Katō on July 12. Two days later Katō handed to Admiral Jean Darlan, the vice premier and foreign minister, a note demanding the following concessions: 1) military cooperation with Japan for the defense of French Indochina; 2) support for Japanese army, navy, and air force personnel dispatched to southern French Indochina; 3) use of eight air bases, including Saigon, and the use of Saigon and Camranh Bay as naval base⌐ together with their complete equipment; 4) freedom of residence, of maneuvers, and of action for troops stationed in Indochina, including the supplying of special requirements necessary for carrying out the required duties; 5) funds for the dispatched troops; and 6) "approval of the general arrangements for the entry of Japanese troops, approval of the principle of consultation between Japan and French Indochina concerning the procedures involved in the entrance of Japanese troops and the withdrawal of French Indochinese troops from the areas where Japanese troops would land in order to avoid conflicts, and other necessary arrangements." The demands were accompanied by the following explanatory note:

> This proposal aims at the joint defense of Indochina. The Empire guarantees that there will be no change in its pledge to respect the territorial integrity of French Indochina and French sovereignty there which was previously guaranteed by the imperial government. This decision has been made after careful consideration and with a firm will. Therefore, we are fully determined to carry it out.

Japan requested that the French government answer the note by July 19. On the 15th Katō met with Premier Henri Pétain and conveyed a message from Prime Minister Konoe promising Japan's commitment to respect the territorial integrity of and French sovereignty in French Indochina.[77]

On July 16 Ambassador Grew informed the State Department of the Japanese demands, which he had learned about through Craigie. Welles at once ordered Leahy, at Roosevelt's suggestion, to talk personally with Pétain and express the hope that France would delay its decision as long as possible. In France, Ambassador Leahy received word of the Japanese demands that same day, during a meeting with Marshal Pétain. The subject was first brought up by Darlan, who was also present. According to the vice premier, there had been no ultimatum, but while Japan spoke "courteously" of a joint occupation for the common defense of Indochina, he was aware that "it amounts to a move by force." France would make a "symbolic defense," Darlan said, but it was unable to resist as it had in Syria. As Leahy left, Pétain remarked privately that "events of the greatest import" were about to occur. Did he mean in the Far East? Leahy asked. To which Pétain only answered, "There and everywhere else."[78]

Leahy carried out Roosevelt's instruction in a meeting with Pétain and Darlan on the 19th, the day the French were due to answer the Japanese demands. The French leaders promised to make an effort to delay giving a definite response but were certain that Japan would not wait more than a week before taking action. While Darlan felt Germany would oppose the establishment of Japanese bases in Indochina and the Dutch East Indies, he did not think seeking advice from Germany would serve as a delaying tactic, since Franco-German relations at the time were strained.[79]

Meanwhile Japan was pressing for a favorable reply. On the 17th Darlan assured Katō that a response would be forthcoming on the 19th. In Berlin Ambassador Ōshima Hiroshi endeavored to persuade the Germans to insure France's acceptance of Japan's demands. Nonetheless, on the 19th Darlan told Katō that, under the terms of the armistice, the French government would have to consult Germany and Italy before giving a definite answer. Katō took this as a rejection of Japan's demands and the following day, upon further instructions from Tokyo, insisted that all the demands be accepted by 6:00 p.m. (French time) on the 22nd, under threat of immediate military action. France had no choice but to submit, and at noon on the 21st Darlan officially accepted the demands. The reply stated that the French government had "no choice but to yield to the demands" of Japan and agreed to "cooperate" with Japan in the defense of French Indochina. France would not, however, "participate in offense strategies." Japan was asked to withdraw its forces as soon as the problem that required their stationing in Indochina was settled and, further, to issue immediately a public statement guaranteeing to "respect the territorial integrity of Indochina and French sovereign rights over the colony."[80]

On the 22nd the negotiations at Vichy were concluded with an exchange of letters, and the following morning talks began in Indochina between Governor-General Decoux and General Sumita concerning the details of the stationing of Japanese troops. By eight o'clock that evening everything had been settled. American and French efforts to delay the occupation had failed.[81]

The United States now began to consider more drastic measures against Japan. On the 21st Hull expressed to Welles his fear that Japan might soon launch a general rather than a piecemeal advance in the Far East. He agreed that Welles should meet with Ambassador Nomura Kichisaburō, if only for the record, and assure him that the new Konoe cabinet would find the United States patient if it truly meant to work for

a peaceful settlement. If not, and if Japan continued to take action showing the world that it was following a policy of force and conquest, then
the Japanese government should declare frankly to the United States
that it could not continue discussions for a peaceful settlement.[82]

Nomura met with Welles on July 23. He explained that the Japanese
move into southern Indochina had been necessitated by the critical
economic situation in Japan and by reasons of military security. With the
western powers cutting off trade, Japan had been forced to find substitute sources of supply or be doomed to collapse. He urged that the
United States not "reach hasty conclusions" and assured Welles that the
new government in Japan was as eager as its predecessor to come to an
agreement with the United States. In reply Welles stated that his government viewed Japan's action toward French Indochina as fundamentally opposed to any policy of understanding with the United States and
regarded the agreement as confirmation of Japan's support of Hitler's
policy of world conquest and domination. Neither Britain nor the
United States constituted any threat to Japan, he continued, therefore
the occupation of Indochina could only signify Japan's intention to pursue "a policy of force and of conquest" and had been undertaken in preparation for an offensive against the South Seas area.[83]

On July 24 the State Department issued a press release condemning
Japan's action in Indochina. It declared in part:

> By the course which it has followed and is following in regard to In-
> dochina, the Japanese Government is giving clear indication that it is de-
> termined to pursue an objective of expansion by force or threat of force.
>   There is not apparent to the Government of the United States any
> valid ground upon which the Japanese Government would be warranted
> in occupying Indochina or establishing bases in that area as measures of
> self-defense.
>   There is not the slightest ground for belief on the part of even the
> most credulous that the Governments of the United States, of Great Brit-
> ain, or of the Netherlands have any territorial ambitions in Indochina or
> have been planning any moves which could have been regarded as
> threats to Japan. This Government can, therefore, only conclude that the
> action of Japan is undertaken because of the estimated value to Japan of
> bases in that region primarily for purposes of further and more obvious
> movements of conquest in adjacent areas.

The announcement concluded with a warning that, in endangering
American access to essential commodities and the security of the Pacific,

including the Philippines, Japan's actions "bear directly upon the vital problem of our national security."[84]

On the 25th President Roosevelt issued an executive order freezing Japanese assets in the United States. The next day Britain took similar action, followed by the Dutch East Indies on the 27th. On the 28th Japanese troops began to move unopposed into French Indochina, which thus came under Japanese control. On the 29th signatures were exchanged on the Japanese-French Protocol Concerning Joint Defense and Mutual Military Cooperation in French Indochina, together with a Note on Mutual Military Cooperation.[85] Thus the negotiations between Japan and France came to an end, and the Indochina problem, hitherto an issue primarily involving Japan and France, now brought Japan and the United States into confrontation.

FIVE

The Navy's Role
in the Southern Strategy

TSUNODA JUN

Translated by
ROBERT A. SCALAPINO

The Navy Eyes the Dutch East Indies

From July 1940 on the diplomatic policies of Foreign Minister Arita Hachirō met with growing opposition from other branches of the government. The navy, in particular, became increasingly critical of his policies and began to advance its own views independently of the government and the Foreign Ministry. These views revolved around the dazzling opportunity Germany's war in Europe was giving to Japan to replace the European Powers in Southeast Asia and the frightening probability that a Japanese advance would bring on war with the United States.

The navy had initiated planning for a southern advance as early as 1936. During the Hirota cabinet's discussions of the draft "Foreign Policy of Imperial Japan," the navy had leaked a plan to seize of the oil fields in Borneo in certain eventualities, a suggestion that had worried Arita and surprised the Army General Staff.[1] At that time the head of the War Guidance Office (*Sensō Shidōhan*) of the Navy General Staff, which was directly responsible to the vice chief of the Navy General Staff, was the so-called "King of the South Seas" Nakahara Yoshimasa, who had persuasively advanced within the Navy General Staff his conviction that Japan's destiny lay to the south. Not surprisingly, he regarded the outbreak of war between Britain and Germany in 1939 as

---

* This essay originally appeared as "Nihon no tai-Bei kaisen (1940-nen–1941-nen)," in *Taiheiyō sensō e no michi*, vol. 7, part I, sec. 1, pp. 16–28 and sec. 2, pp. 44–53, 65–88, 109–18.

Japan's golden opportunity. On the very day war began Nakahara exulted:

> Finally the time has come. This maritime nation, Japan, should today commence its advance to the Bay of Bengal! Moss-covered tundras, vast barren deserts—of what use are they? Today people should begin to follow the grand strategy of the navy, altering their old bad habits.
>
> Japan must be brought back to its maritime tradition, placing the main emphasis on the development of the navy. (We should not hesitate even to fight the United States and Britain to attain that end.)[2]

A few days later his desire was elaborated in greater detail:

> Under present circumstances, Japan must advance east of the Dutch East Indies to Malaya (naturally Australia will come under our control) and to the British islands in the South Seas. . . . The empire must take this opportunity to advance in the South Seas. . . . For this purpose, an arms replenishment program must be promoted in accordance with the following plan, so that we shall be prepared for any eventuality.
>
> 1) An arms replenishment program must be promoted so that active maneuvers in the south may begin from August 1 of next year.
>
> 2) For this purpose the remodeling and repair of naval vessels now under way must be completed by April 1 of next year. From April Guard Squadrons will be revived. From June 1 crews will be fully stationed on all naval vessels and full-scale exercises on a war footing will be undertaken.
>
> 3) On August 1 the 5th Fleet will be prepared for operations against Hong Kong. The 1st Fleet will support the 5th Fleet, the 2nd Fleet will wait in the Gulf of Tonkin for the next advance to Singapore, while the 4th Fleet will advance to the Palaus and the 5th Fleet to Ponape.

As this document shows, Nakahara had drawn up a concrete schedule for military operations in the south.

The arms replenishment program discussed in Nakahara's plan was viewed as one stage in the navy's planning for war, paralleling the army's mobilization plan. Since August 23, 1937, following the outbreak of war with China, the navy had carried out similar replenishment programs on three occasions. On September 16, 1939, one week after Nakahara submitted his plan to the Navy General Staff, it was decided to put a fourth such program into effect.

In the meantime the Navy General Staff had several times attempted to obtain the Navy Ministry's agreement to a fleet reorganization, to begin on November 15, 1939. The reorganization was to be based upon a "first alert" status, an intermediate stage between a peacetime and wartime footing and constituting about 60 percent of a wartime structure. (A "second alert" status would have constituted about 80 percent of the wartime organization.) Eventually the Navy Ministry did agree to a gradual reorganization whereby the fleet would reach "first alert" status by April 1940, and preparations began for the execution of this plan.

On October 20 the Naval Affairs Bureau presented to the Foreign Ministry, with the approval of Navy Minister Yoshida Zengo, its "Outline of Policy toward America." The draft contained the following sentence: "In view of the unpredictability of American diplomacy, as shown by the sudden notice of termination of the Treaty of Commerce and Navigation, an arms replenishment program must be promoted to provide against any emergency."[3] Nakahara's idea was thus not merely a private proposal but expressed attitudes shared by middle-echelon officers within the navy.

On November 15, 1939, as Nakahara had anticipated, a new, independent 4th Fleet was organized and charged with the topographical investigation and training in the South Seas. It was assigned to forward (blue water) operations and, like the Combined Fleet and the China Fleet, was under the direct supervision of Imperial Headquarters. It was also planned to increase the fleet's strength by attaching to it the 17th Squadron (submarine tenders), the 18th Squadron (light cruisers), the 30th Destroyer Squadron, the 5th Submarine Squadron, and the Yokohama Air Corps.

By the beginning of April 1940, the target date set by the Navy Ministry, the ministry had concluded that there would be no drastic change in the war situation in Europe and therefore withheld the order putting the fleet reorganization on a "first alert" basis. The Navy General Staff also decided merely to strengthen the fleets for forward operations to the approximate level of a "first alert" in its 1941 reorganization plan. Then, on April 9, Germany invaded Norway and Denmark, and the attitude of the Navy Ministry and General Staff changed abruptly. At this time the influence of section chiefs within the Navy General Staff was very great, and decisions taken at section chief conferences often determined the policy of the General Staff. At conferences held on April 11 and 12 the section chiefs asserted that "the time has come to occupy the Dutch East Indies," and on the 20th discussions again centered around the Dutch East Indies. On April 24 Chief of Staff Prince Fushimi Hiroyasu reported to the emperor:

> In view of the present critical international situation, an internal instruction has been dispatched to make preparations to organize the fleet on a first and second alert basis. The preparations are being carried out so that the first stage may be completed within one and a half months and the second within about three months of the issuance of the order. At present everything is almost ready, except for air force crews and a few other matters. After receipt of the order the navy will require at least five to six months to prepare for war, needing time to requisition and equip special vessels.

Needless to say, the navy's plans for the occupation of strategic points in the Dutch East Indies and its preparations for placing the fleet on "alert" status were accelerated by the launching of Germany's western offensive on May 10. That same day the Navy General Staff decided that the 4th Fleet should prepare to be dispatched southward and that studies should be made of the need to organize the fleet on an "alert" basis in case of possible violations of the neutrality of the Dutch East Indies by Britain, France, or Germany. Early on the morning of May 11 Navy Vice Chief of Staff Kondō Nobutake sent the following cable to 4th Fleet Commander Katagiri Eikichi: "It has been decided internally that the 4th Fleet will be sent to the Palaus as required so that it may be dispatched to the Dutch East Indies. Therefore preparations for sailing should be made immediately." He also ordered orally the Yokohama Air Corps attached to the 4th Fleet to proceed with preparations for war as quickly as possible.

The 4th Fleet left Yokosuka for the Palaus between the 15th and 17th of May. The navy's enthusiasm at its departure is apparent from the fact that Kondō's mobilization order was also circulated to the commanders of the Combined Fleet, the 2nd Fleet, the 1st and 2nd China Fleets, and the naval bases. It can also be seen in the statement made in the name of Navy Minister Yoshida on Navy Day, May 27, when he asserted that "Japan's naval power, which was demonstrated in the great victory of the Battle of the Japan Sea thirty-five years ago, will now be exhibited in the Pacific."[4]

It was generally agreed among naval officials that a military occupation of the Dutch East Indies with its important natural resources was possible at any time so long as Britain and the United States did not intervene. Following the events that took place in Europe in May, such a military occupation of resource areas or even a more general occupation of the entire Dutch East Indies, whose sovereign government fled from home, was considered not impossible in view of the difficulties Britain was then facing and providing that the United States remained a passive spectator.[5] Since May 20 Nakahara had emerged as a central figure on the Navy General Staff's Committee to Study Southern Policies and after June 20 as a staff member of the Naval Affairs Bureau, a post which he held simultaneously. The only element in Nakahara's program of the previous year that had not yet been put into effect was his plan for large-scale naval maneuvers. In place of such maneuvers, between May 15 and 21 map exercises involving southern operations were carried out by the Navy Ministry, Naval Aviation Headquarters, and Ship Procurement Headquarters. The only major map exercises on this scale to be conducted before the outbreak of the Pacific War, they were based on the most accurate data available and concerned the adequacy of the mobilization plan, the timing of the opening of war, basic strategies, and the construction plan of warships and other vessels during a war. The war game proceeded along the following lines:

It was recognized that relations among the United States, Britain, and the Netherlands were fundamentally inseparable. However, assuming the possibility of separating them, if there were some sign of a violation of the status quo of the Dutch East Indies by Britain, France, or Germany, the Japanese navy would proceed to occupy beforehand such important natural resource areas as the petroleum fields in Borneo and the nickel mines in the Celebes on the pretext of guaranteeing the neutrality of the Dutch East Indies, regardless of whether such a request came from the Indies. For this objective, when Blue (the Japanese navy) singlehandedly launched a surprise attack from the Palaus by a fleet on a war footing, labeling it a naval exercise in order to keep its real purpose secret, the operation was frustrated by a Red (the hypothetical enemy, the U.S. navy) counterattack, due to the inadequacy of Blue's military preparation for a decisive battle. The strategy of attacking only the Dutch East Indies while taking every precaution to avoid hostilities with the United States resulted ultimately in war with the United States, Britain, and the Netherlands, developing into an attack on Malaya and a protracted war against the U.S. navy, whose base was in Hawaii.[6]

The conclusions, reported to the navy chief of staff on the 23rd and to the navy minister on the 24th, were:

> 1) If U.S. exports of petroleum are totally banned, it will be impossible to continue the war unless within four months we are able to secure oil in the Dutch East Indies and acquire the capacity to transport it to Japan.
>
> 2) Even then, Japan would be able to continue the war for a year at most. Should the war continue beyond a year, our chances of winning would be nil.[7]

Upon receiving this report Navy Minister Yoshida asked Operations Division Chief Ugaki Matome whether the proposal for an attack upon the Dutch East Indies was not "nonsense if, in spite of occupying their important resource areas, it is difficult to secure the sea routes to bring back their natural resources." Yet in spite of the grave conclusions that grew out of the map exercises, Yoshida alone questioned the opportunistic plan for a military invasion toward the south. Meanwhile, this very project was being advanced secretly, independently of the cabinet, and completely ignoring the diplomatic policies of Foreign Minister Arita.

Army-Navy Strategic Plan of July 1940

Within the Army General Staff plans for military operations in French Indochina were being enthusiastically promoted by Tominaga Kyōji, chief of the Operations Division, and his subordinates, although their views had so far had little influence on senior officers of the General Staff. But the idea of formulating a broader, more fundamental southern advance policy and the creation of a national structure in preparation for the execution of such a policy were gaining currency within the General Staff and the Army Ministry at this time. Such ideas were given new impetus by the remarkable success of Germany's western campaign and the collapse of French resistance in June 1940, events that astonished military observers all over the world. Most impressed by the German victories were Japanese middle-ranking army officers who, far from the scene of the hostilities, lost all capacity for detached observation and, convinced that there had been changes in the world situation, began hastily to draft a program for coping with them.

On May 19, the day the German army broke through the Maginot
Line, Iwakuro Hideo, chief of the Army Ministry's Military Affairs Section, ordered a staff officer, Nishiura Susumu, to draft a grand strategic
plan taking these changes into account. That same day, and again early
in June, Nishiura drafted a short statement warning of the need for
careful study in preparation for the southern advance. As a result, on
June 21 a preliminary plan was drafted by the War Guidance Office of
the Army General Staff, under the guidance of Usui Shigeki, chief of the
Subversion and Propaganda Section, who was in charge of matters relating to national policy at the time. The following day a draft was completed after consultations among responsible officials of the Army Ministry and General Staff. Two days later it was discussed further in talks
between Iwakuro and Military Affairs Section Chief Kawamura Saburō,
representing the Army Ministry, and Usui and Operations Section Chief
Okada Jūichi, representing the General Staff. The plan that emerged
from these discussions was completed by the Operations Section on the
25th. On July 1 this document was presented to a conference of division
chiefs of the Army General Staff, who gave their approval the next day.
When on July 3 it received the joint approval of key individuals in the
Army Ministry and General Staff, the "Outline of the Main Principles
for Coping with the Changing World Situation" became the basis for the
national policies advocated by the army.[8] The policies followed by the
army until war broke out in December 1941 were based largely on the
program set forth in the "Outline." Indeed, it was to exercise a fatal influence upon subsequent events, in the sense that the entire scenario
had been set forth therein.

The army's aims were clearly revealed in an explanation attached to
the draft handed to the navy on July 4, when representatives of both
services met to discuss the "Outline." Japan's fundamental problem, it
was asserted there, was "to free itself from its dependence upon Britain
and the United States . . . through the establishment of a self-sufficient
economic sphere centering upon Japan, Manchuria, and China" and
stretching from the Indian Ocean to the South Seas north of Australia
and New Zealand. In establishing such an economic sphere, moreover,
the empire would have to sever the ties that intimately bound the
region to Britain. Japan, it was urged, should act before the European
conflict ended, when "British and American pressure against Japan will
be greatly increased . . . , when Britain will seek its revival through

securing territories in the Pacific, and when the United States attains the level of military strength through which it hopes to dominate the world." Japan should therefore not hesitate to go to war with Britain and the Netherlands but should take advantage of America's indecision and Britain's difficulties in Europe to attack Malaya and Hong Kong and expel British forces from the Far East and the southern areas. In addition, the resources of the Dutch East Indies should be brought under Japan's control so that Japan might become economically independent of Britain and the United States. The explanation concluded with a plea that, in a period when "the entire world is experiencing historic change," Japan "should not miss the opportunity to establish a self-sufficient economic sphere. The rapid changes taking place in the world do not permit a moment's hesitation. . . . Never in our history has there been a time like the present, when it is so urgent to plan for the development of our national power. . . . We should grasp the favorable opportunity that now presents itself." [9]

The army's position was further developed by Operations Section Chief Okada, who stated that Japan was very likely to have to undertake southern operations before the China War was settled. The southern advance should be given priority, he went on, even if it meant a less desirable settlement in the China conflict. War preparations should be completed by the end of August, because the European war would reach its climax during the summer or might be concluded even earlier should Germany launch an attack across the Channel. An attack on Hong Kong, however, was not to be made until it was certain that it would not lead to war with the United States. An attack on Singapore might follow that on Hong Kong, particularly if a "favorable opportunity" should arise, such as Britain's thorough defeat by Germany.

Okada and his colleagues continued to advocate these views until the end of August, the date they had set as a target for the completion of war preparations. On August 28, in a meeting with members of the Operations Section of the Navy General Staff, they stated: "The capture or bombing of Hong Kong and/or Singapore should be carried out as soon as there is any sign of British submission and a peace settlement with Germany, to establish Japan's right to participate in the peace conference. But such an attack should be directed only against Britain, so that there will be no war with the United States." In a note of September 11, answering a query from the Navy General Staff, they repeated these views: Japan should not be overly concerned with war preparations and thereby "miss the opportunity presented by Britain's defeat following an attack on the British Isles or its exhaustion as the result of a prolonged war."

From the "Outline" and the oral and written explanations of it, it is evident that the drafters, dazzled by Germany's achievements, had lost all capacity for objective judgment. Thereafter, driven by the desire to obtain economic self-sufficiency, by a determination to seize this "golden opportunity," and by a bullish confidence stemming from their firm belief in a German victory, they began to plan the establishment of a new world order.

On September 13 American Ambassador Joseph C. Grew described their program:

> Whatever may be the intentions of the present Japanese Government, there can be no doubt that the army and other elements in the country see in the present world situation a "golden opportunity" to carry into effect their dreams of expansion; the German victories have gone to their heads like strong wine; until recently they have believed implicitly in the defeat of Great Britain; they have argued that the war will probably end in a quick German victory and that it is well to consolidate Japan's position in greater East Asia while Germany is still acquiescent and before the eventual hypothetical strengthening of German naval power might rob Japan of far flung control in the Far East; they have discounted effective opposition on the part of the United States although carefully watching our attitude. . . .[10]

That the "Outline" was a hastily prepared policy drawn up by officers confident that Germany's victory over Britain was certain is attested to by the fact that no careful study was ever made of Japan's material ability to carry out a comprehensive policy of southern expansion. On July 29 Army Vice Chief of Staff Sawada Shigeru reported to the emperor that the policy, "which depends entirely upon the achievements of the Germans, will be put into effect only in case of German success in their operations against Britain." The next day a similar statement was made to the emperor by his chief military aide-de-camp Hasunuma Shigeru, who commented: "Japan does not attempt to solve the southern problem by itself; its real intention is to benefit itself at the expense of others." In speaking of "the expense of others," Hasunuma referred primarily to German aid. But he also had in mind the Japanese navy. In the months that followed, the weakness and ambiguity of the planners' policy of southern advance was to emerge in the course of negotiations with the navy.

On July 25 Mutō Akira, chief of the Army Ministry's Military Affairs Bureau, called on the new prime minister, Prince Konoe Fumimaro, and expressed the view that "a war with the United States must be avoided" and his hope that Japan would be able to join the German-Italian Axis and at the same time secure materials both from the south and from the United States. But while the army planners insisted that a war should involve only Britain, on the "hopeful chance" that Britain and the United States could be separated, they knew that the capture of Singapore would necessarily involve naval operations, which meant that an agreement with the navy was essential. The navy's reaction to the "Outline" was therefore a matter of great concern to the army.

In early June, after receiving Nishiura's second statement of warning, Takatsuki Tamotsu, a member of the Operations Section of the Army General Staff, had called on Kawai Iwao in the Operations Section of the Navy General Staff to explain the draft "Outline." On July 4 Usui, Okada, and Nagai Yatsuji, a senior official of the Military Affairs Section, met at navy headquarters with Ōno Takeji, head of the War Guidance Office, and Nakazawa Tasuku, chief of the Operations Section, and with Shiba Katsuo, Ōmae Toshikazu, and Miwa Yoshitake of the First (War Preparations) Section of the Naval Affairs Bureau. Various amendments were proposed by the navy, and on July 9 Kawai explained these amendments to the Army General Staff. At a second army-navy conference on July 15 agreement was almost reached, and it was left to four representatives of the Operations sections of both sides to prepare an amended version and draft an explanatory statement. Usui was also to draw up an explanation of the final document.[11] One day after agreement was achieved, the Yonai cabinet resigned.

The navy's amendments were related primarily to relations with the United States, with the object of expressing a firmer attitude toward that nation. Thus, the navy accepted the army's judgment that "the most opportune time" to solve the problem of the south was near and that it would still be possible to wage war with Britain alone while not refraining "from facing the inevitable aggravations" in relations with the United States that would result. While the plan specified that military operations would be restricted "insofar as possible . . . to Britain alone," the navy was aware, as a result of its war games in May, that a war with the Netherlands would inevitably lead to war with Britain and the United States, and that southern operations would therefore end with the involvement of the United States. As a result, the navy proposed to add to the section dealing with Hong Kong the following sentences: "A military offensive is to be avoided insofar as possible. But if the situation permits, an offensive will be carried out with a firm resolution for war against Britain (or even against the United States)."

In the meeting of July 15, moreover, the navy insisted that the army draft be amended to avoid creating any impression that no military offensive was planned. Accordingly, the army's statement that although Japan would "endeavor insofar as possible to avoid war with the United States, all necessary preparations must be made for the opening of a war against the United States," was offered in view of the navy suggestion that the position be phrased even more explicitly: "While operations should be structured so that no war against the United States results, sooner or later military action against the United States may become inevitable.

The previous October, immediately after the opening of the Anglo-German war, Nakahara had written in his personal diary that Japan should not fear to wage war against the United States and Britain in carrying out an advance to the south. His view was shared by other middle-grade officers in the navy, who during the map exercises in May agreed that "war with the United States may become inevitable sooner or later" in the course of any southern operation. Now they agreed to the army's plan for war with Britain, on condition that the navy was given time to complete its war preparations. They had grown increasingly confident that Japan would triumph even over the United States, should war with that nation result from southern operations, so long as sufficient military preparations had been made.

When he received the report on the army-navy discussion of the "Outline" on July 4, Operations Division Chief Ugaki Matome commented that war with Britain meant that Japan would have to make full preparations for war with the United States. War Guidance Chief Ōno agreed with the principle of "northern defense and southern advance," but he expressed doubts that the army would be willing to prepare for war with the United States at the expense of its posture of preparedness against Russia in the north.

Within the navy, unknown to the government and the army, plans for an invasion of the Dutch East Indies were already being prepared. Thus, the army's proposal for a southern advance aroused some feelings of resentment among naval planners at this preemption of their own long cherished ideas. At the same time, they had no grounds for opposing totally the army's plan, nor was there any group within the navy desiring to raise any overall objections. Opposition to a southern advance might have meant "southern defense and northern advance," implying possible war with the USSR based on the posture of no war with the United States and resulting in a substantial shift of military budget to the army. On the other hand, cooperation with the army's southern advance plan would enable the navy to achieve its policy of "northern defense and southern advance" and at the same time to expand its armaments significantly. Therefore a posture of war with the United States became an internal necessity in strengthening the navy's position vis-à-vis the army.

Another reason for the absence of navy opposition to the army's proposals was the feeling among officers of admiral rank in the ministry and General Staff, particularly since Yoshida's appointment as navy minister, that interservice cooperation was in the national interest and that disputes, such as those in the past between Yonai Mitsumasa and Itagaki Seishirō over the strengthening of the Anti-Comintern Pact, had to be avoided. The few objections they did raise to the strong demands of the army were so muted and indirect that policy on the question gradually came under the control of the army.

Holding such an attitude toward relations with the army,[12] the navy planners therefore acknowledged the possibility of waging war against the United States provided that "satisfactory preparations" were made. And with agreement in principle achieved, they hoped the army would cooperate in providing the materials, manpower, and industrial capacity necessary to strengthen the naval arm. Thus, while the navy was willing to assert the possibility of managing the war satisfactorily, this conclusion was probably not based upon any substantial strategic calculations but rather derived from a realization that it would necessitate the strengthening of the naval force. In short, it was an argument of convenience, with little basis in reality.

An acceptance of the need for compromise with the army, the request for time to complete war preparations, and a substantial ambiguity about ultimate victory over the United States—these were to characterize the attitude of the navy in policy discussions with the army and the government in the year and a half that preceded the outbreak of the Pacific War. Thus, when the army, unaware of internal conditions within the navy, presented a proposal which depended upon the navy to carry out, the navy quickly acquiesced and twisted it in a policy of increasing firmness toward the United States. However grandiose and statesmanlike their language, the plans that resulted from interservice conferences in the months to come were based upon the one-sided and mutually contradictory dreams of each side.

This pattern began to emerge at their first meeting on July 4, when Okada, speaking for the army, called for a "powerful politics" to be carried out by a prime minister not chosen from the army. He expressed anxiety that an imperial order would call for an army man to form a new cabinet, although it was his hope that Prince Konoe would be given the mandate and would name Tōjō Hideki or Yamashita Tomoyuki as army minister and Matsuoka Yōsuke as foreign minister. This proposal meant the overthrow of the Yonai cabinet as the first step toward a "powerful politics." The suggestion met with no challenge from the navy, which had sent Yonai to the premiership. Thereafter the army began to pursue openly Yonai's overthrow as the prerequisite to the achievement of its plans.

Naval Preparations against the United States: September

Meanwhile, in May 1940, the 4th Fleet had assembled at the Palaus and the 2nd China Fleet, the naval force closest to the Dutch East Indies, had been ordered to guard the 4th Fleet in the event of a sudden attack on the Dutch East Indies. Anticipating a possible violation of the Indies' neutrality by Britain, France, or Germany, the navy hoped to take advantage of such a situation to launch its planned southern advance. The opportunity did not, however, arise, and the "Outline" as finally agreed upon by the army and navy stated merely that "with respect to the Dutch East Indies, for the present efforts will be made to acquire needed resources by diplomatic means." In their meetings with army officials in July, the navy representatives urged that the army plan for a military invasion of the Dutch East Indies be scrapped. In the end the two services agreed upon a formulation stating that military operations aimed at winning control of the region would be used if favorable circumstances should in the future arise, when the Dutch East Indies would of course be an important target; but "for the present, diplomatic means" would be used.

In accordance with this decision, Prime Minister Konoe requested General (Res.) Koiso Kuniaki, who had been minister of overseas affairs in the former cabinet, to head an economic mission to the Dutch East Indies. On July 30 Koiso submitted to the prime minister a document entitled "The Urgent Policy of the Empire," in which he recommended that the negotiations be underwritten by a full display of military might. The mission was to travel to the Dutch colony on a war vessel and would be accompanied by a "substantial contingent" of marines. The navy, however, refused to agree, and on August 1 Vice Minister of Overseas Affairs Tanaka Takeo remarked that it seemed that the Navy was hoping "that negotiations will be conducted in the manner of regular trade negotiations, whoever is dispatched as envoy." When Koiso asked Navy Minister Yoshida on August 19 whether the navy would send in troops if the lives of Japanese residents in the Dutch East Indies were endangered, Yoshida replied that troops would of course be sent. But, he added, "before dispatching a large number of troops, we should be very cautious." Could war vessels be sent to the area? Koiso asked. To which Yoshida replied, "Right now it is not possible." [13]

The navy, it seems, had changed its attitude on policy toward the Dutch East Indies. Not only did it refuse to mobilize militarily, but it even opposed conducting diplomatic negotiations under threat of military action. Its plan for a sudden attack upon the Dutch East Indies as the first target in the southern advance had, it indicated, been postponed. But this did not mean that the navy no longer regarded the Indies as a target in the southern advance, and in August, when the United States threatened to strengthen its embargo against Japan in an effort to forestall a Japanese attack on the Dutch East Indies, the navy once more considered an invasion of the islands.

On July 30, two days before negotiations were opened in Tokyo between Foreign Minister Matsuoka and French Ambassador Charles Arsène-Henry concerning the passage of Japanese troops through French Indochina, the Operations Section of the Navy General Staff began to discuss the question. On August 1 its views were formulated for submission to the Army and Foreign ministries in the following "Study of Policy toward French Indochina."

The advantages of stationing troops in French Indochina for the purpose of a southern advance are:
1) It will represent a firm step forward in the southern advance (control over Thailand, Burma, and Malaya).
2) It will be of great strategic advantage in a war against the United States and Britain.
3) Products necessary for defense (coal, rubber, rice, iron ore, and phosphorus) will be secured.
Assuming this to be correct in principle, it has been decided that if our aims cannot be obtained by diplomatic negotiations, military power should be mobilized to achieve our purpose.
If, after delivering an ultimatum, Japan occupies all of French Indochina, there is a strong possibility that the United States will tighten its embargo. An American embargo on scrap iron and oil would be a matter of life or death to the empire. In that event the empire will be obliged to attack the Dutch East Indies to secure oil.
The following countermeasures should therefore be planned:
1) Mainly in view of the empire's war preparations, military operations against French Indochina should begin after early November.
2) While all necessary measures should be taken to limit military operations to French Indochina, if this is not possible Japan must be resolved to wage war against other powers.
3) If the situation develops very favorably for Japan, military operations in French Indochina might begin earlier than November. The time and details of military operations can be decided later.
4) The navy should be placed on an emergency war footing when appropriate, with all preparations made for mobilization of the fleet.[14]

In short, the navy was advocating a policy that foresaw military operations against French Indochina, leading to a more rigid American embargo against Japan, whereupon Japan would launch an attack upon the Dutch East Indies, accepting the risk of war with the United States and making preparations for such a war. Thus, while it postponed the attack upon the Dutch East Indies until stronger economic sanctions were imposed by the United States, the navy now established its resolve and began to accelerate its preparations for war with the United States.

On August 2 representatives of the Navy General Staff, the Navy

Ministry, Ship Procurement Headquarters, and Naval Aviation Headquarters met to discuss full-scale planning for a naval war. With regard to the fleets themselves, it was soon clear that, as of September, of the combat fleets on the forward line (that is, the Combined Fleet, the 1st and 2nd China Fleets, and the 4th Fleet) only 57 percent of the principal ships would be available for actual operations, and even if guard squadrons (excluding reserve ships) at naval stations were included, only 77 percent would be available. If an order were issued for "preparatory fleet mobilization" (equivalent to an army mobilization order) to begin on August 15, by the end of September 33 war vessels, including 4 battleships, 5 heavy cruisers, 3 light cruisers, and 4 aircraft carriers, would still not be ready. By the end of March of the following year, however, all but one remodeled aircraft carrier and 4 submarines could be made ready for action, although all new ship building would have to be postponed in the meanwhile. By the end of September 356 requisitioned merchant vessels totaling 650,000 tons could be made ready, and by the end of March 1942, 984 vessels weighing 2 million tons. As for the naval air force, crews almost sufficient for "second alert" status could be trained by the end of March, still 39 percent short of the number needed for full wartime operations.

With respect to war materials, the outlook was gloomy. If the United States should cut off all oil supplies to Japan, the navy's stocks of aviation fuel would last for only a year, and in the second year of an embargo, Mishuku Yoshimi, chief of the Navy Ministry's Munitions Bureau, estimated that 4 million tons of crude petroleum would have to be acquired. Stocks of nickel, molybdenum, tungsten, copper, zinc, mercury, mica, asbestos, aluminum, cobalt, and crude rubber were sufficient for only a year and a half, should all trade with the United States and Britain be halted. "Such a situation would finish us," Ship Procurement Headquarters Chief Toyoda Soemu declared. "The navy could barely fight for one year."

Nevertheless, on August 4 the Navy General Staff met to discuss placing the fleet on a wartime footing, with September 1 as the target date. Further conferences were held between top officials of the ministry and General Staff on the 15th and 17th, when it was decided that "promotion of war preparations" should begin immediately. In particular, a fleet reorganization was to be initiated, the aim being to complete the work necessary for "preparatory fleet mobilization" by November

15. This involved equipping and preparing the navy for operations in the early period of hostilities. The decision was reported to the Throne by the navy minister on the 21st and by the navy chief of staff on the 24th, and to the chiefs of staff of the fleets and naval stations on the 27th.

Preparation for war and the decision to wage war are closely related, and a decision to execute a "preparatory mobilization" order clearly indicated that the navy had taken the first step in its gradual resolve to wage war with the United States, even before the conclusion of the Tripartite Pact and the stationing of troops in French Indochina had led to a drastic deterioration in relations with that country. Moreover, the decision naturally heightened the alarmist mood toward the United States within the navy.[15]

Navy Minister Yoshida took issue with the logic of the General Staff. "The Japanese navy can continue the fight against the United States for only one year—is this not a very unreliable navy?" he asked at the August 2 meeting. But the United States would probably plan for a protracted war; therefore, he went on, "I trust that the Navy General Staff will seriously investigate the relationship between the extent of our naval armaments and our prospects in a protracted war." On the 15th he warned that even if Japan did complete its preparations by the target date of November 15, this did not mean that immediate operations in the South Seas could begin. Other factors must first be considered, in particular whether Britain's defeat was certain and whether a total United States embargo against Japan was likely. In the latter case, he continued, "I would not be wholly in favor of military operations."

While Yoshida considered carefully all the issues involved in a possible confrontation with the United States, Navy Chief of Staff Prince Fushimi, in contrast, viewed the question in much simpler terms. "Since, after a decision to wage war is taken, at least eight months will be needed to prepare," he told the emperor, "the later war comes, the better."[16]

Yoshida also called for further discussions with the army, urging on the 2nd that the navy state openly "its own firm position with respect to the execution of national policies" and not allow itself to be "pulled by the army." "There are major differences between the army and navy in interpreting the 'Outline of the Main Principles for Coping with the Changing World Situation,' " he told the Navy General Staff on August 27. "One reason for this is that the two general staffs had different ideas when they drafted the plan. I hope both sides will continue to discuss the matter."

Discussions did continue—between the chiefs of both Operations sections on the 28th and between top officials of the two services on the 29th—but the significant issues were not raised; and while a document drawn up by the navy on the 27th was partially discussed by the Operations Section chiefs, it was not brought up at the conference on the 29th, which adjourned without discussing the core issues.

The navy's document was concerned largely with Japan's prospects in a war with the United States. In keeping with the army's "Outline," it at first foresaw the commencement of military operations if a "favorable opportunity" presented itself or if hostilities were unavoidable for the sake of the empire's prestige. Then the navy departed from the "Outline" to enumerate the circumstances in which it believed Japan would be forced to undertake military operations "for the survival of the empire, whether we like it or not." These were:

1) If the United States institutes a complete embargo against Japan and is followed by other powers, resulting in a situation in which Japan is forced to wage war to acquire necessary materials.
2) If the United States and Britain cooperate to apply pressure against Japan or clearly intend to do so.
3) If the United States and Great Britain take measures that directly threaten our existence.

This document shows that the navy intended to clarify to the army chiefs its views on national policy, a task that Yoshida himself, because of his troubled psychological state, did not accomplish. At the same time, even though the document was not handed to the army, the navy was obviously convinced of the inevitability of the process of American embargo leading to Japanese military operations in the South Seas and ultimately to war with the United States, "for the survival of the empire, whether we like it or not." Already the navy's views had gone beyond those expressed in the "Outline of the Main Principles."

As to Japan's chances of victory in a war with the United States, the navy planners were confident "if the United States wants to decide the war quickly." But they did not expect this to be the case, and if, as they thought likely, "the United States bases its strategy on a protracted war, then we are not very confident of our capacity for endurance." Nonetheless, they asserted that if Japan's resolve were firm and if the nation's energies were concentrated on the production of naval armaments in preparation for hostilities against America, there was no need for undue pessimism. The "Outline" had already decided on a shift in policy emphasis toward the South Seas, therefore "it is natural that national energies should be directed toward this policy. Consequently, some adjustments must be made between the armaments of the army and those of the navy." Precisely when the navy would be ready for war depended upon the speed with which naval armaments could be prepared, which in turn depended upon how easily the necessary materials and labor could be acquired. The navy's requirements for war in the South Seas would be less if it did not involve a direct conflict with the United States. But, they warned, "if we undertake war, we must be prepared in the final analysis for a direct confrontation with the United States," therefore "all of the armaments demanded by the navy must be prepared and supplied." In concluding that the navy's maximum requirements must be met, however, the planners had somehow forgotten the most important question—could Japan defeat America?

Even if a positive answer were implied, could the navy actually have persuaded the army and the government of the need to focus the nation's energies on the preparation of naval armaments? After all, it was the customary practice in the Shōwa era to balance the needs of the army and the navy. And even if the navy's demands were largely fulfilled, could Japan hope to match the rapid naval expansion that would certainly take place in America in a protracted war? Was there any possibility that Japan could win such a war? To these crucial questions the navy seems intentionally to have avoided providing answers. Instead, it began with the question of the possibility of victory as a convenient argument in support of its demands for naval armament.

Twenty years before, at the time of the Washington Conference, the then navy minister Katō Tomosaburō had warned the ministry of the potential strength of the United States: "If Japan continues to build new ships, the United States will not just stand by and watch without developing its own naval building plans. Eventually it will develop new plans. Japan must be prepared for this. Should this happen, the gap in naval power between the two nations will increase steadily; it will never decrease. At that point Japan will be threatened tremendously."[17]

Now, on August 26, Admiral Nomura Kichisaburō, who in a few

months was to depart for negotiations with the United States in Washington, issued a similar warning to Navy Minister Yoshida: "We are already in the fourth year of the China Incident and our national strength has been considerably exhausted. A war [between Japan and the United States] would, of necessity, be a long one, and this would be very disadvantageous to Japan. There is therefore a limit to the hard attitude Japan can adopt toward the United States. In my opinion, these are facts fundamental to both political and strategic considerations."[18] That the navy's data failed even to take note of such warnings points to the conclusion that it had intentionally evaded the central question for its own immediate interests.

At the naval planning conference on August 2 Vice Minister Sumiyama Tokutarō called for a revision of the 1940 materials mobilization program, as an initial step in the new national emphasis on naval armaments. The following day, and again on the 6th and the 26th, Operations Section Chief Nakazawa Tasuku and Mobilization Section Chief Hashimoto Shōzō called on Army General Staff Operations Section Chief Okada Jūichi to obtain approval of the navy's requests for new allocations. A proposal for a new materials mobilization program, entitled "Promotion of Preparatory Fleet Mobilization," was presented to the cabinet on September 26 by Navy Minister Oikawa Koshirō and approved, subject to Army Minister Tōjō's proviso that the effect upon army procurements would be minimized. On December 10 the cabinet agreed to a new materials mobilization program for the third and fourth quarters of the year which, for the first time, gave the navy priority over the army in allocation of war resources.[19] In supplies of steel products, for example, the balance was:

	Army		Navy	
	3rd Quarter	4th Quarter	3rd Quarter	4th Quarter
Base Tonnage	20.8	20.8	15.7	15.7
Current Allocation	18.4	18.4	13.7	13.7
Demanded Increase	4.3	4.3	15.0	15.0
New Allocation	2.0	1.8	11.5	7.8
Total Allocation	20.4	20.2	25.2	21.5

Unit = 10,000 tons

Apart from the immediate needs for naval building, there were other reasons for altering the materials mobilization plan. Japan's worsening economic relations with Britain and the United States had made it increasingly difficult to obtain vital imports. Moreover, by late June it appeared that the foreign exchange available would fall some 20 percent short of what was needed to fulfill the original materials mobilization program. How then could the navy continue to assert that there was no need for undue pessimism in a war against the United States?

Another question is what the cabinet understood it had agreed to on September 26. What did the navy mean by the phrase "preparatory fleet mobilization" (*suishi jumbi*)? Had Oikawa explained it fully to the cabinet? What was Konoe's understanding of it when he presented the revised plans in a report to the Throne on December 17?

At each stage the phrase was interpreted as referring to the need for preparedness in terms of matériel and applied to the revision of the materials mobilization program and the completion of naval armaments. But while this may have been the assumption of civilian officials ignorant of naval terminology, to the navy it implied a state of preparedness close to full mobilization for war. Thus, the issuing of a "preparatory fleet mobilization" order indicated that the navy was taking its first step in its gradual resolution to wage war. Moreover, its August 17 decision for the "promotion of war preparations" (*sembi sokushin*)—to commence the first stage of work prior to issuing a "preparatory fleet mobilization" order, in order to reduce the time required to carry out the order—in fact meant that the navy, independently of the army and the government, had taken its first step toward war with the United States.

The "Outline of the Main Principles for Coping with the Changing World Situation" had not directly confronted the issue of war with the United States, but it had raised two important questions: If the United States placed an embargo on all trade with Japan, should Japan go to war or adopt a policy of concessions to obtain a relaxation of the embargo? And given the probability of a complete American embargo, should Japan abandon its plan for military operations in the South Seas or take the risk?

These were matters of life or death for Japan and deserved exhaustive research and consideration before any decision was made. But rather than discussing them with the government and the army, the navy had arbitrarily resolved to wage a war that it had concluded would inevitably follow a Japanese advance toward the South Seas—then American embargoes and a Japanese attack on the Dutch East Indies.

And its preparations for that war had begun. The perilous significance of this posture was clearly revealed in July 1941, when the anticipated embargo was imposed following the stationing of Japanese troops in southern French Indochina. The navy then forced the government to accept its earlier analysis and acquiesce in its resolution for war. By this time it was too late to reconsider these two crucial issues. There were already almost immovable faits accomplis. The navy had accelerated its planning for a "preparatory fleet mobilization" and the embargo order had been issued.

The Navy Supports the Tripartite Pact

These forces and attitudes explain the navy's decision this same month to support the Tripartite Pact. With the outbreak of the China War, anti-British sentiments suddenly appeared within the middle echelons of the navy. These sentiments received formal expression at a conference of Navy General Staff section chiefs the following year and had a profound effect upon the thinking of the General Staff. Thenceforth Britain was targeted in map exercises as a hypothetical enemy second to the United States. The mood of hostility could not be restrained by the chief of the Operations Section Kusaka Ryūnosuke, nor by the successive chiefs of the Operations Division, Kondō Nobutake and Ugaki Matome. Simultaneously, pro-German sympathies became widespread, fueled by an illusion that Germany supported Japan's aims.[20] The top officials of the Navy Ministry—Navy Minister Yonai, Vice-Minister Yamamoto Isoroku, and Naval Affairs Bureau Chief Inoue Shigeyoshi—did not share the emotional feelings that permeated the General Staff, and in the discussions that took place between August 1938 and August 1939 concerning the strengthening of the Anti-Comintern Pact, they remained opposed to a military alliance aimed against Britain, France, or the United States. On August 20, 1938, Yamamoto asked the First (War Preparations) Section of the Naval Affairs Bureau, which was charged with drafting a naval policy on the issue, several blunt questions: Was not an attempt to strengthen relations with Germany and Italy disadvantageous to Japan's relations with Britain and the United States in attempting to reach a solution of the China problem? What countermeasures were available to Japan if the United States, Britain, and France brought economic pressures to bear against the Axis powers? What would be the result if we restrict it to the USSR? Since Japan could not expect substantial help from Germany in case of war with the USSR, what benefit would there be? Would it not be disadvantageous for Japan to conclude an agreement quickly? If a pact were concluded, would Japan have to give to Germany and Italy some rights and interests in China?[21]

Yamamoto later summarized his opposition to a pact: "To take sides with Germany, which aims at the establishment of a new world order, necessarily involves Japan in the war by which Germany is attempting to destroy the old order centered upon the United States and Britain. But for some years to come there is no hope that Japan could win a war against the United States with its existing naval force, particularly given the preparedness of its air force."[22]

In meetings of the cabinet Yonai took the same position. Japan, he contended, could not possibly win a war against Britain and the United States, and on this point, he told Prime Minister Hiranuma Kiichirō on May 15, 1939, "there is no room for the navy to concede."[23] His stand was in strong opposition to Army Minister Itagaki Seishirō, to whom he remarked, "If you venture to fight against Great Britain, I will oppose you even at the cost of my position."[24] When asked by Ambassador Grew at a dinner in honor of the crew of the ship *Astoria* in April 1939 if Japan intended to fight the United States, Yonai answered it had consistently "no intention whatsoever since the days of the Washington Conference."[25]

Within the Navy Ministry, however, the views of the General Staff were shared by the First Section of the Naval Affairs Bureau, headed by Oka Takazumi, which was responsible for policy on the issue.[26] In a conference with army officials on May 15, 1939, Oka made numerous concessions "to accommodate to the army's position," although he added that these were his own "private opinions."[27] This division in the navy's ranks soon became obvious to outsiders, including officials of the Foreign Ministry, who took note of Yonai's insistence that Japan must retain the right to decide if and when to join with Germany and Italy in a war. In contrast, they reported, subordinate officials dealing with the matter felt that while Japan hoped to avoid being forced automatically to enter the war in Europe, "the question of whether or not to enter a war must be decided in terms of the *common interests of the three countries* and in consultation with Germany and Italy."[28]

So long as Yonai, Yamamoto, and Inoue were in charge of naval policy, their views, although those of a minority, prevailed. The navy's fundamental policy against war with the United States likewise remained unchanged. With the resignation of the Hiranuma cabinet, however, Yonai left his post as navy minister and in January 1940 voluntarily assumed reserve status when he was asked to organize his own cabinet. Yamamoto and Inoue were ordered to sea duty, and with the departure of this triumverate, the ministry's determination not to wage war against the United States suddenly collapsed. Their successors—Navy Minister Yoshida Zengo, Vice Minister Sumiyama Tokutarō, and Naval Affairs Bureau Chief Abe Katsuo—were unable to counter the growing anti-British and pro-German sentiments in the middle echelons. Moreover, the Naval Affairs Bureau's "Outline of Policy toward America," presented to the Foreign Ministry on October 20, indicated that an anti-American policy was increasingly seen as the corollary of this anti-British line. "In view of the fact that the United States and Britain cannot be dealt with separately," this document stated, "Japan should not pursue a deliberate policy of friendship toward the United States while alienating Great Britain."[29] The navy's policy toward the United States had been fundamentally altered.

Admiration for Germany within the navy, especially among middle-ranking officers of the General Staff, was heightened with the invasion of Norway and Denmark and the lightning success of the western campaign.[30] Renewed pressure for a strengthened German alliance, with the United States as a target, now arose within the General Staff, beginning with Vice Chief of Staff Kondō Nobutake.[31]

Even as the Army General Staff was drafting its "Outline of the Main Principles for Coping with the Changing World Situation" in mid-June, the Navy General Staff was preparing its own policy to deal with the new situation in Europe. Entitled "The Empire's Policy in View of the Decline of Britain and France," it was concerned with the need to define Japan's sphere of influence as well as to reach an "overall diplomatic settlement with the Soviet Union" and advocated rapprochement with Germany and Italy, concluding that the idea of simultaneously seeking an accommodation with the United States was unrealistic. Consequently, when Okada stated at the first interservice meeting on the "Outline of the Main Principles" on July 4 that policy toward Germany, Italy, and the USSR must be given "first priority," the navy's representatives concluded that the army favored a tripartite alliance and therefore expressed no substantive opposition. Meeting with army, navy, and Foreign Ministry officials on the 12th and 16th to consider strengthening Japan's ties with the Axis, Shiba Katsuo of the First Section of the Naval Affairs Bureau enthusiastically agreed with a policy calling for "a concrete political understanding on strengthening diplomatic and economic ties" with Germany and Italy. He asserted that the navy would be able to adjust its policies to this goal,[32] a view which Ōno Takeji thought he could persuade senior officers of the Navy General Staff to accept.

The draft of "The Empire's Policy" had in fact been carefully studied by Naval Affairs Bureau Chief Abe and Navy Minister Yoshida, who had expressed no opposition. Shiba was therefore justified in his assumptions.[33] At a meeting of senior officials of both services on July 22 Military Affairs Bureau Chief Mutō Akira declared that "if Germany and Italy propose a military alliance, we must accept." He was backed up by Army Vice Chief of Staff Sawada Shigeru, who stated that Japan must "resolve to share our fate with Germany and Italy." In the end naval representatives agreed to amend the Foreign Ministry's "Proposal for Strengthening Cooperation between Japan, Germany, and Italy," adopted by middle-echelon officials on the 16th, to provide that for the present Japan would "proceed to strengthen political ties."[34]

On July 30 a new proposal "On Strengthening Cooperation between Japan, Germany, and Italy" was drafted by the Foreign Ministry at the behest of Matsuoka, who had a week before taken charge at the ministry. The document was sent to the army and navy for approval, and on August 6 responsible officials of both services met to discuss it. At this meeting it was apparent that Navy Minister Yoshida was virtually alone in his stand against the Axis pact. Even Naval Affairs Bureau Chief Abe remarked that "in the rapidly changing international situation Japan is becoming isolated from the world powers. Nor are its relations with the United States good. Thus, it is natural for Japan to look to other powers for support. The alliance cannot be avoided."[35] On the question of war with the United States, however, Yoshida yielded to pressure from the Navy General Staff and at the August 17 conference with top officials of the Army General Staff agreed to the immediate "promotion of war preparations" in anticipation of a "preparatory fleet mobilization" order on November 15. The first step toward a determination for war with the United States had been taken. But Yoshida's opposition to the tripartite alliance, while he simultaneously set in motion preparations for war with the United States, soon placed him in an untenable position with respect to others both within and outside the navy.

In opposing a tripartite pact in order to avoid war with the United States, Yoshida was carrying on the policy of his predecessor Yonai Mitsumasa, as Yonai and Konoe had expected when he was appointed. But his views met with little support within the navy. According to Enomoto Shigeharu, an international law specialist and adviser to the navy, "it is argued from time to time that the navy has been left behind in the current situation and must join the general trend of the times. Such opinions are often expressed by extremists who advocate intimate relations with Germany and Italy. Their purpose is to force the navy to adopt an agressive policy."

Pushed by two opposing factions, increasingly passive and inconsistent in his own policies, and fundamentally disliking politics, Yoshida progressively withdrew from the pressures around him until, on September 3, he was hospitalized; the following day he resigned. During the preceding month the navy's circular logic—of military operations against French Indochina, leading to a more rigid American embargo against Japan, forcing Japan to attack the Dutch East Indies, making inevitable hostilities against the United States—had set in motion concrete preparations for war. The only problem now remaining was the question of the tripartite alliance, to which Yoshida remained the only stumbling block. The choice of his successor was naturally influenced by that issue.

In the selection of Oikawa Koshirō as navy minister Captain Ishikawa Shingo, then a section chief on the Asia Development Board, appears to have been influential. When asked which admiral he thought "would unconditionally support the tripartite alliance," he answered unhesitatingly, "Oikawa."[36] Matsuoka also seems to have influenced the choice, and on August 23 he met with Ishikawa.[37] In November Oikawa appointed Ishikawa chief of the newly created Second Section within the restructured Naval Affairs Bureau, charged with foreign and defense policy and liaison with the army.

On the 5th Oikawa went to see Konoe and after only 16 minutes of discussion accepted the post of navy minister. The Foreign Ministry's proposals for an Axis alliance had been stymied by Yoshida's opposition.

However, Prime Minister Konoe had given his approval to Matsuoka's amended version of a tripartite pact by the afternoon of the 4th, and he was doubtless eager to end the impasse over the issue. Moreover, Oikawa was related by marriage to Shiratori Toshio, leader of the pro-Axis faction within the Foreign Ministry, and therefore should have been intimately acquainted with attitudes in the Foreign Ministry.[38] Oikawa's appointment signified that the navy would no longer block the proposed alliance with Germany.

On September 6 Matsuoka asked the Four Ministers Conference for authority to begin negotiations for a strengthened tripartite alliance, emphasizing that this was the only way for Japan to overcome the difficulties it faced. Oikawa, "after a brief, silent reflection on his responsibility as a cabinet minister, agreed, without asking the opinion of his subordinates."[39] Thus agreement was finally reached, and Matsuoka was able to begin talks with the German special envoy, Heinrich Stahmer, who arrived in Tokyo the next day.

On the 12th Matsuoka reported to the Four Ministers Conference on the progress of the negotiations, recommending that Japan accept "as it stands" the proposal for a clearly military alliance that Stahmer had presented the previous day. Oikawa withheld an immediate answer, saying, "Let me think it over."[40] On the afternoon of the 13th Vice Navy Minister Toyoda Teijirō together with Oka Takazumi, the pro-German chief of the Navy General Staff Intelligence Division, visited Matsuoka secretly at his private residence to discuss several amendments the navy wished made to the document. Matsuoka agreed, whereupon Oikawa asserted there was "no further reason for the navy to oppose the alliance, since all our conditions have been accepted."[41] At the Four Ministers Conference held that evening he gave his support to the new alliance and continued to support it at the Liaison Conference the following day, at the Imperial Conference on the 19th, and finally before the Privy Council on the 26th.

Navy Minister Oikawa was a scholarly, soft-spoken individual, who seldom spoke out firmly on important issues. Unlike Yonai and Yamamoto, he was reluctant to press his own views but seemed anxious to avoid friction with others and offered little resistance to internal and external pressures.[42] Not surprisingly, his more aggressive, politically adept vice minister Toyoda Teijirō soon began to take the initiative within the navy.

As commander-in-chief of the naval base at Sasebo in 1938, Toyoda had made a secret request to then Vice Minister Yamamoto that he be appointed Yamamoto's successor; instead, in November he was named head of Naval Aviation Headquarters. He soon became exasperated by what he regarded as Sumiyama's inept handling of affairs as vice navy minister[43] and in September 1950 took over the latter's duties with enthusiasm, only to grow impatient at Oikawa's indecisiveness and to begin himself to play the leading role within the ministry. His activities led Oikawa to remark to Yamamoto that "Toyoda plays too many games. It would be better to replace him soon."[44] Oikawa failed to take any action to replace Toyoda, while the vice minister ignored such complaints and continued to go his own way, often without consulting Oikawa.[45] Toyoda's meeting with Matsuoka on the tripartite alliance is a case in point, and his success in this endeavor could hardly fail to give him a sense of triumph and satisfaction.[46]

Toyoda was a schemer, an opportunist, skillful in adapting to circumstances, but unencumbered by any consistent principles or policies.[47] Thus, the amendments he proposed to Matsuoka were merely technical, drafted to accommodate various opinions within the navy rather than being based on a firm policy, such as Yonai's and Yamamoto's insistence that war with the United States must be avoided.[48] Toyoda's sole concern was that Japan avoid being obligated under the Tripartite Pact automatically to join in a European war. "If we wish to amend the main body of the treaty," he said to Shiba, "the treaty itself will be weakened. This is opposed by both Germany and Matsuoka. Therefore the navy has decided to satisfy its concern by providing for mixed commissions to determine the extent of cooperation and assistance and for an exchange of letters" stipulating that "the question, whether an attack within the meaning of article 3 of the Pact has taken place, must be determined through joint consultation of the three contracting parties."[49]

In actuality, a nation decides on its own initiative when and how it will exercise military power, whatever its treaty obligations. In the Imperial Conference on the 19th Prince Fushimi approached the issue somewhat obliquely when he asked Matsuoka: "Even if Japan should be compelled to participate in the European war because the United States participates in it, it is essential for us to choose independently our own time for beginning hostilities. What assurances does our government have in this regard?" It was an unnecessary and foolish question. The question he should have asked was not whether Japan could decide voluntarily when to declare war but whether it was obligated automatically to enter the war.

In his reply, Matsuoka adroitly shifted the issue from Japan's obligation under the pact to the method of dealing with that obligation, whereby, he argued, Japan retained its autonomy of decision:

> It is clear that Japan is obligated automatically to enter the war. However, it has been agreed that the question of whether or not the United States has participated in the war will be decided by consultation among the three countries. Besides, a joint army-navy commission will study the appropriate action to be taken and its decision will be reported to the respective governments. Thus the final decision will be made by the respective governments. It will be an independent decision.[50]

Thus Matsuoka avoided the difficulties inherent in Fushimi's question. But ambiguities still remained, and the question of Japan's obligations or autonomy under the Tripartite Pact was to reappear as the crucial issue in the Japanese-American negotiations the following year.

The navy's approval meant that the last obstacle to the conclusion of the Tripartite Pact had been removed. Nonetheless, the navy was still concerned to avoid war with the United States. In the course of the Imperial Conference Prince Fushimi had expressed the hope that, following the signing of the treaty, "every possible measure must be taken to avoid war with the United States."[51] Yet the conclusion of a treaty obligating Japan automatically to enter the war on Germany's side if the United States joined in the hostilities meant that the United States, then providing extensive support to Britain and on the brink of war with Germany, was seen as a quasi-enemy. Did the navy's leaders think it would be possible then to avoid war with the United States while supporting Germany? The answer is related to the navy's strategic judgment regarding the Anglo-German war.

On May 21, the day after the first German forces reached the Strait of Dover, Nakahara wrote:

> I think Germany . . . will launch air and submarine attacks against the British Isles as soon as it has increased its submarine strength (about September) and equipped its air force. The German naval force will destroy the British fleet and merchant marine, increasing the stress on the domestic front in Britain. The Germans will then take advantage of that stress to cross the Dover Strait. . . . If Germany's air attack on Britain is

successful and causes great destruction to British naval power, Germany
may advance the date of landing troops in Britain. It is expected to take
place about October.

A week later he wrote:

For the landing operations [against Britain] it is necessary for Germany to
step up its attacks on British ships or to develop the means for adopting
such tactics by building up its submarine fleet. . . . To prepare for the
Strait crossing will take Germany about two months (until August).

Soon after this Nakahara was attached to a section in charge of policy
relating to Britain within the Intelligence Division of the Navy General
Staff. War Guidance Office Chief Ōno Takeji was likewise convinced of
the inevitability of an Axis victory in Europe. Discussing the pact with
French Indochina on July 12 he commented, "Given the present situation, it is almost certain that Germany and Italy will win the war."

The navy memorandum of August 27, drafted for use by the Operations Sections chiefs of both services the following day, but actually not
presented, had stated: "Britain may yield sometime during the summer
or autumn (if Germany occupies the British Isles). . . . Although in the
end Germany will win, ideally we hope the war will be prolonged . . .
so that we may seize any favorable opportunities that arise during this
period." Apparently the navy was not anxious that Britain surrender too
quickly. Ōno and Nakahara had concluded that if Germany's air attacks
continued until the end of August, a German cross-Channel invasion
would succeed and Britain would surrender.[52] Shiba Katsuo also believed the German air war and naval blockade would eventually force
Britain to surrender, although he thought expectations of a German invasion in August were premature.[53] Similar conclusions concerning the
efficacy of the pact and the certainty of a German victory were common.
Matsuda Chiaki, in charge of intelligence concerning the United States
for the Navy General Staff, stated immediately after the alliance was
concluded, "It is sufficient if this treaty can prevent the United States
from declaring war only for this year." Commenting on his remark,
Yoshida Zengo later said, "It should mean that Germany will defeat Britain within the year."[54] In other words, if the treaty prevented the
United States from entering the war on Britain's side for only one year,
Germany would defeat Britain and the war in Europe would be over.

This judgment was predominant within the navy in the summer of 1940.[55] And doubtless it provided the means by which the navy reconciled the contradiction between its support for the Tripartite Pact, aimed against the United States, and its belief that war with the United States could be avoided.

How well founded were the navy's judgments concerning the battle then in progress between Germany and Britain? On July 2 Hitler had issued his first order calling for military staff studies of the possibility of a cross-Channel invasion. At first the high commands urged caution, pointing to the strength of the British fleet and air force and to the geographic difficulties involved. Then on July 12 General Alfred Jodl, chief of operations of the German high command, expressed a more confident outlook in his "First Thoughts on a Landing in England." To circumvent the German navy's inferiority to the British fleet, he recommended a landing on the south coast, where "we can substitute command of the air for the naval supremacy we do not possess, and the sea crossing is short there." To deal with the British land forces and the impossibility of a surprise attack, the landings should "take place in the form of a river crossing in force on a broad front. In this operation, the role of artillery will fall to the Luftwaffe. . . ." The army command now evidenced more enthusiasm for the proposed invasion, and on July 16 Hitler issued his Operation Sea Lion Directive No. 16, followed on the 31st by orders that preparations were to be completed for September 15. Luftwaffe leaders agreed that strategic bombing tactics would put an early end to the war, a judgment supported by two preliminary studies in August 1939 of the problems involved in an air war against the British Isles. On August 13, 1940, Operation Eagle was launched, with the aim of completely destroying the British air forces.[56]

The German navy, however, had from the beginning had doubts about the feasibility of the planned invasion. "The British Home Fleet will always be able to appear in greater strength than our own fleet, if the will is there," it had replied to an army invasion plan on January 8, 1940. Even if extensive air and naval operations were undertaken to render the British navy ineffective, "it cannot be expected that it will be possible, with some degree of certainty, to achieve this object and thus to secure continuous control of the supply lines" of the operation.[57] Moreover, the Luftwaffe, established in 1933 as an independent branch of the German armed services, was not structured and trained to cooperate effectively with the navy under the special circumstances of naval warfare, and its leaders tended to conceive and execute operations against Britain independently of the planning for the invasion, which would be essentially a naval operation. Nor was the Luftwaffe able to achieve the two prerequisites the navy regarded as essential for an invasion: absolute command of the skies over the Channel and southern England and the crippling of the British fleet. So long as British planes were in the air and the Royal Navy was operating in the Channel, there was no guarantee that the invading forces could be landed safely or that, once landed, they could be supplied and reinforced.[58]

The German navy also faced tactical difficulties. Since it possessed no suitable landing craft, the landings would have to be accomplished by towed barges not fitted with ramps for beach landings. They would therefore have to anchor off the British coast for 36 hours while unloading, an impossible feat as long as the British air force survived. The barge convoys would consist of 33 tugs each towing 2 barges and could not be expected to make better than 2 to 3 knots against a current that might run up to 4 to 5 knots. They would have to navigate 40 to 50 miles, which would take at least 15 hours. Protection would be poor, for tides and currents in the Channel rendered mines largely ineffective and only a small number of destroyers, torpedo boats, and minesweepers were available.[59]

The frank recognition by the German navy that it would not carry out the landings successfully or provide protection for the landing forces persuaded Hitler to rethink this strategy. On September 14 he issued an order postponing the operation indefinitely. In effect, this meant that the invasion had been given up.

As if aware of this decision, the British navy, toward the end of October, lifted restrictions on the movement of the Home Fleet and ordered the battleships *Hood* and *Nelson*, which had been sent south to the Firth of Forth on September 13, to return to Scapa Flow in the Orkneys.[60] On October 31 Admiral Sir C. Forbes, commander-in-chief of the Home Fleet, declared to Prime Minister Winston Churchill that "while we are predominant at sea and until Germany has defeated our fighter force invasion by sea is not a practical operation of war."[61]

Both British and German naval leaders were thus aware that Germany lacked the prerequisites for successful landing operations against the British Isles. Most Japanese naval officers, however, failed to reach this obvious conclusion and persisted in their expectation of an early

British surrender. This failure of judgment may have been due to the anti-British and pro-German sentiments that had taken root in the navy since 1938, an emotional bias that rendered its officers incapable of viewing the European situation rationally. Not only did Japan's naval strategists fail to recognize Germany's western successes for what they were, merely local ground war victories, but they failed to note the basic strategic fact that, although British ground forces had been forced to withdraw to the British Isles, behind them was the sea, where British warships and merchant vessels continued to move freely, with little opposition from the German army and its air force. In short, the Japanese Navy General Staff had failed in its responsibility to judge the naval situation and reached a wishful, amateurish conclusion on the naval aspects of the war in Europe.

Both Yonai and Yamamoto continued to oppose this trend in naval thinking. "Abstract opinion, without reference to the concrete situation and its management, can bring only harm, not profit," Yonai commented in the spring of 1940, referring to the need to take a serious view of relations with the United States and at all costs to remain at peace with that nation. When told that the Tripartite Pact had been signed, however, he admitted to Ogata Taketora, "Our opposition was a useless effort. It was like paddling against the rapids only a few hundred yards upstream from Niagara Falls." Supposing that he and Yamamoto still controlled the navy, Ogata asked Yonai, "did you truly oppose it?" Yonai answered with a sigh, "Of course, but we might have been killed."[62]

Even during the period of the Hiranuma cabinet Yamamoto was aware of assassination plots for his stubborn resistance to general opinion in the navy. His will, left secretly in an office safe when he was vice navy minister and discovered after his death during the war read:

It is the supreme satisfaction for a soldier to sacrifice his life for the imperial nation. There is no difference between battlefields and the home front. . . . How lofty is the heavenly benevolence! How eternal is our imperial nation! When one considers the eternal prosperity of our imperial nation, there is no time to think of one's own pride or shame, life or death. . . . My body may be destroyed, but my will shall never be obliterated.[63]

Just before the collapse of the Hiranuma cabinet in August 1939 the outgoing navy minister appointed his deputy to the important post of commander-in-chief of the Combined Fleet. Thus it was that Yamamoto attended a conference of naval chiefs on the evening of September 15, the day after the Liaison Conference had agreed to Stahmer's private plan presented by Matsuoka. Yamamoto was determined to question whether suitable military preparations for war with the United States had been made and to query those responsible—Navy Minister Oikawa, Vice Minister Toyoda, Chief of Staff Prince Fushimi, and Vice Chief Kondō—"whether they are really confident that they will be able to develop rapidly military requirements sufficient to win the war." That morning, however, Oikawa and Toyoda had requested that Yamamoto, as the representative of the Combined Fleet, agree to the proposal which the senior member of the army and navy councilors' conference was expected to approve. Yamamoto remained silent.[64] At the evening meeting Toyoda, who was in the chair, gave Yamamoto little opportunity to speak, Oikawa concluded quickly that the navy had agreed to the alliance, and the meeting was ended.[65] This signaled the end of the Yonai-Yamamoto policy of avoiding war with the United States. On October 14 Yamamoto exclaimed fatalistically to Harada: "It's out of the question! To fight the United States is like fighting the whole world. But it has been decided. So I will fight my best. Doubtless I will die on board the Nagato [his flagship]. . . . Konoe and the others may be torn to pieces by the people. I wonder!"[66]

Soon after the decision was reached Konoe told Yamamoto of a conversation he had had with Toyoda. If there had been difficulties relating to matériel and other war preparations, the prime minister had asked, why had Toyoda not opposed the alliance? "If the navy had registered its opposition at that time," Toyoda had replied, "the navy and the army would have come into conflict and the national policy would have become confused, resulting in grave problems. So, with the larger view in mind, we did not oppose." Forgetting that he himself was responsible for appointing the weak Oikawa as navy minister, Konoe told Yamamoto reproachfully: "The navy must express its opinion on the basis of naval considerations. It does not have to consider domestic problems; those I can handle." Yamamoto later wrote bitterly that "I felt he had made a fool of me. But Konoe is always like this and it was no surprise to me. After all, it is dangerous for the navy to rely on Konoe and Matsuoka and to lose a firm grip on reality."[67]

The army's original "Outline of the Main Principles" had in view military operations against Britain. This had been expanded by Konoe and Matsuoka into a plan to wage war against both Britain and the United States, and the navy had given official support to such a plan. Without considering seriously the consequences, the navy had tossed aside the realistic policies of Yonai and Yamamoto and had lost its "firm grip on reality."

Preparatory Naval Mobilization

Navy Minister Yonai, asserting that the Japanese navy would "have no chance to win a war" against the United States and Britain, had tried desperately to maintain the policy of avoiding hostilities with the United States. His successor, Yoshida, had at least been concerned about Japan's preparedness and ability to sustain itself in a protracted war with the United States. In contrast, Oikawa's views concerning such a war were not only ambiguous, but also irresponsible. Answering questions in the Privy Council on September 26, Oikawa declared: "Today our fleets are completely equipped and in no way inferior to those of the United States. But," he went on, "if the war is protracted, we would have to make more complete preparations, as the United States would certainly augment its naval armaments. With regard to this point, the navy is doing its best, using all possible methods. . . . At present, if we aim at a quick war and a quick victory, we have a good chance to win. With respect to war in the future, we are now undertaking a plan for expansion in various areas."

Concerning oil supplies, he first said they were sufficient "for a fairly long period of use. On the other hand, if the war is prolonged, we must think of ways in which to economize on the use of petroleum. We are also now testing synthetic substances. . . . However, since we have just started research on synthetic petroleum, it is not available for immediate use. The navy recently established a special branch to do research on high octane petroleum and we are now manufacturing it ourselves. We have a considerable quantity of such petroleum in stock." [68]

In a later statement he was equally vague: "Although it is difficult to increase the supply of munitions and other materials necessary for a protracted war, we have to find a way out somehow. . . . We have enough heavy oil for a fairly long war. . . . Synthetic oil alone will not be enough. . . . We expect oil from the Dutch East Indies and northern Sakhalin . . . not sufficient, but enough for a fairly long time." Councillor Fukai Eigo later commented: "From what Oikawa said, he seemed to expect victory in a short war, but he did not seem to have much confidence with respect to a long war. On this point he sounded rather timid."[69] In mid-September, queried about the future by a worried Yamamoto, Oikawa answered, "There is a danger that we shall pick Germany's chestnuts out of the fire. But the United States will *hesitate* to wage a war. I think it's *probably* safe."[70]

Navy Chief of Staff Prince Fushimi was similarly uncertain about the navy's prospects. He believed that a war between Japan and the United States would probably develop into a protracted conflict, which Japan could not hope to win given its existing petroleum stocks. Was the government, he asked, developing concrete plans for ameliorating this situation? "We must avoid war with the United States," he told the emperor at the Imperial Conference on September 19. "I cannot ascertain the chance of victory." Whereupon Vice Chief Kondō added, "We cannot expect a victory such as we achieved in the Russo-Japanese War. Even if we win, considerable losses can certainly be expected."[71] Yet once the treaty had been concluded, Prince Fushimi assumed an attitude of resignation. "It cannot be helped," he remarked to Yamamoto. "We must do what we can."[72]

Naval leaders had already begun to advocate an early deadline for commencing hostilities. At the September 14 Liaison Conference Vice Chief of Staff Kondō volunteered that while the navy was not yet fully prepared for war with the United States, by April it would be ready. "Vessels already built will have been equipped and merchant ships totaling 2.5 million tons will have been converted to war vessels. Once all these preparations are completed, we have a chance of victory over the United States, if we aim for a quick war and a quick victory. But if the United States prolongs the war," he warned, "then we will face grave difficulties. The United States will build more ships as time passes, and Japan will hardly be able to catch up with it in such a competition. On the contrary, the gap will become wider. In this sense, it is better to fight now."[73]

Middle-ranking navy officers were even more optimistic about Japan's prospects in an early war with the United States. On October 28 Kami Shigenori, a senior official of the Operations Section of the Navy

General Staff, declared enthusiastically to his opposite numbers in the Army General Staff that the Dutch East Indies would be attacked first. Should the United States and Britain thereby become enemies, by April Japan would be prepared to fight them as well. By December, he predicted, "70 percent of the fleet assigned to forward defense will be ready, and 100 percent by mid-January. Therefore, if we fight the Dutch East Indies alone, we will succeed. By mid-April we shall achieve approximately 75 percent readiness vis-à-vis the United States. Hence, it is the navy's view that we must commence hostilities against the United States by April or May." To wait until the end of the next year, he said, would mean more ships in need of repair. In addition, "from the standpoint of internal control" it was important to begin operations in the south before April, and by then, he concluded, "we are confident that we can defeat the United States. By then we shall be 75 percent ready."

Behind such statements, preparations for a naval war were proceeding rapidly. When he spoke up in support of the Tripartite Pact at the Liaison Conference on September 14, Oikawa urged that the government and the army "take the replenishment of naval armaments into consideration." [74] At the Imperial Conference on the 19th Prince Fushimi similarly asked for "earnest cooperation" between the government and the navy in the "strengthening and promotion of naval armaments."

The navy, as we have seen, succeeded in having altered to its benefit the materials mobilization program for the latter half of that year. The "diplomatic turnabout" in its attitude on the Tripartite Pact was apparently related to the navy's feverish expansion of naval armaments and its ambiguous calculations concerning war with the United States. In the process, a mutual understanding seems to have been reached between Vice Navy Minister Toyoda and Foreign Minister Matsuoka who, as a reward for Toyoda's support of the pact, offered to intervene on the navy's behalf with the government and the army in altering the materials program. [75]

With agreement reached on increased allocations for the navy, Vice Chief Kondō on September 21 ordered Mobilization Section Chief Hashimoto to lay the administrative groundwork for issuance of a "preparatory fleet mobilization" order. On the 23rd and 24th representatives of the Navy Ministry and General Staff held preliminary meetings, followed on October 1 by a full-scale conference to discuss the preparatory mobilization. As a result, the General Staff presented to the ministry a formal request to begin immediately "promotion of war preparations" aiming at the issuance of a "preparatory fleet mobilization" order on November 15. By the end of March arrangements were to be completed to place the fleet on a "second alert" status, and by November 1941 it was to be prepared for full wartime operations. The first stages of preparation involved the following:

1) Completing Preparation of Naval Forces:
    a) All necessary construction must be undertaken as a matter of urgency so that vessels are ready for military operations (this involves the transfer to the active fleet of reserve vessels in the first to fourth categories).
    b) Remodeling of vessels and completion of unfinished vessels must be hastened (e.g., bringing submarine tenders up to second condition).
    c) Vessels which were to have been built during wartime must be constructed.
    d) Essential crews must be supplemented and other preparations completed.
2) Completing Preparation of Armed Merchant Vessels:
    a) Armed merchant vessels must be put in order quickly (with equipment provided and planned adjustments completed, and the vessels transferred to the wartime fleet).
    b) Special units must be established and equipped quickly (special base units, guard corps, small ships with cannons, minesweepers, observation towers, communication corps, etc.).
3) Bringing personnel to full strength (mobilizing reserves).
4) Procuring munitions, matériel, and raw materials required for the immediate prewar period and for the first two years of war.
5) Completing Preparation of factories.
6) Other items: transportation, communications, budgets, laws and edicts, etc., for wartime.

Some of these tasks had been underway since August, in the name of "promotion of war preparations," in particular the remodeling of merchant ships for wartime use. The *Kasuga-maru* was requisitioned in September and by September 1941 had been transformed into the aircraft carrier *Taiyō*. In October the *Kashihara-maru* and the *Izumo-maru* were similarly taken over while still on their building slips and by May and July respectively had become the carriers *Shunyō* and *Hiyō*.

Work proceeded in accordance with plan. On November 15 Navy Minister Oikawa reported to the Throne and a preparatory mobilization order was issued, preparations to be completed by the end of March.

Immediately Yamamoto demanded that the Navy General Staff begin map exercises for operations in the South Seas, but "they hesitated, saying it was too late." Thereupon Yamamoto himself called together officers of the General Staff and the Navy War College for tabletop exercises relating to operations against the Dutch East Indies. Queried on November 30 by Prince Fushimi as to the results of these exercises, Yamamoto drew up a written report which concluded that the United States, and ultimately Britain as well, would inevitably be drawn into any war between Japan and the Netherlands. Therefore, he told Fushimi, "without resolution and sufficient preparation we should not start operations in the South Seas." Fushimi replied, "I quite agree with you." Oikawa, too, after seeing Yamamoto's report, expressed agreement and added, "We must handle the situation in anticipation of such developments."[76] But if Yamamoto hoped to deny the logic of middle-grade officers—that military operations in French Indochina would lead to a more rigid American embargo, in turn requiring Japan to seize the Dutch East Indies, and therefore demanding preparations for the war with the United States that would then result—he was disappointed. For while Fushimi and Oikawa agreed verbally with Yamamoto's assertion that Japan could not defeat the United States and therefore should not attack the Dutch East Indies, their actions supported the views of the middle echelon.

After the issuing of the order on November 15, the first stage of preparations was carried out smoothly. In a sense the order was merely an administrative matter, since actual preparations had been in progress since August. But in that it established the authority for the work to proceed and gave official approval for the use of materials allocated for preparatory mobilization, it stimulated those in charge and simplified clerical operations. In addition, the November 15 order contained new instructions: the submarine tender *Kenzaki* was to be remodeled as an aircraft carrier (in January 1942 it went into service as the *Shōhō*); additional vessels totaling 180,000 tons were to be requisitioned for use in forward fleet operations;* air fields, ports, defense installations, fuel storage depots, submarine bases, and communications facilities were to be fully equipped both in Japan proper and especially in the mandated territories in the Pacific.

---

* This brought the total requisitioned tonnage up to 562,000 tons, including general vessels (72,000 tons), special vessels requisitioned since the start of the Sino-Japanese War (240,000 tons), and ships being remodeled as aircraft carriers (70,000 tons).

Particular attention should be paid to the accompanying order for reorganization of the fleet. It had originated in an August 24 report to the Throne on preparations for reorganization from Prince Fushimi and was followed on October 28 by an "execution of reorganization" report; the final order was issued on November 15. Under the reorganization a new 6th Fleet, consisting primarily of 3 submarine squadrons (2 of them newly created at this time), was established and placed under the direction of the Combined Fleet, together with the 4th Fleet formerly under the control of Imperial Headquarters. The 2nd Squadron (2 battleships), the 3rd Air Squadron (2 aircraft carriers), and the 7th Air Squadron (2 submarine tenders) was transferred to the 1st Fleet, while the 6th Air Squadron (2 submarine tenders), the 2nd Combined Air Squadron, and the 4th Combined Air Squadron were transferred to the Combined Fleet. Almost all of Japan's naval force was now part of the active fleet, making it, as Fushimi stated in his August 24 report, "the largest naval organization in Japanese history. Almost all the navy's vessels will be transferred to the fleet on the forward or inner defense. The Combined Fleet will likewise be the largest force in the history of the Japanese navy. Excluded from the Combined Fleet are only 3 battleships, 2 heavy cruisers, 1 aircraft carrier, 5 light cruisers, 3 destroyer flotillas, and 2 submarine squadrons." The excluded vessels were to be reconstructed, repaired, and equipped for war, but once this was completed, "all are to be transferred to the Combined Fleet."

On November 16 the problems involved in the reorganization were explained at an unofficial meeting of the Navy Council:

To organize the fleets exactly in accordance with the 1941 reorganization, vessels totaling 2.4 million tons must be requisitioned from outside the navy. An investigation in May, however, revealed a civilian tonnage of only 5.4 million tons in Japan, of which the army has already taken 700,000 tons. If we order the authorities to supply us with 2.4 million tons, only 2.3 million tons will be left for civilian use (for materials mobilization). The final decision concerning the time of executing the 1941 reorganization should take into consideration our national strength (based on materials mobilization) and other factors. The Navy General Staff is now investigating these problems with the Navy Ministry.

Preparations for mobilization naturally attracted the attention of outside observers. On November 13, two days before the actual order was issued, Admiral Thomas Hart, commander in chief of the U.S. Asiatic Fleet in Manila, wrote Chief of Naval Operations Admiral Harold R. Stark:

> There seems no doubt that Japan is resolved on a southward movement—employing force if necessary. Her most important early objective is the oil supply from the East Indies. . . .
>
> In so far as it seems possible to differentiate between courses of action open to Japan, there are two:—
>   a. A direct jump to N.E.I., by-passing the British.
>   b. An advance against the British, primarily, either wholly waterborne, direct against Singapore or step by step—Indochina, Thailand, Burma and Malaya to Singapore.

Either course, he predicted, "will eventually take in" the Netherlands East Indies.[77] Both the British and American ambassadors in Japan similarly advised their governments of the likelihood of an early Japanese advance in the south.[78]

As planning for the preparatory mobilization proceeded, significant personnel changes occurred in the navy's organization. As vice navy minister, Toyoda Teijirō had worked closely with Oka Takazumi, chief of the Navy General Staff Intelligence Division and long an advocate of the Axis alliance. Now, in October, on Toyoda's recommendation, Oka was appointed to the key post of chief of the Naval Affairs Bureau, which was restructured the following month. As head of the newly-created Second Section, charged with matters of foreign and defense policy and liaison with the army, Oka appointed another pro-German officer, Captain Ishikawa Shingo; and to head the reorganized First Section he named a former section official who had earlier served in Germany, Captain Takada Toshitane.

Takada was convinced of the need to create within the navy an organization to provide unified direction of war planning and execution. He had therefore recommended the establishment of three ad hoc committees, staffed by both the Navy Ministry and the Navy General Staff: the first was to discuss and recommend policy, the second to consider matters of military preparations, and the third to be concerned with the direction of public opinion and information. His plan was approved, and in mid-November the three committees began to operate. The activities of the First Committee were particularly noteworthy. It was composed of four officers: Takada, Ishikawa, War Guidance Office Chief Ōno, and

Tomioka Sadatoshi, the newly appointed chief of the Operations Section. All four were young, energetic officers, determined that their views should predominate in navy policymaking. Before long, every major policy had its origins in the First Committee. Indeed, top naval leaders eventually came to ask whether documents awaiting their approval had been approved by the First Committee; those which had were accepted without question.[79]

These developments—the order for preparatory mobilization, reorganization of the fleet, the new assignments given Takada and Ishikawa, and the establishment of the First Committee—indicated to many of the junior officers that "the time is ripe for southern operations."[80] One of them, Commander Kami Shigenori of the Navy General Staff Operations Section, on December 13, argued that Japan must begin to strengthen the fleet reorganization and even to carry out full mobilization in accordance with the 1941 organization plan if the following circumstances should arise:

> 1) When diplomatic negotiations to secure strategic bases in southern French Indochina become deadlocked, forcing us to exercise military means, if we judge that the United States definitely intends to declare war on Japan or to take military action against Japan.
>
> 2) If the war in Europe develops in Germany's favor by next spring and Britain's fighting strength is weakened considerably, or when Germany begins landing operations in the British Isles and the situation becomes favorable to the empire; should we then adopt forceful diplomatic measures toward the Dutch East Indies and should the Dutch East Indies and the United States remain intransigent, war with the United States will be inevitable if we are to attain our demands and if the empire resolves to achieve its demands nevertheless (that is, if Japan is prepared to accept war with the United States in the process of carrying out an active policy toward the Dutch East Indies).
>
> 3) If the United States applies all-out economic pressure against Japan and the empire resolves that its survival necessitates an active policy toward the Dutch East Indies.

Even the vacillating Oikawa suddenly began to share the bellicose attitudes of the middle echelons. In mid-January he remarked to the Japanese ambassador to Germany Ōshima Hiroshi that the navy would "follow an active policy based upon the triple alliance," assuring him that "War preparations have also been greatly advanced."[81] On the 26th, during House of Representatives discussions on the budget, he expressed confidence that the navy was "carefully prepared to meet the worst situation." He pointed out to the Diet members that "Quantity is not the only factor with respect to armaments, quality is important as well. . . . Herein lies Japan's opportunity. The navy has established armaments sufficient to meet almost every conceivable exigency."[82]

The Navy and the Thai-French Indochina Border Dispute

This, then, was the situation within the navy when Japan became involved in the border dispute between Thailand and French Indochina (see Ch. 2). The First Committee responded with a customarily aggressive attitude, and the original drafts of the "Policy of the Empire toward Thailand and French Indochina," adopted by the Liaison Conference on December 26, and the "Outline of Emergency Measures to Deal with the Thailand-French Indochina Border Dispute" of January 19 emanated from the navy. (A slightly different version of the origins of these documents, stressing the Foreign Ministry's role, is given in essay 2.) The latter document took a far harder line toward the French authorities, demanding that "necessary pressure"—that is, a demonstration of naval might—be brought to bear to win acceptance of Japan's demands, whereas the earlier policy had referred only to "necessary steps" accompanying the destruction of the Matsuoka-Henry Pact of August 30. The naval planners proposed that the 15th Squadron (1 heavy and 1 light cruiser) be dispatched from Japan and the 5th Torpedo Flotilla (1 light cruiser and 4 destroyers) from Hainan to the South China Sea under the direction of the commander of the 2nd China Fleet, arriving off the coast near the border on the 25th. In addition, a newly-organized unit, designated "S," composed of the 7th Squadron (4 heavy cruisers), the 1st Torpedo Flotilla (1 light cruiser, 12 destroyers), and the 7th Air Squadron (2 submarine tenders), was to be sent from Kure to Hainan by the end of the month and the 2nd Air Squadron (2 aircraft carriers) to Kaohsiung on Taiwan early in February. The navy also drew up plans for landing 700 marines at each of three places along the central and southern coast of French Indochina, with the aim of seizing the air bases in the colony. This purpose was expressly stated in a communication from the Operations Section to their counterparts in the Army General Staff on January 24:

Our objective in dispatching troops is to overawe [the French]—or so it has been reported to the Throne. In fact, our real intention is to use military force in central and southern French Indochina. The chief of the Operations Division has already sent a telegram instructing that military means are to be exercised if necessary. The navy's hope is to secure permanent bases near Saigon and Camranh Bay, once we dispatch the marines.

And on February 1 Hasunuma Shigeru informed Kido, on the basis of a report by his majesty's naval aide-de-camp, that "the navy aims to use Camranh Bay and the air base near Saigon."[83]

With the Liaison Conference's adoption of the "Outline of Emergency Measures," the army and navy began planning to put the new policy into effect. To an Army General Staff proposal of the 22nd stating that whether French Indochina "accepts our mediation or not, we will force them to accept certain military demands," the Navy General Staff added, "If they do not accept our demands, we will take military measures if necessary." Army leaders appear to have been impressed by the strong posture of the navy. Vice Chief of Staff Kondō asserted to the Liaison Conference on January 30, "If the building of air bases and ports in French Indochina is delayed, it will hinder all other development."

Neither the proposed naval landing nor the naval demonstration was carried out as the navy had hoped, however, and on February 20 the units dispatched to the area were recalled to Japan to participate in war exercises of the Combined Fleet. Following the acceptance by Thailand and French Indochina of Japan's mediation proposals, the Liaison Conference met on January 30 and adopted a new "Outline of Policy toward French Indochina and Thailand." With the adoption of this policy, Navy Chief of Staff Nagano Osami remarked, at the November 1, 1941, conference where the naval chiefs reached their final determination for war with the United States, "Japan had already started down the road to war."

Yamamoto was alarmed at the belligerent attitude the new policy expressed toward the United States. On February 15 he wrote to Oikawa:

No one will doubt that the "military demands," which seem to be the most important point of the "Outline," imply a military advance against the United States and Britain. Therefore, whether or not we exercise military means in order to make them accept our demands, we will in the end confront the United States and Britain. In the final analysis, *the "Outline" contains the dangerous probability that events will develop into a war between Japan and the United States and Great Britain.* I trust, therefore, that those who have made this decision are prepared for such an eventuality. To judge from the fact that the United States apparently is no longer merely posturing . . . , if we were to decide that we must apply military pressure in French Indochina because our demands have not been accepted, we may suddenly find ourselves in a critical situation. I presume that you too are bearing this possibility in mind.[84]

Yamamoto thus attempted to make certain that the decision makers were prepared themselves for the risks inherent in their policies.

By now Oikawa had accepted the logic of the inevitability of war with the United States that permeated the lower echelons of the navy. The need to exercise military power had not materialized, but the opportunities presented by the Japanese mediation effort seemed to be carrying events in the same direction—toward a Japanese advance into central and southern French Indochina. And an increasingly confident Oikawa paid little attention to Yamamoto's worries. In Liaison Conference discussions it was he who pressured Matsuoka to utilize the threat of military force to obtain Japan's demands. For while Yamamoto and Oikawa agreed that a military advance into French Indochina might eventually lead to war with the United States, Yamamoto saw this as an argument against military action, whereas Oikawa continued zealously to support such action despite the dangers. Yamamoto's warning was echoed by a representative of the Foreign Ministry at a conference of responsible division chiefs from the Foreign Ministry and the Army and Navy ministries and general staffs on the evening of February 15. Japan alone, he declared, will "decide relations between us and the United States and Britain. Our destiny will be decided by the decision as to whether we establish military bases in French Indochina and Thailand." He was challenged by Oka and Ugaki: "Our action will not decide the development of this situation. Whether the United States carries out a complete embargo against Japan, once it has completed strategic preparations, is the key issue that will determine the future." This was the logic that, since August, had persuaded Oikawa and now guided his decisions.

Oikawa's optimism was undoubtedly based upon the conclusions reached by his subordinates in the Navy General Staff concerning Germany's prospects in the war with Britain. We have already noted the superficiality and absence of realism that characterized those judgments during the summer and fall of 1940. As late as January 1941 Yamaguchi Bunjirō and Horiuchi Shigetada, in charge of intelligence relating to the United States and Britain respectively, confidently predicted to their army colleagues a German victory over Britain and asserted that thereafter combined action by the American and British navies would not pose a threat to Japan. Ōno Takeji based his earlier expectations of an Axis victory on vague grounds, but on the strength of a report from a military attaché in Berlin on Germany's equipment for a cross-Channel invasion, strengthened his conviction. On March 1 the American naval attaché in Tokyo reported to Washington that Japanese naval officers had "expressed in conversation the opinion that in the anticipated German spring offensive British defeat is a foregone conclusion; that British sea power will probably be diminished to such an extent that control of the Atlantic will be lost to the British; and that as a result thereof a part of the American fleet will be withdrawn from the Pacific Ocean, enabling the Japanese to carry out their plans for expansion in southeast Asia without substantial opposition."[85]

Those observers who reached a contrary conclusion were ignored. For example, Yokoi Tadao, who arrived in Germany as naval attaché in October 1940, took note of the discouraged attitude of German naval officers, who seemed at a loss to find an effective strategy against Britain. One of them asked him "how, under the circumstances, could Japan have concluded an alliance with us? It is very advantageous for us, but what about for your navy?"[86] Even Ōshima reported, on March 18, that Admiral Erich Raeder, commander in chief of the German navy, had bemoaned the German navy's inferiority in battleships to the British navy. "Though we are confident of our submarine strength," he went on, "even with our superiority in the air we cannot fully protect our ships at sea. Thus we have had great difficulty in finding a way to attack Britain."[87]

The Japanese Navy General Staff, however, was more willing to be persuaded by the propagandistic arguments of Ambassador Eugen Ott, who declared to Kondō on March 4 that before long "submarine and air operations will begin. Preparations for landings in Britain have already been completed. We await only the Führer's decision as to the date on which we do it."[88]

The Services Formulate A New Southern Advance Policy: April 1941

The first draft of the "Outline of Policy toward French Indochina and Thailand" approved by the Liaison Conference on January 30 was drawn up by the War Guidance Office of the Army General Staff at the request of Army Chief of Staff Sugiyama Gen. This version had in view the establishment of military bases in Thailand and French Indochina through Japanese mediation of the border dispute. While it did not spell out fully a concrete policy for the entire southern region, this had been done in the "Main Principles for Coping with the Changing World Situation" of the previous July, which still constituted the army's basic policy for a southern advance. And since the earlier policy had been aimed against Britain and the Netherlands, the issue could not now be limited, even temporarily, to French Indochina and Thailand.

As a result of personnel changes instituted by Army Minister Tōjō in the fall of 1940, there had been shifts in the leadership and staff of the Operations Division and Section of the General Staff. Despite the changes, planning for the southern advance continued as before, developments such as the border dispute being considered within that framework as issues of secondary importance. By February 1941 plans had been worked out within the Operations Division for the deployment of forces in the southern advance.

Until the China Incident was concluded, the basic operation plan for 1940 had stated, operations in the south would be determined by Japan's involvement in China. Subsequent strategic planning therefore provided for the following distribution of ground forces: out of a total of 53 divisions, 11 were to be prepared for a confrontation with the Soviet Union, 28 were tied down in China, and 11 would be made available for the southern advance. Designated as the core of the southern forces were: the 5th Division, which was recalled from northern French Indochina to Shanghai, placed under the direct control of Imperial Headquarters, and, on October 12, ordered to "train primarily for landing operations" (Imperial Headquarters Army Order 467); the Imperial Guard Division, which was ordered on October 22 to assemble at Shant'ou (Swatow); the 48th Division, reorganized on October 22 from the Taiwan Mixed Brigade and ordered to advance to Hainan island; and the 18th Division at Canton. These arrangements were completed by the end of December. On January 6 the commander of the South China Army was instructed (Imperial Headquarters Army Instruction 791) to begin training the Imperial Guard Division, the 18th Division, and the 48th Division for landing operations in tropical zones and on the 16th to undertake "the study of the critical problems involved in southern operations."

With respect to the air arm, the Operations Section on December 7 drew up plans for the following deployment of 920 planes in 99 companies: 34 companies totaling 300 planes against the USSR, 80 planes in 8 companies for the war in China, and 540 planes in 57 companies to military operations in the south. Planning was also advanced concerning the accumulation of weapons, ammunition, fuel, transport, and landing craft in the rear, and the army's communications system was reorganized and expanded. At the end of March joint army-navy maneuvers for an attack on Singapore following a Malaya landing were practiced; the landing force (primarily the 5th Division and the 5th Air Force Group in Manchuria) advanced from the Choushan islands near Shanghai, broke through the enemy's naval and air lines in the East China Sea, where they were joined by the 2nd Fleet, and landed in northern Kyushu to attack the base at Sasebo.

While the Operations Division set in motion these plans for an advance in the entire south, the War Guidance Office began to question such a policy. On November 26 its investigations led to the conclusion that the war in the south would not be decided rapidly but would develop into a prolonged struggle, a judgment that War Guidance Chief Arisue Yadoru reported to Sugiyama on the 29th. The following day the chief of staff told Arisue that the emperor had advised Sugiyama that "the southern advance problem must be considered very carefully." At the subsequent meeting with Sugiyama on December 3, when Okada Kikusaburō, chief of the Army Ministry's War Preparations Section, reported on Japan's material strength, Arisue took the opportunity to clarify "the particularly tight situation that exists with respect to matériel needed for military operations in the south." Under the circumstances, the War Guidance Office recommended that for the present pressure should be limited to Thailand and French Indochina.

The Operations Section, however, absorbed in its planning for military operations throughout the south, was not satisfied with such a conclusion, and on November 20 Operations Section Chief Doi Akio advocated in a conference of ministry and General Staff officials that the advance into southern Indochina be made a stepping stone to an advance into the entire south. On December 4 he urged concerned army section chiefs to commence the southern advance in the spring, beginning with operations in Thailand and Indochina. His views were opposed by the War Guidance Office which, on December 10, argued in the preface to an outline on military operations in the south that "preparations alone should be carried out, no actual decisions should be made." The Army Ministry's Military Affairs Section agreed, stating on the 12th that it was "impossible to decide definitely upon southern operations. Therefore, without making such a resolution, preparations alone should be advanced as much as possible."

In the effort to reach a consensus within the army, the War Guidance Office on the 16th proposed the following compromise policy: "Military operations will be carried out if the nation's material strength can sustain them. Meanwhile, preparations will be advanced within the present materials mobilization plan and budget."

Officials of the War and Guidance Office and the Operations Section discussed the compromise statement on January 7. The Operations Section wanted the planning for southern operations to proceed on the assumption that military operations would be conducted, since "a southern program without a decision to conduct military operations would lack direction." "That is quite true," the War Guidance Office replied. "However, the difficulty in operating a state lies in the fact that it is difficult to reach firm conclusions. The prevailing situation will decide the issue." In a further attempt at compromise, the War Guidance Office on the 9th changed the first sentence to read "military operations will be conducted" in the south. But its basic position remained unchanged. "Even if the word 'conducted' is used," it declared, "this is only a matter of terminology. A decision concerning military operations will still depend on the current situation. This problem will come up again."

By the 11th general agreement on the compromise plan had been achieved within the Army General Staff, and on the 19th a draft "Outline for Dealing with the Southern Areas" emerged from the War Guidance Office and was officially handed to those in charge of the matter in the Army Ministry—from the Military Affairs Section, Chief Kawamura Saburō and Nagai Yatsuji, and from the Military Section, Chief Iwakuro Hideo and Nishiura Susumu—accompanied by an explanation from Arisue. Although Doi continued to argue strongly that a military stationing in southern French Indochina should begin at once, his views were not accepted. On February 6 a final draft, "revised to relate to the actual development of the situation and clarifying the circumstances under which military operations could be exercised," was approved by the War Guidance Office and presented the next day to the sections concerned in the Army Ministry and General Staff.

On the 8th the General Staff and the Army Ministry's Military Affairs Bureau reached agreement on a policy providing: "1) that while the United States and Britain might be dealt with separately, Britain and the Netherlands were not separable; 2) that Japan should 'take advantage of the favorable opportunity' presented by the Anglo-German war; and 3) that military operations toward Malaya and the Dutch East Indies would be undertaken."

In the course of two months the War Guidance Office had shifted from a policy of "preparations without decision" concerning military operations to one that would "take advantage of a favorable opportunity" to launch military operations. Doubtless the War Guidance Office was influenced by the prevailing view within the General Staff that war with Britain did not necessarily mean war with the United States as well. For example, Intelligence Division Chief Wakamatsu Tadakazu commented, on February 18, that "the United States will not go so far as to commit double suicide with Britain. Thus, an alliance between the United States and Britain is not developing." Chief of Staff Sugiyama too seemed to be moving toward acceptance of this opportunistic policy. When asked by Army Minister Tōjō at an army conference on January 16 whether the Greater East Asia Co-Prosperity Sphere included the southern areas, Sugiyama replied, "Japan, Manchuria, China, Thailand, French Indochina, and, if possible, the Dutch East Indies and Malaya." On the 30th he emphasized in the Liaison Conference that in its policy toward Thailand and French Indochina, Japan should take advantage of the war between Germany and Britain to advance the southern operation.

When he gave his final approval to the army's "Outline of Policy toward the South" on February 8, Military Affairs Bureau Chief Mutō Akira expressed the opinion that, in view of the circumstances since the "Main Principles" had been adopted the previous year, it might be better if this plan were to be proposed by the navy first. Accordingly, on the 10th Arisue met with his navy colleague and presented the army's final draft as his own private plan, urging Ōno to draw up a plan on behalf of the navy. Any plan for military operations in the south would have to recognize two fundamental points, Ōno asserted: first, that it would mean war with both Britain and the United States, since it was impossible to consider them separately; and second, that a southern advance should be executed only in case of an American naval advance in the Far East, endangering the empire's defense. A week later he reiterated to Arisue that these two points were the core of any southern advance policy. It was "the general opinion of the navy," he said, that the United States and Britain were inseparable, thus overt military operations in the south would mean war with the United States. Preparations for military operations against Britain and the Netherlands had already been completed, he went on. "The important thing now is preparation for war against the United States." Ōno did not, however, present a written plan at this time. Arisue strongly urged him to do so, whereupon Ōno tentatively agreed. Days passed, but still no navy proposal materialized. On February 24 Army Vice Chief Tsukada Osamu made the same request of Kondō, and the next day Arisue once against asked Ōno for a written plan. Nearly three weeks more went by, then on March 15 the two War Guidance offices began joint discussions on the question. The army's impression was that the navy favored military operations in the south only if they were "unavoidable"; they were not particularly interested in "taking advantage of a favorable opportunity."

At this first meeting the army asked for the navy's reaction to several documents. A reply was given when an official of the navy's War Guidance Office visited the army's office on the 20th. He made it clear that the navy would not consider Britain's defeat a "favorable opportunity" to launch military operations, since such a defeat would only increase the military pressure by other powers against Japan. Military operations in the south, he went on, would unquestionably mean war with the United States. Thus, it was the navy's view that only under circumstances of extreme military pressure by the United States, that is, a complete embargo, should military operations be undertaken.

Reluctantly, Arisue and other army advocates of a southern advance were forced to acknolwedge what to the navy had been self-evident since its war games the previous May, despite the national policy enunciated in the "Main Principles." To the navy, military operations in the south meant war with the United States, and such operations should be permitted only under circumstances of military necessity, such as a complete American embargo against Japan would produce, regardless of the situation between Britain and Germany. But although this view had been firmly adhered to by the First Committee ever since its establishment,[89] it had not hitherto been communicated to the army, nor had the army planners been apprised of the conclusions of the map maneuvers and the paper aimed for the August 27 meeting. Consequently, they were surprised at the navy's blunt reply, a reply utterly at variance with the "Main Principles."

Thus, after painstaking efforts to achieve a compromise between the Operations Section, the War Guidance Office, and other sections concerned in the wording of its policy on southern operations, the army unexpectedly found its compromise plan flatly rejected by the navy, which made war with the United States wholly dependent on American embargo moves. Its reaction was one of puzzlement and mistrust, coupled with suspicion that the navy's reply masked some "political plot." Nonetheless, it was clear that the army's draft policy would have to be dropped. The question now was how the army was to respond to the navy's position. Its reply was greatly influenced by a study of Japan's material strength conducted by the Army Ministry's War Preparations Section in March and reported on by a section official, Shibafu Hideo, to relevant officials of the ministry and General Staff on the 18th and 22nd and to Army Minister Tōjō on the 19th, and by section Chief Okada Kikusaburō to leaders of the General Staff including Sugiyama on the 25th and 26th.

The report advised that Japan should advance the economic negotiations with the Dutch East Indies in order to establish swiftly a "self-sufficient sphere in East Asia." Unnecessary provocations of the United States and Britain were to be avoided while the empire continued to acquire from them the resources necessary to increase its national strength, although preparations must be made "for the war that might occur." Should Japan become involved in a war with the United States, Britain, and the Netherlands, the report continued, "it cannot be denied that the empire's material strength would be insufficient for a long war. While we have munitions sufficient to defeat the enemy within a period of two years, by the end of the second year liquid fuels will become short at least temporarily, and should the war be further prolonged, our economic capabilities might be strained."[90]

Okada supplemented this report with the following oral comments to Tōjō and Sugiyama:

Our fundamental national policy should be decided in the light of all circumstances, not merely in accordance with material considerations. However, if we limit ourselves to the materials problem, the question of oil supplies will have the greatest effect upon our national defense. And any cessation of trade will have a decisive impact upon oil supplies. Under present circumstances we still should not wage war. If we wage war, oil and other important materials will last only for the initial two years. It is not possible at present to predict the precise situation with respect to matériel after the initial two years because it will depend upon developments in the war. Under any circumstances we will face a tight situation. In particular, we must pay attention to the situation with respect to marine transport, which is the foundation of our economy. If we lose too many ships or if we cannot maintain a balance between transportation for war operations and transportation for general materials mobilization, we will be unable to continue the war.

According to records in the Military History Office, the First (Fleet Mobilization) Section of the Navy Ministry's Naval Ordnance Bureau had calculated that of a total requisitioned tonnage of 2.5 million, 800,000 tons would be lost during the first year of war, 600,000 tons during the second, and 700,000 during the third. If it was true, as Okada stated, that it was a matter of life or death that marine transport be maintained, this report should have led the Army General Staff to seek guarantees from the navy. However, a judgment that Japan had no hope of victory in a war with the United States did not accord with the army planners' emotional bias in favor of war. Both Okada and Shibafu, who was influenced by his father-in-law General Araki Sadao, supported a decision for war. Even while Okada commented to Military Affairs Section Chief Satō Kenryō on March 11, "In the end, we are no match for the United States and Britain in the event of war," the War Preparations Section's report could conclude wishfully, "if military operations cannot be avoided, we will manage by one means or another." Another official of the Military Affairs Section, Ishii Akiho, after listening to Okada on several occasions, judged that while war with Britain and the United States would be "a most difficult undertaking and, if possible, should be avoided," if war did break out, Japan could "continue to fight for three or four years without being defeated, although it will be very difficult. *If this operation is successful,* as expected, and if the fundamental conditions underlying such a war do not change, we should be able barely to make it." Tōjō and Sugiyama likewise came to accept a blind judgment that was completely opposed to the conclusions of the report on Japan's material strength. They too were prepared to assert, "If it becomes unavoidable, we will resort to war."

The real shortcoming of the War Preparations Section's estimates was that they calculated the material power of Japan alone, without relating it to that of the United States and Britain. Such a comparison would have made clear the folly of army policymakers in thinking they could wage war against the two western powers. On April 2 Churchill attempted to point this out in a message to Matsuoka: "Is it true that the production of steel in the United States of America during 1941 will be 75 million tons and in Great Britain about 12½ million tons, making a total of nearly 90 million tons? If Germany should happen to be defeated as she was last time, would not the 7 million tons of steel production of Japan be inadequate for a single-handed war?"[91] His query was dismissed as "extremely arrogant and rude" and ignored by the Army Ministry and General Staff.

They could not ignore the navy's rejection of an immediate military advance in the south, however. On March 22 the War Guidance Office once more changed its position to accord with that of the navy: "Regardless of the situation in Europe, it is better not to undertake military operations in the south. Only if absolutely unavoidable should such military operations be allowed. Given the situation in which the empire now finds itself, the Main Principles for Coping with the Changing World Situation must be altered. It is out of the question to conduct military operations in the south." The next day it decided that "there should be no military operations to take advantage of a favorable opportunity." On the 27th Hattori Takushirō and Nishiura Susumu agreed on behalf of the Operations and Military sections respectively. The army and the navy, it appeared, were now in accord on policy toward the south: military operations were to be undertaken only if "absolutely unavoidable," not in response to a "favorable opportunity." But this meant giving up any plan for southern operations, except in French Indochina and Thailand, and went counter to fundamental army policy ever since the "Main Principles" was drafted. Thus the possibility of a divergence in aims between the two services still remained.

On March 26 the navy advised the army that it was drafting a statement on policy toward the south. On the 30th officials of the two War Guidance offices discussed the question, and on April 5 an "Outline of Policy toward the South" was handed to the army. The essential principle of this navy draft was still that military operations were not to be undertaken to take advantage of a favorable opportunity, but only for the sake of Japan's "self-existence and self-defense." Ten days later, following deliberations within the army, Arisue brought forward an amended version for negotiations with the navy, and on the 17th agreement was reached (see Appendix 3 for the full text).

In this document, which, according to the supplement, was to replace the earlier "Main Principles for Coping with the Changing World Situation," the navy's position was clearly enunciated: that military operations against the United States would be undertaken only if Japan's "self-existence and self-defense" were threatened. But while this suggests that an army-navy compromise had resulted in a new southern policy, in actuality the army tended to interpret the document to accord with its continuing desire to begin an advance in the south. According to the army, the new policy would still permit a southern advance so long as it did not provoke war with the United States.

The "Outline of Policy toward the South" was regarded by the navy and the army as an internal document and was therefore not shown to Foreign Minister Matsuoka or other members of the cabinet. At the time of its adoption, however, Matsuoka harbored quite different intentions toward the United States, while in Washington negotiations that ran counter to the designs of both the services and the foreign minister had been opened by Ambassador Nomura Kichisaburō. Thus the stage was set not only for a clash of divergent national policies toward the southern areas and the United States but also for a fundamental disagreement among the country's top decision makers.

Appendixes

APPENDIX I

Text of Semi-Official Communication from Foreign Minister Matsuoka to Foreign Commissar Molotov, April 13, 1941 *

My dear Mr. Molotov:

With reference to the Treaty of Neutrality signed today, I have the honor to state that I expect and hope that a commercial agreement and a fisheries convention will soon be concluded and that at the earliest opportunity we, Your Excellency and myself, shall endeavor, in the spirit of conciliation and mutual accommodation, to solve in a few months the question of the liquidation of the concessions in northern Sakhalin under the contracts signed at Moscow on December 14, 1925, with a view to removing the various questions not conducive to the maintenance of cordial relations between our two countries.

In the same spirit I should like to point out that it will be well for our two countries, as well as Manchukuo and Outer Mongolia, if we find at the earliest possible date a means of instituting joint or mixed commissions of the countries concerned, with the object of settling the boundary questions and of handling disputes and incidents along the border.

* Japan, Foreign Ministry, *Nihon gaikō nempyō narabi ni shuyō bunsho* (Chronology and Major Documents of Japanese Foreign Relations), 2:492.

APPENDIX 2

The Matsuoka-Henry Pact, August 30, 1940 *

1. Letter from Arsène-Henry to Matsuoka

Tokyo, August 30, 1940

Excellency:

I have the honor to inform Your Excellency that the French Government recognizes the supreme interests of Japan in the economic and political spheres in the Far East.

Hence the French Government expects that the Imperial Government of Japan will give assurances to the French Government to the effect that Japan will respect the rights and interests of France in the Far East, particularly the territorial integrity of Indochina and the sovereignty of France over the entire area of the Indochinese Union.

Concerning the economic sphere, France will make efforts to accelerate trade between Indochina and Japan. At the same time, France is prepared to negotiate promptly as to the means to guarantee to Japan and its people the most favorable status possible and in any event a status superior to that of any third country in Indochina.

Concerning the procurement of special military facilities that Japan has requested, France notes that the Imperial Government of Japan intends to use the foregoing procurement solely for the purpose of resolving the conflict with Generalissimo Chiang Kai-shek, and consequently the aforementioned procurement is temporary and will be terminated with the resolution of the conflict, and that the above is applicable only to the Indochinese provinces along the China border. Under the aforementioned conditions, the French Government is prepared to order the commander of the French army in Indochina to settle the aforementioned military matter with the commander of the Japanese Army. None of the requests made by the Imperial Government of Japan shall be excluded beforehand, and the orders issued, to the responsible officer of the French army shall not restrict their authority in this regard. The aforementioned negotiations shall be conducted on the following conditions:

The commanders of both armies, in true military spirit, shall exchange information in order accurately to inform each other as to what the Japanese army requires and how these requirements can be met. Those items which are required by the Japanese Army shall be limited to items which

---

* Japan, Foreign Ministry, *Nihon gaikō nempyō narabi ni shuyō bunsho* (Chronology and Major Documents of Japanese Foreign Relations), 2:446–48.

are related to military operations in the Chinese provinces along the Indochina border.

After the exchange of the above information, mutually trustworthy contacts shall be made between the military authorities of Japan and France in order to provide the Japanese army with the required military facilities. The French Government shall not bear any financial burden arising from the procurement of these various facilities for the Japanese army. The foregoing procurement of facilities shall not have the character of a military occupation and, being strictly limited to those items which are necessary for operations, it shall be conducted through the mediation and under the control of the authorities of the French army.

Lastly, the Imperial Government of Japan shall pledge itself to take responsibility to compensate for those damages to Indochina which may arise from its own military action and from the action of enemy troops in Indochina caused by the presence of the Japanese Army.

I avail myself of this opportunity to submit my highest respect and courtesy to Your Excellency.

> Envoy Extraordinary and Ambassador
> Plenipotentiary of France
> Charles Arsène-Henry

2. Reply from Matsuoka to Arsène-Henry

Tokyo, August 30, 1940

Excellency:

I have the honor to acknowledge receipt of Your Excellency's letter dated the 30th of August 1940 with contents as follows:

(Repeats *verbatim* the text of the above Arsène-Henry letter to Matsuoka of the same date, then adds):

As an answer to the foregoing letter, I have the honor to inform Your Excellency that the Japanese Government has every intention of respecting the rights and interests of France in the Far East, particularly the territorial integrity of Indochina and the sovereignty of France over the entire area of the Indochinese Union and that Japan accepts the proposal made by the French Government; that Japan hopes that negotiations designed to meet satisfactorily the requests made by Japan will be begun without delay and will accomplish speedily the expected results; and that Japan hopes that the French Government will issue the necessary orders to the Indochinese authorities for this purpose.

I avail myself of this opportunity to submit my highest respect and courtesy to Your Excellency.

> The Foreign Minister of Japan
> Matsuoka Yōsuke

APPENDIX 3

Outline of Policy toward the South

Army-Navy Draft Policy of April 17, 1941*

1). The objective of policy toward the south, in accordance with the process of strengthening the Greater East Asia Co-Prosperity Sphere, is the rapid strengthening of Japan's defense posture for the sake of the empire's self-existence and self-defense. To this end:
   a) Close relations with Thailand and French Indochina must be established in the military, political, and economic spheres.
   b) Close economic relations with the Dutch East Indies must be established.
   c) The empire must endeavor to maintain normal commercial relations with other nations of the south.
2) The empire's aim is to attain the above objectives by diplomatic means. In particular, with Thailand and French Indochina efforts will be made for the early establishment of military relations.
3) If in the pursuit of the above policies the developments stated below occur, and if no other means are available, the empire will exercise military means for the sake of its self-existence and self-defense. The objectives, targets, dates, and methods of such military means will be decided quickly, in accordance with developments in the European war and the situation in diplomatic relations with the Soviet Union.
   a) If the empire's self-existence is threatened by embargoes imposed by the United States, Britain, the Netherlands, and others.
   b) If the United States, alone or in cooperation with Britain, the Netherlands, and China, gradually increases its pressures to contain the empire, making it impossible for the empire any longer to bear those pressures in the light of its self-defense.
4) If it is judged that Britain's collapse in the European war is certain, this policy, particularly diplomatic activities toward the Dutch East Indies, will be further strengthened and the empire should make renewed efforts to accomplish its purposes.
5) Reform of the empire's organization for war will be accomplished swiftly in accordance with the "Outline of Fundamental National Policy" of July 1940.

* Japan, Foreign Ministry, Nihon gaikō nempyō narabi ni shuyō bunsho (Chronology and Major Documents of Japanese Foreign Relations), 2:495–96.

Supplement

1) Policies toward French Indochina and Thailand will be conducted in accordance with the "Outline of Policy toward French Indochina and Thailand" approved by the emperor on February 1, 1941.

2) If the China Incident cannot be settled as set forth in the "Main Principles for Coping with the Changing World Situation" adopted in July 1940, policies toward the south will be conducted in accordance with this "Outline of Policy."

3) Should the China Incident be settled or the world situation change suddenly and drastically, policies toward the south will then be reexamined.

Notes

(Full English-language titles, publication information, Japanese characters, and abbreviations used may be found in the Bibliography)

PART I.

Northern Defense

Introduction (Berton)

1. The importance of this documentation can be judged from the special volume of documents appended to the *Taiheiyō senso e no michi* series and from Nobutaka Ike's translation of the proceedings of high-level policy conferences in 1941, published under the title *Japan's Decision for War* (Stanford, Calif.: Stanford University Press, 1967).

2. Ott to German Foreign Office, May 6, 1941, in U.S. Department of State, *Documents on German Foreign Policy, 1918–1945*, series D, 12:725.

3. Report by Ambassador Konstantin Smetanin in Foreign Policy Archives of the USSR (hereafter SFP Archives), File 0146, Document 1376, p. 205, quoted in Leonid N. Kutakov, *Istoriia sovetsko-iaponskikh diplomaticheskikh otnoshenii*, p. 282.

4. SFP Archives, File 0146, Document 413, p. 17, quoted in Leonid N. Kutakov, *Portsmutskii mirnyi dogovor*, p. 256.

5. This reaction, documented in Soviet scholarly writings, was substantiated by the Soviet historian Leonid Kutakov in a private interview April 1969 in New York at United Nations headquarters, where Dr. Kutakov was serving as deputy secretary general.

6. SFP Archives, quoted in B. N. Ponomarev et al., eds., *Istoriia vneshnei politiki SSSR*, 1:375.

7. SFP Archives, File 436B, vol. 11, document 48, p. 7, quoted in Kutakov, *Istoriia*, p. 284.

8. See the full text of this document in Joseph Gordon, "The Russo-Japanese Neutrality Pact of April, 1941," p. 100.

9. Interview cited in n. 5 above. In response to a direct question, Kutakov also claimed that no secret assurances had been given by Molotov when he explained the neutrality treaty to the Chinese ambassador in Moscow in April 1941.

10. Kutakov, *Istoriia*, p. 288.

11. Kh. T. Eidus, ed., *Ocherki noveishei istorii Iaponii*, p. 226.

12. Kutakov, *Istoriia*, p. 263.

13. See Chapter 7, "The Fruits of Espionage," particularly pp. 154–62, in Chalmers Johnson, *An Instance of Treason: Ozaki Hotsumi and the Sorge Spy Ring*.

14. I. M. Korol'kov, *Chelovek dlia kotorogo ne bylo tain (Rikhard Zorge)*, p. 180.

15. Korol'kov, p. 196. See also M. S. Kolesnikov, *Takim byl Rikhard Zorge*, and I. N. Dement'eva et al., *Tovarishch Zorge*.

16. John Erickson, "Reflections on Securing the Soviet Far Eastern Frontiers: 1932–1945," *Interplay*, Vol. 3, No. 2 (August/September 1969), 57. Editor's note: Alvin Coox identifies the probable source of this information as "Japanese Intelligence Planning against the USSR," Vol. 10, 1955, in "Japanese Special Studies on Manchuria," prepared by the U.S. Army's Japanese Research Division, p. 108, n. 12.

17. Editorial in *Izvestiia*, April 14, 1941.

18. See, for instance, M. E. Airapetian and G. A. Deborin, *Etapy vneshnei politiki SSSR*, p. 259.

1. The Japanese-Soviet Neutrality Pact

1. On January 12, 1932, the Soviet ambassador to Japan, Alexandre Troyanovsky, sounded out Prime Minister Inukai Tsuyoshi (who concurrently held the post of foreign minister) about a nonaggression pact. Again, on March 16 at a disarmament conference in Geneva Foreign Commissar Maxim Litvinov told Ambassador Matsudaira Tsuneo: "The Soviet government is still concerned over the present situation in Manchuria. Somehow, through a Japanese-Soviet nonaggression treaty or through some other means, it is necessary to remove mutual suspicions.." On May 15 Karl Radek in an article in *Izvestiia* advocated the conclusion of a treaty between Japan and the Soviet Union. When the Japanese delegate to the League of Nations, Matsuoka Yōsuke, stopped in Moscow, November 4 – 6, on his way to Geneva, Litvinov, Radek, and Leo Karakhan all emphasized the Soviet desire to consider the question of recognizing Manchukuo along with a Japanese-Soviet nonaggression treaty. Japan, Foreign Ministry (hereafter JFM), "Soren ni yoru fushinryaku jōyaku teigi mondai" (Concerning Soviet Proposals for a Nonaggression Treaty), in JFM Archives.

2. *Ibid.*

3. Japan, National Defense Agency, Military History Office (hereafter JDA Archives).

4. JFM, ed., *Nisso kōshō shi* (A History of Japanese-Soviet Negotiations), p. 519.

5. *Ibid.*, p. 520; Tōgō Shigenori, *Jidai no ichi-men* (One View of an Era), p. 128.

6. JFM, *Nisso kōshō shi*, p. 521; memorandum of a conversation between Japanese Ambassador to Italy Shiratori Toshio and German Counselor Johann von Plessen on September 4, 1939, reported by German Ambassador to Italy Hans Georg von Mackensen, in U.S., Department of State, *Documents on German Foreign Policy, 1918–1945, from the Archives of the German Foreign Ministry*, Series D (1937– 45), pp. 8–11 (hereafter cited as *DGFP*).

7. JFM, *Nisso kōshō shi*, pp. 521–22.

8. *Ibid.*, p. 522.

9. U. S., Department of State, *Nazi-Soviet Relations, 1939–1941: Documents from the Archives of the German Foreign Office* (hereafter cited as *Nazi-Soviet Relations*), pp. 52– 53 and p. 58.

10. *Nazi-Soviet Relations*, pp. 72–73.

11. Ōshima to Arita, telegram 832, August 23, 1939, in JFM Archives. For Oshima's conversation with State Secretary Ernst von Weizsaecker, see *Nazi-Soviet Relations*, pp. 71–72.

12. Ōshima to Abe, telegram 945, September 7, 1939, in JFM Archives; Ribbentrop to Ott, telegram of September 9, 1939, *DGFP*, 8:36–38.

13. Schulenburg memorandum, September 7, 1939, and Schulenburg to Weizsaecker, telegram of September 16, 1939, *DGFP*, 8:77–79.

14. Ott to Ribbentrop, telegram of September 16, 1939, *DGFP*, 8:75–76.

15. Ott to Ribbentrop, telegram of May 10, 1940, *DGFP*, 9:310–11.

16. JFM, *Nisso kōshō shi*, p. 526.

17. Shiratori Toshio, *Nichi-Doku-I sūjiku ron* (On the Japanese-German-Italian Axis) (Nazi Series, Vol. 15, 1940); Kyokutō Kokusai Gunji Saiban Kōhan Kiroku (Records of the International Military Tribunal for the Far East), Exhibit 2234, in Japan, Justice Ministry (hereafter JJM), War Crimes Materials Office (hereafter cited as IMTFE Records).

18. Konoe Papers.

19. This plan, which included the concept of a division of the world into spheres of influence, differed slightly from the grand design later formulated by Ribbentrop, which

called for the formation of a simple anti-British bloc. These two approaches were reconciled a year later in the four-power entente advocated by Foreign Minister Matsuoka.

20. Harada Kumao, *Saionji kō to seikyoku* (Prince Saionji and the Political Situation), 8:66–67.

21. See n. 6.

22. JDA Archives; Harada, 8:112; as part of his educational campaign Shiratori went on a provincial speaking tour from November 24 to 29 (such activities of Shiratori and his associates were supported by the *Kokumin shimbun*); and Ott to German Foreign Office, telegram of October 24, 1939, *DGFP*, 8:335–36.

23. Harada, 8:117–18.

24. Kōno Mitsu, "Dainanajūgo Gikai to Nisso mondai" (The 75th Diet and the Japanese-Soviet Problem), *Gekkan Roshia*, Vol. 6, No. 5 (May 1940), pp. 15–19.

25. Harada, 8:67.

26. Harada, 8:81–82.

27. Harada, 8:73. Counselor Plessen of the German embassy in Rome reported that, according to Shiratori, the August 31 cable from Abe (then serving concurrently as foreign minister) had instructed Tōgō: "If in the course of conversations about a trade treaty Russia should let it be known that she wishes to conclude a nonaggression pact with Japan, then Ambassador Tōgō should immediately ask whether Russia would be inclined to refuse future aid to Chiang Kai-shek." See the memorandum cited in n. 6.

28. Harada, 8:107.

29. Konoe Papers.

30. Harada, 8:112.

31. JFM, "Gaikō shiryō: Nisso gaikō kōshō kiroku no bu" (Diplomatic Documents: The Record of Japanese-Soviet Negotiations), p. 24 (hereafter cited as JFM, "Nisso gaikō kōshō").

32. Schulenburg to Weizsaecker (see n. 13).

33. Tōgō, *Jidai no ichi-men*, p. 132.

34. JFM, *Nihon gaikō nempyō narabi ni shuyō bunsho* (Chronology and Major Documents of Japanese Foreign Relations), 2:241–24.

35. U.S., Department of State, *Papers Relating to the Foreign Relations of the United States: Japan, 1931–1941*, 2:37–38 (hereafter cited as *FR: Japan*).

36. *Asahi shimbun*, January 17, 1940.

37. Ever since he had been chief of the Asia Bureau (1927–30), Arita was concerned about the danger of the bolshevization of China. As vice foreign minister (1932–33) he is said to have been conscious of the need for Japan to be first of all ideologically and militarily prepared for the Soviet Union. Araki Takeyuki, *Shōwa gaikō henrinroku: Arita gaishō no maki* (Glimpses of Diplomacy in the Shōwa Era: Foreign Minister Arita), pp. 27–28.

38. *Ibid.*, p. 36. For Arita's greetings at the meeting on November 24, 1938, sponsored by the Comrades for the Strengthening of the Anti-Comintern Pact to commemorate the signing of the Anti-Comintern Pact, see pp. 216–23.

39. Kita Reikichi, "Nisso kankei no genjitsu-teki mokuteki" (Realistic Objectives in Japanese-Soviet Relations), *Gekkan Roshia*, Vol. 6, No. 1 (January 1940), pp. 8–22.

40. JDA Archives.

41. JDA Archives.

42. JDA Archives.

43. JDA Archives.

44. Harada, 8:249–50.

45. JFM, "Teikoku no taigai seisaku kankei ikken" (Documents Relating to Japanese Foreign Policy), in JFM Archives (hereafter cited as JFM, Foreign Policy Documents).

46. Max Beloff, *The Foreign Policy of Soviet Russia, 1929–1941*, 2:314.

47. Harada, 8:226. On April 21 Vice Foreign Minister Tani told Harada that "it seems the Soviets . . . would like to stabilize the eastern front for a while through diplomatic negotiations with Japan" (8:226–27).

48. Steinhardt's cable of February 28, 1940, quoted in a memorandum by the assistant chief of the Division of European Affairs, Loy W. Henderson, in U.S., Department of State, *Foreign Relations of the United States: Diplomatic Papers, 1940, The Far East*, 4:6 (hereafter cited as FR, 1940).

49. William L. Langer and S. Everett Gleason, *The Challenge to Isolation, 1937–1940*, p. 642.

50. Tōgō to Arita, telegram 554, April 28, 1940, in "Nisso chūritsu jōyaku kankei ikken" (Documents Relating to the Japanese-Soviet Neutrality Pact), JFM Archives (hereafter cited as JFM, Neutrality Pact Documents).

51. JDA Archives.

52. JDA Archives.

53. Ott to German Foreign Office, telegram of May 10, 1940, DGFP, 9:325–26.

54. Harada, 8:244.

55. JDA Archives.

56. JFM, Neutrality Pact Documents.

57. JDA Archives.

58. Tōgō to Arita, telegram 826, June 19, 1940, and telegram 842, June 22, 1940, in JFM, Neutrality Pact Documents.

59. JFM, Neutrality Pact Documents, and in JFM, "Nisso gaikō kōshō," pp. 24–25.

60. "Sempan kankei shiryō" (Materials Relating to War Crimes), in JJM, War Crimes Materials Office (hereafter cited as JJM, War Crimes Materials).

61. Ott to German Foreign Office, telegram of June 24, 1940, DGFP, 10:5.

62. JDA Archives. See the partial translation of the "Outline" given in Vol. 3 of this series, pp. 203–5.

63. Knoll memorandum, June 20, 1940, DGFP, 9:635.

64. Tōgō to Arita, telegram 879, July 4, 1940, in JFM, Neutrality Pact Documents.

65. Two very interesting documents have been found in the Foreign Ministry Archives. Both are copies of cables exchanged between the People's Commissariat for Foreign Affairs in Moscow and the Soviet ambassador in Tokyo, procured by Japan from the Soviet consulate in Harbin.

The first, telegram 204 of June 22, 1940, from Kubota Kan'ichirō, the consul-general in Harbin, to Arita, summarizes a cable of June 14 sent by the commissariat in Moscow to the Soviet ambassadors in Japan and China:

"Aside from the fact that Japan was persuaded to accept the basic arguments of the Soviet-Mongolian side, two additional reasons why we compromised in the settlement of the border [this refers to the June 9 agreement on the demarcation of the Manchurian-Mongolian border—author's note] were: 1) the need to prepare for positive action on our western border; 2) Japan is now making concessions to the Soviet Union because it seeks security in Manchuria in order to apply pressure on China, as well as on foreign interests in the southern regions. Should Japan undertake such action, the foreign powers will resist, and this will be to our and Chinese advantage.

"We are prepared to discuss several administrative problems with Japan. If Japan relieves its pressure on the Soviet Union and China, we will alleviate our pressure along Manchukuo's northern frontier. In our relations with China, and especially taking into consideration the changes in the European situation, the United States looms extremely important. This is so because we can defend our Far Eastern borders only in cooperation with the United States and China. Therefore, *in order not to damage American-Soviet relations, we cannot discuss* [*with Japan*] *all the problems pending between the two countries. We should agree to all treaties that would promote a clash between Japan and the United States, but we cannot sanction treaties that might cause the United States to take anti-Soviet action.* In such a situation we should limit our negotiations with Japan to secondary problems that have no political significance. Furthermore, we have already reached an agreement with the American government regarding our policies vis-à-vis Japan.

"We want to avoid treaties that would give the United States the impression that we are entering into close political cooperation with Japan. On the other hand, we must take positive measures to give Japan a feeling of security in the north and so stimulate their determination to advance in the south. To stabilize diplomatic relations with Japan, the Soviet government supports the formula of a neutrality treaty but firmly opposes the formula of a nonaggression treaty."

This cable helps clarify the motives behind the Soviet government's policy of forming a weak political combination with Japan.

The second cable, dated June 28, was from the Soviet ambassador in Tokyo to the People's Commissariat for Foreign Affairs:

"Although the Chungking government is now in a critical situation, we anticipate that Japan will make a favorable peace offer to China. According to certain available intelligence, Japan will acquiesce in the extension of our influence and the establishment of any political form we may wish in Outer Mongolia, in the western part of Ninghsia province, and in Kansu, Tsinghai, Sikang, and Sinkiang provinces. While extending its own sphere of influence to a maximum extent, Japan will agree to stop at Lanchow. Because of this situation, *we must grasp this opportunity* before Japan starts positive action to destroy the Chungking government. *If we should negotiate for the determination of the above-mentioned spheres of influence, we expect to succeed.* In this case, there will be no fear of disputes on the Soviet and Mongolian borders, and Japan may not be opposed to the withdrawal of a considerable number of troops from Manchuria."

In reply to this report, the People's Commissariat for Foreign Affairs on July 1 sent the following instructions (Kubota to Arita, telegram 233, July 12, 1940):

"The various negotiations concerning general problems between Japan and the Soviet Union are, after all, nothing more than a sounding-out of mutual intentions. A general agreement with Japan that would involve the issue of peace between Japan and China would harm American-Soviet relations. Considering also the possibility that a dispute may break out in the future between Germany and the Soviet Union, we don't want to harm our friendly relations with the United States, therefore we cannot conclude the above-mentioned general agreement with Japan. Furthermore, an agreement with Japan will not only have a disastrous effect on our continuing activities among the oppressed peoples of Asia, but *it will also needlessly incite Japan to advance in the south. It will guarantee Japan's freedom of action in China and in the Pacific and will not lead to the Japanese-American war we would like to see occur. Therefore our policy is to endeavor to soften our position toward Japan without bringing Japanese-Soviet negotiations to the point of signing an agreement.* The conclusion of our agreement with Germany was dictated by the need for a war in Europe. Our present policy toward France takes into consideration the possibility of a future dispute between Germany and the Soviet Union, the need, in the worst case, to prepare French reserves in Germany's rear, to save France from destruction, and to protect the French Communist Party."

66. Tōgō to Arita, telegram 967, July 19, 1940, JFM, Neutrality Pact Documents.

67. Tōgō to Mutsuoka, telegram 999, July 23, 1940, ibid.

68. Jane Degras, ed., Soviet Documents on Foreign Policy, 3:468.

69. Konoe Papers, published in JFM, Nihon gaikō nempyō, 2:435-36; and Nihon Kokusai Seiji Gakkai, Taiheiyō Sensō Gen'in Kenkyūbu (Japan Association on International Relations, Study Group on the Causes of the Pacific War), ed., Taiheiyō sensō e no michi: Bekkan shiryō hen (The Road to the Pacific War: Supplementary Volume of Documents), pp. 319-20 (hereafter cited as TSM: Bekkan).

70. Tōgō's telegram of July 23, 1940, cited in n.67.

71. Tōgō to Matsuoka, telegram 1019, July 25, 1940, and Matsuoka to Tōgō, telegram 1086, August 5, 1940, in JFM, Neutrality Pact Documents.

72. Tōgō to Matsuoka, telegram 1139, August 16, 1940, ibid.

73. Ibid.

74. Tōgō, Jidai no ichi-men, p. 133.

75. Tōgō to Matsuoka, telegram 1150, August 18, 1940, in JFM, Neutrality Pact Documents.

76. In file entitled "Nichi-Doku-I dōmei jōyaku kankei ikken" (Documents Relating to the Treaty of Alliance between Japan, Germany, and Italy), JFM Archives.

77. JFM, Europe-Asia Bureau, "Matsuoka gaishō to Otto taishi to no kaidan yōryō" (Summary of the Matsuoka-Ott Conversation), August 2, 1940, presented to the IMTFE as Exhibit 545, in JFM Archives.

78. Matsuoka's explanation at the Imperial Conference of September 19, 1940, in the Foreign Ministry study, "Nichi-Doku-I sangoku jōyaku" (The Tripartite Pact), in JFM Archives (hereafter cited as JFM, Tripartite Pact Study); published in TSM: Bekkan, pp. 337-42.

79. See the summary of their conversations, compiled by Matsuoka and confirmed by Stahmer: JFM, "Kaidan yōshi" (Summary of Conversations), in JFM, Tripartite Pact Study.

80. Harada, 8:350.

81. Statement by Toyoda Teijirō, December 1957, in JDA Archives.

82. See n. 78.

83. On September 20 Konoe told Harada: "Since Germany has concluded a nonaggression treaty with the Soviet Union, it will serve as a go-between. Direct negotiations between Japan and the Soviet Union are impossible. They will be possible only if Germany mediates. Germany will also make an effort to facilitate peace maneuvers toward China." Harada, 8:350.

84. JFM, Tripartite Pact Study, pp. 211-33.

85. Ibid., p. 60; Saitō Yoshie, "Nichi-Doku-I dōmei jōyaku teiketsu yōroku" (Summary Record of the Conclusion of the Tripartite Pact), in JFM Archives.

86. JDA Archives.

87. Galeazzo Ciano, The Ciano Diaries, 1939-1943, p. 293.

88. JFM, Tripartite Pact Study, p. 102.

89. "Nisso kokkō chōsei an ni kansuru setsumei" (Explanation of the Plan for the Adjustment of Japanese-Soviet Diplomatic Relations), October 2, 1940, in JFM, Foreign Policy Documents.

90. The draft contained the following passage: "Even if we should yield temporarily in the matter of our concessions, this would simply be because we foresaw before long the arrival of a day when a thoroughgoing settlement would be reached in accordance with our overall desires."

91. The original October 9 draft of Matsuoka's cable to Kurusu (later cancelled) expresses well what the Foreign Ministry had expected from German diplomatic mediation: "Although the draft for adjusting relations with the Soviet Union is still under study, its essence is as follows: a) our first objective is the conclusion of a nonaggression pact; b) Japan and the Soviet Union will mutually respect each other's position in China; c) Japan will recognize the Soviet advance into central Asia in return for Soviet recognition of Japan's advance to the south. . . .

"In order to curb present Soviet demands and accomplish a speedy adjustment of diplomatic relations, Japan, taking into consideration the terms of the Tripartite Pact, is now especially anxious that Germany should make positive efforts at mediation." JFM, Neutrality Pact Documents.

92. JDA Archives. Present at the conference were: from the Foreign Ministry, Narita Katsushirō, acting head of the First (Soviet) Section of the Europe-Asia Bureau, and Kakitsubo Masayoshi; from the Army Ministry, Lieutenant-Colonels Takayama Hikoichi and Ninomiya Yoshikiyo; and from the Navy Ministry, Commander Shiba Katsuo.

93. "Nisso kokkō chōsei an ni taisuru iken kōkan kiroku" (Record of the Exchange of Opinions Concerning the Plan for the Adjustment of Japanese-Soviet Diplomatic Relations), October 3, 1940, in JFM, Foreign Policy Documents.

94. "Nisso kokkō chōsei yōkō an" (Draft of Basic Principles for the Adjustment of Japanese-Soviet Diplomatic Relations), October 4, 1940, in JFM, Foreign Policy Documents.

95. Harada, 8:364, 383.

96. Harada 8:334. For the Soviet view of General Tatekawa's appointment, see the translator's introductory essay.

97. Hashimoto Kingorō, "Shintaisei to Nisso mondai" (The New Order and the Japanese-Soviet Problem), Gekkan Roshia, October 1940, pp. 34–37.

98. JFM, "Nisso gaikō kōshō," pp. 26–28.

99. Ibid.

100. Nazi-Soviet Relations, pp. 207–13.

101. Schulenburg to German Foreign Office, telegram of October 22, 1940, ibid., p. 216.

102. JFM, "Nisso gaikō kōshō," p. 28.

103. Ott to Ribbentrop, telegram of November 11, 1940, DGFP, 11:512–13.

104. JFM, "Nisso gaikō kōshō," p. 28.

105. Ott's telegram of November 11 (see n. 103).

106. JFM, "Nisso gaikō kōshō," p. 28.

107. Nazi-Soviet Relations, pp. 217–25.

108. Ibid., pp. 234–47.

109. Ibid., pp. 255–58.

110. Ibid., pp. 251–52.

111. Schulenburg to Ribbentrop, telegram of November 26, 1940, ibid., pp. 258–59.

112. William L. Shirer, The Rise and Fall of the Third Reich, p. 798.

113. Shirer, pp. 799–800.

114. Joachim von Ribbentrop, The Ribbentrop Memoirs, pp. 146–50.

115. JFM, "Nisso gaikō kōshō," pp. 28–29.

116. *Ibid.*, pp. 29–30.

117. *Ibid.*, p. 30.

118. Ott to German Foreign Office, telegram of November 21, 1940, *DGFP*, 11:645.

119. JFM, "Nisso gaikō kōshō," pp. 30–31. The Japanese intention related only to fishery rights, but Molotov capitalized on Ribbentrop's mistake.

120. Japan, Army General Staff (hereafter AGS), War Guidance Office, "Daihon'ei kimitsu sensō nisshi" (Confidential War Diary of the Imperial Headquarters), entry for December 13, 1940, in JDA Archives (hereafter cited as AGS, *Confidential War Diary*).

121. Ott's telegram of November 21 (n. 118).

122. Kurusu spoke in this vein to Weizsaecker on November 29. See Weizsaecker memorandum of November 29, 1940, in *DGFP*, 11:744.

123. In view of the need for closer liaison between the government and the high command, the army had suggested that the Liaison Conference meet at the prime minister's official residence every Thursday. The first regularly scheduled meeting took place on November 28. See JDA Archives.

124. Ott's telegram of November 21 (n. 118); also, AGS, *Confidential War Diary*, entry for December 13, 1940.

125. AGS, *Confidential War Diary*, entry for December 13, 1940.

126. Statement by Lieutenant-Colonel Takayama Hikoichi in the Foreign Ministry record cited in n. 93.

127. AGS, *Confidential War Diary*, entry for November 21, 1940.

128. *Ibid.* The entry for December 17 contains the following passage: "The adjustment of Japanese-Soviet diplomatic relations is at a standstill. We have not made any sweeping adjustment. Alas!" See also Ott to German Foreign Office, telegram of December 18, 1940, *DGFP*, 11:886.

129. Vice Navy Minister Toyoda also suggested that Matsuoka visit Europe. Toyoda statement, cited in n. 81. And Harada, 8:356.

130. Ott to German Foreign Office, telegram of December 19, 1940, *DGFP*, 11:907; IMTFE Records, Exhibit 568.

131. "Tai-Doku-I-So kōshō an yōkō," in JDA Archives.

132. See AGS, *Confidential War Diary*, entries for January 13, 15, and 18, 1941.

133. JDA Archives; the conference proceedings have been published in *TSM: Bekkan*, pp. 362–65; and in AGS, comp., *Sugiyama memo* (Sugiyama Gen Memorandum), 1:173–77.

134. The draft published in JFM, *Nihon gaikō nempyō*, 2:480–82, differs in some respects—e.g., the conditions for transfer of the oil concessions in northern Sakhalin—from the one that was finally approved.

135. "Shitsumu hōkoku" (Administrative Report), in JFM Archives. Vice Minister Ōhashi wrote in his memoirs that "these negotiations between Germany and the Soviet Union had an important effect on the course of the Second World War. Yet Germany did not provide Japan with information before the negotiations began. Even after the negotiations no more than a bare outline was transmitted to Japan through Ambassador Ōshima, with the important points left obscure." Ōhashi Chūichi, *Taiheiyō sensō yuraiki* (Origins of the Pacific War), pp. 84–85.

136. Tatekawa to Matsuoka, telegram 101, January 27, 1941, in JFM, Neutrality Pact Documents.

137. Tōgō, *Jidai no ichi-men*, pp. 136, 138; and Matsuoka, "Shitsumu nisshi" (Office Diary), in JFM Archives. At a meeting of army and navy officers of full general and admiral

rank on January 18, 1941, Tōgō explained the problems involved in having Germany act as a mediator to bring about Japanese negotiations with the Soviet Union. JDA Archives.

138. Saitō Yoshie, *Azamukareta rekishi: Matsuoka to sangoku dōmei no rimen* (History Deceived: The Inside Story of Matsuoka and the Tripartite Pact), p. 192; Kurihara Ken, *Tennō: Shōwa shi oboegaki* (The Emperor: A Note on the History of the Shōwa Period), p. 154.

139. Kurusu Saburō, *Hōmatsu no sanjūgo-nen* (Vain Endeavor), p. 43.

140. Kido Kōichi, *Kido Kōichi nikki* (Diary of Kido Kōichi), entry for February 7, 1941, 2:855 (hereafter cited as *Kido Diary*).

141. According to Vice Minister Ōhashi, Matsuoka took with him instructions for concluding a Japanese-Soviet neutrality treaty, in case the establishment of a four-power entente proved impossible. Ōhashi, p. 80.

142. Hasegawa Shin'ichi, "Matsuoka gaishō to-O nikki" (Diary of Foreign Minister Matsuoka's European Trip), published in the May 1941 issue of *Kōron*. The following account of the trip is based largely on this record by Hasegawa, who was a member of the foreign minister's party.

143. *Ibid.*; and Saionji Kinkazu, *Kizoku to taijō* (The Exit of the Aristocracy), pp. 62–76.

144. Steinhardt to Hull, telegram of March, 24, 1941, in *FR: Japan*, 2:143–45.

145. Matsuoka mentioned these comments to Stalin during his conference with Hitler on March 27. See IMTFE Records, Exhibit 577.

146. *DGFP*, 12:219 (italics in original); conference between Ribbentrop and Ōshima on February 23, 1941; IMTFE Records, and Ribbentrop to Ōshima, February 27, 1941, Exhibits 571 and 572.

147. Matsuoka-Ribbentrop conference of March 27, 1941; Matsuoka-Hitler conference of March 27; Matsuoka-Ribbentrop conference of March 28; Matsuoka-Ribbentrop conference of March 29; in IMTFE Records, Exhibits 578, 577, 579, and 580, respectively.

148. *DGFP*, 12:408.

149. *DGFP*, 12:413.

150. To-Ō fukumei naisō" (Report to the Throne on the Journey to Europe), Matsuoka's private report to the emperor, in JFM, Neutrality Pact Documents; Tatekawa to Konoe, telegram 431, April 10, 1941, in the Konoe Papers.

151. Matsuoka's report to the emperor and Tatekawa's telegram, cited in n. 150; report by Colonel Nagai Yatsuji, a military member of the foreign minister's party, in JDA Archives.

152. Matsuoka's report to the emperor; Tatekawa to Konoe, telegrams 442 and 444, April 12, 1941, in the Konoe Papers.

153. Matsuoka's report to the emperor; also Matsuoka's report to the Liaison Conference on the evening of April 22, 1941, in JDA Archives, published in AGS, *Sugiyama memo*, 1:199–202.

154. JFM, *Nihon gaikō nempyō*, 2:491–92.

155. Hubertus Lupke, *Japans Russlandpolitik von 1939 bis 1941*, pp. 125–26.

156. F. C. Jones, *Japan's New Order in East Asia*, p. 214.

157. *Nazi-Soviet Relations*, pp. 322–23. See also Matsuoka's explanation to the Privy Council on April 24, 1941, in Fukai Eigo, *Sūmitsuin jūyō giji oboegaki* (Notes on Important Sessions of the Privy Council), p. 151; Lupke, pp. 119–25.

158. John M. Maki, *Conflict and Tension in the Far East*, p. 90.

159. Henry Wei, *China and Soviet Russia*, pp. 152–54.

160. For example, Kh. T. Eidus, *Ocherki novoi i noveishei istorii Iaponii*, p. 221.

161. D. I. Gol'dberg, *Vneshniaia politika Iaponii, Sentiabr' 1939-Dekabr' 1941gg*, p. 114.

162. Jones, p. 215.

163. *Kido Diary*, entry for June 6, 1941, 2:879.

164. Matsuoka Yōsuke, "Konoe shuki ni taisuru setsumei" (Explanation of the Konoe Memorandum), in JJM, War Crimes Materials.

165. JDA Archives; AGS, *Sugiyama memo*, 1:225–26.

166. Ōhashi, p. 97.

167. Fukai, p. 152; JFM, Research Division, Third Section, "Soren kankei kokusai jōsei handan" (Analysis of the International Situation with Regard to the Soviet Union), April 19, 1941, in JFM Archives.

168. Shidehara Heiwa Zaidan (Shidehara Peace Foundation), ed., *Shidehara Kijūrō*, pp. 516–21. Konoe was a recipient of this letter, a copy of which is in the Konoe Papers.

169. AGS, *Confidential War Diary*, entries for April 14 and 18, 1941.

170. Fukai, pp. 150–51.

171. Consul-General Yano Seiki in Hong Kong to Matsuoka, telegram 211, April 28, 1941, in JFM, Neutrality Pact Documents.

172. Beloff, p. 376.

173. Joseph C. Grew, *Ten Years in Japan*, pp. 381–82; under the heading "The Japanese-Russian Pact," the *New York Times* on April 14 wrote that it was a diplomatic victory for the Axis.

174. *FR: Japan*, 2:186.

175. Shirer, pp. 822–30.

176. Gerhard L. Weinberg, *Germany and the Soviet Union*, pp. 155–56, 160; Shirer, p. 843.

177. Weinberg, pp. 158–60.

178. *Nazi-Soviet Relations*, p. 324.

179. Weinberg, p. 161; Shirer, p. 840.

180. Shirer, p. 845.

181. Schulenburg to German Foreign Office, telegram of June 14, 1941, *Nazi-Soviet Relations*, pp. 345–46.

182. In reply to a question on this point at a Privy Council meeting, Matsuoka said: "There is a contradiction from a legal point of view. In this case, although we should consult with Germany, Japan must decide on the basis of its own position." Fukai, pp. 150–51.

183. Ōshima to Konoe, telegram 413, April 16, 1941, in the Konoe Papers.

184. *Ibid.*

185. *Kido Diary*, entry for April 18, 1941, 2:869.

186. JDA Archives.

187. *Ibid.*

188. AGS, *Confidential War Diary*, entry for May 13, 1941.

189. JDA Archives.

190. AGS, *Confidential War Diary*, entry for May 15, 1941.

191. *Ibid.*, entry for May 12, 1941.

192. Matsuoka to Ōshima, telegram 458, May 28, 1941, in the Konoe Papers.

193. Ōshima to Matsuoka, telegrams 638 and 639, June 5, 1941, *ibid.*

194. He said it was sixty percent for the conclusion of an agreement and forty percent for war. See n. 163.

195. JDA Archives; AGS, *Sugiyama memo*, 1:218.

196. JDA Archives.

197. AGS, *Confidential War Diary*, entries for June 5–14, 1941.

198. "Kaisen made no kokusaku no keii, shūsen kettei no keii oyobi kaigun daijin kōtetsu kankei bunsho" (Documents Concerning National Policy Prior to the Outbreak of War, the Decision to End the War, and the Replacement of the Navy Minister), in JJM, War Crimes Materials.

199. Konoe Fumimaro, *Ushinawareshi seiji* (Politics that Failed), p. 83.

200. *Kido Diary*, entry for June 21, 1941, 2:883.

201. Konoe Fumimaro, *Heiwa e no doryoku* (My Struggle for Peace), pp. 25–26.

202. Hattori Takushirō, *Dai Tōa sensō zenshi* (A History of the Greater East Asia War), 1:142.

203. AGS, *Confidential War Diary*, entries for June 23 and 24, 1941; Hattori, 1:142–43.

204. JFM, *Nihon gaikō nempyō*, 2:531.

205. JDA Archives; AGS, *Sugiyama memo*, 1:243–46; Hattori, 1:144–48.

206. Matsuoka, "Konoe shuki."

207. AGS, *Confidential War Diary*, entry for June 27, 1941.

208. JDA Archives; AGS, *Sugiyama memo*, 1:246–48.

209. JDA Archives; AGS, *Sugiyama memo*, 1:248–50.

210. Foreign Minister Ribbentrop's proposal of June 30, 1941, in the Konoe Papers; Ribbentrop to Ott, June 28, 1941, *DGFP*, 13;40–41.

211. Ōshima to Matsuoka, telegrams 784 and 785, June 27, 1941, and telegram 798, June 28, in the Konoe Papers. On June 27 Ott met with Matsuoka and Ohashi.

212. JDA Archives; AGS, *Sugiyama memo*, 1:248–50.

213. A copy of the Japanese reply to the German government is in the Konoe Papers, published in AGS, *Sugiyama memo*, 1:252–53.

214. JDA Archives; AGS, *Sugiyama memo*, Hattori, 1:152.

215. The "Outline of National Policies in View of the Changing Situation" has been published in JFM, *Nihon gaikō nempyō*, 2:531–33; also in AGS, *Sugiyama memo*, 1:254–64.

216. JDA Archives; AGS, *Sugiyama memo*, 1:227.

217. JDA Archives.

218. Ambassador to Manchukuo Umezu Yoshijirō to Matsuoka, telegram of June 27, 1941, in JFM, "Doku-So kaisen kankei ikken" (Documents Relating to the Outbreak of War between Germany and the USSR), in JFM Archives.

219. Satō Kenryō, *Tōjō Hideki to Taiheiyō sensō* (Tōjō Hideki and the Pacific War), pp. 182–88.

220. JDA Archives.

221. Grew, pp. 403–4.

222. Ōshima to Matsuoka, telegram 825, July 2, 1941, in the Konoe Papers.

223. Tatekawa to Matsuoka, telegrams 848 and 854, July 4, 1941, *ibid.*

224. JDA Archives.

225. JDA Archives.

226. AGS, *Confidential War Diary*, entries for August 2 and 3, 1941; Hattori, 1:154.

227. AGS, *Confidential War Diary*, entry for August 3, 1941; Hattori, 1:155.

228. JDA Archives.

229. JDA Archives, see also AGS, *Confidential War Diary*, entries for August 4–6, 1941; and Hattori, 1:155–56.

230. AGS, *Confidential War Diary*, entry for August 9, 1941; Hattori, 1:156.
231. Presented to the Liaison Conference on August 6, 1941, in JDA Archives.
232. Diary of Ambassador Konstantin Smetanin, entry for June 25, 1941, IMTFE Records, Exhibit 792.
233. For a discussion of the Soviet intelligence network in Japan, see the translator's introduction to this essay.
234. Konoe Papers.
235. JDA Archives, AGS, *Sugiyama memo*, 1:281 and 283.
236. AGS, *Confidential War Diary*, entries for June 26 and 27, 1941.
237. JFM, Neutrality Pact Documents.
238. Konoe Papers, AGS, *Sugiyama memo*, 1:284–89.
239. JDA Archives; AGS, *Sugiyama memo*, 1:293.

PART II

Southern Advance

2. Economic Demands on the Dutch East Indies (Nagaoka Shinjirō)

1. JFM, "Nichi-Ran tsūshō jōyaku kankei ikken: Shōwa jū-nen ikō jūgo-nen made no Nichi-Ran kan kōshō kankei" (Documents Relating to the Commercial Treaty between Japan and the Netherlands: Negotiations, 1935–40), in JFM Archives (hereafter cited as JFM, Netherlands Commercial Treaty Documents, 1935–40).
2. JFM, Netherlands Commercial Treaty Documents, 1935–40—the source for the material here and in the preceeding paragraphs.
3. JFM, "Teikoku nampō seisaku kankei ikken" (Documents Relating to the Southern Policy of the Empire) (hereafter cited as JFM, Documents on Southern Policy); the translation here is taken from the press release issued by the Japanese embassy in Washington on April 15, 1940, *FR, Japan* 2:281.
4. JFM, Netherlands Commercial Treaty Documents, 1935–40.
5. *FR, 1940*, 4:9.
6. *FR, Japan*, 2:282.
7. *FR, 1940*, 4:9–10.
8. *Ibid.*, pp. 11–12.
9. Ernst L. Presseisen, *Germany and Japan*, p. 238.
10. Ott to Foreign Office, telegram of April 15, 1940, *DGFP*, 9:175–76.
11. Harada, 8:208 and 224.
12. Langer and Gleason, *The Challenge to Isolation*, p. 587.
13. *FR, Japan*, 2:283–84.
14. Langer and Gleason, *Challenge to Isolation*, p. 588.
15. JFM, Netherlands Commercial Treaty Documents, 1935–40.
16. *FR, 1940*, 4: 13.
17. JFM, Netherlands Commercial Treaty Documents, 1935–40.
18. *Ibid.*
19. JFM, Documents on Southern Policy.
20. *FR, Japan*, 2:285.
21. JFM, Netherlands Commercial Treaty Documents, 1935–40; *FR, 1940*, 4:17–18.

22. *FR, 1940*, 4:15, 18–19.

23. JFM, Netherlands Commercial Treaty Documents, 1935–40.

24. Langer and Gleason, *Challenge to Isolation*, p. 592.

25. JFM, Netherlands Commercial Treaty Documents, 1935–40.

26. Weizsaecker memorandum, May 17, 1940, *DGFP*, 9:360–62.

27. JFM, Netherlands Commercial Treaty Documents, 1935–40; Ribbentrop to Ott, telegram of May 20, 1940, *DGFP*, 9:385–87.

28. *FR, Japan*, 2:67–71.

29. JFM, "Shina jihen kakkoku no taido: Nichi-Bei kankei dakai kōsaku" (Attitudes of the Powers toward the China Incident: Efforts to Find a Way Out in Relations between Japan and the United States), in JFM Archives; *FR, Japan*, 2:79–80.

30. JFM, "Shina jihen kakkoku no taido"; *FR, Japan*, 2:83–87.

31. JFM, "Shina jihen kakkoku no taido"; *FR, Japan*, 2:88–92.

32. JFM, *Nihon gaikō nempyō* 2:433–34; the full text of the official English translation, followed here, is in *FR, Japan*, 2:93–94.

33. JFM, *Nihon gaikō nempyō* 2:431.

34. Ishii Itarō, *Gaikōkan no isshō* (The Life of a Diplomat), pp. 345–46.

35. JFM, "Nichi-Ran tsūshō jōyaku kankei ikken: Shōwa jūgo-nen jūroku-nen *Nichi-Ran kaishō kankei* (Documents Relating to the Commercial Treaty between Japan and the Netherlands: Negotiations, 1940–41), in JFM Archives (hereafter cited as JFM, Netherlands Commercial Treaty Documents, 1940–41).

36. Sumner Welles, *Seven Decisions That Shaped History*, pp. 89–90.

37. JFM, "Shina jihen kakkoku no taido."

38. *Ibid.; FR, Japan*, 2:95–101.

39. JFM, Netherlands Commercial Treaty Documents, 1940–41.

40. "Sempan kankei shiryō," JJM, War Crimes Materials.

41. JFM, Netherlands Commercial Treaty Documents, 1940–41; see Grew's reports on Koiso's appointment in *FR, 1940*, 4:60 and 72; also Hubertus J. Van Mook, The Netherlands Indies and Japan, p. 74.

42. *FR, 1940*, 4:61–62.

43. Netherlands Commercial Treaty Documents, 1940–41. When the *Asahi shimbun* published a report of these disagreements in its issue of August 15, the article was suppressed by the government on the grounds that it would place Japan in a disadvantageous position in the negotiations with the Dutch East Indies.

44. *FR, 1940*, 2:55–56 and 58–59.

45. *Ibid.*, pp. 73, 83.

46. *Ibid.*, pp. 75–79.

47. *Ibid.*, p. 85.

48. *Ibid.*, pp. 108–09 and 147–48.

49. JFM, *Nihon gaikō nempyō*, 2:440.

50. Netherlands Commercial Treaty Documents, 1940–41.

51. *Ibid.*

52. JFM, "Nichi-Ran tsūshō jōyaku kankei ikken: Shōwa jūgo-nen jūroku-nen Nichi-Ran kaishō kankei: sekiyu kankei" (Documents Relating to the Commercial Treaty between Japan and the Netherlands: Negotiations, 1940–41—Petroleum), in JFM Archives (hereafter cited as JFM, Documents on Petroleum Negotiations).

53. Itagaki Yoichi, "Taiheiyō sensō to sekiyu mondai" (The Pacific War and the Petroleum Problem), in Nihon Gaikō Gakkai (Association for the Study of Japanese Diplomacy), ed., *Taiheiyō sensō gen'in ron* (The Origins of the Pacific War), p. 659.

54. U.S., Department of State, *Foreign Relations of the United States: Diplomatic Papers, 1941, The Far East* (hereafter cited as *FR, 1941*), 4:814.

55. *Ibid.*, pp. 806–07 (italics in original).

56. JFM, Documents on Petroleum Negotiations.

57. JFM, Netherlands Commercial Treaty Documents, 1940–41.

58. Yoshizawa Kenkichi, "Itsuwari no gaikō shi: Nichi-Ran kōshō no shinsō" (False Diplomatic History: The True Story of the Japan-Netherlands Negotiations), *Chūō kōron,* December 1950, p. 176; Netherlands Commercial Treaty Documents, 1940–41.

59. See the summary of the Japanese proposals cabled to the Department of State by the U.S. consul-general in Batavia on January 21, 1941, in *FR, 1941,* 5:25–27.

60. JFM, Netherlands Commercial Treaty Documents, 1940–41; see also Grew's report of Matsuoka's remarks in *FR, Japan,* 2:303–07.

61. See reports of the Dutch protest in *FR, 1941,* 5:51 and 54.

62. JFM, Netherlands Commercial Treaty Documents, 1940–41.

63. *FR, 1941,* 5:27–28; and see Hornbeck's memorandum of his conversation with Loudon on January 23 on p. 37.

64. JFM, "Shina jihen kakkoku no taido," Vol. 2, "Tai-Bei gaikō kankei shuyō shiryō-shū" (Major Documents Relating to Diplomacy toward the United States), in JFM Archives.

65. *Ibid.; FR, Japan,* 2:222–48.

66. JFM, Netherlands Commercial Treaty Documents, 1940–41.

67. *FR, 1941,* 4:814.

68. JFM, Netherlands Commercial Treaty Documents, 1940–41.

69. *Ibid.*

70. *Ibid.*

71. *Ibid.;* also *FR, 1941,* 5:141.

72. JFM, Netherlands Commercial Treaty Documents, 1940–41.

73. *Ibid.;* see also the cable to the British embassy in Washington forwarded to the Department of State on May 23, 1941, in *FR, 1941,* 5:161.

74. JFM, Netherlands Commercial Treaty Documents, 1940–41.

75. Hattori Takushirō, *Dai Tōa sensō zenshi* (A History of the Greater East Asia War), 1:133.

76. See Grew's report of Matsuoka's talk with Craigie on June 10, in *FR, 1941,* 5:175.

77. *FR, 1941,* 5:173–74.

78. *FR, 1941,* 4:251.

79. JFM, Netherlands Commercial Treaty Documents, 1940–41; see *FR, 1941,* 5:174, for Grew's summary of the Dutch reply.

80. Hattori, 1:135.

81. JFM, Netherlands Commercial Treaty Documents, 1940–41.

3. The Army's Move into Northern Indochina (*Hata Ikuhiko*)

1. Materials in the JDA Archives—unless otherwise indicated, the source for all material in this chapter, including undocumented quotations and telegrams.

2. Kido Kōichi, *Kido Kōichi nikki* (Diary of Kido Kōichi), entry for June 19, 1940, 2:794.

3. The original plan drawn up by the Operations Division called for a force of 500. Intelligence Division Chief Tsuchihashi was opposed to so large a unit, however, and the

number was reduced, first to 100 and finally to 40, including 23 from the army, 7 from the navy (to be headed by Captain Yanagisawa Kuranosuke), and 10 from the Foreign Ministry (headed by Yosano Shigeru). In the course of the discussions relations between Tsuchihashi and Tominaga became severely strained.

The "Preliminary Directives for the Commission Dispatched to French Indochina," drawn up on June 24, delineated the responsibilities of the army head: "to command the army members of the commission, simultaneously to manage the naval members, and to control the entire operation, which is to supervise the French Indochina authorities who are to stop the flow of supplies to Chiang Kai-shek." Those assigned to the commission's headquarters in Hanoi were Colonel Koike Ryōji and Colonel Nakai Masutarō (special duties), Major Tokuo Toshihiko (general administration), Captain Nakajima (communications and codes), Military Police Major Ariga Jingorō (inspection unit), and Intendant Captain Yabe Toshio (budget); dispatched as inspectors at important transit points were Commander Motoki Jun'ichi (Haiphong), Lieutenant-Colonel Oka Yoshio (Lang Son), Major Yokoyama Hikozane (Cao Bang), Major Yasumura Isao (Ha Giang), Major Sakai Wataru (Lao Cai), and Lieutenant-Commander Fukuoka Takeshi (Mong Cai). Editor's note: Japanese text lists Tien Yen instead of Mong Cai as given in Jean Decoux, *A la barre de l'Indochine.* Mong Cai seems more likely to be correct since it is closer to the border.

4. Satō Kenryō, "Hokubu Futsuin shinchū no keii" (The Stationing of Troops in Northern French Indochina) (1958) JDA Archives.

5. Koike Ryōji, "Nishihara kikan kara mita Hokubu Futsuin shinchū no shinsō (Nikki)" (The truth about the stationing of troops in Northern Indochina as seen by the Nishihara agency, Diary), 1958. JDA Archives. About June 25 the Army General Staff Operations Section reported the navy's plan:

"a) If the government of French Indochina approves the passage of Japanese troops through Indochina, in early or mid-July the 5th Division and the Imperial Guard Division will advance via land and sea to Hanoi and Haiphong. Immediately thereafter the main force of the 22nd Army will be assembled in French Indochina and will prepare to attack Mengtzu and K'unming. Troops at Nanning and Ch'inhsien will be withdrawn.

"b) If the French Indochina authorities do not accept our demands, in early or mid-July the main force of the 22nd Army (the core of the 5th Division) will invade Indochina by land while the 18th Division and other forces invade by sea, with the aim of occupying the country."

6. According to Nishihara to Army Chief of Staff, telegram 14 of July 1 and telegram 16 of July 2, 1940, the terms of the border inspection agreement were: 1) transit of materials from French Indochina to China was to be stopped completely; 2) reports were to be made each time commodities were supplied to the French and American embassies in Chungking; 3) from July 2 observers would be assigned to Haiphong and five places along the border.

7. Nishihara to Army and Navy Vice Chiefs of Staff, telegram 45, July 5, 1940. According to a telegram of the 14th from Consul-General Suzuki Rokurō at Hanoi to Foreign Minister Arita, the idea of a defensive alliance was first advanced in an exchange of opinion between Nishihara and Thiébaut.

8. This was urged, for example, in the General Staff's draft "Outline for Obtaining French Aid in Handling the China Incident," dated June 1, 1940.

9. See, for example, the General Staff document of July 7, 1940, entitled "Maneuvers to Utilize France."

10. Telegram 45, July 7, 1940.

11. Nishihara to Army and Navy Vice Chiefs of Staff, telegram 75, July 9, 1940; Nishihara to Vice Chiefs, telegram 91, July 11, 1940.

12. Satō, "Hokubu Futsuin shinchū."

13. Nishihara to Chief of General Affairs Division, telegram 103, July 13, 1940. Additional articles are omitted here.

14. The proposed supplementary supply route was to run by road from Nanning via Paise and Mengtzu to K'unming. Catroux also promised to supply Japanese troops landed at Haiphong. But when the Keijō-maru entered Haiphong, the authorities refused to permit it to be unloaded because it carried soldiers as well as goods. The ship remained in port for some time and eventually left without unloading.

15. Satō Kenryō, Tojō Hideki to Taiheiyō sensō (Tōjō Hideki and the Pacific War), p. 126.

16. Satō later wrote that after he arrived in Hanoi he "found that Hanoi is just another part of French Indochina, but the real center is Saigon." He therefore suggested to the central command that the entire territory be included in the stationing and actually made such a demand in late July, when he was conducting the negotiations in Nishihara's absence. Satō, "Hokubu Futsuin shinchū."

17. Nishihara to Chief of General Affairs Division, Army General Staff, telegram 103, July 13, 1940.

18. Nishihara to Army Vice Chief of Staff, telegram 169, July 25, 1940.

19. Nishihara was informed of Decoux's appointment in mid-July and reported it to the central command in Tokyo on the 16th. Official public announcement was made around July 20. One rumor to explain the change held that Catroux had exceeded his authority in proposing the defensive alliance; another linked him to de Gaulle's government-in-exile and opposed to Pétain. Koike, "Nishihara kikan" (entry of July 24).

20. See Nishihara telegram 169 (n. 18).

21. Satō to Chief of General Affairs Division, Army General Staff, telegram 183, July 28, 1940.

22. Army and Navy Vice Chiefs of Staff to Satō, telegram of July 30, 1940; Satō to Army Vice Chief of Staff, telegram 197, July 31, 1940; Army Vice Chief of Staff to Satō, telegram of August 2, 1940.

23. According to materials in the JDA Archives, in July an officer of the General Staff Operations Section visited the Army Ministry Military Section and proposed to its chief, Colonel Iwakuro Hideo, and to Lieutenant-Colonel Nishiura Susumu that the 22nd Army should be withdrawn via Indochina, since a withdrawal via Ch'inchou Bay was impossible. Due to circumstances since the Nanning operation, he found it difficult to propose the matter to the Army Ministry directly. Iwakuro and Nishiura agreed that the army could not be endangered simply to save face and promised to approach the army minister so that the withdrawal could be accomplished following diplomatic negotiations. However, earlier in the spring the Ch'inning road had been repaired, easing the army's supply situation despite the fact that Ch'inchou Bay was not a good port, and the concern for its safety may therefore have been exaggerated. Nishiura Susumu, "Hokubu Futsuin shinchū senshiteki kansatsu" (Historical survey of the stationing of troops in Northern Indochina) (1955). JDA Archives.

24. Nakamura Aketo, Futsuin shinchū no shinsō (The Truth Concerning the Stationing of Troops in French Indochina). Tokyo, Ground Self-Defense Forces Staff Headquarters, 1954.

25. Secret telegram 767 from Chief of Staff of 2nd China Fleet, received by Chief of First Division, Navy Division of Imperial Headquarters, June 19, 1940.

26. Nakamura, *Futsuin shinchū*.

27. Wakamatsu to Army Vice Chief of Staff, telegram 996, July 11, 1940.

28. Nemoto to Army Vice Chief of Staff, telegram 669, July 19, 1940.

29. Nakamura, *Futsuin shinchū*.

30. Nemoto to Satō, telegram 824, July 30, 1940.

31. Satō to Army Vice Chief of Staff, telegram 213 of August 2 and telegram 222 of August 3, 1940.

32. Nakamura, *Futsuin shinchū*.

33. Copy of a note from Matsuoka to Ambassador Arsène-Henry Navy General Staff, "Futsuin mondai Keii."

34. Matsuoka to Horinouchi, telegram U.S. 1705, August 1, 1940, *ibid.*

35. AGS, *Confidential War Diary*, entry for August 26, 1940.

36. Just before Tominaga's departure, two plans were drafted, which Tominaga took with him to Hanoi. The "Outline for the Management of the French Indochina Problem" stated that negotiations were to be conducted on the spot by Nishihara, as the representative of the navy and the army, on the basis of the Matsuoka-Henry Pact. The date on which the stationing of Japanese forces would commence was to be decided in consultation with the French authorities, after which the stationing would begin. The second, a draft of a note to be exchanged once agreement had been reached, was much the same as the "Details Concerning Military Demands" Nishi had presented to Arsène-Henry on August 21, with the additional provision that the date of stationing would be agreed to by the army and navy central command once it had been determined by the commander of the South China Army in consultation with the commander-in-chief of the 2nd China Fleet. Navy General Staff, "Futsuin mondai keii."

37. Although we do not know the contents of the instructions given to Tominaga, he was apparently empowered to command the troops on the spot in the name of the chief of the Army General Staff. Article 5 of the instructions to Nishihara stated that "details will be communicated by the chief staff officer," who in this case was Tominaga. A similar situation arose at the time of the Hsuchou operation, when Hashimoto Gun, chief of the Operations Division of the Army General Staff, was sent to direct the forces on the spot.

38. The original telegram, as sent by Satō to General Nemoto at 11:40 p.m. on September 2, read:

1) At this time, the evening of the 2nd, negotiations on the spot have almost reached the point of breakdown.

2) As transmitted by Tominaga, chief of the First Division, the following instructions have been issued by the chief of the General Staff: Based on Imperial Headquarters Army Order——(preparations for operations against a third power), I instruct you as follows: The commander of the South China Army is to complete preparations immediately for an attack on northern French Indochina.

Chief of Army General Staff

Prince Kan'in Kotohito

39. AGS, *Confidential War Diary*, entry for August 26, 1940. Other entries in the *Diary* reveal how confused the situation at headquarters was. August 1: "A chaotic situation prevails concerning the French Indochina problem. No agreement can be reached between the Army Ministry and the General Staff." August 8: "Major-General Nishihara has returned to his duties. Nothing has been settled. Of those who welcomed him and those who saw him off, none knows what is going on. The French Indochina problem is still in confusion."

40. Tominaga to Army Vice Chief of Staff, telegram 321, September 3, 1940.

41. Shirahama to Chief of First Division, Navy Division of Imperial Headquarters, secret telegram 99, September 2, 1940.
42. Army Vice Chief of Staff to Nishihara, telegram sent at 5:00 p.m. on September 3, 1940.
43. Tanemura Sakō, *Daihon'ei kimitsu nisshi* (Confidential Record of the Imperial Headquarters), p. 25.
44. Navy General Staff, "Futsuin mondai keii." Before the telegram signed by both vice chiefs was sent, the Army General Staff had already sent essentially the same instructions in the name of the army vice chief of staff (see n. 42).
45. AGS, *Confidential War Diary*.
46. *Ibid.*
47. Nakamura, *Futsuin shinchū*.
48. *Ibid.*
49. *Ibid.*
50. *Ibid.*
51. Satō, *Tōjō*, p. 129.
52. Nakamura, *Futsuin shinchū*.
53. According to the army penal code, violation of a border was subject to harsh punishment as a "crime of the arbitrary use of power." Morimoto should have been under the jurisdiction of the 22nd Army, but by Tōjō's order his courtmartial was transferred to the South China Army. After being warned by the French officer, Morimoto admitted to having crossed the border, but when the area was investigated later the border marks had disappeared. The court concluded that it was not clear whether Morimoto had crossed the border and he was acquitted. Satō, *Tōjō*, p. 133.
54. A version drafted by the Army General Staff on September 9 set the time the stationing was to begin at 0:00 hours on the 15th. The navy opposed this. Following interservice consultations, a document of the 12th entitled "Principles for Managing the French Indochina Problem" stated that the stationing would begin around the 20th, although the navy agreed to setting a time limit for acceptance of Japan's demands. The army insisted that the stationing was to be based upon the Matsuoka-Henry and Nishihara-Martin pacts, in the hope that the negotiations could be kept to the line of the Matsuoka-Henry Pact after Tominaga returned to Tokyo, although another army plan of the 12th stated that "the on-the-spot decision of September 4 has been set aside by the French Indochina negotiators." The final version, "On the Future Management of the French Indochina Problem," was approved by a conference of army and navy division and bureau chiefs on the 13th.
55. Following the decision of the Four Ministers Conference, Foreign Minister Matsuoka reported to the emperor at 11:00 a.m. The next day the chiefs of the Army and Navy General Staffs went to the imperial palace and asked the emperor to approve the decision and to issue an imperial order for the use of military force.
56. In addition to transmitting the details of the army instructions, Tominaga, as before, was empowered by instructions to command the troops on the spot in the name of the army chief of staff. However, the instructions were ambiguous, apparently having been drafted by Tominaga himself and then approved formally by higher officers. After Tominaga's departure Imperial Headquarters reported the decision of the Four Ministers Conference to the Nishihara unit, which was under its direct control, instructing Nishihara that he was "responsible for the on-the-spot negotiations as the representative of the army and the navy, based upon separate instructions." Responsibility for the on-the-spot negotiations should therefore have lain with Nishihara but, as we shall see, Tominaga interpreted his command over the troops on the spot to include Nishihara.

57. Nakamura, *Futsuin shinchū*.

58. For example, in an official document the word "yesterday" would not normally be used. The date of the Four Ministers Conference was also erroneous.

59. Nakamura, *Futsuin shinchū*. The remainder of the document is omitted here.

60. *Ibid.*

61. Satō, *Tōjō*.

62. In the end the stationing was carried out without an agreement between the army and navy, except that the army changed the date for the stationing by sea to the deadline plus two days.

63. Interview with Ōi Atsushi, February 11, 1961.

64. Tanemura, *Daihonei kimitsu nikki*, p. 28. These developments in the negotiations were reported to central headquarters in two telegrams sent from Hanoi by either Tominaga or Nishihara. Telegram 440 concerns the withdrawal of the Nishihara unit and the repatriation of Japanese residents. Telegram 441 stated that it would be impossible to have only the Nishimura corps (i.e. those forces dispatched to Indochina by sea) stationed in French Indochina, and if no reply had been received by the 18th troop stationing in limited areas would commence. This telegram came as a great shock (AGS, *Confidential War Diary*, entry for September 18, 1940), and Sawada immediately drafted an order countermanding it. Although telegram 441 does not make it clear, it is presumed that the 5th Division was to be among the forces stationed in Indochina and that some of the troops at Ch'innankuan were to be used to threaten the French authorities.

65. Tanemura, *Daihonei kimitsu nikki*, p. 28.

66. The navy high command reported this on September 16 to Captain Chūdō Kan'ei, who had succeeded Captain Yanagisawa as head of the naval inspection contingent, and on the 19th to Nishihara.

67. To Japan's proposal of September 17 the French on the 18th agreed to the utilization of five air bases, excluding Hanoi, but rejected the increase in numbers and any stationing in the Hanoi region. That night Nishihara met with Martin and demanded acceptance of the Japanese proposal, declaring that the stationing would begin on the 23rd (one day earlier than Tokyo had decided) and that if a satisfactory reply had not been received by noon on the 20th, his unit would withdraw to Haiphong. Martin thereupon conceded the right to use the air base at Hanoi and to station up to 6,000 soldiers around Hanoi. Nishihara presented a compromise plan proposing that 25,000 men might be stationed at first, the number to be decreased gradually to 5,000 to 6,000. This plan was opposed by Tominaga, and the French side refused to yield.

68. The full text of the Nishihara-Martin Pact of September 22, 1940, is given in Japanese in JFM, *Nihon gaikō nempyō narabi ni shuyō bunsho*, 2:454–56.

69. Army and Navy Vice Chiefs of Staff to Nishihara, telegram of September 20, 1940.

70. Nakamura, *Futsuin shinchū*. Nishihara ordered Ariga to report to Nakamura that "further negotiations with the authorities of French Indochina will be required to reach a final settlement and agreement on the passage through Indochina of the Nakamura corps." Ariga flew via Lang Son to Ch'innankuan, where the advance force was given this report. It was then transmitted through channels to Nakamura, who received it about 11:00 p.m., just as he was about to leave his headquarters at P'inghsiang for Ch'innankuan. Nakamura was at a loss how to react, but in the end 22nd Army Chief of Staff Wakamatsu, who was at P'inghsiang, took the report to headquarters at Ningming, and Nakamura went to Ch'innankuan as planned.

71. Interview with Sawada Shigeru, August 4, 1953.

72. Army General Staff telegram 79.

73. It is alleged that the South China Army command had calculated beforehand that if orders to halt the land stationing were to reach the front line forces in time, they would have to arrive at command headquarters by 4:00 p.m. Interview with Shirai Masatoki, former staff officer of the South China Army, November 26, 1962.

74. Ōi interview.

75. Nakamura, *Futsuin shinchū*.

76. *Ibid.*

77. Nishihara sent an urgent wire concerning the operation to the vice chiefs of the Army and Navy General Staffs and to the chiefs of staff of both armies involved in the fighting. He reported that he had sent Colonel Koike to Dong Dang to prevent expansion of the hostilities. His wire reached the Navy General Staff at 3:40 a.m., half an hour before an earlier wire that stated: "According to a report from Indochina, Japanese troops in front of Ch'innankuan crossed the border a little after 0:00 hours on the 23rd and a struggle is now taking place at Dong Dang. Please take necessary action." The Army General Staff apparently received word of the incident earlier than the navy.

78. See n. 75. These instructions were dropped from a plane in accordance with the request of the South China Army, but they were communicated to Nakamura in the name of Colonel Akiyama Toyoji, head of the 1st Air Squadron. Nakamura wrote that it "seemed very strange. These instructions were different from those the 22nd Army had issued after the crossing of the border." The fact that they came from Akiyama gave Nakamura a good pretext for disregarding the instructions.

79. In the course of the fighting that morning Colonel Koike, who had been dispatched to the front by Nishihara, actually moved in front of the Japanese troops in an effort to get them to cease firing. Since he did not have command authority, however, the excited Japanese troops paid no attention to him, and in the end he returned to Haiphong to report his failure to Nishihara. The 22nd Army had told Nakamura that "although Colonel Koike has been dispatched to the front line, this order cannot be countermanded by him."

80. See n. 75.

81. Nishimura asked Fujita for support in his planned surprise attack. Fujita, however, required a special order from the commander-in-chief of the 2nd China Fleet and therefore withheld his agreement. In addition, at 4:15 p.m. on the 23rd Ugaki Matome, the chief of the Navy General Staff Operations Division, had notified the commander of the fleet that military operations could be launched only on orders from the central command.

82. Nishihara transmitted the French appeal to central headquarters and asked that "proper consideration" be given to it (Hanoi telegram 494). The reply from Captain Chūdō stated: "We have accepted this proposal. We request that you order the transport ships of the Nishimura corps to wait for a while." (Telegram 208, Secret, from the Operations Division, Navy Division of Imperial Headquarters.) Presumably Nishihara then accepted the French proposal, speaking as the head of the inspection unit. The South China Army later accused him of taking what they termed unauthorized action.

83. Secret telegram 544 issued by the 2nd China Fleet at 6:10 p.m. Telegram 549 issued at 10:30 p.m. stated: "The hostilities in which the Nakamura corps is engaged have been limited to the immediate area. The Nishimura corps is to be strongly urged to postpone its landing." This telegram indicated that the order "represents agreement reached between the *Nami* Group [South China Army] and the 2nd China Fleet," although whether such agreement had actually been reached is not clear. According to Satō Kenryō, Nemoto did not consult his subordinates before conferring with staff officer Ōi and giving his approval.

84. Fujita to Takasu, secret telegram 557, sent at 9:10 p.m. on September 23, 1940.

85. 2nd China Fleet secret telegram 551, sent at 12:35 a.m. on September 24, 1940.

86. Andō to Takasu, South China Army telegram 102, September 24, 1940.

87. Chief of Staff of 2nd China Fleet to Chief of Operations Division, Navy General Staff, secret telegram 555, September 24, 1940; secret telegram 558; and secret telegram 559.

88. Chief of Operations Division, Navy General Staff, to Chief of Staff of 2nd China Fleet, telegram sent at 7:00 a.m. on September 24, 1940; telegram sent at 3:15 p.m.

89. Fujita transmitted the misinterpreted cable to Nishimura and returned to his flagship, the *Sendai*, a light cruiser. When he noticed his mistake, he went to Nishimura's ship, the *Shinshū-maru*, and apologized.

90. Chief of Staff of 2nd China Fleet to Chief of Operations Division, Navy General Staff, secret telegram 569, sent at 11:40 a.m., September 24, 1940.

91. Fujita to Chief of Operations Division and to Commander-in-Chief of 2nd China Fleet, secret telegram 584, sent at 4:00 p.m. on September 25, 1940; secret telegram 595 from 2nd China Fleet, sent at 7:00 p.m. on September 25, 1940.

92. Secret telegram 601 from 2nd China Fleet, September 25, 1940.

93. Nishihara telegram 512, sent from Hanoi on the afternoon of September 25, 1940. Nishihara is said to have addressed his appeal to Kanda because he feared that Vice Chief Sawada would not be able to control the conflict between the Operations and Intelligence divisions, and he hoped that Kanda, who was senior in rank to the chiefs of those divisions, would exercise his influence within the Army General Staff to halt the South China Army's plans.

94. Shirahama to Operations Division, Navy Division of Imperial Headquarters, telegram sent at 7:30 p.m. on September 25, 1940.

95. Satō, *Tōjō*.

96. Ōi interview.

97. Imperial Headquarters Navy Order 238, issued at 12:20 p.m. on September 26, 1940: "Military operations in accordance with Section 2 of Imperial Headquarters Navy Order 232 will be suspended until a further order is issued. Halt operations against French Indochina and wait at the position fixed by order of the commander-in-chief of the 2nd China Fleet."

98. Sawada interview.

99. Imperial Headquarters Army Order 461, issued on September 27, 1940: "In executing the troop stationing in northern French Indochina, the commander of the South China Army is not to engage in aerial bombing except on receipt of a special order."

100. The destroyer *Nenohi* with the Nishihara party on board entered Haik'ou harbor on the evening of the 26th, to a warm welcome from Commander-in-Chief Takasu and his officers. The proposal for the telegram was made by Colonel Koike at the dinner table, following drinks, and Nishihara immediately accepted it. Chief of Staff Hara Chūichi, who was asked to send the wire, was concerned about its harsh tone. Ōi interview, February 11, 1961.

101. AGS, *Confidential War Diary*, entry for September 29, 1940.

102. In accordance with the Army Division order of October 1 the Nanning region was to be abandoned, and on the 12th the Army Division ordered an advance to Shanghai via French Indochina. By the 15th detailed agreement had been reached between Sumita and the government of French Indochina concerning the passage of the 5th Division.

103. A conversation between Tōjō and Satō, quoted in Satō, *Tōjō*, p. 139.

104. Tanemura Sakō, "Daihon'ei konran su" (Imperial Headquarters in Confusion), in *Bessatsu Chisei 5: Himerareta Shōwa shi*, December 1956, pp. 301–11.

105. A War Guidance Section had been established in June 1936 as part of the Operations Division but was abolished in October 1937, after it came into conflict with the Operations Section, and was replaced by a War Guidance Office under the Operations Section. This too was abolished in August 1940, when the problem of troop stationing arose.

106. On October 7 a joint army-navy conference to investigate the problems that had arisen was held at the Suikōsha under the leadership of the two vice chiefs of staff with Colonel Satō and Commander Ōi among the participants. The army's proposal of a unified command was rejected by the navy. According to Satō, he had attempted to appeal directly to the emperor through Vice Chief Sawada, but although Sawada and Tōjō had at first supported the idea, they changed their minds and the proposal was dropped.

4. The Drive into Southern Indochina (Nagaoka Shinjirō)

1. FR, 1940, 4:74–75.
2. Ibid.
3. FR, 1940, 4:79, 83–84.
4. FR, 1940, 4:98–99, 104.
5. Jean Decoux, A la barre de l'Indochine, pp. 132–33.
6. FR, 1940, 4:107–8.
7. Paul Baudouin, The Private Diaries of Paul Baudouin, pp. 237–38.
8. JFM, "Shina jihen: Futsuryō Indoshina shinchū mondai" (The China Incident: Problems Concerning the Stationing of Troops in French Indochina), September 4, 1940, in JFM Archives.
9. Decoux, p. 130.
10. FR, 1940, 4:113–15, 117.
11. FR, 1940, 4:118.
12. FR, 1940, 4:122–23, 126.
13. FR, 1940, 4:127–28, 140.
14. FR, 1940, 4:135.
15. FR, 1940, 4:164–67.
16. FR, 1940, 4:130–31, 143–47, 152–53.
17. Baudouin, p. 254; FR, 1940, 4:170.
18. JDA Archives.
19. JFM, "Taikoku-Futsuryō Indoshina kan kokkyō funsō ikken: Tōkyō chōtei kaigi kankei bessatsu chōsho" (Documents Relating to the Border Dispute between Thailand and French Indochina: Notes on Talks Concerning Mediation in Tokyo), in JFM Archives (hereafter cited as JFM, Documents on Border Mediation).
20. FR, 1940, 4:162, 176–77, 187–88.
21. FR, 1940, 4:177–78.
22. FR, 1940, 4:178–79.
23. FR, 1940, 4:191, 204.
24. FR, 1940, 4:125, 138.
25. Cordell Hull, The Memoirs of Cordell Hull, 1:907.
26. Egbert Haas, Frans Indo-china en de Japanse expantiepolitiek, 1939–1945, p. 105.
27. FR, 1940, 4:172–73.
28. JDA Archives.
29. JFM, "Taikoku-Futsuryō Indoshina kokkyō funsō ikken: Nichi-Tai kan Nichi-Futsu

kan hoshō oyobi seiji-teki ryōkai ni kansuru giteisho teiketsu kankei wo fukumu" (Documents Relating to the Border Dispute between Thailand and French Indochina, including protocols on the guarantee and the political understanding between Japan and Thailand, and Japan and France), in JFM Archives (hereafter cited as JFM, Documents on Border Protocols).

30. JDA Archives.

31. JFM, "Nihon-Taikoku kan yūkō kankei no sonzoku oyobi sōgo ryōdo sonchō ni kansuru jōyaku kankei ikken" (Documents Relating to the Treaty of Frendship and Respect for Territorial Integrity between Japan and Thailand), in JFM Archives.

32. JFM, Documents on Border Protocols.

33. JFM, Documents on Border Mediation.

34. Ibid.

35. DGFP, 11:831–32.

36. FR, 1940, 4:235–36, 239–40.

37. FR, 1940, 4:238.

38. FR, 1940, 4:241–42, 239.

39. FR, 1940, 4:246; Decoux, p. 142; FR, 1941, 5:3.

40. For reports on Japanese war matériel supplied to Thailand, see FR, 1940, 4:247–50, and FR, 1941, 5:1–2. And see JDA Archives.

41. JFM, Documents on Border Protocols.

42. FR, 1941, 5:2–5.

43. FR, 1941, 5:31–32 and 31 n.

44. FR, 1941, 5:10–11.

45. FR, 1941, 5:7, 19.

46. FR, 1941, 5:11–12, 20–21.

47. FR, 1941, 5:20, 16–17.

48. FR, 1941, 5:18.

49. JFM, Documents on Border Mediation.

50. JFM, Documents on Border Protocols.

51. JFM Documents on Border Mediation; see also FR, 1941, 5:34–35.

52. JFM, Documents on Border Protocols.

53. Hattori, 1:96.

54. JFM, Documents on Border Mediation.

55. Ibid.

56. FR, 1941, 5:28–31.

57. FR, 1941, 5:32–34.

58. JFM, Documents on Border Protocols.

59. DGFP, 11:1,125.

60. See FR, 1941, 5:20–21, 38.

61. Kyokutō Kokusai Gunji Saiban Kōhan Kiroku (Records of the International Military Tribunal for the Far East) in Japan, Justice Ministry, War Crimes Materials Office (hereafter cited as IMTFE Records), Exhibit 629.

62. Aoki Tokuzō, Taiheiyō sensō zenshi (The Historical Background of the Pacific War), 2:775.

63. JFM, Documents on Border Mediation.

64. FR, 1941, 5:48, 57, and 70–71.

65. Konoe Papers, published in JFM, Nihon gaikō nempyō, 2:479–80.

66. IMTFE Records, Exhibit 1303.

67. Editor's Note: According to Grant (FR, 1941, 5:86–87), the terms of the Japanese

proposal were: 1) cession of Luang Prabang and Pakse on the right bank of the Mekong, Thailand's "official territorial claim"; 2) cession in Cambodia of all of the province of Battambang, two-thirds of Siem-reap, and one-third of Kampongthom, totaling some 70,000 square kilometers; 3) payment to France of baht 10 million by Thailand; 4) establishment of a boundary commission; 5) Japanese control and application of the treaty.

68. Editor's Note: The second Japanese plan made no reference to an indemnity payment by the Thais, although it still provided for the territorial cessions by France in Laos and Cambodia. See the report of the American consul at Hanoi on February 27 and Leahy's report of March 1 (FR, 1941, 5:94–95 and 99–101).

69. "Nichi-Ei gaikō kankei zassan" (Miscellaneous Materials Relating to Japanese-British Relations), in JFM Archives (hereafter cited as JFM, Materials on British Relations).

70. JDA Archives.

71. JDA Archives.

72. JFM, Materials on British Relations.

73. Hattori, 1:106–07.

74. Hattori, 1:139–40.

75. JFM, Nihon gaikō nempyō, 2:531.

76. Decoux, pp. 150–51.

77. JFM, "Dai Tōa sensō kankei ikken: Nichi-Futsuin kyōdō bōei oyobi kore ni motozuku teikoku guntai no Futsuin shinchū kankei" (Documents Relating to the Greater East Asia War: The Stationing of Imperial Forces in French Indochina on the Basis of the Japan-French Indochina Joint Defense Agreement), in JFM Archives (hereafter cited as JFM, Indochina Defense Agreement Documents).

78. FR, 1941, 5:212, 213–14.

79. FR, 1941, 5:218.

80. JFM, Indochina Defense Agreement Documents; see also FR, 1941, 5:220.

81. JFM, Indochina Defense Agreement Documents.

82. Langer and Gleason, The Undeclared War, p. 643. At the time Welles was acting secretary of state in Hull's absence for medical treatment. On July 18 Konoe had formed his third cabinet, with Admiral Toyoda Teijirō replacing Matsuoka as foreign minister.

83. Nomura Kichisaburō, Beikoku ni shishite: Nichi-Bei kōshō no kaiko (Ambassador to the United States: Reminiscences of the Japanese-American Negotiations), pp. 74–75; for Welles's report of the interview, see FR: Japan, 2:522–26.

84. FR, Japan, 2:315–17.

85. JFM, Nihon gaikō nempyō, 2:538–39.

5. The Navy's Role in the Southern Strategy (Tsunoda Jun)

1. Interview with Andō Yoshirō, November 11, 1961.

2. JDA Archives—unless otherwise indicated, the source for all material in this chapter (including undocumented quotations).

3. Konoe Papers.

4. Tōkyō Asahi shimbun, evening edition, May 27, 1940.

5. Interview with Shiba Katsuo, April 8, 1961.

6. Interview with Odagiri Masanori, January 24, 1962.

7. Interview with Miyo Kazunari, December 10, 1960; "Sempan kankei shiryō" (Materials Relating to War Crimes), in JJM, War Crimes Materials.

8. The "Outline" has been partially translated in Vol. 3 of this series, *Deterrent Diplomacy*, pp. 208–9; the full text is published in *TSM: Bekkan*, pp. 322–24.

9. Published in *TSM: Bekkan*, pp. 317–18.

10. Joseph C. Grew, *Turbulent Era*, 2;1225.

11. Both explanations are published in *TSM: Bekkan*, pp. 323–25.

12. This discussion is based upon interviews with Miyo, December 10; Kawai Iwao, May 13, 1961; Takada Toshitane, December 5, 1961; and Rear Admiral Takagi Sōkichi, April 4, 1962.

13. JFM, Netherlands Commercial Treaty Documents, 1940–41.

14. Published in *Gendai shi shiryō 10: Nitchū sensō 3* (Source Materials on Contemporary History, 10: Sino-Japanese War, 3).

15. JJM, War Crimes Materials.

16. Kido Diary, entry for August 10, 1940, 2:814.

17. In the records of the Navy General Staff, held by the Shiryō Chōsakai (Documentary Research Society) (hereafter cited as NGS Archives), published in *TSM: Bekkan*, pp. 3–4.

18. Nomura Kichisaburō, *Beikoku ni shishite: Nichi-Bei kōshō no kaiko* (Ambassador to the United States: Reminiscences of the Japanese-American Negotiations), p. 12.

19. When he reported the cabinet's decision to the emperor on December 17, Prime Minister Konoe explained that amendment of the materials mobilization program was necessitated by the expansion of the European war, by Japan's worsening economic relations with the United States and Britain as a result of the Tripartite Pact, which had made it increasingly difficult to secure vital commodities, and by the need to develop armaments, particularly naval armaments, in preparation for a possible war in the south.

The navy, he reported, had demanded 370,000 tons of steel, and proportionate increases in other materials, in preparation for the fleet mobilization. By reducing non-naval allocations, and notably by the army's voluntary reduction of its requests by 200,000 tons, it had with difficulty been possible to provide 283,000 tons of steel for the navy. Its other requests had been largely fufilled. "For the present," Konoe concluded, "no difficulties are anticipated in connection with the preparations for fleet mobilization." Konoe Papers.

20. Interviews with Ōi Atsushi, February 10, 1961; Shiba Katsuo, March 25, 1961; Kawai Iwao, May 13, 1961; and Inoue Shigeyoshi, November 8, 1961.

21. Papers of Takagi Sōkichi.

22. Fukudome Shigeru, *Kaigun no hansei* (A Self-Examination by the Navy), p. 61.

23. Harada Kumao, *Saionji kō to seikyoku* (Prince Saionji and the Political Situation), 8:367.

24. Ogata Taketora, *Ichi gunjin no shōgai: kaisō no Yonai Mitsumasa* (The Life of an Admiral: Reminiscences of Yonai Mitsumasa), p. 43.

25. Inoue interview.

26. *Ibid.*; Shiba interview, March 25; and interview with Yokoi Tadao, July 8, 1961.

27. Konoe Papers.

28. *Ibid.* (italics in original).

29. *Ibid.*

30. Takagi Sōkichi interview.

31. Interview with Onoda Sutejirō, October 14, 1961.

32. Kyokutō Kokusai Gunji Saiban Kōhan Kiroku (Records of the International Military Tribunal for the Far East), Exhibit 528, in JJM, War Crimes Materials, IMTFE Records.

33. Shiba interview, March 25.

34. *Ibid.;* see also *TSM: Bekkan* pp. 325–29.
35. Shiba interview, March 25.
36. Takada Toshitane interview.
37. Shiba interview, March 25; Takagi Sōkichi interview.
38. Shiba interview, March 25.
39. Saitō Yoshie, "Nichi-Doku-I dōmei jōyaku teiketsu yōroku" (Summary Record of the Conclusion of the Tripartite Pact), in JFM Archives.
40. Konoe Papers.
41. Shiba interview, March 25; JJM, War Crimes Materials; JDA Archives.
42. Inoue and Shiba (March 25) interviews.
43. Shiba interview, March 25.
44. Yamamoto Isoroku to Koga Mineichi, letter of January 23, 1941, in NGS Archives.
45. Inoue interview.
46. Shiba interview, March 25.
47. Interview with Oi Atsushi, November 6, 1961.
48. JJM, War Crimes Materials.
49. Shiba interview, April 8; for the exchange of letters accompanying the Tripartite.
50. Published in *TSM: Bekkan,* p. 339. Pact, see Vol. 3, Appendix 7.
51. *TSM: Bekkan,* p. 341.
52. JJM, War Crimes Materials.
53. Shiba interview, April 8.
54. JJM, War Crimes Materials.
55. Shiba interview, April 8.
56. Ronald Wheatley, *Operation Sea Lion,* pp. 32–36, 49, 54–55, 63–64.
57. Wheatley, p. 10.
58. See Erich Raeder, "The Campaign for a Naval Air Arm," pp. 83–92, and "Operation Sea Lion," pp. 177–89, in *Struggle for the Sea;* also Karl Klee, "The Battle of Britain."
59. Friedrich Ruge, *Sea Warfare, 1939–1945,* p. 85.
60. J. R. M. Butler, *Grand Strategy,* 2:288, 293; Basil Collier, *The Defence of the United Kingdom,* p. 229.
61. S. W. Roskill, *The War at Sea, 1939–1945,* 1:257.
62. Ogata, pp. 70, 60–61.
63. *Ibid.,* p. 60.
64. Yamamoto to Koga.
65. Fukudome, p. 62.
66. Harada, 8:365.
67. Yamamoto Isoroku to Shimada Shigetarō, letter of December 10, 1940, in NGS Archives.
68. IMTFE Records, Exhibit 552.
69. Fukai Eigo, *Sūmitsuin jūyō giji oboegaki* (Notes on Important Sessions of the Privy Council), pp. 74–75 and 98.
70. Yamamoto to Koga (italics added).
71. Tomioka Sadatoshi, *Taiheiyō sensō Nihon kaigun senshi* (The Japanese Navy in the Pacific War), 1:96.
72. Yamamoto to Koga.
73. Konoe Papers.
74. Konoe Papers.
75. As former head of the Kure Naval Yard, Toyoda had a personal interest in the ma-

terials mobilization program. In April 1941 Konoe appointed him minister of commerce and industry.

76. Tamamoto to Shimada.

77. *FR, 1940*, 4:208–09.

78. See Grew to Secretary of State, November 25, 1940, *FR, 1940*, 4:444–46.

79. Takada interview; interview with Miyo Kazunari, January 28, 1961.

80. Yamamoto to Shimada.

81. Interview with Ōshima Hiroshi, March 10, 1962.

82. *Tōkyō Asahi shimbun*, January 27, 1941.

83. *Kido Diary*, entry for February 1, 1941, 2:853–54.

84. NGS Archives (italics added).

85. See Berle to Grew, March 15, 1941, in *FR, 1941*, 4:79–80.

86. Yokoi interview.

87. Konoe Papers.

88. *Ibid.*

89. Shiba (April 8) and Miyo (January 28) interviews.

90. IMTFE Records, Exhibit 767.

91. JFM, *Nihon gaikō nempyō narabi ni shuyō bunsho* (Chronology and Major Documents of Japanese Foreign Relations), 2:489–90; Churchill's letter is printed in English with Japanese translation.

Glossary

Abe Katsuo 阿部勝雄
Abe Nobuyuki 阿部信行
Abo Kiyokazu 安保清種
Akiyama Toyoji 秋山豊次
Amano Masakazu 天野正一
Andō Rikichi 安藤利吉
Andō Yoshirō 安東義良
Araki Sadao 荒木貞夫
Arao Okikatsu 荒尾興功
Ariga Jingorō 有賀甚五郎
Arisue Yadoru 有末次
Arita Hachirō 有田八郎
Asada Shunsuke 浅田俊介
Banzai Ichirō 坂西一良
Chang Ch'ün 張群
Chiang Kai-shek (Chieh-shih)
　蔣介石(中正)
Ch'ien Yung-ming 銭永銘
Chō Isamu 長勇
Chūdō Kan'ei 中堂観恵
Doi Akio 土居明夫
Enomoto Shigeharu 榎本重治
Fujita Ruitarō 藤田類太郎
Fujiwara Takeshi 藤原武
Fukuoka Takeshi 福岡武
Fushimi-no-miya Hiroyasu (Prince)
　伏見宮博恭
Futami Yasusato 二見甚郷
Gondō Seii 権藤正威
Hara Chūichi 原忠一
Hara Yoshimichi 原嘉道
Harada Kumao 原田熊雄
Hashimoto Gun 橋本群
Hashimoto Kingorō 橋本欣五郎
Hashimoto Shōzō 橋本象造
Hasunuma Shigeru 蓮沼蕃
Hata Shunroku 畑俊六
Hattori Takushirō 服部卓四郎
Hayashi Raisaburō 林頼三郎
Hiranuma Kiichirō 平沼騏一郎
Ho Ying-ch'in 何応欽
Horinouchi Kensuke 堀内謙介
Horiuchi Shigetada 堀内茂忠
Iida Shōjirō 飯田祥二郎
Inoue Shigeyoshi (Shigemi) 井上成美

Inukai Tsuyoshi (Ki) 犬養毅
Ishii Akiho 石井秋穂
Ishii Itarō 石射猪太郎
Ishii Yasushi (Kō) 石井康
Ishikawa Shingo 石川信吾
Ishizawa Yutaka 石沢豊
Isomura Takesuke 磯村武亮
Itagaki Seishirō 板垣征四郎
Iwakuro Hideo 岩畔豪雄
Kakitsubo Masayoshi 柿坪正義
Kami Shigenori 神重徳
Kanda Masatane 神田正種
Kan'in-no-miya Kotohito (Prince)
　閑院宮載仁
Karakawa Yasuo 唐川安夫
Katagiri Eikichi 片桐英吉
Katō Sotomatsu 加藤外松
Katō Tomosaburō 加藤友三郎
Kawai Iwao 川井巌
Kawamura Saburō 河村参郎
Kido Kōichi 木戸幸一
Kita Reikichi 北昤吉
Kiyose Ichirō 清瀬一郎
Kobayashi Ichizō 小林一三
Koike Ryōji 小池龍二
Koiso Kuniaki 小磯国昭
Kondō Nobutake 近藤信竹
Konoe Fumimaro 近衛文麿
Kōtani Etsuo 甲谷悦雄
Kubota Kan'ichirō 久保田貫一郎
Kubota Seitarō 窪田静太郎
Kuno Seiichi 久納誠一
Kurusu Saburō 来栖三郎
Kusaka Ryūnosuke 草鹿龍之介
Kusumoto Sanetaka 楠本実隆
Matsuda Chiaki 松田千秋
Matsudaira Tsuneo 松平恒雄
Matsumae Misoo 松前未曽雄
Matsumiya Jun 松宮順
Matsuoka Yōsuke 松岡洋右
Miki Bukichi 三木武吉
Miki Kichinosuke 三木吉之助
Minami Hiroshi 南弘
Minoda Fujio 蓑田不二夫
Mishuku Yoshimi 御宿好

Miwa Yoshitake 三和義勇
Miyama Yōzō 美山要蔵
Miyo Kazunari 三代一就
　(Tatsukichi 辰吉)
Morimoto Takuji 森本宅二
Motoki Jun'ichi 根木純一
Mukai Tadaharu 向井忠晴
Mushakōji Kintomo 武者小路公共
Mutō Akira 武藤章
Nagai Yatsuji 永井八津次
Nagano Osami 永野修身
Nakahara Yoshimasa 中原義正
Nakai Masutarō 中井増太郎
Nakamura Aketo 中村明人
Nakayama Motoo 中山源夫
Nakazawa Tasuku 中沢佑
Narita Katsushirō 成田勝四郎
Nemoto Hiroshi 根本博
Ninomiya Yoshikiyo 二宮義清
Nishi Haruhiko 西春彦
Nishihara Issaku 西原一策
Nishimura Takuma 西村琢磨
Nishiura Susumu 西浦進
Nomura Kichisaburō 野村吉三郎
Ōhashi Chūichi 大橋忠一
Ōi Atsushi 大井篤
Oikawa Koshirō 及川古志郎
Oka Yoshio 岡芳郎
Oka Takazumi 岡敬純
Okada Jūichi 岡田重一
Okada Kikusaburō 岡田菊三郎
Okamoto Kiyotomi 岡本清福
Okamoto Shizuomi 岡本鎮臣
Ōmae Toshikazu 大前敏一
Ōno Takeji 大野竹二
Ōshima Hiroshi 大島浩
Ozaki Hotsumi 尾崎秀実
Saitō Kiura 斎藤輝宇良
Sakai Wataru 酒井弥
Sakamoto Mizuo 阪本瑞男
Sakawa Shūichi 酒匂秀一
Satō Kenryō 佐藤賢了
Satō Naotake 佐藤尚武
Sawada Renzō 沢田廉三

Sawada Shigeru 沢田茂
Shao Li-tzu 邵力子
Shiba Katsuo 紫勝男
Shibafu Hideo 芝生英夫
Shidehara Kijūrō 幣原喜重郎
Shigematsu Nobuo 重松宣雄
Shigemitsu Mamoru 重光葵
Shirahama Eiichi 白浜栄一
Shiratori Toshio 白鳥敏夫
Suetsugu Nobumasa 末次信正
Sugiura Kajū 杉浦嘉十
Sugiyama Gen (Hajime) 杉山元
Sumita Raishirō 澄田睞四郎
Sumiyama Tokutarō 住山徳太郎
Sun Fo 孫科
Sung Tsu-liang 宋子良
Suzuki Rokurō 鈴木碌郎
Suzuki Sōsaku 鈴木宗作
Takada Toshitane 高田利種
Takagi Sōkichi 高木惣吉
Takasu Shirō 高須四郎
Takatsuki Tamotsu 高月保
Takayama Hikoichi 高山彦一
Tamura Hiroshi 田村浩
Tanaka Shin'ichi 田中新一
Tanaka Takeo 田中武夫
Tani Masayuki 谷正之
Tanomogi Keikichi 頼舟木桂吉
Tatekawa Yoshitsugu 建川美次
Tōgō Shigenori 東郷茂徳
Tōjō Hideki 東条英機
Tokuo Toshihiko 徳尾佟芳
Tokutomi Soho 徳富蘇峰
Tominaga Kyōji 富永恭次
Tomioka Sadatoshi 富岡定俊
Torigoshi Shin'ichi 鳥越新一
Tōyama Mitsuru 頭山満
Toyoda Soemu 豊田副武
Toyoda Teijirō 豊田貞次郎
Tsuchihashi Yūichi (Yūitsu) 土橋勇逸
Tsukada Osamu 塚田攻
Ugaki Matome 宇垣纒
Umezu Yoshijirō 梅津美治郎
Ushiroku Jun 後宮淳

Usui Shigeki 臼井茂樹
Wakamatsu Tadakazu (Tadaichi)
若松只一
Wakasugi Kaname 若杉要
Wang Ching-wei 汪精衛
Wang Ch'ung-hui 王寵恵
Watanabe Kumeichi 渡辺粂一
Watanabe Saburō 渡辺三郎
Yabe Toshio 矢部敏雄
Yamada Yoshiji 山田義次
Yamaguchi Bunjirō 山口文次郎

Yamaji Akira 山路章
Yamamoto Isoroku 山本五十六
Yamashita Tomoyuki 山下奉文
Yanagisawa Kuranosuke 柳沢蔵之助
Yano Seiki 矢野征記
Yasumura Isao 安村紗
Yokoyama Hikosane 横山彦真
Yonai Mitsumasa 米内光政
Yosano Shigeru 与謝野秀
Yoshida Zengo 吉田善吾
Yoshizawa Kenkichi 芳沢謙吉

Bibliography

I. Archives

Note: Major archival documents cited in the notes are listed separately in Section III below.

Japan, Foreign Ministry Archives. Cited as JFM Archives.

The following collections of documents are noteworthy:

"Dai Tōa sensō kankei ikken: Nichi-Futsuin kyōdō bōei oyobi kore ni motozuku teikoku guntai no Futsuin shinchū kankei" 大東亜戦争関係一件 日仏印共同防衛及ビコレニ基ゾク帝国軍隊、仏印進駐関係 (Documents Relating to the Greater East Asia War: The Stationing of Imperial Forces in French Indochina on the Basis of the Japan-French Indochina Joint Defense Agreement). Cited as JFM, Indochina Defense Agreement Documents.

"Doku-So kaisen kankei ikken" 独ソ開戦関係一件 (Documents Relating to the Outbreak of War between Germany and the USSR).

"Nichi-Doku-I dōmei jōyaku kankei ikken" 日独伊同盟条約関係一件 (Documents Relating to the Treaty of Alliance between Japan, Germany, and Italy).

"Nichi-Ei gaikō kankei zassan" 日英外交関係雑纂 (Miscellaneous Materials Relating to Japanese-British Relations). Cited as JFM, Materials on British Relations.

"Nichi-Ran tsūshō jōyaku kankei ikken: Shōwa jū-nen ikō jūgo-nen made no Nichi-Ran kan kōshō kankei" 日蘭通商条約関係一件 昭和十年以降十五年マデノ日蘭間交渉関係 (Documents Relating to the Commercial Treaty between Japan and the Netherlands: Negotiations, 1935–40). Cited as JFM, Netherlands Commercial Treaty Documents, 1935–40.

"Nichi-Ran tsūshō jōyaku kankei ikken: Shōwa jūgo-nen jūroku-nen, Nichi-Ran kaishō kankei" 日蘭通商条約関係一件 昭和十五年十六年日蘭会商関係 (Documents Relating to the Commercial Treaty between Japan and the Netherlands: Negotiations, 1940–41). Cited as JFM, Netherlands Commercial Treaty Documents, 1940–41.

"Nichi-Ran tsūshō jōyaku kankei ikken: Shōwa jūgo-nen jūroku-nen Nichi-Ran kaishō kankei: sekiyu kankei" 日蘭通商条約関係一件 昭和十五年十六年日蘭会商関係, 石油関係 (Documents Relating to the Commercial Treaty between Japan and the Netherlands: Negotiations, 1940–41— Petroleum). Cited as JFM, Documents on Petroleum Negotiations.

"Nihon Taikoku kan yūkō kankei no sonzoku oyobi sōgo ryōdo sonchō ni kansuru jōyaku kankei ikken" 日本タイ国間友好関係、存続及ビ相互領土尊重ニ関スル条約関係一件 (Documents Relating to the Treaty of Friendship and Respect for Territorial Integrity between Japan and Thailand).

"Nisso chūritsu jōyaku kankei ikken" 日ソ中立条約関係一件 (Documents Relating to the Japanese-Soviet Neutrality Pact). Cited as JFM, Neutrality Pact Documents.

"Taikoku-Futsuryō Indoshina kan kokkyō funsō ikken: Tōkyō chōtei kaigi kankei bessatsu chōsho" 泰国仏領印度支那間国境紛争一件　東京調停会議関係別冊調書 (Documents Relating to the Border Dispute between Thailand and French Indochina: Notes on Talks Concerning Mediation in Tokyo). Cited as JFM, Documents on Border Mediation.

"Taikoku-Futsuryō Indoshina kokkyō funsō ikken: Nichi-Tai kan Nichi-Futsu kan hoshō oyobi seiji-teki ryōkai ni kansuru giteisho teiketsu kankei wo fukumu" 泰国仏領印度支那国境紛争一件（日泰間日仏間保障及ビ政治的了解二関スル議定書締結関係ヲ含ム）(Documents Relating to the Border Dispute between Thailand and French Indochina, including protocols on the guarantee and the political understanding between Japan and Thailand, and Japan and France). Cited as JFM, Documents on Border Protocols.

"Teikoku nampō seisaku kankei ikken" 帝国南方政策関係一件 (Documents Relating to the Southern Policy of the Empire). Cited as JFM, Documents on Southern Policy.

"Teikoku no taigai seisaku kankei ikken" 帝国ノ対外政策関係一件 (Documents Relating to Japanese Foreign Policy). Cited as JFM, Foreign Policy Documents.

Japan, Justice Ministry, War Crimes Materials Office.

Here are located the "Sempan kankei shiryō" 戦犯関係資料 (Materials Relating to War Crimes). Cited as JJM, War Crimes Materials.

These archives also contain the Kyokutō Kokusai Gunji Saiban Kōhan Kiroku 極東国際軍事裁判公判記録 (Records of the International Military Tribunal for the Far East). Cited as IMTFE Records.

Japan, National Defense Agency, Military History Office. Cited as JDA Archives.

Japan, Navy General Staff Archives, held by the Shiryō Chōsakai 史料調査会 (Documentary Research Society), Tokyo. Cited as NGS Archives.

Papers of Konoe Fumimaro, held in the Yōmei Bunko 陽明文庫, the private library of the Konoe family, Kyoto.

Papers of Takagi Sōkichi, held by the War History Division, National Defense College.

II. Interviews

Andō Yoshirō 安東義良, former chief of the First (Soviet) Section, Europe-Asia Bureau, Foreign Ministry, November 11, 1961.

Inoue Shigeyoshi 井上成美, former chief of the Naval Affairs Bureau, Navy Ministry, November 8, 1961.

Kawai Iwao 川井巌, former member of the Operations Section, Navy General Staff, May 13, 1961.

Miyo Kazunari 三代一就, former member of the Operations Section, Navy General Staff, December 10, 1960 and January 28, 1961.

Odagiri Masanori 小田切政徳, former member of the Navy General Staff,

January 24, 1962.

Ōi Atsushi 大井篤, former member of the Navy General Staff and staff officer of the 2nd China Fleet, February 10, 1961; February 11, 1961; and November 6, 1961.

Onoda Sutejirō 小野田捨二郎, former member of the First Division, Navy General Staff, October 14, 1961.

Ōshima Hiroshi 大島浩, former ambassador to Germany, March 10, 1962.

Sawada Shigeru 沢田茂, former vice chief, Army General Staff, August 4, 1953.

Shiba Katsuo 柴勝男, former member of the First Section, Naval Affairs Bureau, March 25, 1961 and April 8, 1961.

Shirai Masatoki 白井正辰, former staff officer of the South China Army, November 26, 1962.

Takada Toshitane 高田利種, former section chief, Naval Affairs Bureau, December 5, 1961.

Takagi Sōkichi 高木惣吉 (Rear Admiral), April 4, 1962.

Yokoi Tadao 横井忠雄, former member of the Navy General Staff, July 8, 1961.

III. Published Works and Major Unpublished Materials Cited

Airapetian, M. E. and G. A. Deborin. *Etapy vneshnei politiki SSSR* (The Stages in the Foreign Policy of the USSR). Moscow: Sotsekgiz, 1961.

Aoki Tokuzō 青木得三. *Taiheiyō sensō zenshi* 太平洋戦争前史 (The Historical Background of the Pacific War). 3 vols. Tokyo: Gakujutsu Bunken Fukyūkai, 1953.

Araki Takeyuki 荒木武行. *Shōwa gaikō henrinroku: Arita gaishō no maki* 昭和外交片鱗録　有田外相之巻 (Glimpses of Diplomacy in the Shōwa Era: Foreign Minister Arita). Tokyo: Shinshosetsu-sha, 1943.

Baudouin, Paul. *The Private Diaries (March 1940 to January 1941) of Paul Baudouin.* Trans. by Sir Charles Petrie; a Foreword by Malcolm Muggeridge. London: Eyre and Spottiswoode, 1948.

Beloff, Max. *The Foreign Policy of Soviet Russia, 1929–1941,* Vol. 2, *1936–1941.* London: Oxford University Press, 1949.

Butler, J. R. M. *Grand Strategy,* vol. 2, *September 1939-June 1941.* In *History of the Second World War,* United Kingdom Military Series, edited by J. R. M. Butler. London: H.M.S.O., 1957.

Ciano, Galeazzo. *The Ciano Diaries, 1939–1943.* Hugh Gibson, ed. Garden City, N.Y.: Doubleday, 1946.

Collier, Basil. *The Defence of the United Kingdom.* In *History of the Second World War,* United Kingdom Military Series, edited by J. R. M. Butler. London: H.M.S.O., 1957.

Decoux, Jean. *A la barre de l'Indochine: Histoire de mon gouvernement général (1940–1945).* Paris: Librairie Plon, 1949.

Degras, Jane, ed. *Soviet Documents on Foreign Policy,* vol. 3. London: Oxford University Press, 1953.

Dement'eva, I. N. et al. *Tovarishch Zorge* (Comrade Sorge). Moscow: "Sovetskaia Rossiia," 1965.

Eidus, Kh. T., ed. *Ocherki noveishei istorii Iaponii* (Essays on Contemporary Japanese History). Moscow: Izdatel'stvo Akademii Nauk SSSR, 1957.

—— *Ocherki novoi i noveishei istorii Iaponii* (Essays in the Modern and Contemporary History of Japan). Moscow: Izdatel'stvo Akademii Nauk SSSR, 1955.

Erickson, John. "Reflections on Securing the Soviet Far Eastern Frontiers: 1932–1945," *Interplay*, vol. 3, no. 2, August/September 1969.

Fukai Eigo 深井英五. *Sūmitsuin jūyō giji oboegaki* 枢密院重要議事覚書 (Notes on Important Sessions of the Privy Council). Tokyo: Iwanami Shoten, 1953.

Fukudome Shigeru 福留繁. *Kaigun no hansei* 海軍の反省 (A Self-Examination by the Navy). Tokyo: Nihon Shuppan Kyōdō Kabushiki Kaisha, 1951.

Gendai shi shiryō 10: Nitchū sensō 3 現代史資料　日中戦争 (Source Materials on Contemporary History, 10: Sino-Japanese War, 3). Tokyo: Misuzu Shobō, 1964.

Gol'dberg, D. I. *Vneshniaia politika Iaponii, Sentiabr' 1939–Dekabr' 1941gg* (Foreign Policy of Japan, 1939–1941). Moscow: Izdatel'stvo Vostochnoi Literaturyi, 1959.

Gordon, Joseph. "The Russo-Japanese Neutrality Pact of April, 1941." Masters thesis, Columbia University, 1955.

Grew, Joseph C. *Ten Years in Japan*. New York: Simon and Schuster, 1944.

—— *Turbulent Era: A Diplomatic Record of Forty Years, 1904–1945*. Edited by Walter Johnson, assisted by Nancy Harrison. 2 vols. London: Hammond, 1953.

Haas, Egbert. *Frans Indo-china en de Japanse expantiepolitiek, 1939–1945*. Leiden: Universitaire Pers Leiden, 1956.

Harada Kumao 原田熊雄. *Saionji kō to seikyoku* 西園寺公と政局 (Prince Saionji and the Political Situation). 8 vols. and supplementary volume of documents: *Bekkan* 別巻. Tokyo: Iwanami Shoten, 1950–52, 1956.

Hasegawa Shin'ichi 長谷川進一. "Matsuoka gaishō to-Ō nikki" 松岡外相渡欧日記 (Diary of Foreign Minister Matsuoka's European Trip). *Kōron*, May 1941.

Hashimoto Kingorō 橋本欣五郎. "Shintaisei to Nisso mondai" 新体制と日ソ問題 (The New Order and the Japanese-Soviet Problem). *Gekkan Roshia*, October 1940.

Hattori Takushirō 服部卓四郎. *Dai Tōa sensō zenshi* 大東亜戦争全史 (A History of the Greater East Asia War). 4 vols., 1953; 8 vols., 1956. Tokyo: Masu Shobō.

Hull, Cordell. *The Memoirs of Cordell Hull*. 2 vols. New York: Macmillan, 1948.

Ike, Nobutaka, trans. and ed. *Japan's Decision for War: Records of the 1941 Policy Conferences*. Stanford, Calif.: Stanford University Press, 1967.

Ishii Itarō 石射猪太郎. *Gaikōkan no isshō* 外交官の一生 (The Life of a Diplomat). Tokyo: Yomiuri Shimbunsha, 1950.

Itagaki Yoichi 板垣与一. "Taiheiyō sensō to sekiyu mondai" 太平洋戦争と石油問題 (The Pacific War and the Petroleum Problem). In Nihon Gaikō Gakkai 日本外交学会 (Association for the Study of Japanese Diplomacy), ed. *Taiheiyō sensō gen'in ron* 太平洋戦争原因論 (The Origins of the Pacific War). Tokyo: Shimbun Gekkansha, 1953.

Japan, Army General Staff, comp. *Sugiyama memo* 杉山メモ (Sugiyama Gen memorandum). 2 vols. Tokyo: Hara Shobō, 1967.

——. War Guidance Office 陸軍戦争指導班. "Daihon'ei kimitsu sensō nisshi" 大本営機密戦争日誌 (Confidential War Diary of the Imperial Headquarters), 1938–45. In JDA Archives. Cited as AGS, *Confidential War Diary*.

Japan, Foreign Ministry. "Gaikō shiryō: Nisso gaikō kōshō kiroku no bu" 外交資料　日「ソ」外交交渉記録ノ部 (Diplomatic Documents: The Record of Japanese-Soviet Negotiations), 1946. Cited as JFM, "Nisso gaikō kōshō."

—— "Kaidan yōshi" 会談要旨 (Summary of Conversations), compiled by Matsuoka Yōsuke. In JFM, Tripartite Pact Study. Published in *TSM: Bekkan*, pp. 334–36. Cited as JFM, Matsuoka-Stahmer Conversations.

—— Europe-Asia Bureau. "Matsuoka gaishō to Otto taishi to no kaidan yōryō" 松岡外相とオット大使との会談要領 (Summary of the Matsuoka-Ott Conversation), August 2, 1940. Presented to the IMTFE as Exhibit 544, in JFM Archives.

—— "Nichi-Doku-I sangoku jōyaku" 日独伊三国条約 (The Tripartite Pact). In JFM Archives. Cited as JFM, Tripartite Pact Study.

—— *Nihon gaikō nempyō narabi ni shuyō bunsho* 日本外交年表並主要文書 (Chronology and Major Documents of Japanese Foreign Relations). 2 vols. Tokyo: Hara Shobō, 1965; first pub. in 1955.

——, ed. *Nisso kōshō shi* 日ソ交渉史 (A History of Japanese-Soviet Relations). Tokyo: Gannandō, 1969; originally issued in 1942.

—— "Shina jihen: Futsuryō Indoshina shinchū mondai" 支那事変　仏領印度支那進駐問題 (The China Incident: Problems Concerning the Stationing of Troops in French Indochina), September 4, 1940. In JFM Archives.

—— "Shina jihen kakkoku no taido: Nichi-Bei kankei dakai kōsaku" 支那事変各国ノ態度　日米関係打開工作 (Attitudes of the Powers toward the China Incident: Efforts to Find a Way Out in Relations between Japan and the United States). In JFM Archives.

Japan, Navy General Staff. "Futsuin mondai keii" 仏印問題経緯 (Details of the French Indochina Problem). In JDA Archives.

Johnson, Chalmers. *An Instance of Treason: Ozaki Hotsumi and the Sorge Spy Ring*. Stanford, Calif.: Stanford University Press, 1964.

Jones, F. C. *Japan's New Order in East Asia: Its Rise and Fall, 1937–1945*. London: Oxford University Press, 1954.

Kido Kōichi 木戸幸一. *Kido Kōichi nikki* 木戸幸一日記 (Diary of Kido Kōichi). 2 vols. Tokyo: Tōkyō Daigaku Shuppankai, 1966. Cited as *Kido Diary*.

Kita Reikichi 北昑吉. "Nisso kankei no genjitsu-teki mokuteki" 日ソ関係の現実的目的 (Realistic Objectives in Japanese-Soviet Relations). *Gekkan Roshia*, vol. 6, no. 1, January 1940.

Klee, Karl. "The Battle of Britain." In Hans-Adolf Jacobsen and Jürgen Rohwer. *Decisive Battles of World War II: The German View*, pp. 73–94. Trans. by Edward Fitzgerald. London: André Deutsch, 1965.

Koike Ryōji 小池竜二. "Nishihara kikan kara mita Hokubu Futsuin shinchū no shinsō. Nikki" 西原機関から見た北部仏印進駐の真相. 日記 (The truth about the stationing of troops in Northern Indochina as seen by the Nishihara Agency. Diary). 1958. In JDA Archives.

Kolesnikov, M. S. *Takim byl Rikhard Zorge* (Such Was Richard Sorge). Moscow: Voennoe Izdatel'stvo Ministerstva Oborony SSSR, 1965.

Kōno Mitsu 河野密. "Dainanajūgo Gikai to Nisso mondai" 第七十五議会と日ソ問題 (The 75th Diet and the Japanese-Soviet Problem). *Gekkan Roshia*, vol. 6, no. 5, May 1940.

Konoe Fumimaro 近衛文麿. *Heiwa e no doryoku* 平和への努力 (My Struggle for Peace). Tokyo: Nihon Dempō Tsūshinsha, 1946.

—— *Ushinawareshi seiji* 失はれし政治 (Politics that Failed). Tokyo: Asahi Shimbunsha, 1946.

Korol'kov, I. M. *Chelovek dlia kotorogo ne bylo tain* (*Rikhard Zorge*) (A Man for Whom There Were No Secrets: Richard Sorge). Moscow: Izdatel'stvo Politicheskoi Literatury, 1965.

Kurihara Ken 栗原健. *Tennō: Shōwa shi oboegaki* 天皇　昭和史覚書 (The Emperor: A Note on the History of the Shōwa Period). Tokyo: Yūshindō, 1955.

Kurusu Saburō 来栖三郎. *Hōmatsu no sanjūgo-nen* 泡沫の三十五年 (Vain Endeavor). Tokyo: Bunka Shoin, 1948.

Kutakov, Leonid N. *Istoriia sovetsko-iaponskikh diplomaticheskikh otnoshenii* (History of Japanese-Soviet Diplomatic Relations). Moscow: Izdatel'stvo Instituta Mezhdunarodnykh Otnoshenii, 1962.

—— *Portsmutskii mirnyi dogovor* (*iz istorii otnoshenii Iaponii s Rossiei i SSSR, 1905-1945gg*) (The Portsmouth Peace Treaty: From the History of Japan's Relations with Russia and the USSR, 1905-1945). Moscow: Sotsekgiz, 1961.

Langer, William L. and S. Everett Gleason. *The Challenge to Isolation, 1937-1940.* New York: Harper, 1952.

—— *The Undeclared War, 1940-1941.* New York: Harper, 1953.

Lupke, Hubertus. *Japans Russlandpolitik von 1939 bis 1941.* Frankfurt: A. Metzner, 1962.

Maki, John M. *Conflict and Tension in the Far East: Key Documents, 1894-1960.* Seattle: University of Washington Press, 1961.

Matsuoka Yōsuke 松岡洋右. "Konoe shuki ni taisuru setsumei" 近衛手記に対する説明 (Explanation of the Konoe Memorandum). In JJM, War Crimes Materials.

—— "Shitsumu nisshi" 執務日誌 (Office Diary). In JFM Archives.

—— "To-Ō fukumei naisō" 渡欧復命内奏 (Report to the Throne on the Journey to Europe). In JFM, Neutrality Pact Documents.

Mook, Hubertus J. van. *The Netherlands Indies and Japan: Battle on Paper, 1940-41.* New York: Norton, 1944.

Nakamura Aketo 中村明人. *Futsuin shinchū no shinsō* 仏印進駐の真相 (The Truth Concerning the Stationing of Troops in French Indochina). Tokyo, Ground Self-defense Forces Staff Headquarters, 1954.

Nihon Gaikō Gakkai 日本外交学会 (Association for the Study of Japanese Diplomacy), ed. *Taiheiyō sensō gen'in ron* 太平洋戦争原因論 (The Origins of the Pacific War). Tokyo: Shimbun Gekkansha, 1953.

Nihon Kokusai Seiji Gakkai, Taiheiyō Sensō Gen'in Kenkyūbu 日本国際政治学会太平洋戦争原因研究部 (Japan Association on International Relations, Study Group on the Causes of the Pacific War), ed. *Taiheiyō sensō e no michi: Bekkan shiryō hen* 太平洋戦争への道 別巻資料編 (The Road to the Pacific War: Supplementary Volume of Documents). Tokyo: Asahi Shimbunsha, 1963. Cited as *TSM: Bekkan*.

Nishiura Susumu 西浦進. "Hokubu Futsuin shinchū no senshiteki kansatsu" 北部仏印進駐の戦史的観察 (Historical Survey of the Stationing of Troops in Northern Indochina), 1930. In JDA Archives.

Nomura Kichisaburō 野村吉三郎. *Beikoku ni shishite: Nichi-Bei kōshō no kaiko* 米国に使して日米交渉の回顧 (Ambassador to the United States: Reminiscences of the Japanese-American Negotiations). Tokyo: Iwanami Shoten, 1946.

Ogata Taketora 緒方竹虎. *Ichi gunjin no shōgai: kaisō no Yonai Mitsumasa* 一軍人の生涯 回想の米内光政 (The Life of an Admiral: Reminiscences of Yonai Mitsumasa). Tokyo: Bungei Shunjū Shinsha, 1955.

Ōhashi Chūichi 大橋忠一. *Taiheiyō sensō yuraiki* 太平洋戦争由来記 (Origins of the Pacific War). Tokyo: Kaname Shobō, 1952.

Ponomarev, B. N. et al., eds. *Istoriia vneshnei politiki SSSR* (History of the Foreign Policy of the USSR), vol. 1, *1917–1945*. Moscow: "Nauka," 1966.

Presseisen, Ernst L. *Germany and Japan: A Study in Totalitarian Diplomacy, 1933–1941*. The Hague: Martinus Nijhoff, 1958.

Raeder, Erich. *Struggle for the Sea*. Trans. by Edward Fitzgerald. London: William Kimber, 1959.

Ribbentrop, Joachim von. *The Ribbentrop Memoirs*. London: Weidenfeld and Nicholson, 1954.

Roskill, S. W. *The War at Sea, 1939–1945*, vol. 1, *The Defensive*. In *History of the Second World War*, United Kingdom Military Series, edited by J. R. M. Butler. London: H.M.S.O., 1954.

Ruge, Friedrich. *Sea Warfare, 1939–1945: A German Viewpoint*. Trans. by Commander M. G. Saunders, R. N. London: Cassell, 1957.

Saionji Kinkazu 西園寺公一. *Kizoku no taijō* 貴族の退場 (The Exit of the Aristocracy). Tokyo: Bungei Shunjū Shinsha, 1951.

Saitō Yoshie 斎藤良衛. *Azamukareta rekishi: Matsuoka to sangoku dōmei no rimen* 欺かれた歴史 松岡と三国同盟の裏面 (History Deceived: The Inside Story of Matsuoka and the Tripartite Pact). Tokyo: Yomiuri Shinbunsha, 1955.

―― "Nichi-Doku-I dōmei jōyaku teiketsu yōroku" 日独伊同盟条約締結要録 (Summary Record of the Conclusion of the Tripartite Pact). In JFM Archives.

Satō Kenryō 佐藤賢了. "Hokubu Futsuin shinchū no keii" 北部仏印進駐の経緯 (The Stationing of Troops in Northern French Indochina). Publication data unverified.

—— *Tōjō Hideki to Taiheiyō sensō* 東条英機と太平洋戦争 (Tōjō Hideki and the Pacific War). Tokyo: Bungei Shunjū Shinsha, 1960.

Shidehara Heiwa Zaidan 幣原平和財団 (Shidehara Peace Foundation), ed. *Shidehara Kijūrō* 幣原喜重郎. Tokyo: Shidehara Heiwa Zaidan, 1955.

Shiratori Toshio 白鳥敏夫. *Nichi-Doku-I sūjiku ron* 日独伊枢軸論 (On the Japanese-German-Italian Axis) (Nazi Series, vol. 15, 1940).

Shirer, William L. *The Rise and Fall of the Third Reich.* New York: Simon and Schuster, 1960.

Smetanin, Konstantin, "Diary," in IMTFE Records, Exhibit 792.

Tanemura Sakō 種村佐孝. *Daihon'ei kimitsu nisshi* 大本営機密日誌 (Confidential Record of the Imperial Headquarters). Tokyo: Daiyamondosha, 1952.

—— "Daihon'ei konran su" 大本営混乱す (Imperial Headquarters in Confusion). In *Bessatsu Chisei 5: Himerareta Shōwa shi* 別冊知性　秘められた昭和史 (Secret History of the Shōwa Era: *Chisei* Special Issue), December 1956.

Tōgō Shigenori 東郷茂徳. *Jidai no ichi-men* 時代の一面 (One View of an Era). Tokyo: Kaizōsha, 1952.

Tominaga Kyōji 富永恭次. Hokubu Futsuin shinchū sakusen no shinsō" 北部仏印進駐作戦の真相 (The Truth about the Stationing of Troops and Operations in Northern Indochina), 1956. In JDA Archives.

Tomioka Sadatoshi 富岡定俊, ed. *Taiheiyō sensō Nihon kaigun senshi* 太平洋戦争日本海軍戦史 (The Japanese Navy in the Pacific War. 14 vols. mimeo.). Tokyo: Maritime Self-defense Force, 1950s.

U.S. Department of State. *Documents on German Foreign Policy, 1918–1945, from the Archives of the German Foreign Ministry*, series D (1937–1945), vols. 8 (1954), 9 (1956), 10 (1957), 11 (1960), 12 (1962), 13 (1964). Washington D.C.: U.S. Government Printing Office. Cited as *DGFP*.

—— *Foreign Relations of the United States: Diplomatic Papers, 1940*, vol. 4, *The Far East.* Washington D.C.: U.S. Government Printing Office, 1955. Cited as *FR, 1940.*

—— *Foreign Relations of the United States: Diplomatic Papers, 1941, The Far East*, vols. 4–5. Washington D.C.: U.S. Government Printing Office, 1956. Cited as *FR, 1941.*

—— *Nazi-Soviet Relations, 1939–1941: Documents from the Archives of the German Foreign Office.* Raymond James Sontag and James Stuart Beddie, eds. Washington D.C.: U.S. Government Printing Office, 1948. Cited as *Nazi-Soviet Relations.*

—— *Papers Relating to the Foreign Relations of the United States: Japan, 1931–1941.* 2 vols. Washington D.C.: U.S. Government Printing Office, 1943. Cited as *FR: Japan.*

Wei, Henry. *China and Soviet Russia.* Princeton: Van Nostrand, 1956.

Weinberg, Gerhard L. *Germany and the Soviet Union, 1939–1941.* Leiden: E. J. Brill, 1954.

Welles, Sumner. *Seven Decisions That Shaped History.* New York: Harper, 1950.

Wheatley, Ronald. *Operation Sea Lion: German Plans for the Invasion of England,*

1939–1942. Oxford: Clarendon Press, 1958.

Yoshizawa Kenkichi 芳沢謙吉. "Itsuwari no gaikō shi: Nichi-Ran kōshō no shinsō" 偽りの外交史　日蘭交渉の真相 (False Diplomatic History: The True Story of the Japan-Netherlands Negotiations), *Chūō kōron*, December 1950.

Contributors

PETER A. BERTON is professor of international relations at the University of Southern California, and since 1970 editor of *Studies in Comparative Communism*. Born in 1922, he was educated in both China and Japan (Waseda University), and received his Ph.D. in 1956 from Columbia University (East Asian and Russian Institutes). A specialist in Soviet-Asian relations and Communist affairs, he is the author of among other works *The Secret Russo-Japanese Alliance of 1916* (1956) and *Nichi-Ro Ryōdo Mondai–The Russo-Japanese Boundary, 1850–1875* (1967), co-author of *Japanese Training and Research in the Russian Field* (1956) and "Japanische Innenpolitik seit 1945" in *Asien im 20. Jahrhundert* (1972), editor of *The Japanese Penetration of Korea, 1894–1910* (1959), and co-editor of *The Russian Impact on Japan: Literature and Social Thought* (forthcoming).

HATA IKUHIKO was born in 1932. With A.B. (1956) and Ph.D. degrees from Tokyo University, he served until 1976 as chief historian of the Ministry of Finance. Among his recent writings are *Nitchū sensōshi* (A history of the Japanese-Chinese war, 1931–1941, rev. 1972); *Gun fashizumu undōshi* (A History of the Japanese Military Fascist Movement, rev. 1972); *Taiheiyō kokusai kankei shi: Nichi-Bei oyobi Nichi-Ro kiki no keifu 1900–1935* (A History of the International Relations of the Pacific: Crises between Japan and the U.S. and Japan and Russia, 1900–1935), 1972; and *America no tai-Nichi senryō seisaku* (America's Occupation Policy toward Japan) (1976; being vol. 3 of *Shōwa zaisheishi: Shūsen kara kōwa made* [Financial History of the Shōwa Period: From the end of the War to the Treaty of Peace, 20 vols.], 1976–79, which Hata edited for the Ministry of Finance).

HOSOYA CHIHIRO is a professor of international relations, Faculty of Law, Hitotsubashi University in Tokyo. He is also president of the Japan Association of International Relations and chairman of the editorial com-

mittee of Nihon gaikō bunsho, the Foreign Ministry's official series of historical documents on Japanese foreign policy. Born in 1920 and educated at Tokyo (A.B., 1945) and Kyoto (Ph.D., 1961) universities, he contributed to *Pearl Harbor as History: Japanese-American Relations, 1931–1941* (1973) and co-edited the Japanese version, *Nichi-Bei kankeishi, 1931–1941* (4 vols., 1971–72). His most recent works include *Taigai seisaku kettei katei no Nichi-Bei Hikaku* (A Comparison of the Foreign Policy Decision-Making Processes of Japan and the U.S.), co-authored and co-edited with Watanuki Jōji (1977), and *Washington taisei to Nichi-Bei kankei* (The Washington Order and Japan-U.S. Relations), co-authored with Saitō Makoto (1978).

NAGAOKA SHINJIRŌ is chief editor of *Nihon gaikō bunsho,* the Foreign Minsitry's official series of historical documents on Japanese foreign policy. He was born in 1916 and was graduated from Taihoku University in 1942. A specialist in Japanese foreign relations, he has published a number of works in Japanese, including "Ōshū sensō sanka mondai" (Japan's Participation in the European War, *Kokusai seiji,* 1958), "Katō Taka'aki" (*ibid.,* 1966, no. 1), and "Ishii-Lansing kyōtei no seiritsu" (The Negotiation of the Ishii-Lansing Agreement, *ibid.,* 1967, no. 2).

ROBERT A. SCALAPINO is Robson Research Professor of Government and director of the Institute of East Asian Studies at the University of California, Berkeley. Born in Kansas in 1919, he received his doctorate from Harvard in 1948. He is also editor of *Asian Survey* and has served as consultant to foundations, government agencies, and research centers. His more recent writings include *Asia and the World Powers* (1972); *American-Japanese Relations in a Changing Era* (1972); *Elites in the People's Republic of China* (editor and contributor) (1972); *Communism in Korea,* 2 vols. (with Chong Sik Lee) (1972), for which they received the Woodrow Wilson Award for the best book published in 1973 on government, politics, or international affairs; *Asia and the Road Ahead* (1975); and *The Foreign Policy of Modern Japan* (editor and contributor) (1977).

TSUNODA JUN is a professor at Kokushikan University, Tokyo, and director of the Japan Commission for International Cooperation. Graduated from Tokyo Imperial University in 1933, he subsequently earned the Dr. Jur. there and has held posts at a number of Japanese universities. He has been active also as board member of various international policy research organizations and as a press and political adviser. Author of many publications in Japanese, he succeeded Dr. Kamikawa Hikomatsu as editor of the series from which the essays in this volume are drawn. Among his works in English are "Japan's Role in East Asia: Domestic and Foreign Constraints" in *National Strategy in a Decade of Change*, edited by William R. Kintner and Richard B. Foster (1973) and "Japan: Quest for Strategic Compatibility" in *Nuclear Proliferation, Phase II*, edited by Robert M. Lawrence and Joel Lanes (1974).

Index

Abe cabinet: "Foreign Policy to be Pursued in Response to the European War," 27; "Principles of Foreign Policy," 28; and relations with USSR, 22, 29
Abe Katsuo, 264, 265
Abe Nobuyuki, 18, 26, 309n27
Abo Kiyokazu, 31
"Actions to be Taken If France Rejects Our Final Mediation Proposal" (Foreign Ministry), 233-34
"Agreement between the Army and Navy High Command Concerning the Stationing of Troops in French Indochina" (Navy Division), 181-82
Akiyama Toyoji, 326n78
Amano Masakaza, 92
Andō Rikichi, 168; removed from command, 183, 204; and troop stationing, 194, 195, 196
Andō Yoshirō, 38-39
Anti-Comintern Pact (November 1936), 16-17, 31
Araki Sadao, 14, 26, 54, 293
Arao Okikatsu, 165, 177, 186, 195, 207
Ariga Jingorō, 192
Arisue Yadoru, 95, 288, 290-91, 295
Arita Hachirō: and Dutch East Indies, 127, 128-29, 132; and Japanese-Soviet nonaggression treaty, 33-34, 37-38; and relations with USSR, 26, 30-31, 36, 309n37; on relations with U.S., 135-37; on Sino-Soviet relations, 37; and trade with Dutch East Indies, 138-39
Army, Japan: and China War, 32-33; "National Defense Policy for Dealing with the Changing Situation," 93, 103; on north Sakhalin concessions, 64; on Operation Barbarossa, 95-96; "Outline of the Main Principles for Coping with the Changing World Situation," 41, 247-49, 250-53, 261-62; on relations with USSR, 41; southern advance policy, 288-95
Army General Staff, 324n44; on army mobilization, 103; and China War, 32-34; and French Indochina, 159, 284, 326n77; on German-Soviet war, 92-93; "Japan's Attitude in Case of War between Germany and the Soviet Union," 90; and Japanese-Soviet neutrality treaty, 38-39, 83; on Matsuoka's European trip, 67; Operations Division, 189, 194, 197-98, 287-88, 289; Operations Section, 208, 322n23, 328n105; personnel changes in, 287; on relations with USSR, 14-15, 32-33, 106, 108; and southern advance policy, 155, 246-50, 290; and troop stationing, 169, 179, 185-86, 323n38, 324n54; War Guidance Office, 93, 208, 247, 288-90, 294, 328n105
Army Ministry: and China War, 32; and French Indochina, 159; on German-Soviet War, 92-93; and Japanese-Soviet nonaggression treaty, 53-54; Military Affairs Bureau, 103, 290; Military Affairs Section, 32, 92, 93, 289; War Preparations Section, 292-94; see also Tōjō Hideki
Army-Navy Draft Policy toward the South, 303-4
Army-Navy relations: and Dutch East Indies policy, 253-54; and French Indochina policy, 161-62, 328n106; conflict on Nishihara negotiations, 175-76; conflict on Nishimura corps landing, 198-99; conflict on southern advance policy, 291-95; conflict on troop stationing, 178; "On the Future Management of the French Indochina Problem," 324n54; "Outline of National Policies in View of the Changing Situation," 96; "Principles for Managing the French Indochina Problem," 324n54; and relations with USSR, 98
Arsene-Henry, Charles: on border closing, 159, 160; and Dutch East Indies, 133; and French Indochina, 172-75; and Thai-French Indochina border dispute, 211, 228, 230

Asada Shunsuke, 219
Asiatic Petroleum Company, 142

Ballantine, Joseph W., 141
Banzai Ichirō, 90
Baudouin, Paul, 222
Butler, Nevile M., 219, 223-24, 231
Butler, R. A., 130

Casey, Richard G., 134
Catroux, Georges: and border closing, 159;
and Japanese troop supply route, 158,
322n14; negotiations with Nishihara,
162-65; replaced, 166-67, 322n19; and
Thai territorial claims, 212
Chang Ch'ün, 84
Chauvel, Maurice, 221-22, 226
Chiang Kai-shek, 32-33, 42, 309n27; see also
China
Ch'ien Yung-ming, 65
China, 32-33, 84-85, 117, 156-59, 287-88; see
also Chiang Kai-shek
Chinese Eastern Railway, 14, 16, 30
Chō Isamu, 203
Chūdō Kan'ei, 191, 193, 325n66, 326n82
Churchill, Winston, 86, 294
Ciano, Galeazzo, 221
Commissariat for Foreign Affairs, 10
Comrades for the Strengthening of the
Anti-Comintern Pact, 31
Confidential War Diary: on army discipline,
205; on army-navy disagreement, 94; on
French Indochina, 323n39; on German-
Soviet relations, 90, 106; on Japanese-
Soviet neutrality treaty, 83-84; on rela-
tions with USSR, 314n128
Craigie, Robert L., 133, 152, 158, 236
Cripps, Sir Stafford, 39
Crosby, Sir Josiah, 210, 212, 214, 216-17,
227

Darlan, Jean, 236-37, 238
Decision-making process, in Japan, 120-21
Decoux, Jean: draft pact on Japanese troop
stationing, 177-78; meeting with Satō,
171; meeting with Sumita, 238; and
Japanese intentions in French Indochina,
236-37; mission to U.S., 217-18; named
governor-general, 166-67, 322n19; ne-

gotiations with Nishihara, 167, 175-76,
183, 190; and Nishimura landing, 199; and
Thai-French Indochina relations, 210-11,
212
"Details Concerning Military Demands"
(Foreign Ministry), 174
Diet, 25
Direck Jaiyanama, Nai, 209-10, 225, 227
Doi Akio, 64, 92, 290
"Draft Outline for the Adjustment of
Japanese-Soviet Diplomatic Relations"
(Foreign Ministry), 51-54
Dunn, James C., 140
Dutch East Indies: Arita views on, 128-29;
French policy on, 130; German policy on,
134-35; Japanese interest in future of, 125;
and Japan in French Indochina, 240; and
Kobayashi mission, 143-44; and trade with
Japan, 137; U.S. policy on, 129-30, 135;
see also Netherlands

"Empire's Policy in View of the Decline of
Britain and France, The" (Navy General
Staff), 40-41, 264-65
Erickson, John, 12

Fisheries problem, 29-30, 43, 77
Flandin, Pierre-Etienne, 226, 229
Foote, Walter A., 141
Forbes, Sir C., 272
Foreign Ministry: "Details Concerning
Military Demands," 174; "Draft Outline
for the Adjustment of Japanese-Soviet
Diplomatic Relations," 51-54; Europe-
Asia Bureau, 69, 125-26; "Guidelines for
Diplomatic Negotiations with the Soviet
Union," 110-12; intelligence effectiveness
of, 68-69; and Japanese-Soviet nonaggres-
sion treaty, 34-35; and Nationalist Chinese
supply routes, 159-60; "On Strengthening
Cooperation between Japan, Germany,
and Italy," 265; "Outline for Negotiations
Concerning Diplomatic Relations between Japan and the Dutch East Indies,"
128; "Outline for the Settlement of the
Northern Problem," 110-12; "Outline of
a Japan-Netherlands Agreement," 128;
"Principles of Foreign Policy, II," 47; on
relations with USSR, 37; on troop station-

ing, 173; see also Arita Hachirō; Matsuoka Yōsuke; Nomura Kichisaburō
"Foreign Policy to Be Pursued in Response to the European War" (Abe cabinet), 27
Four Bureau and Two Division Chiefs Conference, 37
Four Ministers Conference: and invasion of French Indochina, 159; and Japanese-Soviet nonaggression treaty, 54; on Japanese-Thai relations, 218-19; "On the Future Management of the French Indochina Problem," 183-84; "Policy toward Thailand and French Indochina," 219-21; on troop stationing, 190
Four-power entente: Foreign Ministry draft on, 51-53; German views on, 51, 55-62; Matsuoka views on, 47, 64-74; Ribbentrop views on, 73-74; Shiratori views on, 23-24; Soviet views on, 60
Fourth fleet, 253
France, 130, 133, 211-12, 215, 229, 238
French Indochina: and border inspection agreement, 321n6; and European War, 158; and Japanese demand for bases, 236-37; and Japanese mediation, 221-34; Japanese policy debate on, 99-101; and Matsuoka-Henry negotiations, 172-75; Matsuoka-Henry Pact concluded, 175; and Morimoto border crossing, 182-83; and Nishihara-Martin agreement, 177-78, 182-85; Nishihara-Martin Pact, 188-92; as supply route for Nationalist Chinese, 158; and territorial integrity question, 166, 173; and Thai territorial claims, 217-18; troop stationing in, 155-203, 321n5, 323n36, 324n54; see also Catroux, Georges; Decoux, Jean; Thailand
Fujita Ruitaro, 199-202, 327n89, 360n81
Fujiwara Takeshi, 168, 171, 195, 203
Fukai Eigo, 276
Fukuoka Takeshi, 321n3
Fushimi Hiroyasu, 49, 257, 268-69, 276, 277
Futami Yasusato, 227, 228

German-Soviet relations: Berlin conference on (November 1940), 57-59; German decision for war, 60-62; Japanese views on, 68-70, 88-94; Matsuoka views on, 74, 87-88, 90-92; nonaggression pact, 17, 18,

19-20; Stalin views on, 56; see also Operation Barbarossa
Germany: and Dutch East Indies, 134-35; and four-power entente, 51, 55-62; and French Indochina, 230; Matsuoka views on, 316n182; and mediation of Japanese-Soviet relations, 48-51, 312n83, 313n91; and Thai border dispute, 221, 222; and war with Great Britain, 271-73; see also Hitler, Adolf; Ribbentrop, Joachim von
Gondō Seii, 197
Gordon, Joseph, 5-6
Grant, Hugh Gladney, 209-10, 212-15, 217
Great Britain: and Dutch East Indies, 129-30, 133, 142-43, 150; and Japanese in French Indochina, 228-29, 240; and Japanese trade with Dutch East Indies, 152; relations with Thailand, 219; on Thai-French Indochina dispute, 210, 216, 222-24, 226, 231; and USSR, 39
Greater East Asia Co-Prosperity Sphere, 9, 122-23
Grew, Joseph C.: on Japan and Dutch East Indies, 133, 139-40; on Japanese domestic situation, 104; on Japanese expansionism, 249; and Japanese in French Indochina, 237; on Japanese-Soviet neutrality pact, 85; on U.S.-Japan relations, 135-37
"Guidelines for Diplomatic Negotiations with the Soviet Union" (Foreign Ministry), 110-12

Haiphong, 204
Halifax, Lord, 216
Hamilton, Maxwell M., 141, 216
Hara Chūichi, 188
Harada Kumao, Baron, 26, 46
Hara Yoshimichi, 101
Hart, Thomas, 281
Hashimoto Gun, 323n37
Hashimoto Kingorō, 54
Hashimoto Shōzō, 260
Hasunuma Shigeru, 249, 284
Hata Shunroku, 159
Hattori Takushirō, 294
Hayashi Raisaburō, 50
Henry-Haye, Gaston, 217-18, 225
Hiranuma Kiichirō, 18

Hirohito, Emperor: on bombing of Haiphong, 204; on German-Soviet relations, 70; and Nomonhan Incident, 17-18; on Operation Barbarossa, 94; on southern advance, 288; on troop stationing, 184, 324n55
Hitler, Adolf, 58, 60-62, 90-91
Hong Kong, 251
Horinouchi Kensuke, 29, 131, 132
Horiuchi Shigetada, 286
Hornbeck, Stanley K., 141-42
Ho Ying-ch'in, 84
Hull, Cordell: on Dutch East Indies, 129-32, 135, 142-43; on Japanese intentions in Thailand, 221-22, 226, 229; on Japanese-Soviet relations, 29, 85; and Japanese troop stationing, 238; on supplies to French Indochina, 217-18

Iida Shōjirō, 168
Imperial Conference: "Outline of National Policies in View of the Changing Situation," 100-1, 236; "Outline of Policy to Deal with the China Incident," 65; on Soviet strength, 105; on war with U.S., 276-77
Imperial Headquarters: Army Instruction 745, 201, 203; Army Instruction 750, 197; Army Instruction 791, 288; Army Order 452, 181; Army Order 458, 184-85; Army Order 461, 327n99; Army Order 467, 287; Navy Order 237, 202
Indochina Army, 181
Inoue Shigeyoshi, 262, 264
Inukai Tsuyoshi, 308n1
Ishii Akiho, 293-94
Ishii Itarō, 125, 126, 138
Ishikawa Shingo, 207, 266, 281
Ishizawa-Hult Pact (April 1937), 137
Ishizawa Yutaka, 147, 153
Isomura Takesuke, 105
Istoriia sovetsko-jiaponskikh diplomaticheskikh otnoshenii (Kutakov), 6
Itagaki Seishirō, 263
Iwakuro Hideo, 247, 289, 322n23

Japanese-French Protocol Concerning Joint Defense and Mutual Military Cooperation in French Indochina, 240

Japanese-Soviet Neutrality Pact (April 1941): abrogated, 114; and German-Soviet war, 109; Japanese reaction to, 82-84, 310-11n65; and Japan-U.S. relations, 81; Kōtani draft of, 38-40; Liaison Conference on, 111-12; Matsuoka-Molotov negotiations on, 75-77; Matsuoka views on, 44-45; signed, 78; text of, 78-79; and Sino-Soviet relations, 80-81; Soviet draft of, 62-63; Soviet views on, 81-82; Stalin's motives for, 10-11; Tōgō views on, 46; U.S. views on, 85
Japanese-Soviet nonaggression treaty, proposal for: Abe cabinet views on, 28; Arita views on, 30-31; Foreign Ministry views on, 34-35; Japanese public opposition to, 54; Japanese reactions to Soviet proposals on, 15-16; proposed, 14; right-wing Japanese support of, 24; sought by Foreign Ministry, 51-54; Tōgō views on, 27-28; Tsuchihashi views on, 33
"Japan's Attitude in Case of War between Germany and the Soviet Union" (General Staff), 90
Japans Russlandpolitik von 1939 bis 1941 (Lupke), 5-6
Jouan, Captain, 222-23, 236

Kakitsubo Masayoshi, 313n92
Kami Shigenori, 165, 188, 207, 276-77, 282
Kanda Masatane, 202, 327n93
Kan'in Kotohito, Prince, 176, 184, 206, 323n38
Kantokuen plan, 102-4, 106-7
Karakawa Yasuo, 186
Karakhan, Leo, 308n1
Katagiri Eikichi, 244
Katō Sotomatsu, 236, 237, 238
Katō Tomosaburō, 259
Kawaii Iwao, 250
Kawamura Saburō, 247, 289
Kido Kōichi, 70, 90
Kita Reikichi, 31
Kiyose Ichirō, 25
Kleffens, E. N. van, 125, 126, 152
Knox, Frank, 139
Kobayashi Ichizō, 141, 143, 144, 146
Koike Ryōji, 191, 321n3, 326n79
Koiso Kuniaki, 25, 140-41, 254

Kondō Nobutake, 233, 244, 262, 264, 276-77, 284

Konoe Fumimaro, Prince: and Dutch East Indies, 140, 254; forms second cabinet, 165; on French Indochina, 237; and German-Soviet relations, 89-90, 95; on materials mobilization program, 331n19; on neutrality pact, 82-83; and Ozaki, 11-12; and relations with Germany, 100-1, 312n83; and relations with USSR, 25, 43-44, 112-13; and war with U.S., 274-75; and Yoshizawa mission, 148-49

Kōtani Etsuo, 33, 38-39

Kōtani-van Mook note (January 1938), 137

Kubota Kan'ichirō, 310n65

Kubota Seitarō, 50

Kuno Seiichi, 168, 170, 198, 206

Kurusu Saburō, 41, 56, 70, 137, 229-30

Kusaka Ryūnosuke, 262

Kusumoto Sanetaka, 168

Kutakov, Leonid N., 6, 11, 307n9

Kwantung Army, 17-18, 102-4, 106-7

Leahy, William D., 226, 237-38

Liaison Conference: "Actions to be Taken if France Rejects Our Final Mediation Proposal," 233-34; on German-Soviet relations, 91-92; "Main Principles for Coping with the Changing World Situation," 44; on Matsuoka's European trip, 67-68; "Measures for Advancing the Southern Policy," 96, 235; "Measures to be Taken by Japan to Deal with the Present Situation in Japanese-Soviet Relations," 107; and neutrality pact, 109, 111-12; on north Sakhalin concessions, 63-64; "Outline of Emergency Measures to Deal with the Thailand-French Indochina Border Dispute," 227-28, 231, 283; "Outline of National Policies in View of the Changing Situation," 98; "Outline of Policy toward French Indochina and Thailand," 231-32, 287; "Policy of the Empire toward Thailand and French Indochina," 223, 283; on relations with Germany, 100; on relations with USSR, 96-99; on Thai-Japanese military alliance, 234; and Tripartite Alliance, 50; on Yoshizawa mission, 152-53

Litvinov, Maxim, 14, 308n1

Lothian, Lord, 129-32, 134, 142-43

Loudon, A., 140, 141

Lozovsky, Solomon, 10

Lupke, Hubertus, 5-6

"Main Principles for Coping with the Changing World Situation" (Liaison Conference), 44

"Manchurian Group," 43

Manchurian Incident, 13-15

Martin, Maurice-Pierre, 180, 191, 325n67

Matsuda Chiaki, 270

Matsudaira Tsuneo, 11, 26

Matsumiya Jun, 226

Matsuoka-Henry Pact (August 1940), 175, 301-2

Matsuoka Yōsuke: and army leadership, 9-10; and choice of navy minister, 266; on Dutch East Indies, 144, 146; European trip of, 64-74; and four-power entente, 47, 57, 308-9n19; and French Indochina, 99-101, 236; on German mediation, 48-50, 56, 313n91; on German-Soviet relations, 74, 87-88, 90-92; and Japanese-Soviet neutrality pact, 7-8, 44-47; and Japanese-Soviet nonaggression treaty, 308n1; on Koiso mission, 140; letter to Molotov, 299; meetings with Hitler and Ribbentrop, 72-74; meetings with Stalin, 71-72, 77-78; negotiations with Arsene-Henry, 165-66, 172-75; negotiations with Molotov, 75-77; and north Sakhalin concessions, 64, 108-9; on oil embargo, 146; on Operation Barbarossa, 82, 94; "Outline for Negotiations with Germany, Italy, and the USSR," 65-68; personal style of, 8; on relations with Germany, 100-1, 151, 316n182; on relations with USSR, 79-80, 96-98; and relations with U.S., 71, 274-75, 295; replaced, 9, 109; on Thai-French Indochina border dispute, 226, 227, 228, 232-34; on Tripartite Pact, 8-9, 269; and troop stationing, 179, 190; and Yoshizawa mission, 150, 153

"Measures for Advancing the Southern Policy" (Liaison Conference), 96, 235

"Measures for Dealing with the New Situation in German-Soviet Relations" (Navy), 93-94

"Measures to be Taken by Japan to Deal with the Present Situation in Japanese-Soviet Relations" (Liaison Conference), 107

Michi Kichinosuke, 196

Miki Bukichi, 25

Minami Hiroshi, 50

Minoda Fujio, 191

Mishuku Yoshimi, 256

Molotov, Vyacheslav: on Japanese-Soviet neutrality treaty, 62-63, 307n9; on Japanese-Soviet nonaggression treaty, 55; meeting with Hitler, 62; meetings with Ribbentrop and Hitler, 57-59; meetings with Tōgō, 22; negotiations with Matsuoka, 75-77; and Nomonhan Incident, 19; on relations with China, 46, 84-85; on relations with Japan, 9, 20, 35-36, 41-44, 58-60

Morgenthau, Henry, Jr., 139

Morimoto Takuji, 182-83, 324n53

Motoki Jun'ichi, 321n3

Mukai Tadaharu, 144-45

Murphy, Robert D., 221, 222

Mushakōji Kintomo, 26

Mutō Akira, 34, 41; on China War, 68; on Operation Barbarossa, 95; on southern advance, 290; on Tripartite Pact, 265; on war with U.S., 250

Nagai Yatsuji, 9-10, 90, 289

Nagano Osami, 100-1, 235, 284

Nakahara Yoshimasa, 241-42, 251, 269-70

Nakai Masutarō, 321n3

Nakamura Aketo, 168; on Morimoto border crossing, 183; and Nishihara orders, 325n70; and troop stationing, 169-71; 192-94, 196-97, 326n78

Nakayama Motoo, 186

Nakazawa Tasuku, 260

Nami Group, see South China Army

Nanning, 158, 168-69

Narita Katsushirō, 313n92

National Alliance for the Reconstruction of East Asia, 54

"National Defense Policy for Dealing with the Changing Situation" (Army), 93, 103

Navy, Japan: "Agreement between the Army and Navy High Commands Concerning the Stationing of Troops in French In-

dochina," 181-82; and Anglo-German war, 272-73; and Dutch East Indies policy, 141, 244-46, 254; First Committee, 281-82, 283; fleet reorganization, 280-82; "Measures for Dealing with the New Situation in German-Soviet Relations," 93-94; on north Sakhalin concessions, 64; and Operation Barbarossa, 95-96; and "Outline of the Main Principles for Coping with the Changing World," 250-53; "Outline of Policy toward the South," 295; preparedness for war, 255-61, 275-83; and relations with USSR, 107; and southern advance, 156, 241-46, 252, 292-95; and Thai-French Indochina border dispute, 232; and Tominaga, 178; on Tripartite Alliance, 49, 262-69; on troop stationing, 190, 321n5; and U.S. oil embargo, 148; and war with U.S., 252-53, 257-59, 269-73

Navy General Staff: and Anglo-German war, 272, 285-86; "The Empire's Policy in View of the Decline of Britain and France," 40-41, 264-65; and invasion of Dutch East Indies, 243-44, 255-57; and fleet reorganization, 242-43; on French Indochina, 284; on relations with Great Britain, 262; "Study" of Policy toward French Indochina," 255; and troop stationing, 201; War Guidance Office, 241

Navy Ministry: Naval Affairs Bureau, 262-63, 264

Nemoto Hiroshi, 168, 179, 195, 326n83

Netherlands: and Dutch East Indies, 127-28, 132, 137-53; and European War, 125-26; maintains neutrality, 128-29; trading policy of, 137; see also Dutch East Indies

"New Diplomatic Policy" (Tsuchihashi), 34

New York Times, 85

Ninomiya Yoshikiyo, 313n92

Nishihara Issaku, 327n100; background of, 160; and bombing of Haiphong, 204; censured, 204-5; and Chinese supply route, 155; difficulties in command, 160-68; on French appeal, 326n82; and French Indochina, 323n39, 325n76, 326n77; meeting with Martin, 325n67; negotiations with Decoux, 175-76; negotiations concluded, 188-92; and Nishimura landing, 199; pow-

ers of, 324n56; and South China Army, 327n93; and southern advance, 156; and troòp stationing, 202, 325n66
Nishihara-Martin agreement, 177-78, 180
Nishihara-Martin Pact, 182, 185, 188-92
Nishi Haruhiko, 174
Nishimura Takuma, 181, 198-99, 200-3, 206, 326n81
Nishiura Susumu, 158, 247, 289, 294, 322n23
Nomonhan Incident, 17-19, 22, 36
Nomura Kichisaburō: and Dutch East Indies, 125, 126-27; and Japanese-Soviet nonaggression pact, 27-28; meeting with Welles, 238-401 and relations with USSR, 26; on war with U.S., 259-60
North Sakhalin concessions, 43, 46, 63-64, 75-78, 108-9

Ogata Taketora, 273
Ōhashi Chūichi, 90; and Dutch East Indies, 146, 151-52; and German mediation, 56-57; on Japanese mediation of border dispute, 232; on Matsuoka European trip, 315n141; on relations with Germany, 314n135; on relations with Thailand, 211, 221; on troop stationing, 173, 174-75
Ōi Atsushi, 188, 195, 199, 328n106
Oikawa Koshirō, 190, 233, 260, 266-67; on China War, 68; and naval preparedness, 275-76, 282-83; and southern advance policy, 100; and war with U.S., 285
Okada Jūichi, 162, 204, 206, 247-49, 253, 260
Okada Kikusaburō, 288, 292-93
Okamoto Kiyotomi, 95
Okamoto Shizuomi, 168
Oka Takazumi, 68, 263, 267, 281, 285
Oka Yoshio, 321n3
Onō Takeji, 270, 281, 286, 291
"On Strengthening the Cooperation between Japan, Germany, and Italy" (Foreign Ministry), 47-48, 265
"On the Future Management of the French Indochina Problem" (Four Ministers Conference), 183-84, 324n54
Operation Barbarossa, 62, 82, 85-89, 94-95
Ōshima Hiroshi: on Anglo-German war, 286; on German-Soviet relations, 82, 89, 90; and Japanese in French Indochina, 238;

meeting with Hitler, 90-91; and relations with USSR, 22; on Soviet army, 104-5
Ott, Eugen, 21-22, 48, 134, 286
Oumansky, Constantine, 36-37
"Outline for Dealing with the Southern Areas" (War Guidance Office), 289-90
"Outline for Negotiations Concerning Diplomatic Relations between Japan and the Dutch East Indies" (Foreign Ministry), 128
"Outline for Negotiations with Germany, Italy, and the U.S.S.R." (Matsuoka), 65-68
"Outline for the Management of the French Indochina Problem," 323n36
"Outline for the Settlement of the Northern Problem" (Foreign Ministry), 110-12
"Outline of a Japan-French Indochina Agreement" (South China Army), 164-65
"Outline of a Japan-Netherlands Agreement" (Foreign Ministry), 128
"Outline of Emergency Measures to Deal with the Thai-French Indochina Border Dispute" (Liaison Conference), 227-28, 231, 283
"Outline of National Policies," 101-2
"Outline of National Policies in View of the Changing Situation" (Army-Navy), 96
"Outline of National Policies in View of the Changing Situation" (Imperial Conference), 236
"Outline of Policy to Deal with the China Incident" (Imperial Conference), 65
"Outline of Policy toward America" (Naval Affairs Bureau), 243
"Outline of Policy toward the South" (Navy), 295
"Outline of Policy toward French Indochina and Thailand" (Liaison Conference), 231-32, 387
"Outline of the Main Principles for Coping with the Changing World Situation" (Army), 41, 247-49, 250-53, 257-59, 261-62
Ozaki Hotsumi, 11-12

Pibul Songgram, Luong, 120; and Japanese mediation, 227, 228; meeting with Crosby, 216-17; meeting with Grant, 212-14; meeting with Tamura, 215-16; and

Pibul Songgram, Luong (*Continued*)
relations with Japan, 218, 219; on Thai-
British relations, 231; and Thai territorial
claims, 209-10, 225
Plessen, Counselor, 309n27
"Policy of the Empire toward Thailand and
French Indochina" (Liaison Conference),
223, 283
"Policy toward Thailand and French In-
dochina Concerning Mediation for
Thailand's Recovery of Its Lost Ter-
ritories" (Four Ministers Conference),
219-21
"Preliminary Directives for the Commission
Dispatched to French Indochina," 321n3
"Principles for Managing the French In-
dochina Problem" (Army-Navy), 324n54
"Principles for Negotiations with the Dutch
East Indies," 143-44
"Principles of Foreign Policy" (Abe cabinet),
28
"Principles of Foreign Policy, II" (Foreign
Ministry), 35, 47
Privy Council, 50
Prom Yodhi, Luang, 211

Radek, Karl, 308n1
Raeder, Erich, 286
Ribbentrop, Joachim von, 9; and anti-British
bloc, 21; on four-power entente, 47,
55-59, 73-74, 308-9n19; on German-
Japanese relations, 99-100; on Japanese-
Soviet relations, 20, 21, 48; meetings with
Molotov, 57-59; on Tripartite Alliance, 51;
on war with USSR, 62
Rising Sun Company, 144-45
Robin, Rene, 226
Roosevelt, Franklin D., 131, 133, 135, 139,
237
Royal Dutch Shell, 144-45

Saitō Kiura, 37
Sakai Wataru, 321n3
Sakawa Shūichi, 140
Satō Kenryō, 92, 168, 176; and Army Instruction 745, 203; and army-navy conference, 328n106; on Morimoto border
crossing, 183; and Nishihara mission,
164-65, 166, 167-68; telegram to Nemoto,

323n38; and troop stationing, 171, 182,
195, 322n16
Satō Naotake, 26
Sawada Shigeru, 328n106; and invasion of
French Indochina, 159; resigns, 206; on
southern advance policy, 249; and To-
minaga, 204; on Tripartite Alliance, 50; on
troop stationing, 189, 194, 201, 325n64
Schmidt, Paul, 72-74
Schulenberg, Friedrich Werner Count von
der, 21, 87
Second China Fleet, 187-88, 199-201, 253
Shiba Katsuo, 207, 265, 270, 313n92
Shibafu Hideo, 292, 293
Shigematsu Nobuo, 35
Shirahama Eiichi, 176, 177, 186, 201,
310-11n65
Shiratori Toshio, 22, 23-25, 47, 54, 309n22
Singapore, 73, 248, 250, 288
Smetanin, Konstantin, 109
Sorge, Richard, 11-12
South China Army: begins military station-
ing, 194-98; description of, 168; and
French Indochina, 180-88; and Nakamura
corps, 326n83; and Nishihara mission,
168, 326n82; "Outline of a Japan-French
Indochina Agreement," 164-65; and troop
stationing, 169-72, 178, 185, 187-88, 190,
326n73
Stahmer, Heinrich, 9, 46, 48-49, 57, 89
Stalin, Joseph: and German attack, 86-87;
and Japanese-Soviet Neutrality Pact,
10-11; and Matsuoka, 10-11, 71-72, 77-78,
79; on relations with Germany, 56; on
relations with Japan, 20; *see also* Union of
Soviet Socialist Republics
Standard Vacuum Oil, 144-45
Stimson, Henry L., 139
"Study of Policy toward French Indochina"
(Navy General Staff), 255
Suetsugu Nobumasa, 25
Sugiyama Gen: on China War, 68; and
Japanese mediation, 233; and Matsuoka,
10; on relations with Germany, 100-1; on
relations with USSR, 97, 102-3, 107; on
southern advance policy, 290; on Soviet
strength, 105; on war with U.S., 294
Sumita Raishirō, 205, 236, 238, 327n102
Sumiyama Tokutarō, 260, 264

Sun Fo, 84
Suzuki Rokurō, 321n7
Suzuki Sōsaku, 205

Takada Toshitane, 281
Takasu Shirō, 196, 199
Takatsuki Tamotsu, 169, 206-7, 250
Takayama Hikoichi, 313n92
Tamura Hiroshi, 215-16
Tanaka Shin'ichi, 92, 95, 103, 107
Tanaka Takeo, 254
Tani Masayuki, 26-27, 128, 160
Tanomogi Keikichi, 25
Tatekawa Yoshitsugu, 11, 54-55, 63-64, 105
Thailand: British policy on, 210, 212, 223-24;
conflict with French Indochina, 226-27,
232-34; French policy on, 211-12, 214;
nonaggression pact with French Indochina, 211-12; relations with Germany,
221, 222; relations with Japan, 211,
215-16, 218-19, 221-34; 329nn67, 68; territorial claims of, 209-11, 215; U.S. policy
on, 209-11, 212-15, 225-26; see also Pibul
Songgram, Luong
Thiebaut, P., 163, 170
Tōgō Shigenori: on German mediation,
314n137; on German-Soviet relations, 69;
on Japanese-Soviet neutrality pact, 39-40,
44, 46; on Japanese-Soviet nonaggression
treaty, 27-28, 37; meetings with Molotov,
22, 29, 46; and Nomonhan Incident, 18,
19, 22; recall of, 8-9; on relations with
USSR, 30
Tōjō Hideki: on Andō dismissal, 204; and
army discipline, 121, 207; on army maneuvers plan, 103-4; on army-navy cooperation, 205-6; on Japanese-Soviet neutrality
pact, 84; and Moriomoto, 183, 324n53; on
relations with USSR, 43, 97; and troop
stationing, 179, 189, 190; on war with
U.S., 294
Tokuo Toshihiko, 321n3
Tokutomi Sohō, 31
Tominaga Kyōji, 121; criticism of, 203-4; and
invasion of French Indochina, 159; and
Nishihara mission, 175-77; powers of,
323n36, 324n56; transferred, 206; and
troop stationing, 178, 183-84, 186-89,
195-96; and Tsuchihashi, 321n3

Tomioka Sadatoshi, 282
Torigoshi Shin'ichi, 218
Tōyama Mitsuru, 31
Toyoda Soemu, 256
Toyoda Teijirō, 109, 113, 267-68, 274, 277
Tripartite Pact, 8-9, 48-51, 95, 262-69
Troyanovsky, Alexandr, 8, 308n1
Tsuchihashi Yūichi, 204, 207; on China War,
33; on Japanese-Soviet nonaggression
treaty, 33; on Japanese occupation of
French Indochina, 320-21n3; and
Nationalist Chinese supply route, 158;
"New Diplomatic Policy," 34
Tsukada Osamu, 100, 233, 291
22nd Army, 168, 170, 198, 206, 326n79

Ugaki Matome, 246, 251, 262, 285, 326n81
Umezu Yoshijirō, 107
Union of Soviet Socialist Republics (USSR):
and aid to Chiang Kai-shek, 42; on four-
power entente, 60; and France,
311-12n65; and Japanese-Soviet neutrality
treaty, 43, 45-46; and Tatekawa, 11
USSR-Japanese relations: under Abe
cabinet, 27, 29; Arita views on, 30; and
border incidents, 17; effect of German-
Soviet Nonaggression Pact on, 16-17,
19-22; effect of Manchurian Incident on,
13-15; effect of Tōgō recall on, 9; effect of
U.S.-Soviet relations on, 36-37; and
fisheries agreement, 16; Japanese Foreign
Ministry views on, 37; and German mediation, 20-21; German views on, 19-22;
Japanese army views on, 41; Imperial Diet
debate on, 25; Japanese Army General
Staff views on, 32-33; Japanese policy
debate on, 23-30, 101-14; Konoe views on,
25, 44; Liaison Conference on, 96-99;
Molotov views on, 35-36, 43-44, 58-60;
and north Sakhalin concessions, 16; and
Soviet intelligence, 11-12; and Soviet rapprochement, 36-37; Soviet reply to
Japanese demands, 113-14; Tatekawa
views on, 69; and U.S., 10, 11, 28-29;
under Yonai cabinet, 30; see also
Japanese-Soviet Neutrality Pact; Japanese-Soviet nonaggression treaty;
Molotov, Vyacheslav
United States, 209-10, 216, 225-26

United States-Japanese relations: Arita-Grew meeting on, 135-37; and Dutch East Indies, 131, 135, 139-43, 150; effect of China War on, 117; and Japanese-Soviet neutrality pact, 81, 85; and oil embargo, 108, 145; possibility of war, 119; and trade embargo, 118, 147-48; and troop stationing question, 238-40; see also Hull, Cordell
"Urgent Policy of the Empire, The" (Koiso), 254
Ushiroku Jun, 204
Usui Shigeki, 247

Van Boetzelaer van Oosterhout, Baron C. G. W. H., 143
Van Hoogstraten, J. E., 147
Van Mook, Hubertus J., 144, 147

Wa Group, see 22nd Army
Wakamatsu Tadakazu, 168, 193-94, 221, 290, 325n70
Walden, George S., 141-42
Wang Ching-wei, 65
Wang Ch'ung-hui, 84
Watanabe Kumeichi, 186
Watanabe Saburō, 158

Weizsaecker, Ernst von, 134, 230, 232
Welles, Sumner: and Dutch East Indies, 130, 139, 143; meeting with Nomura, 238-40; on Thai-French Indochina dispute, 210, 225-26
Wilkinson, Sir Harold, 142

Yabe Toshio, 321n3
Yamada Yoshiji, 193
Yamaguchi Bunjirō, 286
Yamaji Akira, 70
Yamamoto Isoroku, 121, 262-64, 273-74, 279, 284-85
Yamashita Tomoyuki, 90
Yanigasawa Kuranosuke, 177, 178, 320-21n3
Yasumura Isao, 321n3
Yokoi Tadao, 286
Yokoyama Hikosane, 193, 321n3
Yonai Mitsumasa, 43, 127, 262-64, 273, 275
Yosanu Shigeru, 320-21n3
Yoshida Zengo, 141, 243-44, 264-65, 275; on Anglo-German war, 270; on Dutch East Indies, 254; and Tripartite Pact, 266; and war with U.S., 257-58
Yoshizawa Kenkichi, 14, 146-53
Yost, Charles W., 145
Yugoslavia, 75

Studies of the East Asian Institute

THE LADDER OF SUCCESS IN IMPERIAL CHINA, by Ping-ti Ho. New York: Columbia University Press, 1962.

THE CHINESE INFLATION, 1937-1949, by Shun-hsin Chou. New York: Columbia University Press, 1963.

REFORMER IN MODERN CHINA: CHANG CHIEN, 1853-1926, by Samuel Chu. New York: Columbia University Press, 1965.

RESEARCH IN JAPANESE SOURCES: A GUIDE, by Herschel Webb with the assistance of Marleigh Ryan. New York: Columbia University Press, 1965.

SOCIETY AND EDUCATION IN JAPAN, by Herbert Passin. New York: Teachers College Press, Columbia University, 1965.

AGRICULTURAL PRODUCTION AND ECONOMIC DEVELOPMENT IN JAPAN, 1873-1922, by James I. Nakamura. Princeton: Princeton University Press, 1966.

JAPAN'S FIRST MODERN NOVEL: UKIGUMO OF FUTABATEI SHIMEI, by Marleigh Ryan. New York: Columbia University Press, 1967. Also in paperback.

THE KOREAN COMMUNIST MOVEMENT, 1918-1948, by Dae-Sook Suh. Princeton: Princeton University Press, 1967.

THE FIRST VIETNAM CRISIS, by Melvin Gurtov. New York: Columbia University Press, 1967. Also in paperback.

CADRES, BUREAUCRACY, AND POLITICAL POWER IN COMMUNIST CHINA, by A. Doak Barnett. New York: Columbia University Press, 1967.

THE JAPANESE IMPERIAL INSTITUTION IN THE TOKUGAWA PERIOD, by Herschel Webb. New York, Columbia University Press, 1968.

HIGHER EDUCATION AND BUSINESS RECRUITMENT IN JAPAN, by Koya Azumi. New York: Teachers College Press, Columbia University, 1969.

THE COMMUNISTS AND CHINESE PEASANT REBELLIONS: A STUDY IN THE REWRITING OF CHINESE HISTORY, by James P. Harrison, Jr. New York: Atheneum, 1969.

HOW THE CONSERVATIVES RULE JAPAN, by Nathaniel B. Thayer. Princeton: Princeton University Press, 1969.

ASPECTS OF CHINESE EDUCATION, edited by C. T. Hu. New York: Teachers College Press, Columbia University, 1969.

DOCUMENTS OF KOREAN COMMUNISM, 1918-1948, by Dae-Sook Suh. Princeton: Princeton University Press, 1970.

JAPANESE EDUCATION: A BIBLIOGRAPHY OF MATERIALS IN THE

ENGLISH LANGUAGE, by Herbert Passin. New York: Teachers College Press, Columbia University, 1970.

ECONOMIC DEVELOPMENT AND THE LABOR MARKET IN JAPAN, by Kōji Taira. New York: Columbia University Press, 1970.

THE JAPANESE OLIGARCHY AND THE RUSSO-JAPANESE WAR,. by Shumpei Okamoto. New York: Columbia University Press, 1970.

IMPERIAL RESTORATION IN MEDIEVAL JAPAN, by H. Paul Varley. New York: Columbia University Press, 1971.

JAPAN'S POSTWAR DEFENSE POLICY, 1947–1968, by Martin E. Weinstein. New York: Columbia University Press, 1971.

ELECTION CAMPAIGNING JAPANESE STYLE, by Gerald L. Curtis. New York: Columbia University Press, 1971.

CHINA AND RUSSIA: THE "GREAT GAME," by O. Edmund Clubb. New York: Columbia University Press, 1971. Also in paperback.

MONEY AND MONETARY POLICY IN COMMUNIST CHINA, by Katherine Huang Hsiao. New York: Columbia University Press, 1971.

THE DISTRICT MAGISTRATE IN LATE IMPERIAL CHINA, by John R. Watt. New York: Columbia University Press, 1972.

LAW AND POLICY IN CHINA'S FOREIGN RELATIONS: A STUDY OF ATTITUDES AND PRACTICE, by James C. Hsiung. New York: Columbia University Press, 1972.

PEARL HARBOR AS HISTORY: JAPANESE-AMERICAN RELATIONS: 1931–1941, edited by Dorothy Borg and Shumpei Okamoto, with the assistance of Dale K. A. Finlayson. New York: Columbia University Press, 1973.

JAPANESE CULTURE: A SHORT HISTORY, by H. Paul Varley. New York: Praeger, 1973.

DOCTORS IN POLITICS: THE POLITICAL LIFE OF THE JAPAN MEDICAL ASSOCIATION, by William E. Steslicke. New York: Praeger, 1973.

JAPAN'S FOREIGN POLICY, 1868–1941: A RESEARCH GUIDE, edited by James William Morley. New York: Columbia University Press, 1973.

THE JAPAN TEACHERS UNION: A RADICAL INTEREST GROUP IN JAPANESE POLITICS, by Donald Ray Thurston. Princeton University Press, 1973.

PALACE AND POLITICS IN PREWAR JAPAN, by David Anson Titus. New York: Columbia University Press, 1974.

THE IDEA OF CHINA: ESSAYS IN GEOGRAPHIC MYTH AND THEORY, by Andrew March. Devon, England: David and Charles, 1974.

ORIGINS OF THE CULTURE REVOLUTION, By Roderick MacFarquhar. New York: Columbia University Press, 1974.

SHIBA KŌKAN: ARTIST, INNOVATOR, AND PIONEER IN THE WESTERNIZATION OF JAPAN, by Calvin L. French. Tokyo: Weatherhill, 1974.

EMBASSY AT WAR, by Harold Joyce Noble. Edited with an introduction by Frank Baldwin, Jr. Seattle: University of Washington Press, 1975.

REBELS AND BUREAUCRATS: CHINA'S DECEMBER 9ERS, by John Israel and Donald W. Klein. Berkeley: University of California Press, 1975.

HOUSE UNITED, HOUSE DIVIDED: THE CHINESE FAMILY IN TAIWAN, by Myron L. Cohen. New York: Columbia University Press, 1976.

INSEI: ABDICATED SOVEREIGNS IN THE POLITICS OF LATE HEIAN JAPAN, by G. Cameron Hurst. New York: Columbia University Press, 1976.

DETERRENT DIPLOMACY, edited by James William Morley. New York: Columbia University Press, 1976.

CADRES, COMMANDERS AND COMMISSARS: THE TRAINING OF THE CHINESE COMMUNIST LEADERSHIP, 1920–45, by Jane L. Price. Boulder, Colo.: Westview Press, 1976.

SUN YAT-SEN: FRUSTRATED PATRIOT, by C. Martin Wilbur. New York: Columbia University Press, 1976.

JAPANESE INTERNATIONAL NEGOTIATING STYLE, by Michael Blaker. New York: Columbia University Press, 1977.

CONTEMPORARY JAPANESE BUDGET POLITICS, by John Creighton Campbell. Berkeley: University of California Press, 1977.

THE MEDIEVAL CHINESE OLIGARCHY, by David Johnson. Boulder, Colo.: Westview Press, 1977.

ESCAPE FROM PREDICAMENT: NEO-CONFUCIANISM AND CHINA'S EVOLVING POLITICAL CULTURE, by Thomas A. Metzger. New York: Columbia University Press, 1977.

THE ARMS OF KIANGNAN: MODERNIZATION IN THE CHINESE ORDNANCE INDUSTRY, 1860–1895, by Thomas L. Kennedy. Boulder, Colo.: Westview Press, 1978.

PATTERNS OF JAPANESE POLICYMAKING: EXPERIENCES FROM HIGHER EDUCATION, by T. I. Pempel. Boulder, Colo.: Westview Press, 1978.

THE CHINESE CONNECTION, by Warren Cohen. New York: Columbia University Press, 1978.

MILITARISM IN MODERN CHINA: THE CAREER OF WU P'EI-FU, 1916–1939, by Odoric Y. K. Wou. Folkestone, England: Wm. Dawson & Sons, 1978.

THE LINS OF WU-FENG, by Johanna Meskill. Princeton: Princeton University Press, 1979.

PERSPECTIVES ON A CHANGING CHINA: ESSAYS IN HONOR OF PROFESSOR C. MARTIN WILBUR, edited by Joshua A. Fogel and William T. Rowe. Boulder, Colo.: Westview Press, 1979.

THE MEMOIRS OF LI TSUNG-JEN, by T. K. Tong and Li Tsung-jen. Boulder, Colo.: Westview Press, 1979.

THIN SMOKE, by Edward Gunn. New York: Columbia University Press, 1979.

UNCERTAIN YEARS: CHINESE-AMERICAN RELATIONS, 1947–1950, edited by Dorothy Borg and Waldo Heinrichs. New York: Columbia University Press, 1980.

YENAN AND THE GREAT POWERS, by James Reardon-Anderson. New York: Columbia University Press, 1979.